Film and Television Analysis

Film and Television Analysis is especially designed to introduce undergraduate students to the most important qualitative methodologies used to study film and television.

The methodologies covered include:

- ideological analysis
- auteur theory
- genre theory
- semiotics and structuralism
- psychoanalysis and apparatus theory
- feminism
- postmodernism
- cultural studies (including reception and audience studies)
- contemporary approaches to race, nation, gender, and sexuality.

With each chapter focusing on a distinct methodology, students are introduced to the historical developments of each approach, along with its vocabulary, significant scholars, key concepts, and case studies.

Other features include:

- over 120 color images throughout
- questions for discussion at the end of each chapter
- suggestions for further reading
- a glossary of key terms.

Written in a reader-friendly manner *Film and Television Analysis* is a vital textbook for students encountering these concepts for the first time.

Harry M. Benshoff is a Professor of Media Arts at the University of North Texas, USA. He is the editor of *A Companion to the Horror Film* (2014) and co-author of the best-selling textbook *America on Film: Representing Race, Class, Gender, and Sexuality at the Movies* (2009).

Film and Television Analysis

An Introduction to Methods, Theories, and Approaches

Harry M. Benshoff

Routledge
Taylor & Francis Group

LONDON AND NEW YORK

First published 2016

by Routledge
2 Park Square, Milton Park, Abingdon, Oxon OX14 4RN

and by Routledge
711 Third Avenue, New York, NY 10017

Routledge is an imprint of the Taylor & Francis Group, an informa business

British Library Cataloguing-in-Publication Data
A catalogue record for this book is available from the British Library

Library of Congress Cataloging-in-Publication Data
Benshoff, Harry M., 1963-
Film and television analysis : an introduction to methods, theories, and approaches / Harry M. Benshoff.
pages cm
Includes bibliographical references and index.
1. Film criticism. 2. Television criticism. I. Title.
PN1995.B347 2015
791.4301'5--dc23
2015007551

ISBN: 978-0-415-67480-5 (hbk)
ISBN: 978-0-415-67481-2 (pbk)
ISBN: 978-0-203-12996-8 (ebk)

Typeset in 10/12pt Bembo MT Pro
by Fakenham Prepress Solutions, Fakenham, Norfolk NR21 8NN

Contents

List of figures and diagrams

Contents

List of figures and diagrams

Diagrams

Foreword: About this book

This book is designed to introduce basic qualitative approaches to the study of film and television, primarily to undergraduate students. It grew out of a need, in the department of Media Arts at the University of North Texas, for an intermediate level critical-cultural studies class in methodologies, one that could take its place in the curriculum between basic introductory classes (usually offered at the freshman level) and more advanced topics classes, offered at the junior and senior levels. The perceived need for such a class arose from the fact that many of our upper division topics classes regularly assigned books and essays that dealt with concepts that were more theoretically advanced than the materials found in our basic freshman introductory class. Thus RTVF 3610, "Film and Television Analysis" was created to fill the gap, in order to ease the transition between simpler and more difficult classes. RTVF 3610 was developed by myself and several colleagues over the course of many years, and it has since become a prerequisite for students wanting to enroll in advanced topics classes that may assign (for example) original essays by Laura Mulvey, Peter Wollen, D. A. Miller, and/or Linda Williams. All of our critical-cultural faculty agree that the class has been a success: students are much more prepared to engage with writings that incorporate psychoanalytic, feminist, and/or poststructuralist ideas (among others) once they have been introduced to them in a class (or a book) such as this one.

This book also had input from the 2010 Society for Cinema Studies conference, during a workshop I created and chaired entitled "Teaching Film and Television Theory to Undergraduate Students." The panelists and the audience had an invigorating discussion on the topic, but what became quickly apparent to me was that very few people in the room even agreed on what the term "theory" meant, let alone how it might best be incorporated into an undergraduate curriculum. Some people expressed the view that "theory"—however defined—was too difficult for undergraduates, while others proudly announced that their students were required to take a year-long sequence of classes wherein they read Gilles Deleuze's *Cinema 1: The Movement-Image* and *Cinema 2: The Time-Image*. I was reminded of a time when I was a teaching assistant for the "Introduction to Film" class at the University of Southern California, and one of my ambitious colleagues handed out Laura Mulvey's "Visual Pleasure and Narrative Cinema" to first-year students. At the time, I wondered what the students would take from the essay, considering it had not been discussed in lecture and that most of them probably had very little exposure to basic psychoanalytic concepts. Surely some sort of "primer" that introduced and explained the essay's basic theoretical concepts could have helped students in that situation—helped them parse the

essay and grasp its meanings. Such a "primer" is exactly what this book aims
to be.

In writing this volume, I have had to confront a fear that it (and I) might be
accused of "dumbing down" and/or misrepresenting the complex and frequently
brilliant ideas expressed by previous writers and thinkers on the subjects of film
and television analysis. Why not just throw students into the deep end of the
theoretical pool (so to speak) and see if they learn to swim? Certainly, there are
some universities where highly prepared students can and do encounter Gilles
Deleuze or Laura Mulvey in highly productive ways (most likely in smaller seminar
settings). However, I also realize there are many other institutions (like mine)
where that is not a practical approach to teaching film and television studies. At
UNT, we process hundreds of majors a year, and those students are interested in
vastly different subject areas—from fictional filmmaking to TV studio production,
and from media management to sports broadcasting. In short, I feel that programs
like ours can and do benefit from an approach that is represented by this book,
and the class it was derived from, RTVF 3610. Even students who do not go on
to take advanced critical-cultural studies classes are exposed to the basic ideas of
the discipline, learning to approach film and television from a variety of different
critical and analytical perspectives. Those who do pursue further education
in critical-cultural studies gain a helpful grounding in the field's central and
historically important concepts, a stepping stone that helps them process the more
complex concepts and readings explored in later classes.

That said, I think there are many different ways a book like this can and could
be useful, based upon varying student abilities and the shape of institutional
curricula. At UNT, the class this book is designed upon is taught each long
semester to approximately ninety junior-level students. Scantron tests are
administered to gauge whether or not the students are learning the concepts at
hand, and a number of short writing exercises, designed to allow the students
to apply those concepts, are also assigned throughout the semester. (Similarly,
questions for discussion are also featured throughout this textbook.) On the other
hand, this book might also be ideal in smaller group settings in conjunction with
a selection of important primary essays, many of which are increasingly available
in excellent anthologies such as Braudy and Cohen's *Film Theory and Criticism*
or Corrigan, White, and Mazaj's *Critical Visions in Film Theory*. This book is not
meant to replace volumes such as those, but rather supplement and introduce
some of the ideas they contain, so that when students do encounter the important
primary literature of film and television studies, they are prepared to engage with
it, and not merely be baffled by it.

The choice of what is included in this volume and how it is presented may
seem somewhat idiosyncratic, but this volume is based upon the perceived needs
of the students at UNT, as well as my own personal interests and emphases in
the area of film and television studies. One of the first things that will become
apparent is that I view this as a book of theor*ies* and method*s*, not a book about
Theory—however one might define that. In class I often liken this approach to
"speed dating": students meet a new method or approach every week. In so doing,
they are not required to "date" or "marry" any one theory, but they are required
to learn the basic concepts and values of any given approach. This book also
stresses the historical development of film and television theories, and in so doing
further underlines the point that there is not one "grand theory" for explaining

all aspects of film and television, but rather an ever-changing and evolving set of ideas that people have used over the years—and continue to use—to approach and explore the various meanings of film and television texts. I am deeply indebted to two previous textbooks that I feel share these goals (and that I continue to use in my own classes): Robert C. Allen's *Channels of Discourse, Reassembled* and Joanne Hollows and Mark Jancovich's *Approaches to Popular Film*. If this volume comes anywhere near the elegance and usefulness of those books, it will be because their clarity and pedagogical brilliance have been my inspiration and my guide.

CHAPTER 1

Introduction to culture and cultural criticism

This book is an introduction to some of the (potentially infinite) ways one might think about film and television texts in relation to the socio-cultural surroundings from which they arise and within which they are consumed. It introduces, in a chapter-by-chapter fashion, some of the more important and well-known schools of thought on the relationship(s) between media texts and culture. It takes for granted that film and television texts exist within ever-changing industrial contexts, and while those parameters are important, this is not a book primarily about the film industry nor the television industry *per se*. It is a book about various approaches to understanding the products of those industries, i.e. individual **texts** or **cultural artifacts**. Indeed, this might be thought of as the goal of **media criticism**: using broad theoretical models or frameworks to examine and explore the meanings of individual media texts. Neither is this book interested in championing a set of exemplary or canonical texts; rather it explores the various theoretical methods that might be used to study any and all media texts. (That said, individual film and television shows are discussed throughout this book as case studies meant to illuminate and/or complicate the theoretical approaches under consideration.) This book is also discerning in which methods it chooses to focus upon: as opposed to approaches that arise from mass communications research or traditional literary theory, the approaches addressed in this volume might best be described as those comprising **contemporary cultural criticism** from a liberal arts perspective. Most importantly this book is designed to introduce students to the various ideas, terms, and concepts that they will encounter in later classes and more advanced readings in the fields of film and television studies.

The various ways of thinking about film and television go by different names and labels, and some of them are considered (as the subtitle of this book notes) "methods," while others might be considered "theories," and still others are referred to as "approaches." This book will not draw strict lines of demarcation between these similar terms, frequently using them somewhat interchangeably. In some cases, certain terms have become attached to certain ways of thinking that perhaps were not originally intended, as in the phrase **auteur theory**; however as that phrase is still widely used, this book will follow that precedent. But what exactly are the differences between these terms? Whereas "approach" and "method" are somewhat colloquial sounding, "theory" has more scientific connotations. According to many definitions, a **theory** is a set of abstract principles drawn from observation and experimentation that is useful in describing—and thus helping us understand and reliably predict—various physical or social phenomena. In the **hard sciences** (fields like biology, chemistry, mathematics, and physics), theories are used to frame and explain physical phenomena like gravity, atomic and molecular structure, or evolution. Often theories cannot be proven *per se*—witness the ongoing debates about evolutionary theory—but they can be shown to more or less account for, describe, and predict the observable and repeatable data found in the material world around us. When new data arises that contradicts pre-existing theories, either the data or the theories must be reexamined. In this way, scientific theories are constantly evolving themselves, as scientists struggle to find accurate ways to describe and understand the world around us.

Some people in the past—and perhaps a few still today—see film and television theories in the same light, as having the weight and "truth claim" of scientific theories. This book does not. At best, film and television studies must be considered a **social science** like anthropology or sociology, because film and television studies attempts to look at the complex relations between human subjects and cultural artifacts—in this case, film and television texts. Unlike the constants, variables, and unknowns that can be strictly controlled in the scientist's laboratory, film and television texts exist in the real world and across history, and are consumed by various people and varying communities in (sometimes surprisingly) different ways. It is thus very hard to make **essentialist claims** about most media texts, such as "All people love the movie *Avatar* (2009)" or even "The science fiction film *Avatar* is a disguised Western." (Essentialist claims tend to reduce the complexity of things into basic, easily assimilated sound bites, and misrepresent reality by oversimplifying it.) Whereas the physical sciences can be fairly certain about predicting that the sun will rise in the east and set in the west tomorrow, or that objects will fall at a given rate of acceleration, it is very hard to predict how various people and communities are going to react to different media texts, or even the same media text. When dealing with human subjects, a whole range of variables becomes significant, including things like personal and regional histories, psychology, and socio-cultural factors such as ethnicity, race, class, age, gender, and sexuality. Thus, the good film and television scholar needs to be aware of the multifarious and complex ways that human beings interact with media texts.

Another way of approaching the difference between scientific theory and media theory—one that will be explored in greater detail a bit later in this book—is by making a distinction between **structuralist** and **poststructuralist** theories. Structuralist theories are concerned with (as the term implies) trying to *construct* a model—quite literally a theoretical structure—that explains a given set of texts or phenomena. Often, structuralist theories are concerned with making broad assertive statements about things, such as "*Stagecoach* (1939) belongs to the Western film **genre** because of x, y, and z." Poststructuralist critics, on the other hand, are more interested in illuminating a range of *meanings* about a given text and its relation to culture and history, such as "*Stagecoach* (1939) reflects x, y, and z about American culture in the years immediately preceding World War II." As explored later in this book, poststructuralist approaches arose out of the need to historicize and complicate basic structuralist models, which were seen as being too rigid (**essentialist**) and therefore limiting. Thus, whereas most physical sciences and structuralist approaches to media study are based on theorizing explanatory structures or frameworks, contemporary film and television theory tends to be more open ended, since it needs to consider a host of variables in the ever-changing real world of humanity and human difference.

The concepts explored in this book are also different from most hard science and many social science approaches, in that the models explored herein are **qualitative** approaches, as opposed to **quantitative** ones. Approaches (or methods, or theories) termed qualitative are closely aligned to liberal arts disciplines like literature and history—they explore a text's unique formal and aesthetic qualities in relation to the cultures that produce and consume them. Quantitative approaches—closely aligned with both the hard sciences and social sciences like economics, sociology, and **mass communication**—use numbers and statistics to try to quantify something significant about media texts and/or the media industries. For example, quantitative mass communication approaches might report on the number of male versus female film directors in Hollywood during a given era, or the number of movie characters who smoked cigarettes in the year 2000 versus the year 2010. (Academics who perform such studies are sometimes derogatorily referred to by their less charitable colleagues as "bean counters.") But what do those kinds of analyses really tell us? They may be a starting point for more complicated types of study, but they also seem to imply something static or essentialist about the gender of film directors, or the meaning of smoking in the movies. Whereas many quantitative researchers are content to report numbers, qualitative researchers are more likely to explore what is meant by gender in the first place, and how that might relate to directing a film. Are all female filmmakers going to make movies in a certain way, simply because of their gender? Probably not. Is the sex of a film director more important than what the film itself is expressing about gender? Similarly, smoking in movies might mean a range of different things—it could be used to evoke an era, a genre, or certain character traits—all things that would be ignored by a simple quantitative approach that just tallies up and reports on the number of characters smoking in a given set of films.

Recently, a pair of economic researchers (Phillip B. Levine and Melissa Schettini Kearney) published findings about the effects of MTV shows like *16 and Pregnant* (2009–) and its *Teen Mom* (2009–12) spinoffs on the overall birthrate for teenage women. Comparing **Nielsen Ratings** with topics trending on Twitter, Google, and Topsy, they concluded that as the teenage birthrate fell from 2009–12, 5.7 per cent of that decline was due to watching and talking about the shows. However, other studies (such as the one by Nicole Martins and Robin Jensen in *Mass Communication and Society*) found that heavy viewers of *16 and Pregnant* and *Teen Mom* felt that the shows glamorized teen pregnancy, and were thus unlikely to deter it or otherwise contribute to a decline in the teen birth rates. So which study is "correct"? Do the shows glamorize teen pregnancy or help prevent it? While these **quantitative** studies reached somewhat opposing conclusions, a **qualitative** study of the phenomenon would most likely acknowledge the multifarious and complicated aspects of reception, in that different people are going to "take away" different messages from the same media texts, or that even single individuals may "take away" mixed messages. Contemporary cultural criticism, with its qualitative approach, would also be highly skeptical of the first study's numerical claim. Reducing a complex cultural phenomenon like teen pregnancy—a phenomenon undoubtedly effected by multiple social institutions including schools, families, churches, governments, and the media, not to mention individual differences like race, class, education, age, etc.—to the simple number 5.7 per cent seems abstract and ultimately foolhardy. It is not that contemporary cultural criticism is not interested in questions related to the mass media's effects on culture—it certainly is—it is just that contemporary cultural critics see most cultural conditions and media effects as too complex to quantify in meaningful ways.

The differences between **contemporary cultural criticism**—the subject of this book—and **media economics** or **mass communication** approaches—are also more than just differences between qualitative and quantitative methodologies. In many respects the goals of each theoretical paradigm are fundamentally different. Mass communication approaches often use numbers and statistics like **box office returns** and **Nielsen ratings** to track the success or failure of media products in the marketplace. As such, they are inherently invested in economic aspects of the media, and the media industries frequently use those types of analyses to produce more of the same type of product, based on the logic that what sold once will probably sell again. On the other hand, contemporary cultural criticism—as perhaps its name implies, is often more *critical* of the media industries. While contemporary cultural criticism still pays attention to the economics of media production and consumption, it is more likely to explore the wider socio-cultural implications of texts, well beyond their economic parameters. (Exploring texts in relation to their industrial-economic concerns as well as their social-aesthetic concerns is an approach sometimes broadly termed the study of media's **political economy**.) To take an historical example, the films of Will Rogers made during the Great Depression were very successful at the box office, perhaps because Will Rogers presented a folksy critique of the previous decade's capitalist excesses, and the current era's political foibles. (Examples include *Judge Priest* [1934] and *Steamboat Round the Bend* [1935].) Because of their monetary success, Fox Films copied the formula repeatedly. But Will Rogers's films are also full of racist stereotypes that critics throughout the years have found troubling (see Figure 1.1). Quantitative approaches to the Will Rogers phenomenon might note those stereotypes as part of a successful formula and leave it at that, whereas qualitative approaches might be more concerned with exploring how and why such

Fig 1.1
Character actor Stepin Fetchit (Lincoln Perry) embodied the racist stereotype of the lazy **coon** in many films such as *Steamboat Round the Bend* (1935).

stereotypes arose in the first place, how they spoke to moviegoers in the 1930s, and what their lingering effects might be upon our understandings of race and racial privilege in the twenty-first century.

The various qualitative methods, theories, and approaches explored in this book are occasionally contradictory, and at other times complementary. It is not this author's belief that any one single model or method can adequately explain the entirety of all phenomena related to the vast worlds of film and television. Rather, different models and methods might be used to answer different types of questions about specific film and television artifacts in specific film and television contexts. If we want to understand the role the director plays in the production of a film's meaning, then the **auteur theory** is probably going to help us do so better than **genre theory**. However, genre theory (as well as **feminist film theory**) might be more appropriate to invoke when exploring how TV shows about female police detectives relate to the history of the police show as a traditionally male-dominated form. In other words, various film and television theories (or methods, or approaches) provide frameworks within which film and television scholars can examine specific texts and ask specific questions about them. There is no single overarching "Theory with a capital T" that explains everything (despite what some film scholars used to think). Instead, the different approaches this book introduces might be thought of as tools in the cultural critic's toolbox. Different tools are useful for examining different aspects of film and TV artifacts.

Problematizing culture, problematizing art

As this section will explore, what we mean by culture and what we mean by art varies from era to era as well as from individual to individual. Culture is a slippery term with different meanings that have changed over the years. We also regularly speak of different kinds of culture. For example, one often hears the terms **popular culture** and **mass culture** in relation to film and television. Both of those terms suggest a wide audience: such artifacts are popular because they are consumed by masses of people. However, another way to think of mass culture is in terms of its production: mass culture in this respect is produced in great quantities—like newspapers, comic books, or TV shows—as opposed to paintings or sculptures which usually exist as single artifacts. Likewise, popular culture might also mean different things—does it solely refer to the amount of money any given cultural artifact has made—i.e. how many people have consumed it—or does popular culture suggest something that is somehow "of the people?" In terms of film and television texts, it is important to note that while movies and TV may be consumed by masses of people and thus referred to as popular culture or mass culture, they are in fact produced by a very small number of media practitioners, what some critics and cultural commentators disparagingly refer to as the "Hollywood elite."

On the other hand, cultural artifacts such as ethnic food or traditional dancing that are both produced *and* consumed by the same communities are often described as **folk culture**. Only in rare cases can we consider film and television examples of folk culture (as when a group of people collectively record their own history for their own needs). The great majority of film and television texts that the public consumes is produced by a small number of people working within vast industrial contexts to which most citizens have little to no access. And while individuals have sometimes been able to make films on their own and have them seen by numerous others, it is almost impossible for a single individual to create, produce, and distribute a television show. (Advances in new media technologies like YouTube and Vimeo are challenging this assertion; however, the film and television industries still control the vast majority of the media landscape, and it is their product that is most regularly circulated and consumed.)

Complicating matters even further is the fact that what was once considered a somewhat unified or singular popular or mass culture (such as Hollywood filmmaking or network television) has shifted into a plethora of **niche cultures** allegedly appealing only to small sections of the population. Hollywood films from the 1930s, for example, were once the mass, popular culture of their era. Today, they might be better described as a niche culture enjoyed by select audiences who access them via DVDs or cable channels like Turner Classic Movies. And what of the most recent box office failure that Hollywood was sure would be so popular with audiences? It might be sold to masses of people through mass advertising campaigns, but if no one goes to see it, can it still be called popular culture? Does it then become part of a niche culture if it is taken up by a cult of "so bad it's good" movie fans? Indeed, today's media marketplace is increasingly made up of niche cultures—there are channels for people who like science fiction, channels for those who like sports, and channels for those who like films and television shows from previous eras. In earlier decades, when film and television was produced and distributed by a handful of studios and three TV networks, media practitioners sought to reach a common audience—as the term "broadcast" suggests, they designed their texts to appeal to a broad general demographic. Today we sometimes use the term **narrowcasting** to refer to how 500 TV channels appeal to various types of niche audiences. And even though Hollywood film companies still control most of what is screened at multiplex theaters, independent art house theaters and straight-to-DVD releases aim at serving more varied niche tastes. Arguably, the development of the Internet and YouTube channels allows for an infinite number of niche audiences (as well as the promise of more singular or individuated productions).

As the film and television industries have changed and evolved over the years, so have our understandings of culture, art, and cultural criticism. **Contemporary cultural criticism** itself is quite different from that of preceding centuries—or even recent decades. Those earlier forms of cultural analysis are sometimes referred to collectively as **traditional cultural criticism**, and they developed in the Western world throughout the eighteenth and nineteenth centuries, the so-called "Age of Enlightenment." Traditional cultural criticism was often centered on the creation and maintenance of literary and artistic canons. The term **canon** refers to a collection of artworks (texts) that are thought to be more important than others—allegedly because they are brilliantly creative and hold universal truths— and are thus full of significance to all people of all ages. (Interestingly, the concept of canon arises from within Medieval Christianity, where it referred to the church's sets of authoritative dogma.) Thus, for many centuries Western scholars studied certain Greek philosophers and poets, who were thought to possess and reveal eternal truths about the human condition. Contemporary literary canons might still include the works of Chaucer, William Shakespeare, and Christopher Marlowe. A canon of great American novelists might include Mark Twain, William Faulkner, and Ernest Hemingway. Similarly, during the early years of academic film studies (circa the 1960s), critics and scholars created canons of great cinema that included work by directors such as Charlie Chaplin, John Ford, Alfred Hitchcock, and Orson Welles. What is implied in any canon formation is that the works it includes are deemed significant artistic texts that have stood (or will stand) the test of time—i.e. they will continue to be relevant and appreciated down through the ages for (allegedly) all people everywhere.

This canonical approach to artistic creation held sway throughout much of the twentieth century, often tweaked and redefined under various labels like **New Criticism**, **Leavisite Criticism** (specifically in literature), or more simply **liberal humanist** approaches to "great art." These approaches almost always centered on **formalist** approaches to the text itself: what was thought to be important were the elements of literary style found on the page, the use of color and brushwork on a canvas, or the elements of rhythm and rhyme in a poem. Unlike most approaches within contemporary cultural criticism, the contexts of a work of art (such as its authorship, reception, or historical moment) were deemed relatively unimportant or even unworthy of consideration. Furthermore, works that were not included in the canon were rarely deemed worthy of study at all. Even today, college classes like "Great American Writers" or "Great Hollywood Film Directors" consistently draw upon and reinforce the idea of canons—that there are great artists and great works that are better and more worthy of study than all the rest.

Over the centuries an entire field of study known as **aesthetics** arose to separate out "great art"—worthy of study, preservation, and reverence—from all the others. Oftentimes "great" or "true art" is held to be so because of its originality, complexity, intensity of affect, and coherence. In other words, good or great art should be and/or express something new; it should be complicated or multifaceted; it should provoke a strong emotional response in the person experiencing it; and it should all come together in some unified meaning or affect. While many of these traits can be applied to some film and television texts (such as some art films or specialized TV shows), they seem somewhat out of touch with much contemporary film and television criticism. The latest explosive action thriller sequel is usually not very original nor coherent, and formulaic TV **sitcoms** rarely invoke intense emotional responses beyond pleasant bemusement. It is apparent that film and television texts are not art forms like classical painting or classical music. In fact, according to many critics schooled only in classical art and aesthetics, films (let alone television) barely qualify as art forms at all. In fact, as noted above, film studies did not become a serious academic discipline until the 1960s, and TV studies took even longer to be accepted within academia. Even today, scholars in other fields sometimes look down on the notion of seriously studying film and television, considering them trash without cultural significance, let alone aesthetic or academic merit. As we shall see, our understanding of art, and more broadly culture itself, had to shift over the years before a serious academic discussion of film and TV could begin. The development of **contemporary cultural criticism** and its various methodologies—the very subjects of this book—were part of this evolution, allowing film and television texts to be taken seriously. The question of whether or not they are "art" *per se* is almost irrelevant.

Hopefully, the drawbacks to these traditional approaches—even when discussing older art forms like painting, sculpture, musical composition, and literature—are glaringly apparent. Today, many critics understand the creation of artistic and literary canons in previous centuries as a form of **cultural imperialism**, whereby one region or nation promoted its own interests and culture as superior to all others. Traditional cultural criticism was and is very judgmental and subjective, promoting Greek ideals and Western European arts as universal forms of culture— and by extension universal markers of human achievement and civilization. Non-Western regions or nations were rarely considered to possess culture at all, let alone be capable of producing great works of art. Such attitudes grew alongside of and contributed to **colonialism**, the conquering of the globe and the subsequent subjugation of native peoples in the names of Western European nations. The economic exploitation of less developed regions around the planet could thus be justified as the spreading of "enlightened" and "superior" Western canonical culture (including Christianity) to "savages" who were in many cases thought to possess no culture whatsoever.

Things began to change during the mid-twentieth century, and so did the definition of culture. Instead of defining most of the earth's population as savages without culture, anthropologists, sociologists, and cultural critics began to recognize that every human community inherently possesses culture, and that Western European cultures were not the only ones that could be so defined, studied, and valued for their unique expressions of humanity. Today, we tend to think of **culture** as the artifacts, belief systems, and social practices that define any group of people, regardless of their allegedly "primitive" or "civilized" components. However, this change in thinking about culture has been slow in coming, and to some extent these older models of culture still pervade much thinking about global politics and art (especially outside of academia). Indeed, the phrases "to have culture" or "to be cultured" usually mean that someone is linked to the arts, mores, and decorum descended from and defined by Western European traditions. The term **Eurocentrism**, explored more fully in Chapter 12, is used to describe the ways that Western European ideals still tend to shape our thinking about other nations and cultures. (For example, the mass media tends to refer to Western "religions" versus Eastern "cults" or "sects.") This book is also guilty of Eurocentrism to the extent that it focuses primarily on concepts developed within the Western world over the last hundred years or so. Perhaps other regions and nations did or do have their own ways of theorizing the relationships between people and media. Regrettably, those topics are beyond the scope of this introductory volume, even as they are being studied by emerging and established scholars in the field.

An implied judgment or evaluation between good, eternal, and universally edifying Western culture and all other forms of (non)-culture still can be found in much mainstream media criticism, as well as in the production and reception of film and television texts. That differential is thoroughly embedded in the debates over what exactly constitutes "art." Who gets to define what art is, and what types of art are valued over others? Even though contemporary cultural criticism tries to eschew such distinctions, we still live in a world that frequently draws classificatory lines between art and non-art, or simply between what is judged as "good art" and what is judged as "bad art." Indeed, **journalistic criticism** of film and television (as found in reviews printed in newspapers or posted on websites) is usually devoted to exactly that type of simplistic judgment: separating out good films and television shows from the bad ones. Journalistic reviews are written to advise their readers whether or not they should spend their time and money on a given film or TV show. However, each journalistic critic usually possesses his or her own subjective values—likes and dislikes, predispositions, favorite genres and directors, etc.—and rates film and television texts accordingly, making this approach to criticism not all that different from canon formation. Such journalistic assessment of film and television texts is outside the purview of this book, as the models explored herein attempt to be more objective (descriptive) than subjective (judgmental).

Even when various aspects of culture *are* considered art, one of the most frequent distinctions made by critics concerns their status as high art versus low art. In simplistic terms, **high art** refers to forms and practices like the ballet, opera, classical music, and serious literature—art forms descended from and/or linked to the older Western canons. High art is often patronized by or associated with elite middle-to-upper class citizens, and it is frequently supported by wealthy institutions and foundations. On the other hand, the term **low art** is used to categorize forms and practices like comic books, graffiti, and popular music. Low art tends to arise from or be associated with the broader populations of working class and/or minority cultures. For example, think of classical music versus popular music. The idea of classical music calls to mind elaborate compositions by Beethoven or Bach, played in a sumptuous concert hall, and supported by wealthy patrons. Popular music, on the other hand (whether rock and roll, tejano, or hip-hop) consists of shorter works created in garages or on the streets by working class or minority cultures (and especially the more youthful members of those communities).

In a related way, high art also tends to be classified by its distance from contemporary mass culture—both temporally (eighteenth-century opera) and spatially (located only in wealthier urban areas). Concert halls, ballet corps, and art museums cost money to build and maintain, and often charge higher prices for admittance than do many low art forms. In recent decades, high art has also become associated with the critical and aesthetic challenges posed by **modernism**, a broad movement in the arts circa the late nineteenth and early twentieth centuries that challenged **classicism** and **realism** (discussed more fully in Chapter 9). Modernist art as a broad label includes works crafted within various schools or methods of creation, such as **impressionism**, **expressionism**, **surrealism**, and **dada**, many of which sought to express new ways of seeing and challenge prevailing social norms. Today, art museums display canvases from the Renaissance as well as works by twentieth-century modernists like Pablo Picasso, Marc Chagall, and Salvador Dali. Like much modernist art, high art is often thought to be more abstract or difficult to understand than are lower art forms. An abstract painting requires time and thought to process, a critical or intellectual assessment; low art rarely asks for or requires such efforts to be enjoyed.

As is often the case with **binary oppositions**, low art tends to be defined as the opposite of high art. Thus lower art forms tend to arise more from within folk or subcultural (not elite) populations wherever they are physically and temporally located—whether it be country music as it developed in rural Appalachia, or hip-hop in 1970s inner city ghettoes. In order to be consumed by working and minority cultures, the price of low art is typically lower than that of high art. Some low art forms do not require an admission price, and may actually present a threat to dominant interests; for example, graffiti or break dancing in urban spaces are free practices that may disrupt the aesthetic status quo envisioned by city planners. Similarly, if high art allegedly appeals to the intellect, low art more regularly appeals to the emotions. High art tends to be associated with the mind and brain, whereas low art tends to be associated with affect and the body. (Here one might think of the verbal wordplay or wit of an Oscar Wilde play versus the antics of a slapstick comedian.) One of the most exciting things about studying culture and art is the innovation and evolution of differing forms: what was once a folk culture may become popular and spread to the masses, while other aspects of mass culture may eventually fade away into history. The complex "how and why" of such phenomena are questions that contemporary cultural analysis attempts to explore and explain.

Yet, who is to say that high art forms are better or more worthy of contemplation than are low art forms? One might argue that it is the low arts that have the most impact on a given culture—at least numerically. They are consumed far more regularly and by far more people than the elite few who attend the opera or the ballet. Thus, in order to sidestep the implications of "high" versus "low" (and even the distinction "art" versus "not-art") contemporary cultural theory uses the terms **cultural artifact** and/or **text** in place of art or artwork. Whereas the terms art and artwork carry all sorts of subjective value judgments rooted in historically classist and ethnocentric discourses, the terms cultural artifact and/or text attempt to be more neutral and objective. However, as much as we might want to avoid debates over what constitutes art, let alone what constitutes high and/or low art, those concepts and debates have been prevalent for centuries. As the next section will explore, different types of films and TV shows are also both consciously and unconsciously understood in terms of high art versus low art.

A brief history of high and low art in film and television

As we shall see throughout this book, the debate over whether or not motion pictures (and especially television) are truly an "art" form is a complex and ever-changing one. When film was first innovated in the Western world at the turn of the twentieth century, it was primarily considered a mechanical novelty and demonstrated to an elite few. Quickly however, screenings in music halls, vaudeville theaters, and specialized storefront theaters called Nickelodeons changed the demographics of the audience: cinema became an entertainment form consumed chiefly by immigrants and working class people in urban settings. Wealthy and educated urban people who attended the live theater (supposedly a higher art form) often sneered at the movies both because of their primitive nature (short, grainy, black and white chases and pratfalls) as well as their clientele. Thus it was perhaps provocative when the American poet Vachel Lindsay published his treatise *The Art of the Motion Picture* in 1915. A bit later psychologists Hugo Munsterberg and Rudolf Arnheim argued that cinema should be considered an art form because of its unique formal properties, and theorized on the ways that cinema might effect human perception and psychology.

The nascent Hollywood industry was quick to agree with Vachel Lindsay's evaluation and throughout the 1910s sought to promote its films as art, and to court a "better class" of clientele. They up-scaled storefront Nickelodeon theaters by building lush cinemas called "movie palaces," and created longer, more complex narrative films (including adaptations of literary classics) in order to give cinema the patina of legitimate, i.e. high, art. In both Europe and America, a brief movement in the 1910s referred to by film historians as **films d'art** devoted itself to filming classical plays, contributing to the up-scaling of cinema and its artistic pretensions. Of course, there was a strong economic motive for these shifts in the industry:

middle and upper class audiences had more disposable income to spend than did working class audiences. Studios and exhibitors could charge higher admission fees for longer "high class" movies accompanied by orchestras and/or pipe organs. Despite such attempts however, many cultural critics continued to view films as just so much mass-produced drivel aimed at the allegedly weaker minds of women, the working class, and immigrant populations. It was not until the mid-twentieth century with the rise of an international art cinema and the development of the **auteur theory** (discussed in Chapter 4) that more people began to think of film as art. As the auteur theory suggested (albeit somewhat tautologically), if people who made movies could be considered authors and artists, then surely what they produced must be art.

Similarly, television was hardly considered an art form during its early years of innovation, and many people today might still balk at calling it so. TV's increasingly prevalent placement in the average citizen's home throughout the 1950s firmly situated it within the sphere of the homely, the common, and the low. Domestic sitcoms, sports events, and variety shows that drew upon decades-old vaudeville traditions furthered TV's status as a low (or mass, or popular) art form consumed by common men and women. One exception to this perception was a spate of highly regarded "playhouse" shows that aped theatrical conventions, presenting original screenplays and live performance aesthetics derived from the "legitimate" stage, from which it also drew many of its actors. Some television historians refer to the 1950s as "The Golden Age of Television" (a term which itself sounds rather high art-ish), precisely because TV seemed to be copying a higher art form, in this case live theater. However, by the early 1960s, television was again being described— perhaps most infamously by the FCC (Federal Communications Commission) Chairman Newton Minnow—as a "Vast Wasteland" allegedly composed solely of trivial game shows, formulaic westerns, and inane sitcoms. In response, the television industry tried briefly to upgrade its artistic standing with documentary-style programming, but by the 1970s sitcoms and police dramas comprised much of the three networks' usual fare. According to some critics still mired in the high–low debate, network television in the twenty-first century has become an even lower art form, mostly because of its focus on cheaply produced and sensationalistic reality programming. In this evaluation, scripted fictional shows—even sitcoms—are seen as higher art forms than reality shows like *Jersey Shore* (2009–12) and *Here Comes Honey Boo Boo* (2012–14).

The discourses of the high/low dichotomy can be found everywhere across our new media landscape. For example, Hollywood films distributed to mass audiences via corporate-owned multiplexes, with saturation advertising campaigns and saturation bookings (i.e. they appear on thousands of screens all over the nation at once) are usually perceived as lower forms of cinema than those playing in urban art houses that specialize in foreign films, documentaries, and American independent films. Many if not most people make culturally evaluative distinctions between the latest Adam Sandler gross-out comedy and prestigious literary adaptations like *Jane Eyre* (2011). Even the exhibition contexts are different for mainstream movies versus art house films, and are supposedly indicative of common mass tastes versus elite ones. At the multiplex, consumers are enjoined to eat hotdogs, nachos, and popcorn covered with "butter-flavored" syrup. At the art house patrons are offered gourmet popcorn with real butter, a selection of bottled waters, and frequently a full service bar. Hollywood might pride itself once a year at the Academy Awards ceremony on producing "art," but it more regularly earns its money from movies that many people might not consider art at all.

Film itself has a higher patina of art than does television. Again this partly is due to the fact that film historically resembles live theater in that people pay to see it in a public venue, whereas TV is located in the home and is allegedly "free." It also has to do with the content of each medium. Films are almost always scripted and allegedly "authored" by their directors (see Chapter 4), whereas TV shows tend to be written by committees or be unauthored altogether. Niche TV stations that play older movies exclusively (like American Movie Classics and Turner Classic Movies) forthrightly announce their cultural significance with the word "classic." Similarly, the Sundance Channel and the Independent Film Channel are perceived as having more high art qualities than something like the Home Shopping Network, precisely because of the elite nature of the cinema they feature. Perhaps all this can be best summed up by the HBO slogan "It's not TV, it's HBO." The statement suggests that HBO is better than TV—despite the fact that HBO is a TV channel—because it is a subscription pay channel, because it shows films, and because it has presented unique and prestigious original programming such as *Sex and the City* (1998–2004), *The Sopranos* (1999–2007), *True Blood* (2008–14), and *Boardwalk Empire* (2010–14). Note that each of those HBO series is also associated with an "author": writer/producer/creators Darren Star, David Chase, Alan Ball, and Martin Scorsese, respectively.

It may seem as though the preceding passages have unduly emphasized a high–low dichotomy in film and television rather than worked to undermine it. The point is to recognize how the dichotomy still functions within the discourses of popular culture, and as the following chapters will explore, how it has functioned throughout the history of film and TV analysis. Today, with the vast and increasingly converging universes of cable and satellite TV, direct-to-DVD sales, multiplex and art house movie theaters, Internet distribution and web-series, questions of high art versus low art may be less relevant, even as much popular and journalistic criticism still use the concepts as evaluative tools. The term **niche culture**, introduced earlier, offers a more neutral and ultimately more descriptive way to talk about various film and television texts rather than simply labeling them as high or low. Finding and exploring more neutral, objective, and complex ways to think about film and television is the purpose of most of the various methods explored in the remainder of this book. Following the case studies that illuminate the high/low debate, we will turn to some ideas basic to contemporary cultural criticism, ideas that seek to eschew evaluative judgments about a text's worthiness as art altogether.

Case study: High, low, and niche

Our first case study is a film that most people might classify not only as film art, but high art. *Ballet Mécanique* (1924) is a short avant-garde film made by Dudley Murphy and Fernand Léger. Léger was a painter, and as with other experimental filmmakers he sought to use the tools of cinema in the same way that he might use a paint brush. These contextual facts immediately help situate the film within the territory of art and not commerce, as does its screening in galleries, salons, or museums as opposed to movie houses. Like many experimental films, *Ballet Mécanique* has no real story to tell—it is a

Fig 1.2
Abstract imagery in *Ballet Mécanique* (1924).

Fig 1.3
Swirling kitchen whisks contribute to the sense of rapid movement captured throughout *Ballet Mécanique* (1924).

seemingly random collection of often-time abstract shots including images of marching feet, spinning gears, mannequin legs, human faces, boater hats, bottles, and even a horse collar (see Figures 1.2 and 1.3). The film invites and requires its viewers to "do work" in understanding it—no simple meaning is implied let alone stated directly—thus its appeal is both intellectual as well as aesthetic. If the title (it translates to "Mechanical Dance") is any clue to the variety of images that we see, we might understand the film to be something about the clash of humans and machines: the film does include various shots of robotic automata, mechanical objects "dancing" via the use of stop-motion animation, as well as human beings forced into mechanized functions (see Figure 1.4). Thus in a broad sense, we might say that *Ballet Mécanique* is about the age of modernity, and what happens to humans when they enter the age of the machine. But the film may also leave viewers puzzled and confused because it does not tell a story or express a moral.

A very different type of film, Walt Disney's *The Flying Mouse* (1934) is a cartoon from Hollywood's classical era (roughly the 1920s–50s), and it is a good example of mass produced or popular art. Like most cartoons produced during this era, it played in movie houses as part of a cinematic "bill of fare" that included feature films, newsreels, and

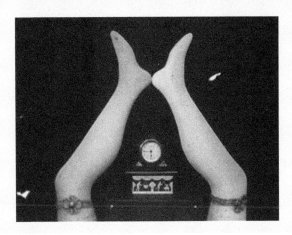

Fig 1.4
Mannequin legs are pixilated (edited together to create movement) in *Ballet Mécanique* (1924) creating a sense of "mechanical dance."

shorts. *The Flying Mouse* was created by the artists at the Disney studio as part of their "Silly Symphonies" series, a group of films that were frequently based on pre-existing fables or nursery rhymes such as *Three Little Pigs* (1933) and *The Ugly Duckling* (1939). As such, many of the "Silly Symphony" films come with an explicit lesson or moral. In *The Flying Mouse*, a young mouse longs to fly, but after his wish is granted by a fairy, he realizes he is an outcast among both mice and birds. He encounters a group of bats who mock him for being "nothin' but a nothin,'" because he does not claim any one group identity (see Figure 1.5). Traumatized and sobbing, the flying mouse begs the fairy to make him a mouse once again, and she grants his wish. Having learned his lesson to "be who you are" and not to wish for other things, the film concludes as the mouse happily reunites with his family (see Figure 1.6). *The Flying Mouse* may be considered a good example of low art. Unlike the ambiguous meanings of *Ballet Mécanique*, *The Flying Mouse* tells you precisely what to think about it, and even provides a moral. It is clearly told in Hollywood narrative style (in which a protagonist desires something, overcomes obstacles, and returns home having learned a lesson), and despite being a cartoon, has an almost realist style to it. (Compared to other cartoon factories of the era, Disney studios promoted a style of animation meant to evoke realism.) Unlike *Ballet Mécanique*'s intellectual appeal, *The Flying Mouse* tells a heartwarming story through physical action and bodily humor, as when the mouse falls from the sky or gets jabbed in the butt by a thorn (see Figure 1.7).

Finally, *Aqua Teen Hunger Force* (2000–) is a television text that muddles notions of high and low, and might better be understood as a text aimed at a niche audience—in this case young people looking for surreal and self-aware entertainment. *Aqua Teen Hunger Force* originally aired during Cartoon Network's "Adult Swim" programming block, a late night segment featuring edgy animated shows definitely not made for children. Its status as television and animation place it more within low art parameters, but its narrative incoherence and invitation to try to make sense of its surreal elements invites a more elite viewer. The show purports to be about a crime fighting fast food "Happy Meal"—comprised of the dimwitted Meatwad, the high-strung Shake, and the more rational Frylock (see Figure 1.8). However, the team rarely solves crimes and each episode

Fig 1.5
In Walt Disney's *The Flying Mouse* (1934), the mouse protagonist encounters hostile bats who tell him he is "nothin' but a nothin'."

Fig 1.6
As with most classical Hollywood narratives, whether animated shorts or full-length features, *The Flying Mouse* (1934) concludes with a happy ending; here, after learning his lesson about wanting to fly, the mouse is reunited with his family.

Fig 1.7
Physical humor and/or slapstick is a hallmark of low art; Disney films are filled with butt humor as characters repeatedly "get it in the end," as in this scene from *The Flying Mouse* (1934).

Fig 1.8
Frylock, Master Shake, and Meatwad, the absurd "crime fighters" who comprise the *Aqua Teen Hunger Force* (2000–).

is usually just a collection of random gags and non sequiturs riffing on pop culture. In an exemplary episode, "Bus of the Undead," Shake becomes convinced that an empty school bus contains the spirit of a reverse vampire (one that can exist in the sun). It is really the hideout of a giant moth-man. At Frylock's insistence, the team travels to Memphis, Tennessee to see the grave of Dracula(?), supposedly to prove that vampires do not exist. Upon their return they discover the moth-man watching *Assisted Living Dracula* on TV, and the episode ends as a cloning device emits a swarm of hybrid brownie/moth-man monsters. Clearly, *Aqua Teen Hunger Force* is not a show for everyone, but it has a loyal cult or niche following. Whether it is high art or low art is of little consequence; it is instead a knowing spoof of popular culture itself.

A contemporary cultural studies framework

While **cultural studies** as an integrated approach to studying media will be discussed more fully in Chapter 10, it is useful to introduce a few of its main ideas here at the start of this book. The idea of using the terms **text** or **cultural artifact** to describe individual films or television shows has already been introduced. These terms allow us to make note of the high or low art connotations associated with a text, but then move on to other concerns related to how film or TV shows intersect with the people who make them, the people who watch them, and the larger cultural contexts surrounding all three. Stuart Hall's well-known "Encoding/ Decoding" model provides a broad yet nuanced framework for understanding film and television, and does not necessarily contradict or conflict with many of the other methods and approaches addressed in the volume. Briefly, Hall's "Encoding/Decoding" model is a modification of an older mass communications model that posits that all media texts involve a sender, a message, and a receiver. We might modify these terms into **media producers**, **texts**, and **audiences/ readers** (see Diagram 1.1). Hall's innovation was to note that as media producers **encode** meaning into a text, they draw upon a range of variables including their own "frameworks of knowledge," "relations of production," and "technical

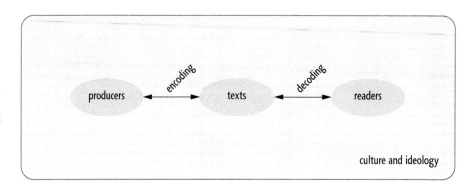

Dia 1.1
An abbreviated version of
Stuart Hall's "Encoding/
Decoding" model, showing
how **cultural artifacts**
(**texts**) circulate between
producers and **readers**
within larger contexts of
culture and **ideology**.

infrastructure." All of which is to say that producers produce texts from certain
points of view, and within varying economic and technical structures such as
a TV studio or an independent film shoot. The process of encoding includes
what the producers consciously want to say within their text, but it also takes
into consideration complex factors of production that go well beyond simply the
author's intent. Likewise, audiences or readers **decode** the text from their own
cultural positions, as well as their own understandings of a text's economic and
technical infrastructure. One of Hall's key points is that the meanings encoded into
a text by its producers may not be the same as the meanings that readers decode
from the text.

Hall's essay proposes three possible ways that readers might draw meanings from
the text. Those three possible reading positions include (1) **preferred** (sometimes
called **dominant**) **readings**, (2) **negotiated readings**, and (3) **oppositional
readings**. When a reader performs a **preferred** reading, he or she decodes the
text according to how the producers encoded it. He or she understands the
text in the way that its producers designed it to be understood, perhaps because
he or she shares many of the same cultural positions and understandings with
the producers (what we will explore as **ideologies** in the next chapter). An
oppositional reading means that an audience member takes away meanings not
necessarily intended by the producers, and in many cases the reader may even
reject the meanings that were encoded by the producers. This may be because
the audience member's own socio-cultural positioning or ideologies are very
different from the producers. In the middle of such extremes lies the **negotiated**
reading position, in which the reader accepts some portions of the text as it was
encoded while rejecting others. In actual practice, it is best to think of preferred
readings and oppositional readings as opposing ends of a continuum. In this
sense all readings are negotiated readings; indeed, we sometimes describe the act
of watching a film or television text as the act of individual readers negotiating
with a text, drawing from it (decoding) meanings based upon his or her personal
subjectivity.

As an example, let us examine the film *The Passion of the Christ* (2004). The
film's **producers** would include everyone involved with the making and marketing
of the film, including Mel Gibson (who helped write the film and also directed).
All of these various film technicians, their frameworks of knowledge, and the
institutions they work within contributed to the meanings **encoded** into the film
text, as does the film's source material, the Holy Bible. At the other end of the
model, are actual **readers** or audience members who **decode** the film according

to their own social positions and frameworks of knowledge. Readers who respond to the film as its producers intended may be said to decode the film in a **preferred** manner. Thus, viewers who decode the film as a violent and visceral retelling of the last days of Jesus Christ and his eventual resurrection, all framed within a Christian-Catholic worldview, could be said to be performing preferred readings.

Readers who do not share similar frameworks of knowledge might have a harder time understanding the film, giving rise to an almost infinite number of **negotiated** readings. It is doubtful whether a Buddhist will decode *The Passion of the Christ* in the same way as an evangelical Christian. Other negotiated readings might include a Catholic woman who agrees with the film's Christian ideals of death and resurrection, but is horrified and appalled by what she considers its excessive and unnecessary violence. Similarly, a self-described atheist gore hound (someone who loves violent horror movies) might reject all the Christian aspects of the film while enjoying the special effects that make the violence so shocking. Finally, **oppositional** readings tend not to "buy into" any aspect of the text. For example, when the film was first in theaters, many Jewish readers not only rejected the film's Christian tenets, but also decoded it as explicitly anti-Semitic for the way in which it depicts its Jewish villains. Such readers were in many cases drawing upon contextual materials along with what they saw and heard on screen: according to a 2006 police report detailing Gibson's arrest for driving under the influence of alcohol, Gibson made several inflammatory anti-Semitic comments. (Mel Gibson's father has also allegedly denied that the Holocaust ever occurred, raising suspicions in some minds that bias against Jews might run in the family line.)

Some people may still want to ask, "Whose reading is correct?" Plenty of ink has been spilled and Internet forums flooded with arguments about the "true" meaning of *The Passion of the Christ*. The point—according to contemporary cultural criticism—is that there is no "true," singular, or **essentialist** meaning to any text. Meanings arise out of the complex negotiation of encoding and decoding, and different readers are going to understand the same text in different ways, based upon their own histories and subjectivities. Ostensibly, one hundred people could watch the same TV show and decode it in one hundred different ways. Yes, we might ask the authors of a text what their actual intentions were, but it does not follow that those are the meanings that enter broader popular culture via various negotiated and oppositional readings. It also does not take into question the fact that most media texts are "authored" not by single individuals but by complex institutions like TV studios or film production companies, nor the fact that artistic creation of any sort might draw upon unconscious urges and desires as much as conscious ones. An author's stated intentionality is only one part of the puzzle of understanding any media text, not the final word on the matter.

The methods explored throughout the remainder of this book, and contemporary cultural studies in general, are not about gauging the quality of a text's artistry, the "genius" or lack thereof of its authors, or whether or not the text is worth the time and money spent to watch it. They *are* about the ways that texts circulate in culture, and activate certain sets of meanings among readers. Stuart Hall's "Encoding/Decoding" model allows us a broad and flexible framework to understand how media texts intersect and interact with audiences and individuals. The following chapters will explore in greater detail more specific and nuanced approaches to the various components of Hall's model.

Questions for discussion

1　How would you define culture? What does culture mean to you? Has this chapter challenged or affirmed your previous ideas about culture and what it means or how it functions?
2　Think about your own preferences in film and television programming. Would you say your favorite texts are more "high art" or more "low art"? Have other people ever been judgmental about your tastes in movies or TV shows?
3　Think about college or high school humanities classes you may have taken. Were any of them focused on a canon of "great works"? What did you take away from those classes? Did any of them explore the cultural artifacts of non-white or non-Western authors or artists?

References and further reading

Allen, Robert C. *Channels of Discourse, Reassembled*. Chapel Hill, NC: The University of North Carolina Press, 1992 (1987).

Arnheim, Rudolf. *Film as Art*. Los Angeles: University of California Press, 2006 (1957, 1933).

Gray, Ann and Jim McGuigan. *Studying Culture: An Introductory Reader*, Second Edition. London and New York: Arnold, 1997 (1993).

Hall, Stuart. "Encoding/Decoding," in *Critical Visions in Film Theory: Classic and Contemporary Readings*, eds. Timothy Corrigan, Patricia White, with Meta Mazaj. Boston and New York: Bedford/St. Martin's, 2011 (1973). Pp. 77–88.

Hollows, Joanne and Mark Jancovich. *Approaches to Popular Film*. Manchester and New York: Manchester University Press, 1995.

Kearney, Melissa Schettini and Phillip B. Levine. "Media Influences on Social Outcomes: The Impact of MTV's *16 and Pregnant* on Teen Childbearing," *National Bureau of Economic Research: Working Paper* (January 2014).

Lindsay, Vachel. *The Art of the Moving Picture*. New York: Modern Library, 2000 (1915).

Martins, Nicole and Robin Jensen. "The Relationship Between 'Teen Mom' Reality Programming and Teenagers' Beliefs about Teen Parenthood," *Mass Communication and Society* 17: 830–52, 2014.

Munsterberg, Hugo. *The Film: A Psychological Study*. New York: Dover Publications, 2012 (1916).

Oswell, David. *Culture and Society: An Introduction to Cultural Studies*. London and Thousand Oaks: Sage, 2006.

Parker, Robert Dale. *How to Interpret Literature: Critical Theory for Literary and Cultural Studies*. New York and Oxford: Oxford University Press, 2008.

Turner, Graeme. *British Cultural Studies: An Introduction*. Boston: Unwin Hyman, 1990.

CHAPTER 2

Concepts of ideology

Ideology is a basic starting point for almost all contemporary cultural theory. **Ideology** refers to the basic ideas and assumptions that help shape a given culture, the preconceived notions and beliefs that structure a given society (as well as its individual members). Ideological beliefs are usually taken as naturally and inherently true by the people, groups, and institutions that hold them. As such, ideology is inherent in all **cultural artifacts**, or **texts**, but it is also something of a free-floating structure that pervades all aspects of culture. If **culture** can be said to consist of the material goods, products, and behaviors of any group of people, ideology is the invisible glue that binds those various objects and behaviors into a coherent and meaningful system of shared relatable experiences. Cultural artifacts always convey ideologies, whether they are consciously encoded into them by their producers or not, and whether their consumers are aware of them or not. Thus, one of the main goals of ideological analysis is to learn to recognize and be able to identify the various ideologies that cultural artifacts convey. And as complex amalgamations of sound and vision, film and television texts can and do convey ideologies in complex and multiple ways. Ideologies are expressed in the ways that stories are told (narrative design), how sets are constructed and lit, how roles are embodied by actors, and how lighting, sound, music, and camera work are deployed. The ideological analysis of a film or TV show therefore often begins with its formal properties, even as it might also encompass a consideration of its means of production (i.e. who made it, for what reasons, and within what socio-historical and industrial contexts).

Ideological analysis immediately asserts that art and culture—indeed all cultural artifacts—have a political dimension. As such, film and television contribute to our understandings of the world around us and the issues we face: film and television texts are part of larger cultural struggles for meaning and understanding. To give one basic historical example, if film and television texts only depict African Americans as butlers and maids (as they mostly did for many decades), those images are going to contribute to a very limited and limiting understanding of African Americans. White viewers might think (either consciously or unconsciously) that those images represent the totality of African American experience, while African American viewers may internalize such messages (consciously or unconsciously) and limit their own lives accordingly. As this one example postulates, the cumulative effects of media images can and do shape how the "real world" understands itself. And those understandings have "real world" consequences in the way that laws are written and passed, and in the basic ways that human beings treat the world around them, including other human beings.

In the mainstream press, ideology is sometimes used to refer to one's political leanings—conservative Republican, liberal Democrat, etc. Furthermore, the popular press likes to pretend that some people and things are free of ideology, while others are biased. However, that understanding of ideology is simplistic and not very nuanced. In fact, people and/or texts that profess to be free of ideology are being naïve if not outright duplicitous. For example, the Fox News Channel's slogan "Fair and Balanced" suggests that they are the only news source free of ideological bias, when by most accounts Fox News is decidedly conservative in its ideology. The slogan is thus itself an **ideological message** that attempts to mask Fox News's conservative agenda. If and when audiences believe the slogan is true, then they are agreeing—consciously or otherwise—with the idea that Fox News's conservative way of seeing the world is actually the one "true" way, when in fact there are infinite ways to see and understand the world around us. While many other (if not most) news channels purport to be objective and free of bias, contemporary ideological theory would insist that none of them really can be so. All news sources—like all cultural artifacts—come with some form of ideological positioning. There is no such thing as being "outside of" ideology. (MSNBC at least hints at its leftist ideological biases: its "lean forward" slogan suggests its "progressive" stance on many social issues.)

As such, any given society is awash in multiple ideologies—some in support of one another, others clashing fairly directly. Texts and people—and we might think of people as complex ever-changing texts in their own right—and the ideologies they contain constantly ebb and flow, interacting and interweaving with one another. Nonetheless, in different cultures and in different historical eras, some ideologies are invariably more prominent or prevalent than others. We call such ideologies **dominant ideologies**: the set of ideas and assumptions that are most prevalent within any given culture at any point in time. In the Western world today, some of our dominant ideologies have been prevalent for many decades if not centuries. The dominant ideology of the Western world is often described as **white supremacist**, **patriarchal**, **Judeo-Christian**, and **capitalist**. This means, respectively, that being racially white or lighter-skinned is usually privileged over belonging to some other race, and that being male tends to afford one extra privilege than does being female. (**Patriarchy** literally means rule by the father.) Our dominant religious ideologies tend to favor those expressed within Judeo-Christian traditions as opposed to Muslim, Shinto, or Hindu. And for several centuries the centrality of capitalism as an economic system and its inherent ideological beliefs—the necessity of unfettered markets, the desirability of amassing wealth, a preference for economic competition rather than economic cooperation—have remained dominant (even as capitalism itself has evolved in various ways).

As noted above, any given society is made up of a huge diversity of ideological positions—in people, in texts, in governing bodies—that necessarily interact with one another in multiple ways. (Scholars call this process **hegemonic negotiation**, discussed more fully below.) This interaction can and does lead to social change. For example, compared to one hundred years ago, women and non-white people have risen to positions of power and prestige within Western cultures, and an African American man has been elected President of the United States. But by most quantitative measures—or by simply examining the ideologies expressed in popular culture—it is apparent that the ideologies of white supremacy (or at least white centrality), patriarchy, Judeo-Christianity, and capitalism continue to structure and dominate most aspects of Western culture. Film and television in the Western world is overwhelmingly produced by white Judeo-Christian men for profit; and many if not most of the texts they produce also express the centrality, importance, and agency of white Judeo-Christian men. Because of this, the intertwining ideologies of white patriarchal capitalism often become naturalized, and remain dominant. (When similar ideological goals are shared and endorsed by multiple texts and social institutions, they are said to be **overdetermined**.) They are taken for granted as "the" way to understand the world. Thus it is one goal of ideological analysis to expose and explore how that happens.

Marx and ideology

Most basic concepts of ideology derive from **Marxism**, a broad set of interrelated ideas that have historically been used to examine and critique capitalism. Marxism takes it name from the ideas and writings of Karl Marx, a German intellectual living in Great Britain during the mid-nineteenth century. Marx's thinking was often collaborative, influenced by that of many others, including his colleague and later editor Friedrich Engels. All of these thinkers shared concerns for the state of the urban **working classes** who were increasingly living under worse and worse conditions as the **Industrial Revolution** progressed throughout Europe and the Americas. Marx and Engels, sometimes referred to as the fathers of Marxism, expressed their ideas in works such as *The German Ideology* (1845), *The Condition of the Working Class in England* (1845), *The Communist Manifesto* (1848), and *Das Kapital* (1867). Since then, hundreds if not thousands of books and treatises have been written on Marx and Marxism, and Marxist thinking has led to various reforms and revolutionary movements throughout the twentieth century. Along with Darwin (evolution) and Freud (psychoanalysis), Marx is often considered to be one of the most influential thinkers of the modern era. However, Marxist ideals (and the concepts that derive from them) remain highly charged and frequently misunderstood subjects. Some commentators are willing to "blame" Marx and Marxism for the Russian Revolution of 1917, and the murderous excesses of Stalinist Russia. Nonetheless, other more nuanced cultural critics continue to find use in the ideas and concepts first theorized by Marx and Engels. What follows will necessarily be highly condensed and rudimentary, an introduction to the ways that basic concepts of Marxism have impacted upon the study of film and television vis-à-vis ideology.

Broadly, Marxism is a system of thought, a philosophy, and/or a critique of economic domination wherein one class—the **ruling class**—controls all aspects of a society at the expense of all others, most significantly the **working class** or the **proletariat**. The middle class or **bourgeoisie** is usually figured as complacent and in league with the ruling class. Importantly—its detractors to the side—Marxism is not the same thing as communism. Marxism is a philosophical critique of capitalism that has been used by some nations to justify **communism**, an economic system in which the state owns and operates all industries and businesses, with the proposed goal of distributing profits fairly across the board to all of its citizens. However, as the history of the twentieth century has shown, nations that attempted to structure themselves along communist economic policies (such as the USSR, Red China, and Cuba) often fell into totalitarianism fairly quickly under the guise of being "Peoples' Republics" or "Democracies." Despite the failure of outright communism *per se* as an economic and/or political system, much Marxist thought still remains relevant to contemporary cultural studies. Basic Marxist principles continue to be useful in the critique of corporate capitalist excesses, as the Occupy Wall Street movement in the twenty-first century has shown. Marxism also offers us a way to understand how cultures and subcultures relate to their economies, and how social changes may and do occur within those cultures and economies.

During the twentieth century, much of the Western world (the so-called **First World**, see Chapter 12) was vocally opposed to communism as both a philosophy and an economic system. In certain eras, such as the 1950s, communism was literally demonized as godless and Satanic by many Judeo-Christian capitalist leaders. This was perhaps inevitable, as many Western nations have generally operated under various forms of capitalism, championing free markets in which everyone has the right to "get ahead" by whatever means they can. However, even in the Western world, capitalism has always been checked or restricted by various laws that limit just how money can be earned, and at whose expense. For example, in the nineteenth century the use of slave labor was outlawed throughout the United States, despite the fact that slavery made good economic sense and created great wealth for those who owned the slaves. Similarly, during the era of Prohibition, the United States government decided that selling alcohol was no longer a legal way to make money; however, those laws only created a huge black market trade for illegal booze and were soon repealed. When the Great Depression occurred after the Stock Market Crash of 1929, many people began to wonder if Marxist ideas might be relevant to American economic policies, and they read books or joined organizations that explored those options. However, after World War II those same people were often ostracized or persecuted during the era of the **Red Scare**, the so-called "communist witch hunts" led by American business owners and politicians like Senator Joseph McCarthy. The anti-communist hysteria of that era had a dramatic impact on the film and television industries: many creative artists lost their jobs and/or were **blacklisted**, while the texts the industries produced were carefully monitored for so called "un-American" ideologies. Others that were produced—such as *My Son John* (1952) and *Big Jim McLain* (1952)—almost verged on propaganda, pitting God, family, country and even John Wayne against cunning communist subversives. This Cold War backlash to communism (and its real or imagined threat to the security of the United States) lasted for many decades, curbing the legitimacy of Marxist thinking in many circles.

In fact, capitalism in the Western World has often been usefully and necessarily regulated via restrictions on the use of slavery and indentured servitude, child labor laws, minimum wage laws, and laws meant to check the despoiling of the environment in the name of profit. The United States, like many European nations, has increasingly used checks and balances on unfettered capitalism in order to protect basic human rights. And while the term **socialism** is almost as demonized as communism in some quarters—witness the recent hysteria and name calling surrounding President Barack Obama's federal health care initiatives—socialism as defined in the West these days represents for many the "happy medium" between capitalism and communism. As practiced in many contemporary cultures, socialism allows for free market capitalism and individual ownership of businesses while also regulating important human services like education, health care, and environmental protections.

As might already be apparent, basic or so-called **vulgar Marxism** is a theory of **economic determinism**—a theory that argues that any given society's economic structure is ultimately the determining factor in shaping, controlling, and governing that particular society. One of the central tenets of Marxism is its **base-superstructure model**, wherein **base** refers to a society's economic system, and **superstructure** refers to the entirety of a society's institutions and beliefs. A short list of superstructural elements might include any given society's political parties and forms of governments, its educational system, its religions, its media, and its institutions devoted to entertainment and leisure, including film, television, and sport (see Diagram 2.1). According to this model, everything in the superstructure arises from the economic base, and exists to support, consolidate, and replicate the economic base. If the economic base is capitalism, then everything in the superstructure will be determined by its subservient and/or supportive relationship to capitalism. To take a relevant example, the contemporary corporate film and television industry has a capitalist base; thus it exists to produce profit and secure the acceptance if not outright desirability of capitalism through its many products that circulate throughout the superstructures of Western and indeed global cultures. According to basic (or "vulgar") Marxism, the only way to change the various elements of the superstructure is to change the economic base that determines it. Thus, twentieth-century revolutionaries who followed basic Marxist thinking often stressed the need to overthrow capitalism altogether, to wrest the means of production from the ruling classes and (allegedly) distribute it among the masses. Later, more nuanced Marxist theories (discussed below) have focused on how some social change is possible without the need for a complete overthrow of the economic base.

As noted above, Marxism arose when it did (the mid-to-late nineteenth century) because of the Industrial Revolution. The machine age created factory jobs in urban areas, and people who may have formerly been artisans or farmers were increasingly employed at assembly lines, working long hours for little pay. They had no sick leave, maternity care, nor life insurance, and if they became ill or died they could immediately be replaced by another worker. (Marx philosophized that workers became **alienated** from their work and from one another, and were increasingly **reified** into cogs in a giant industrial machine, losing their humanity.) Meanwhile, the ruling class of wealthy factory owners continued to get richer and richer. While the working class had few options, they were also compelled to participate in industrial capitalism because of the way it was promoted ideologically.

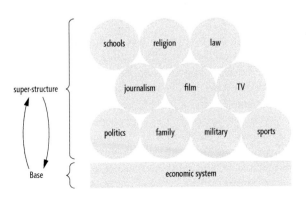

Dia 2.1
The economic **base** (capitalism, communism, socialism, etc.) shapes and **overdetermines** the various elements of the **superstructure** (the spheres of culture and ideology), a theory of **economic determinism**. In turn, the superstructure helps maintain the base by expressing its ideologies.

Among the era's more in/famous tracts that unabashedly promoted capitalism were novels by a man named Horatio Alger. His books promoted the idea that young white men could rise to positions of wealth and power through hard work (and often a little help from the benign ruling class itself). These "rags to riches" narratives have been popular throughout Hollywood history and have helped to promote capitalism throughout the twentieth century, as have multiple TV shows like *Lifestyles of the Rich and Famous* (1984–95) or *MTV Cribs* (2000–11). To a certain extent, many film and television texts (and not just advertisements) celebrate wealth and possession; many are designed to create consumer envy and the desire for material goods. Marx used the term **commodity fetishism** to describe the way that material goods produced under capitalism take on an almost religious or magical aura; their **use-value** (what they do) is often transcended by their **exchange-value** (the price that people will pay for them). To take a contemporary example, one can buy a shirt to clothe oneself (the shirt's use-value) or one can buy an expensive designer shirt to clothe oneself *and* make a social statement about one's own wealth and prestige. People often pay more for expensive designer goods not because their use-value is different from less expensive products, but because they have a higher exchange-value.

It was within these frameworks that Marx formulated his ideas about ideology. Basic Marxism understands ideology to be a form of "false consciousness" that can be unlearned, or somehow shrugged off. In this formulation, alienated workers just need to understand the actual conditions of their exploitation, and then they will (allegedly) become free of the ruling class's ideological dominance. This was one goal of the Soviet formalist filmmakers of the 1920s—men like Sergei Eisenstein, Dziga Vertov, and Alexander Dovzhenko—who theorized film in Marxist terms and attempted to use it as a way to educate, inform, and arouse the proletariat. (In another era, as many commentators have noted, the science fiction hit *The Matrix* [1999] also invokes this notion of Marxist ideology, wherein people are deceived about the actual conditions of their everyday existence.) However, this version of ideology is far less nuanced than the ones we use today, in that contemporary theorists of ideology reject the notion that we can ever "step outside" of ideology. We can become aware of the ideological messages that surround us—permeating all aspects of our culture—but doing so does not exactly make us free from them. Ideologies are pre-existing social and political structures that surround us from the moment we are born to the moment we die. They shape our lives and how we think about the world around us whether we are aware of them or not.

The Frankfurt School: Marxism and the media

The next important step in the theorization of ideology—and specifically how ideology intersects with cultural artifacts like radio and film—came from a group of thinkers who are collectively known as the **Frankfurt School**. The term refers to a group of (mostly) ex-German intellectuals, including Theodor Adorno, Max Horkheimer, Erich Fromm, and Herbert Marcuse, living and writing in the West before and after World War II. Their thinking was shaped by what they understood to be the hijacking of classical Marxist theory by communist despots such as Joseph Stalin, as well as the role mass media had played in the rise of European fascism. Some of them had seen first hand how the Nazis had nationalized German media industries and used them successfully to promote their ideologies. Ultimately, the

Frankfurt School desired to create a more nuanced critique of capitalism as it was being practiced in the West by the mid-twentieth century. They were especially interested in the role mass media played in politics, and stressed the importance of knowing who controlled the means of production vis-à-vis the mass media. Extrapolating from basic Marxist principles, they argued that popular "art" forms like radio and film—as part of the capitalist base's superstructure—were dangerous ideological instruments in the service of capitalist interests. Perhaps most famously, the Frankfurt School coined the term "**culture industry**" to refer to the institutions that mass produced cultural artifacts like film and popular music. Those institutions included the Hollywood studios, radio networks like NBC and CBS, as well as the Wall Street corporations (AT&T, RCA) that backed them. And just as Marx had applied his critique of capitalism to a factory system that mass produced material goods, the Frankfurt School endeavored to theorize how culture itself was mass produced in the twentieth century, and more importantly what the ideological effects of such mass produced culture were on those who consumed it.

Perhaps unsurprisingly, most of the Frankfurt School theorists were quite pessimistic about the culture industry, arguing that mass produced culture could only inculcate ideologies of sameness, conformity, and passivity among its consumers. The Frankfurt School argued that even though there might appear to be a variety of pop songs available on the radio (or different types of Hollywood films available at the local cinema), they were all basically just minor variations on one another that promoted the same ideological messages. Under this model, mass culture is figured as a distraction from actual reality. Similar ideas had been sounded during preceding centuries—at least as far back as the Roman Empire, from whence the phrase "**bread and circuses**" arose. The phrase refers to the way that control over a given society can be maintained by supplying the populace with basic physical needs ("bread") *and* ample distraction from the actual means of governance ("circuses"). Likewise, the Frankfurt School theorists noted that the standard of living in most mid-twentieth-century Western democracies allowed people to meet most of their physical needs, and that the culture industries produced a great many opportunities for diversion or entertainment. As per the Frankfurt School's critique, rather than potentially creating some form of critical or aesthetic awareness, the culture industries only encourage passive people to consume the same ideological messages over and over again. Some of the Frankfurt School theorists also used Freudian or psychoanalytical ideas to theorize these processes, concluding that twentieth-century Westerners masochistically desired to be dominated by strong authoritarian rulers who controlled the means of cultural production, thus explaining the rise of Fascism in Europe and populist demagogues elsewhere.

As later critics have pointed out, the Frankfurt School's critique of the culture industry is fairly essentialist. Their critique is sometimes referred to colloquially as the "**hypodermic needle**" model, a term meant to suggest passive audience members being shot up with dominant ideologies. (Later critics have argued that audiences need not be so passive in the consumption of popular art; see Chapters 10 and 11.) The Frankfurt School also fell back into ongoing debates about (good) high art versus (bad) low art, arguing that only the former could awaken the people from their mass-media-induced slumber. In that respect the Frankfurt School shared ideas espoused by one of their contemporaries: German playwright and Marxist **Bertolt Brecht**. Similarly to the Frankfurt School, Brecht saw dominant forms of theatrical (and by extension cinematic) realism as being complicit with dominant ideologies. Theatergoers confronted with such works might laugh or cry at the comedy or drama being presented, but because of what might be called **classical realist** style, they are never invited to question the means of production involved, or more broadly, the political issues that might be raised by the work. Instead, Brecht argued for a form of "epic theater" that would make use of self-reflexive distanciation devices—commonly called **alienation effects**—such as direct address to the audience (breaking the imaginary "fourth wall"), breaking character altogether, and/or the insertion of songs or comedy routines that might comment upon the production and its political ramifications. Such devices were meant to break up the realist flow of a production, and invite audiences to think about the work's ideological meanings and political underpinnings.

While Brecht wrote his own plays in that style, later filmmakers associated with the rise of the postwar international art cinema (1950s–1970s) would make films according to similar principles. (In fact, there were films made according to Brechtian principles in earlier decades, but they usually screened only within avant-garde and experimental venues.) In response to the so-called "invisible style" of Hollywood filmmaking—with its continuity editing meant to hide (literally) the means of its own production—filmmakers like Jean-Luc Godard, Ingmar Bergman, Federico Fellini, Rainer Werner Fassbinder, and Pedro Almodovar made films that revealed their means of production, and challenged audiences to think more directly about politics. For example, Godard's *Weekend* (1967) includes absurdist characters (some of whom actually read political manifestos directly at the camera), as well as political slogans printed on inter-titles. Other directors explicitly and/or implicitly referenced the act of film production, as in Bergman's *Persona* (1966) and *Hour of the Wolf* (1968). And although Fellini began his career within the Italian Neo-Realist movement, his later films became increasingly formalist and self-reflexive as with *8 ½* (1963), *Satyricon* (1969), and *Casanova* (1976); this tendency arguably culminates in a shot that pans around the film studio revealing the (already apparent) artifice of a diegetic ocean liner in *And the Ship Sails On* (1983) (see Figure 2.1). Likewise, filmmakers like Fassbinder and Almodovar pushed the conventions of cinematic melodrama to their breaking points,

Fig 2.1
A self-reflexive gesture at the end of Federico Fellini's *And the Ship Sails On* (1983); one camera pulls back from the diegetic ocean liner to reveal another camera filming the set of the ship.

accentuating bombastic musical cues, rigid formal compositions, and outlandish, over-the-top characterizations.

Luis Valdez's play *Zoot Suit* (and the film made from it in 1981) also make excellent use of Brechtian alienation effects, allowing the spectator the chance to examine the ethnic and economic exploitation of Mexican Americans that occurred in Los Angeles during Word War II. Through songs, sketches, an unreliable narrator, and multiple endings, *Zoot Suit* exposes the means of its own production and invites viewers to think about the issues at hand, both historically and perhaps as they still exist in contemporary America. However, both historically and today, most mainstream Western film and television texts still remain invested in some form of diegetic realism, and usually eschew Brechtian devices meant to alienate or challenge viewers. In some cases—such as within the broad category of reality television—direct address, actors breaking character, sketch comedy and musical performances, and even shots of the studio audience function not to distance viewers from the text, but instead create a new reality effect: that of televisual performance. Far from **deconstructing** the experience of a text, such devices within many television shows authenticate them as "live," or at least "shot before a live audience." In this way they capture another sense of reality, one that is highly constructed but rarely questioned or challenged by most viewers. In many cases, reality TV game shows forthrightly celebrate the capitalist values of individuality, competition, and consumerism.

Are the ideas of the Frankfurt School still relevant today? As unidirectional, outdated, and/or essentialist as their critiques might be, their ideas are also still fairly persuasive (and perhaps even prescient), especially when looking at the contemporary consumption of "entertainment" products in many developed nations. If anything, we live in an era of proliferating media and increasing distraction, a culture where many see voting for an *American Idol* (2002–) contestant as more important (or interesting) than voting for a President or a Senator. New media technologies have also increased this "potential to distract" exponentially, with many people unable to unplug from simulated worlds that bear little to no relevance to the larger political issues that surround them (not to mention the living and working conditions of the **Third World** workers who in many cases labor to produce those devices in the first place). Many new media technologies actively teach their users how to be good consumers and, in the case of many video games, good workers and/or soldiers. New media has the potential to unite and inform, as demonstrated by the democratic uprisings during the so-called Arab Spring of 2011, but new media can also distract and isolate human beings from one another. And as many political theorists, including most of the Frankfurt School have pointed out, democratic or representational governments are dependent upon informed and involved populations. When the populace unplugs from politics and retreats into mediated worlds of ideological distraction—whether it be spectator sports, blockbuster movies, or Internet gossip—those in power see little need to change the way things work. The interests of the ruling classes and the culture industries remain aligned, and firmly in place. As the science fiction film *The Final Programme* (aka *The Last Days of Man on Earth* [1973]), based on the work of acclaimed British novelist Michael Moorcock once put it: "It's much easier to run a hospital with all the patients sleeping." Ideological analysis would urge us to wake up and pay attention, not just to media, but to all cultural texts and the ideological assumptions they promulgate.

Althusser and Gramsci: Hope for social change without revolution?

The next important developments in thinking about culture and ideology arose from the works of **Louis Althusser** and **Antonio Gramsci**. Althusser was a French Marxist who theorized how Marxism might be applied and/or modified in order to critique twentieth-century Western democracies, not Imperialist Russia or Europe during the Industrial Revolution. The idea that one had to overthrow a society's economic base in order to make any meaningful change in its superstructure (a central tenet of basic Marxism) seemed less and less relevant. Most of the revolutionary movements that had tried that tactic had failed or were failing, having turned into communist dystopias. Written in the political and countercultural foment of the 1960s and 1970s, Althusser's work is pivotal in the development of contemporary cultural criticism in that it addressed ideology by synthesizing ideas from linguistics, structuralism, and psychoanalysis. In so doing, it sought to explain how people in Western nations learned to "submit to the rules of the established order," acquiesce to the dominant ideologies surrounding them, and reproduce those ideologies for future generations.

One of the more important ideas Althusser introduced into the study of ideology was the idea of the **subject** rather than the **individual**. This idea—drawn from psychoanalysis and other spheres of social psychology and philosophy—was a shift in how we understand the nature of human identity, how we define what it means to be a person. For centuries, Western models of human identity had tended to be somewhat essentialist, asserting that identity is stable and determined chiefly by birth or biology. If one was born a serf or a nobleman, one would remain so based upon inherent inherited qualities. One the other hand, the subject is a model of identity that is constantly in flux. Whereas the individual is mostly static and unchanging, the subject is continually being constructed by all of the experiences in his or her life. (Many psychoanalytic concepts of the subject will place special emphasis on one's early childhood experiences—see Chapter 6.) Within Althusser's reformulation of identity, human beings are both *subject to* and *subjects of* the cultures into which they are born and live. On one level, this seems fairly obvious, but Western notions of individualism tend to stress the opposite: that we are self-determining, that we make our own destinies, and that anyone can grow up to be President of the United States. According to those ideological beliefs, the failure to do so is a personal failure and not a failure of the system. The idea of the subject, on the other hand, suggests that who we are and how our lives transpire is determined to a great extent by the social forces and ideologies within which we circulate.

Furthering this model of the subject is Althusser's concept of **interpellation**, which suggests that ideological structures automatically construct us as subjects with or without our knowledge or consent. Interpellation suggests that there is no "outside" of ideology, that human beings are "always-already" in ideology from the moment we are addressed by it. For example, the minute many Western children are born they are placed into a pink or blue blanket—pre-existing symbolic structures that define and determine gender—and from that moment on the subject will be treated differently as either a girl or a boy. Another way to understand interpellation is to understand that ideology is carried by and/or conveyed through structures that constantly surround us. For example, if you enter a classroom and sit down in a chair or desk facing the front of the room, you have just been interpellated into an ideological structure that constructs you as "student," with all of the concomitant ideological meanings that might accrue to such a subject position. In this way, we move through space and time. We are constantly passing into and through various ideological structures that interpellate us as subjects in various ways. How we behave (or who we are) within the structure of a fraternity party is perhaps very different from how we might behave in church or at a family gathering.

Althusser named the various structures that constantly interpellate subjects **ideological state apparatuses** (or **ISAs**). In contrast to **repressive state apparatuses** (**RSAs**), which maintain social control though violence or the threat of violence (forces that would include armed conflicts, war, assassinations, terrorism, the death penalty, etc.), Althusser proposed that social order in most Western nations was actually maintained by ideological state apparatuses—those elements of the superstructure that act by way of example and education rather than force. (In the West, repressive state apparatuses are usually only called into use when the ideological ones fail: witness the police abuses—and the rioting—that welled up in the aftermath of the shooting death of Michael Brown in Ferguson, Missouri during the summer of 2014.) Ideological state apparatuses include religions, educational systems, social organizations and political parties, family structures, and perhaps most importantly the mass media, including film and television. Each of these ideological state apparatuses works in different ways to maintain and recreate the status quo. Sometimes they work in opposition to one another, but more often they work in tandem to create a unified sense of national or regional culture: in this way dominant ideology is sometimes said to be overdetermined, that is to say constructed by various different-but-similar ideologies working at different times and places. In so doing the contradicting elements of each ideological structure may be downplayed (or in psychoanalytic terms **repressed**) in order to create or maintain a unified consensus. For example, if you are a Christian who lives in a state that executes prisoners for major crimes, a contradiction might occur between that aspect of local governance and the Christian mandate that "Thou shalt not kill." One solution to this paradox might be to downplay or repress the meaning of "Thou shalt not kill" in favor of some other Christian tenet, such as the belief that the punishment should fit the crime, the so-called "eye for an eye" doctrine. In this way, the ideological state apparatuses of government and religion work to justify and maintain a belief in the necessity and justice of the death penalty.

Two other important concepts of neo-Marxist theory are often associated with Althusser: **relative autonomy** and **uneven development**, both of which challenge the unidirectional economic determinism of basic Marxist thinking. Relative autonomy suggests that even though the economic base is still the final arbiter of the nature and form of a society's superstructural elements (its culture), various institutions and ideologies within the superstructure can and do potentially influence one another. In other words, elements in the superstructure have relative autonomy from the base (and from one another). This means that one text can influence another text, a given subject can create something that critiques or subverts the dominant ideology, or that organized political campaigns can and do impact on the nature of culture and society. To take one historical example, Frederick Wiseman's famous 1967 documentary *Titicut Follies* exposed the cruel and barbaric conditions in a Massachusetts State correctional institution for the criminally insane. Lawsuits that surrounded the film for years eventually gave rise to new standards for prisoner safety and privacy. Many people feel that the film played an important part in humanizing the way state institutions offer mental health care (not to mention basic human rights) to patients and inmates. In this way, change in the superstructure can occur even though the economic base remains the same.

Similarly, uneven development suggests that the various elements of the superstructure can and do exist in uneven relationships to the economic base; that is to say, some are more closely determined by the economic base while others are less so. For an example, compare network television and independent filmmaking in America. One could safely say that network television programming, highly dependent on advertisers and the right kind of audiences (i.e. those with money to spend), is more closely tied to the economic base of capitalism than is a small independent or even artisanal avant-garde film made on the remote edges of the media industry. According to this logic, superstructural elements that are closer to the economic base will be more likely to promote the ideological agendas that support and uphold that base, much more so than those superstructural elements distanced from the base. Many decades ago President Dwight D. Eisenhower spoke of the developing "military industrial complex" to refer to the close collusion between U.S. military forces and the broader economy. We might note that those two apparatuses have grown even closer together in recent decades: the Armed Forces remain very close to the economic (capitalist) base. Military spending helps fuel the American economy in ever-increasing ways, and the ideologies of God, nation, and patriotism are thus linked to capitalism and corporate profits in overdetermined ways that most Americans never question. (On the other hand, critics further from the economic base of American capitalism have critiqued this state of affairs, among them novelist, playwright, and essayist Gore Vidal whose book *Perpetual War for Perpetual Peace* hypothesizes that the United States actively seeks out military skirmishes in order to maintain the health of its military industrial complex.) One might argue that the idea of the military industrial complex has become so thoroughly ingrained in American capitalism that it is rarely even spoken of anymore.

In more recent years, the term "military entertainment complex" has also been introduced into the lexicon, and that term is suggestive of the ways that Hollywood's economic interests and technologies continue to overlap with those of the U.S. military, and vice versa. Since at least the 1980s, the Armed Services have offered their resources to Hollywood producers whose films promote the military in a positive light, while withholding those same resources from filmmakers who might be critical of military or foreign policy. Similarly, cinematic advertisements to join the Armed Services have appeared in movie theaters throughout the United States, many of which suggest that joining the Marines is not that different from playing a fantasy video game or starring in a heroic Hollywood war film. (Indeed, the technologies used to produce blockbuster special effects and digital gaming systems are also used to train military personnel.) The point of all this is that many large national institutions, both private and public, have many shared goals, and are situated very close to the nation's economic base, capitalism. As such they share ideologies which tend to promote not only the dominant values of capitalism, but also those of whiteness, patriarchy, and American exceptionalism. All of these ideologies are overdetermined because they are expressed in many intertwining ways by many different cultural structures, apparatuses, and individual texts.

One final set of ideas about ideology is necessary at this point, and these are drawn from the writings of Italian Marxist **Antonio Gramsci**. Gramsci wrote most of his cultural theory while a prisoner under the fascist regime of Benito Mussolini during the 1920s and 1930s, but his works were not translated into English until decades later. Most importantly, Gramsci theorized the concept of **cultural hegemony**. Before Gramsci, hegemony simply meant "rule," but Gramsci developed a more nuanced model of how rule is maintained in Western nations through cultural institutions and ideologies (a position not dissimilar to Althusser's theorizing several decades later). According to the model of cultural hegemony, rule over any nation or population is not assured or static, but must be won and re-won in an ongoing struggle, one that occurs by constantly **negotiating** with subcultural artifacts, ideas, and/or social movements that may be in opposition to dominant ideologies. One way to picture cultural hegemony might be to think of it as a constantly evolving and fluctuating **dominant ideology**. To take another historical example, American patriarchy is not the same thing as it was one hundred years ago: even though it remains a dominant ideology in culture, it has also had to negotiate with and adapt to social changes such as women earning the right to vote and the changes to gender and sexuality brought about by the sexual revolution. Western culture may still be patriarchal, but not in the same way as it was one hundred years ago, or even the same way that it was yesterday.

Later thinkers have tended to be either more optimistic or pessimistic about the concept of cultural hegemony. While on one level it means that social change is possible as dominant ideologies are challenged or opposed (the optimistic position), it also means that dominant ideologies—albeit somewhat tweaked—nevertheless remain firmly in place (the pessimistic position). Critics point out that when oppositional ideals and concepts are allowed to enter the mainstream (i.e. achieve cultural hegemony), they often do so through processes of **incorporation** and **commodification**. Incorporation refers to the ways that oppositional ideas might be "allowed" to appear as mainstream, as long as they are situated within larger structures of dominance. In the 1970s for example, African American actors were finally allowed to appear in leading roles in Hollywood films. While that might be thought to be a good thing for racial equality, most of those roles also promoted dominant ideologies of aggressive masculinity, and of course those films were made primarily to fill the coffers of white Hollywood, not uplift the black race. That is what commodification means: literally turning an oppositional ideology into a product that can then be sold for profit. Through incorporation and commodification, alternative or opposing ideologies are often "watered down" or "de-clawed" for consumption by the wider population. Alternative or oppositional political points become reduced to a style or a fad. For example, many African American cultural artifacts—from jazz to hip hop to gangsta rap—have repeatedly passed through these processes throughout the twentieth century.

Yet, whether the glass is half full or half empty, the process of hegemonic negotiation does allow us to theorize cultural change without revolution and without violence. Cultural change (however small or great) can occur because of a film or television text, a poem or a petition. The world and the ideas we use to express our understanding of it are constantly changing, and some contemporary cultural critics see great potential in how media might shape a better future for us all. As Judith Halberstam writes in her book *The Queer Art of Failure*—a work that explores the cultural ramifications of *Dude, Where's My Car?* (2000), *Chicken Run*

(2000), and *Finding Nemo* (2003)—among many other cultural artifacts both high and low:

> The dream of an alternative way of being is often confused with utopian thinking and then dismissed as naïve, simplistic, or a blatant misunderstanding of the nature of power in modernity. And yet the possibility of other forms of being, other forms of knowing, a world with different sites for justice and injustice, a mode of being where the emphasis falls less on money and work and competition and more on cooperation, trade, and sharing animates all kinds of knowledge projects and should not be dismissed as irrelevant or naïve.

For those film and television students wishing to address social issues and/or change the world with their work, contemporary theories of hegemonic negotiation allow for such possibilities. For the contemporary media critic, hegemonic negotiation allows us to follow the ebb and flow of cultural change, how film and television (amid a plethora of other social apparatuses) impacts upon the real world, and *vice versa*.

Where to "find" ideology in film and television texts

Because ideology is pervasive and structural, it can be located at every level of the film and television industries, from federal and corporate policy to the smallest camera angle, sound cue, or lighting design. In the Western world today, six huge global corporate entities—Time Warner, the Walt Disney Company, Rupert Murdoch's News Corporation, Sony Corporation, Viacom/Paramount, and NBC Universal—control almost the entire film and television industry, not to mention the music and publishing industries as well. The ideological agendas of these conglomerate entities are situated directly on the economic base: these global corporations exist to make money, and in so doing they embody the dominant ideologies of capitalism. Furthermore, they rarely challenge other aspects of dominant ideology, such as white centrality or patriarchy, as those ideologies have historically been closely associated with capitalism (and commercial success). It is true that more specialized niche television channels like HBO, Oxygen, or Logo seem designed to express alternative ideologies, but these companies are themselves part of one (or more) of the six larger corporate entities that structure and control the entertainment industry. Some thinkers, including those of the Frankfurt School, have observed how the culture industry only *pretends* to offer significant choices to consumers, when in fact the products it sells are all basically the same. (This process is sometimes referred to as **pseudo-individuation**.) Even independent films have come increasingly under the control of the six major corporations; since the 1990s, each of the six corporate conglomerates has produced and/or distributed "independent" films under boutique subsidiary labels (either acquired or created) such as Fox Searchlight Pictures, Focus Features (part of Universal), and Miramax (currently owned by Disney). More "truly" independent films not made by divisions of these corporate giants do get made and may be able to express ideological viewpoints further from the dominant ones, but then they also have the problem of being seen—i.e. getting distributed very far within the global corporate media scape.

As Chapter 5 will explore, ideology also inheres within textual structures like film **genres** (westerns, musicals, gangster films) or television **formats** (game shows, the sitcom, etc.). It is a central tenet of **genre theory** that different genres attempt to negotiate or express a specific set of cultural concerns, for example what is normal versus monstrous in the horror film, or the meaning of civilization versus the wilderness in the western. As such, genre structures express ideologies related to those concerns, and both the horror film and the western have been critiqued for upholding the centrality of white masculinity at the expense of racial and gendered minorities. Similarly, the very shape of certain television formats might be understood as ideological, regardless of their content. Many of the classic **sitcoms** of the late 1950s and early 1960s, for instance, rarely tackled the serious political issues of that era, instead they expressed a worldview of happy white suburban stasis where nothing ever changed. **Serial television** formats like soap operas on the other hand, have often been more able to express differing ideological perspectives, partly because of their larger casts and ongoing weekly (or daily) structures that have the potential to explore things in greater depth. On the other hand, most game shows are all about capitalism and competition, in which contestants vie with one another to win cash or other valued prizes. *The Price is Right* (1972–) explicitly rewards its players (and by extension its viewers) for their detailed knowledge of what consumer goods are worth in the free market.

Ideology can also be located at the level of individual films or TV episodes, often through the stories they tell and the ways that those stories are represented and resolved. The average Hollywood blockbuster centers on a white protagonist with some form of special power as he defeats the villain and wins the girl. Yes, Hollywood protagonists in the last few decades are sometimes non-white and even female, but those are exceptions that prove the rule. Television—because of its more diffuse and ubiquitous structure—as well as the variety of diverse formats and genres it can encompass—can arguably present a larger range of ideologies than do Hollywood films. As noted above, ongoing serial narratives can explore more complicated issues than can a two-hour Hollywood blockbuster, while more specialized channels like HBO, Showtime, and AMC have been able to offer provocative shows that challenge (or at least tweak or question) some aspects of dominant ideologies. *Sex and the City* (1998–2004) may or may not be an empowering image of women compared to the usual depiction of women in film and television, but shows like *Queer as Folk* (2000–5) or *The L Word* (2004–9) did break new ground in representing more diverse images of gay and lesbian people onscreen. The Netflix original series *Orange is the New Black* (2013–) does similar cultural work, bringing multiple "silenced voices" to the screen: telling until now rarely told stories about women, people of color, and the abuses of the industrial prison system. Similarly, *Six Feet Under* (2001–5) featured a story line about an interracial gay couple raising several children. A few years later, a similar storyline— albeit played for laughs and with a less challenging racial angle—would be central to a popular network hit, ABC's *Modern Family* (2009–). Such media images have played a part in changing the meaning of homosexuality in contemporary Western cultures, and those changes ultimately play out in the "real world" of state legislatures and Supreme Court decisions.

Ideology also can be read not only in narrative patterns and story resolutions, but it might be expressed through specific formal properties such as costume, make up, lighting, editing, etc. Many of these representational codes predate and/or extend beyond film and television, but others have become "shorthand" in visual storytelling. For example, drawing upon cultural and cinematic codes about the meanings of light and dark, consistently dressing a character in black and/or shooting him or her in shadowy spaces, is a very easy way to arouse suspicions in the audience's mind about the character's potential villainy. In a famous example from the history of broadcast television, the producers of *Sixty Minutes* (1968–)—a magazine show that often investigated possible criminal and ethical violations among businessmen and politicians—routinely placed their cameras closer to the person being investigated (closer than to the segment's host, for example), in order to capture every bead of sweat, nervous tick, or sideways glance. In this way, the show suggested that the person being grilled was possibly guilty, even if he or she were not.

Since ideological analysis is dependent upon reading—that is to say **decoding** the sounds and images of film and television texts to see what meanings and effects they create in the mind of the audience member—it is highly dependent on *who* is doing that reading. As the cultural studies "Encoding/Decoding" model introduced in the last chapter suggests, it is rare that there is one dominant meaning that any given text gives out to all of its viewers. Individuals approach any given text from within their own ideological and historical subject positions, to some extent taking from the text what they want to see in it. This facet of media studies opens into the arena of **reception studies** (discussed more fully in Chapters 10 and 11), but it does complicate ideological analysis. For example, is *The Sopranos* (1999–2007) a critique of the violent patriarchal and capitalist ideologies embodied by its gangster anti-hero Tony, or a celebration thereof? Actual viewers and fans of the show have expressed both opinions. Similarly, the AMC period drama *Mad Men* (2007–15) is often read as a critique of the sexist and racist parameters of the Madison Avenue world of 1960s commercial advertising. However, a few critics in the popular press have also written nostalgic elegies about the show, expressing a longing for the allegedly kinder and gentler world the show depicts (before the advent of feminism and the civil rights movement), when sleeping with the secretary was a perk of a man's profession, and not sexual harassment.

As these examples illustrate, some texts are more open to a variety of interpretations than are others, a state of affairs explored in greater detail in later chapters. That is because all texts are made up of a variety of images, sounds, and messages ordered in certain ways; media theorists use the term **structured polysemy** to refer to this aspect of a text. The term means that all film and television texts are made up of many signs ("poly" meaning "many" and "seme" meaning "sign"), and that those signs are ordered or structured in a certain way during the processes of textual creation (**encoding**). As such, some texts are structured to give off explicit meanings, while others are more diffuse. In performing ideological analysis, it is thus perhaps more accurate to say that the critic's job is to express the range of meanings that any single text might express, and how those meanings either derive from or deviate from dominant ideologies. In many cases, ideological analysis will reveal texts that do both: uphold dominant ideologies in multiple ways, while perhaps negotiating with non-dominant ideologies. In this way, cultural hegemony is usually maintained.

Case study 1: Revisiting *Ballet Mécanique*, *The Flying Mouse*, and *Aqua Teen Hunger Force*

Let us return to the three short texts we examined in the previous chapter: the modernist art film *Ballet Mécanique* (1924), the Disney "Silly Symphony" *The Flying Mouse* (1934), and an episode from the TV show *Aqua Teen Hunger Force* (2000–). Those three texts were discussed as examples of (respectively) "high" art, "low" or "mass" art, and a niche artifact that complicated the presumptions of high versus low art. But what can ideological analysis tell us about these texts? Of the three, the episode of *Aqua Teen Hunger Force* seems the most diffuse in its ideological meanings. Its incomplete and almost surreal narrative resists closure and thus lacks a lesson or moral (as with *The Flying Mouse*). As a pop culture text, it appears to be "about" little more than pop culture itself, with its multiple references to TV, Dracula, Elvis, as well as science fiction themes popularized by movies like *Alien* (1979) and *The Fly* (1986) (see Figure 2.2). One might argue that it rewards its viewers for being good media consumers, as catching the pop culture references is part of the pleasure of the show. One might also note the complete absence of female characters from the episode, and its racial ambiguity: the show's theme song and its wrap-around bumpers suggest urban ethnicities, even as its non-human characters are not given racial markers *per se*. (Some viewers think Frylock "sounds black," i.e. is voiced by an African American actor.) *Aqua Teen Hunger Force* seems almost ideologically incoherent, even as one might note certain specific ideological inflections (such as those around gender, race, and pop culture). In this case, one might argue that *Aqua Teen Hunger Force* has less of an explicit **ideological message** and more of an **ideological problematic**. Unlike the former term, which is more precise, the term ideological problematic refers to a range of ideas and ideologies a text may contain or activate, often in an unclear or even contradictory way.

Ballet Mécanique might seem equally diffuse ideologically upon first viewing. Some parts of the film—such as the horse collar coupled with the placard "Someone has stolen a pearl necklace worth 5 million"—might just appear surreal, or nonsensical (one goal of the dadaist movement with which the film is often associated). However, on

Fig 2.2
Random pop culture references in *Aqua Teen Hunger Force* (2000–): a billboard to see Dracula's grave in Memphis(?), here somehow improbably advertised with a vampiric Elvis Presley.

Fig 2.3
In *Ballet Mécanique* (1924), living things—in this case a parrot—are refigured by the modern technology of cinema, literally refracted by the camera's distorting and mechanizing lenses.

Fig 2.4
A washer woman carries a heavy burden up a long flight of steps in *Ballet Mécanique* (1924); in Marxist terms one might say she has become **reified** into a machine-like part, her physical labor (and being) reduced to a cog in the wheel of a larger capitalist enterprise.

repeated viewings *Ballet Mécanique* can be shown to convey an ideological critique of early twentieth-century European modernity. In its images of organic beings (birds and humans) refracted through distorting lenses, and its emphasis on automata and human beings made up to look like automata, *Ballet Mécanique* depicts an overly mechanized world that reduces human beings to cogs in a machine (see Figure 2.3). The famous "loop" sequence of the old worker-woman ascending a long staircase while carrying a heavy burden suggests the never-ending drudgery of the life she lives; to use Marxist terms, she has become **reified** into a mechanism in the capitalist machine (see Figure 2.4). Perhaps the most disturbing shot in *Ballet Mécanique* is a shot of precisely marching feet stomping down (what one may presume to be) a Parisian boulevard. The shot not only suggests the machine-like nature of military units as they functioned throughout World War I, but also foreshadows the industrialization of murder that would occur during the Holocaust two decades later (not to mention the Nazi invasion of France) (see Figure 2.5). The age of modernity may have given rise to the mass media and other mass produced goods and services, but it also laid the groundwork for the assembly line-like mass murders of the Nazi death camps.

Fig 2.5
In *Ballet Mécanique* (1924), the feet of marching soldiers suggests a mechanized approach to warfare, recalling the devastating effects of military technology in World War I, as well as eerily foreshadowing the mechanized death chambers of Nazi Germany.

Of the three films, *The Flying Mouse* is probably the most explicit in its ideological message. Based as it is on a classic fable, the film seems to dramatize its own moral lesson: be careful what you wish for because (chances are) you are better off being who and what you are already—or as the wish-granting-fairy puts it, "Be yourself." Under some circumstances, the message to "Be yourself" might be thought to be a good one, encouraging someone to be true to their own desires and sense of self. However, this moral lesson becomes especially conservative when read in conjunction with the film's other ideological messages. For example, the mouse and his family are clearly poor and rural in their class standing. They wear patched clothing and the single mother works hard to take care of her many children (see Figure 2.6). On the other hand, the birds that the protagonist wants to emulate are given more middle (or even upper) class signifiers such as top hats, canes, and bonnets. Furthermore, the bird community is literally higher than the mouse's family: the birds occupy the upper branches of a tree while the mice live on the ground (see Figure 2.7). These are two separate worlds that the short cartoon suggests should not or will not mix. Everywhere the newly winged mouse goes—to the birds, to the bats, even back to his family—he is rejected as a strange hybrid. Rather than celebrate the flying mouse as a unique individual, the film suggests he is better off staying in his original status, as part of a poor (wingless) rural family. The attempt to mix social classes (or species) produces only heartache.

The Flying Mouse is also filled with elements that promote white patriarchy, as it can be assumed that the flying mouse is both male and whatever is racially normative, which in the Western world of the 1930s, is whiteness. The most powerful figure in the film—the fairy—is female but she embodies an almost Aryan ideal of pale skin, blond hair, and blue eyes (see Figure 2.8). She also appears as a delicate butterfly who needs to be saved by the mouse from a rapacious black spider, a situation that suggests a veiled threat of **miscegenation** (or racial mixing), a very prominent racist fear in 1930s America. Aside from the mouse's mother and several of the birds, the only other significant female in the film is the flying mouse's sister, who appears onscreen for one sight gag and then disappears from the film altogether! (During the family reunion of mice at the end, she is nowhere to be seen) (see Figure 2.9). Likewise, the bats who later berate the flying mouse as "nothin' but a nothin'" are associated with darker visuals and a jazz-inspired

Fig 2.6
The mouse's family in Walt Disney's *The Flying Mouse* (1934) are poor and rural, and generally happy, although one mouse longs to fly.

Fig 2.7
The birds in *The Flying Mouse* (1934) are drawn with middle or upper class **signifiers** such as top hats, canes, fancy bonnets, and nicer clothing than that worn by the mice.

Fig 2.8
The fairy who grants the mouse's wish for wings in *The Flying Mouse* (1934) seems modeled on a blonde-haired, blue-eyed, 1930s-era woman in a sleekly elegant gown.

Fig 2.9
In *The Flying Mouse* (1934) the family of mice apparently does contain a daughter, although she is only onscreen for one sight gag; by the happy ending she has disappeared from the film altogether. (Refer back to Figure 1.6.)

performance as they taunt the mouse for thinking he could be like them (refer back to Figure 1.5). Thus, while one ideological message of the film could be that "there's no place like home" (as a more famous 1939 Hollywood fantasy film would have it), the film also expresses subtle ideological messages about gender, race, and class. Namely: that women are somewhat peripheral to masculine quests, and that attempts to mix class or race will probably result in heartache, and thus they should not be attempted in the first place.

Case study 2: *Never Let Me Go* (2010)

Film scholars often agree that every British film is in some way about class, as class is an issue deeply embedded in the history and culture of Great Britain. The film *Never Let Me Go*, based on the acclaimed novel by Kazuo Ishiguro (also the author of *Remains of the Day*, published in 1989 and filmed in 1993) and directed by Mark Romanek (*One Hour Photo* [2002]) is no exception to that assertion. Deeply symbolic, poetic, and ultimately powerfully moving, the film centers on a love triangle between Tommy (Andrew Garfield), Kathy (Carey Mulligan), and Ruth (Keira Knightley), three young adults who were raised together in what appears initially to be a British boarding school called Hailsham. However, as the tale progresses, the story shifts into science fiction territory: Tommy, Kathy, and Ruth are being raised by the Hailsham school to be living human organ donors, expected to submit to their roles as such, even when they "complete" their lives at a young adult age. The film offers a range of interpretations and contains multiple ideological assertions about the importance of love and the preciousness of our time on earth. It also functions quite nicely as a metaphor or allegory for the ways in which ideology works to create subjects who are willing to submit to the dominant order, and accept their place within a socio-economic structure that literally feeds off their lives as a means of sustaining itself.

The first half of the film focuses on the three protagonists at Hailsham in 1978. Here the institutional structure, ideology, and limitations of the boarding school are stressed: the clever scholar might note the very name "Hailsham" seems to allude to Althusser's notion of the subject being interpellated ("hailed") into some sort of false belief ("sham"). At Hailsham, the individuality of the students is downplayed: they wear drab gray school uniforms and only have last initials, not last names. They are kept inside the school grounds at all times, monitored by electronic bracelets but also dissuaded from leaving by terrible horror stories of what has supposedly happened to other children who attempted to leave the school—a good example of how stories (the media, ideology) influence behavior and understanding. The students are kept busy with what appear to be lessons in geography, art, and sport, and they seem relatively happy as they are told they are special, consume identical meals, ingest pills, and are entertained by old black and white movies—in this case a British musical called *Let George Do It* (1938) in which popular crooner George Formby sings—quite pointedly—a song entitled "Count Your Blessings and Smile." The song recalls the 1980s pop song "Don't Worry, Be Happy" by Bobby McFerrin, and both contain similar ideological exhortations to accept blithely one's place within the social structures in which one might find oneself. However, whereas the Bobby McFerrin song is a good example of how the culture industries ideologically create passive and conformist subjects (*a la* the Frankfurt School), in *Never Let Me Go*, that same process is being exposed for what it is: an ode to passivity and conformity via the ideological indoctrination of the media.

The students at Hailsham are also trained in the ways of capitalism as they compete to have their artworks featured in "The Gallery," and earn tokens that they then may spend on toys and other sundries. (The title of the film refers to a music cassette that Tommy buys for Kathy at such a sale, a recording of an old love song of the same name.) The children are even taught—via playacting—how to go into a tea shop and order something to eat and drink. Most remarkably, when renegade teacher Miss Lucy finds it within her conscience to try to explain to the children exactly what their fates will be, they respond almost without emotion (see Figure 2.10). They have already been trained to accede to and never question their spot within the structure of things. In Althusserian terms, they have been interpellated as subjects destined to be organ donors, and even take pride in that role.

When Tommy, Kathy, and Ruth turn eighteen, they leave Hailsham for a rural working class abode known as The Cottages. Here they meet other young adults similar to themselves, experiment with sexuality, and learn proper codes of gendered behavior

Fig 2.10
When the children in *Never Let Me Go* (2010) hear about their ultimate fate as organ donors, they remain unmoved, having already learned not to question their lot in life.

from an inane sitcom they apparently watch all the time, to the point where they begin to mimic the characters on TV (see Figure 2.11). (Again, a better visualization of the Frankfurt School's theories of ideological indoctrination by the mass media would be hard to find.) Tommy seems to be the most naïve of the three, and allows himself to be drawn into a sexual relationship with Ruth, even though a greater (and "truer") love seems to be shared between Tommy and Kathy. This romantic entanglement fills their lives and gives some sense of hope for the future, especially when they learn of a rumor that donors who are truly in love may receive a "deferral"—extra years of life before their donations must start. Tommy especially clings to that hope, and begins to create art as did the children at Hailsham. Tommy believes that such art was encouraged at Hailsham as a way of fathoming the children's souls, and could thus be used to "prove" his true love for Kathy, earning them both a deferral.

When the story shifts to 1994, Kathy has become a "carer," someone who helps donors through their last years of life before she herself returns to her status as a donor. The three protagonists briefly reunite, even though Tommy and Ruth are suffering the effects of multiple organ donations. Ruth, realizing she has kept Tommy and Kathy from sharing their love, gives them the address of Madame, the woman who was in charge of The Gallery all those years ago at Hailsham. Then, in a cold and stark medical scene we see Ruth's last viable organ removed from her as she "completes" her destiny. Tommy and Kathy do locate Madame, but she tells them there never was such a thing as deferral, that the artworks the children created for The Gallery were not used to gauge "true love," but whether or not the children even had souls at all. Shocked but acquiescent, Tommy leaves and eventually "completes," and Kathy is left alone to ponder—along with the audience—the meanings of life, death, mortality, love, and our place within the social order.

Fig 2.11
Children and young adults in *Never Let Me Go* (2010) are socialized partially by the **ideological state apparatuses** of film and television; at "The Cottages" they literally mimic the behavior and speech of an inane TV sitcom.

Never Let Me Go is part of a long line of thoughtful and imaginative British science fiction texts. Its focus on ideological manipulation, surveillance, and dystopia suggests George Orwell's seminal novel *1984* (published in 1948) and its subsequent film adaptations (1956, 1984), while the children's uniforms and narrative predicaments also recall *These are the Damned* (1963) and *Children of the Damned* (1963), two other classic British science fiction films centered on extraordinary children. Although *Never Let Me Go*, like these other films, is easily classified as science fiction, it is an everyday, realist

science fiction film rather than a futuristic or otherworldly one. Partly this is expressed via the film's remarkable production design, which suggests an almost untimely and uncanny feel. Although its scenes are allegedly set in 1978, 1985, and 1994, the film's visual design suggests an even older era, one that suggests post-World War II Britain, and even earlier. Indeed, it is partly this visual design that gives the film so much of its broad emotional resonance: this story might be an allegory of Cold War communism (as was *1984*), or even more readily a critique of the British class system in the years before and after World War II. Indeed, the children and young adults they become are resolutely poor, relegated to (literally) second class citizenship, a point movingly dramatized when the "bumper crop" of toys they are allowed to purchase with their tokens is revealed to be a collection of incomplete game sets, broken dolls, and other detritus that most second-hand shops would reject (see Figure 2.12).

Perhaps the film also suggests a dystopian present in which medical science— as in *Frankenstein*—has run amok, thus relating it to contemporary concerns over abortion, euthanasia, in vitro fertilization, stem cell research, prosthetic limb design, and cloning itself (which the film suggests is the origin of its donors but never makes explicit). Perhaps the film can be read as a critique of socialized medicine and Britain's National Health Service in particular: the film's "National Donor Program" is depicted as a cold and socialist bureaucracy literally providing extra years for the rich and powerful while sacrificing the bodies of the poor. (In this way the film might also appeal to those who think President Obama's Affordable Care Act will inevitably lead the way to state sanctioned "death panels.") Ultimately, *Never Let Me Go* suggests that whatever allegorical reading one might make of it, it is love, compassion, and connection that matters the most in our short times here on earth. We are all going to "complete"—what matters most is what we do while we are still alive. Of course "love," "compassion," and "connection" are themselves ideologically loaded terms, and can themselves be used to limit or oppress subjects in yet various other ways. Nonetheless, as presented within the film, they seem to be one possibly hopeful response to the cold dehumanizing ideological structures that surround us, whether at the fictional Hailsham or in the real world. *Never Let Me Go* invites us to see and understand those ideological structures, and to free ourselves as best we can from their limiting and even abusive ends.

Fig 2.12
In *Never Let Me Go* (2010), the children clamor over the chance to purchase broken and ill-used toys; they have been conditioned to think that this is a rare treat and not a pitiful display of junk.

Questions for discussion

1   What is your own positioning vis-à-vis dominant ideologies? In what ways does your identity accord with dominant ideologies, and in what ways does it perhaps clash or contradict with dominant ideologies? How aware are you of how film and television transmits normative ideas about race, class, gender, sexuality, etc.?

2   Can you think of other fantasy, science fiction, or horror films that "dramatize" certain concepts of ideology (as do *The Matrix* and *Never Let Me Go*)? Do they uphold or critique other aspects of dominant ideologies such as patriarchy, capitalism, and white supremacy?

3   How do sports—both spectator sports and participant sports—intersect with dominant ideologies? Would you say—in general—that sports or film and TV is more likely to uphold dominant ideologies? If so, why and how?

References and further reading

Althusser, Louis. *Lenin and Philosophy, and Other Essays*. Trans. Ben Brewster. New York: Monthly Review Press, 1972 (1971).

Althusser, Louis. *On the Reproduction of Capitalism: Ideology and Ideological State Apparatuses*. Trans. G. M. Goshgarian. London and New York: Verso, 2014 (1971).

Cantor, Paul A. *The Invisible Hand in Popular Culture: Liberty vs. Authority in American Film and TV*. Lexington, KY: University of Kentucky Press, 2012.

Eagleton, Terry. *Ideology: An Introduction*. London and New York: Verso, 2007 (1991).

Engels, Friedrich. *The Condition of the Working Class in England*. Oxford: Oxford University Press, 2009 (1845).

Gebhardt, Eike and Andrew Arato, eds. *The Essential Frankfurt School Reader*. London: Bloomsbury Academic, 1982.

Gramsci, Antonio. *Selections from Cultural Writings*. Trans. William Boelhower. Cambridge, Massachusetts: Harvard University Press, 1985.

Gramsci, Antonio. *Prison Notebooks*. New York: Columbia University Press, 1992.

Halberstam, Judith. *The Queer Art of Failure*. Durham and London: Duke University Press, 2011.

Heywood, Andrew. *Political Ideologies: An Introduction*. London: Palgrave Macmillan, 2012.

Marx, Karl and Friedrich Engels. *The German Ideology*. New York: International Publishers, 1970 (1845).

Marx, Karl and Friedrich Engels. *The Communist Manifesto*. Printed by Createspace, 2010 (1888, 1848).

Marx, Karl. *Das Kapital*. Printed by Createspace, 2011 (1867).

Nichols, Bill. *Ideology and the Image: Social Representation in the Cinema and Other Media*. Bloomington, IN: Indiana University Press, 1981.

Ryan, Michael and Douglas Kellner. *Camera Politica: The Politics and Ideology of Contemporary Hollywood Film*. Bloomington, IN: Indiana University Press, 1988.

Vidal, Gore. *Perpetual War for Perpetual Peace: How We Got to Be So Hated*. New York: Nation Books, 2002.

CHAPTER 3

Semiotics, structuralism, and beyond

Semiotics (or as some prefer, **semiology**) refers to the study of signs—of signification—of how material things (words, images, sounds) make meanings (mental understandings). While some of this chapter may seem rather abstract and theoretical, concepts from semiotics form the basic building blocks of film and television analysis. Semiotics seeks to explain and explore what happens when we look at a word or image or hear a certain sound, and how that word or image or sound creates meaning. Semiotics was originally a theory of how language works, and is thus part of **linguistics** or the study of language, but over the course of the twentieth century various theorists have sought to apply its concepts to the study of other **cultural artifacts**, including film and television. Some semiotic concepts work perfectly well when applied to film and television, while others do not. Semiotics also gives rise to **structuralism**, another broad interdisciplinary term that refers to the ways various human systems or cultural networks (literally social and ideological *structures*) are organized to create meaning. As we will discover in this and subsequent chapters, models of analysis such as **auteur** or **genre theory** gain further sophistication when the principles of semiotics and structuralism are applied to them. Finally, structuralist approaches to culture have themselves been critiqued as being too essentialist and ahistorical; thinking that moves beyond structuralism is generally called **poststructuralism**. As this chapter explores, while structuralist theories tend to discover and uphold a structure or framework as the explanatory basis of meaning, poststructuralist theories are often concerned with how those structures *fail* to create unified meanings. Poststructuralists focus on the "wiggle room" within structures, and try to create more precise and nuanced analyses of complex cultural phenomena like films and TV shows, and especially how they are understood within varying social, industrial, and historical contexts.

Unlike structuralism and poststructuralism, semiotics in its basic forms is unconcerned with culture and politics. Its earliest theorists saw its principles as abstract and removed from content *per se*; instead semiotics focused on the *how* of meaning production, not the *what*. However, as semiotic concepts were applied to the real world around us (informing structuralism and other models of sociological analysis), concerns of culture and politics (**ideology**) inevitably arose. One of the most important interventions in mid-twentieth-century anthropology was instrumental in this shift: **Claude Lévi-Strauss**'s formulation of **structural anthropology**. Recall that most forms of studying culture previous to the mid-to-late twentieth century had been very **Eurocentric**, and were highly judgmental about non-Western values and practices. Lévi-Strauss's application of structuralism to the field of anthropology suggested a more objective approach. Theorizing that all human cultures could be understood in relation to various opposing terms—such as male/female, inside/outside, etc.— Lévi-Strauss revealed that human cultures possess deeper structures that allow us to make sense of the world around us. Similar to how the use of language is based on deeper structures of grammar and syntax, Lévi-Strauss and others like him explored the deeper structures of various cultural formations, as exposed in cultural artifacts like myth, storytelling, and marriage/kinship relations. Eventually the various ideas germane to structuralism found their way into thinking about film and television. Some film theorists, for example, attempted to explain and explore the western film genre in terms of a series of **binary oppositions** such as the west versus the east, male versus female, and/or the wilderness versus civilization.

Although the binary approach to thinking about structuralism has perhaps become less central in recent decades (as the very notion of "binary opposite" has itself been critiqued by poststructuralist thinkers), the basic idea that social phenomena can be studied in terms of their underlying structures is still quite useful. In this sense we might say that the western film genre does have a structure, one both similar to and different from the structure of musicals or gangster films. However, as more recent theorists have argued, simply identifying a given structure is not the end of analysis, but merely a part of it. So called **poststructuralist** critics—as the name implies—draw on structuralism but also complicate it with the addition of other contextual parameters such as history, psychology, nation, region, industry, and reception, to name just a few. Poststructuralist thinkers find the idea of structure important, but are often more interested in picking that structure apart than upholding it as the ultimate or essentialist explanation of any given phenomenon. This unraveling or problematizing of structures is sometimes referred to broadly as **deconstruction** or **deconstructive criticism** and is associated most directly with the work of theorist **Jacques Derrida**.

Thinking about film genres is a good way of illustrating the differences between structuralist and poststructuralist approaches. A structuralist might be content to identify what he or she feels are the basic structuring principles underlying all westerns, and then use that formula to categorize films accordingly, reducing the many meanings of the western film genre to some essentialist structure or formula. A poststructuralist critic, on the other hand, might acknowledge that same structure, but then go on to complicate it by noting that silent westerns are both similar to and different from sound westerns, that John Wayne and Clint Eastwood westerns also have many differences as well as similarities, or that the so-called "**spaghetti westerns**" made in Europe during the 1960s tweak the underlying structure(s) of the western film genre in yet other ways. In other words, as with some other approaches explored within this book, structuralism was eventually critiqued as being ahistorical and therefore essentialist. The shift to poststructuralism was an attempt to redress what were understood to be structuralism's shortcomings. Whereas many structuralist approaches are interested in explicating the *meaning* of some particular system, poststructuralist approaches are usually more interested in explicating an entire range of *meanings*. But before we get to post/structuralist analysis, it is important to know how the various sights and sounds of film and television texts create meaning in and of themselves.

Basic terms and concepts of the sign

Semiotics has been around since before the turn of the twentieth century, and is usually said to have begun with the work of American philosopher Charles S. Peirce and Swiss linguist **Ferdinand de Saussure**. Both of these men—though working separately—were interested in studying how communication works—how letters and words and other signs create meaning for their users. Although the work of Peirce and de Saussure had somewhat different emphases and each man used somewhat different terms to describe their ideas, the following section represents a synthesis of their work as it is understood within introductory semiotic theory; as such, it presents an overview of the basic concepts germane to contemporary thinking about semiotics.

The first thing to understand about semiotics is the dual nature of the **sign**. A sign can be a word, an image, a sound, or a symbol—actually anything and everything in the entire world might be thought of as a sign, because when someone encounters it, it creates meaning of some sort for whoever encounters it. Basic semiotics suggests that every sign is made up of two parts: the **signifier** and the **signified.** The signifier is that part of the sign that exists in the material world, while the signified refers to the concept that arises in the mind of the person who encounters the sign. Let us take as an example the word "dog." The word itself is the sign under consideration, and the signifier is that specific arrangement of letters upon the page that spell out "d-o-g." The signified of the sign "dog" is located in the reader's mind: the *thought* of the furry four-legged pet that chases cats. Similarly, a drawing of a dog is a sign that—although it uses a different signifier (sketch marks rather than letters)—will give rise to a similar signified: the *thought* of the furry four-legged animal. (More on the different types signs below.) Basic semiotic theory suggests that we further understand the word "dog" (or a drawing of one) because we have already encountered dogs in the real world. Those real dogs are termed the **referents** to the sign "dog," since they allow us to link the processes of signification to our previous knowledge of things in the real world.

But what about a sign like the word "faith"? The signifier of the sign is still the specific combination of letters on the page that spell out the word, but its signified is a lot more diffuse and complicated. For example, the multiple signifieds of the sign "faith" might include further terms such as loyalty, confidence, or adherence to a certain religious dogma. Furthermore, "faith" is not a material thing in the real world: one cannot purchase a bucket of faith or hold faith in your hand. Thus the referents of faith are not material things that exist in the real world (as with the referents for "dog"), they are instead further signs—more words and concepts— that are used to explain the first sign. We call these new signs **interpretants**. In this way each sign gives rise to more signs, and complex meanings are thus created along a chain of signs, wherein each sign is explained by yet others in succession. Theoretically, these **chains of signification** are infinite. Another important axiom that arises at this juncture is that all signs are in the end defined by and against other signs. Even "dog" may be understood without its actual real world referent, if it is defined by other signs such as words or drawings. It is not necessary to have actually encountered a dog in the real world to understand what a dog is. After all, none of us have ever encountered a dinosaur in the real world, yet many of us have a fairly complex understanding of what a dinosaur is or was. That understanding has been generated by things like fossilized remains of dinosaurs, scientific theories of the planet's evolution, and even science fiction films like *Jurassic Park* (1993) that use computer generated special effects to imagine what dinosaurs might actually have been like.

Another important point about basic signification is that not all signs are made up of the same types of material elements. This was hinted at above in our discussion of "dog" versus a sketch or a photograph of a dog. Semiotics suggests that there are three types of signs that differ from one another vis-à-vis how they are produced and understood: symbolic signs, iconic signs and indexical signs. The **symbolic sign** or **symbol** is a sign based in language: there is an arbitrary or culturally agreed upon relation between its signifier and its signified (its meaning). For example, the sign "dog" only means the furry four-legged pet that chases cats *in English*, because we as an English-speaking culture all agree that it does. (We could just as easily agree that the sign "tjkw" signifies a dog, but we do not.) In France, the signifier "chien" is what gives rise to the signified of the furry four-legged animal; in Spain, it is the signifier "perro" that gives rise to the same concept. Furthermore, a symbolic sign such as "dog" tends to be rather vague without other words to make it more specific. Different people will call to mind different signifieds based upon their own history with or knowledge of dogs—some may think of a beagle, others a collie, still others a terrifying attack dog. All can be the signified that arises from the symbolic sign "dog," and thus symbolic signs are highly dependent upon their unique reception contexts (see Figure 3.1).

The second type of sign theorized by semioticians is the **iconic sign** or **icon**. With this type of sign, the signifier in some way resembles the thing it signifies: this would be the sketch of the dog as mentioned above. Theoretically, iconic signs can be and are understood outside of language, which is why you might see drawings or shapes rather than words indicating male and female restrooms in an international airport. Iconic signs are the basic building blocks of all comic strips, graphic novels, and animated films (even as each of those forms also usually uses symbolic signs—i.e. words and language). Iconic signs can be a bit more specific than symbolic signs: a drawing of a beagle does not suggest a collie, and

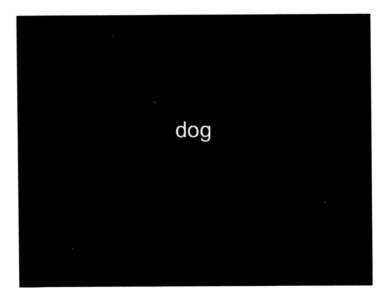

Fig 3.1
Symbolic sign: the word "dog." This sign potentially signifies many different types of dogs.

Fig 3.2
Iconic sign: a drawing of Snoopy. Iconic signs form the basis of animated films.

vice versa. A drawing of the dog Snoopy from Charles Schulz's famous comic strip *Peanuts* is going to signify a very particular dog (assuming one is familiar with the comic strip) (see Figure 3.2). Thus, even with iconic signs, there is still a cultural knowledge or competence at play: a person who encounters a drawing of Snoopy but has never heard of *Peanuts* will probably not understand the sign in the same way as will a fan of the comic strip. Formal qualities in film and television like color or pitch or volume should also be considered iconic signs, as they too create meaning without the use of language *per se*. Instead they create meaning based on graphic qualities that are also generally culturally coded; for example, in the West the color red may suggest passion or danger. On the other hand, red signifies happiness or luck throughout much Chinese culture.

Finally, the third type of sign is the **indexical sign,** or the **index**. An indexical sign can only be produced when the thing that it signifies was there to produce it. In this respect, one might say there is an existential bond between the signifier and the signified of indexical signs. To continue with our examples related to dogs, indexical signs of dog would therefore include a paw print, dog fur on the carpet, or for our purposes in film and television studies, a photographic or video image of a dog. Indeed, indexical signs are the basis of all non-animated film and television texts, based as they are upon the mechanical reproduction of events actually staged before some type of camera. Of course, most contemporary film and television texts make simultaneous use of indexical signs, iconic signs, and symbolic signs (language)—making it difficult to attend to the different types of signification occurring all at once. You may have heard the old expression that "a picture is worth a thousand words." In film and TV analysis this is certainly true: one might easily use a thousand words describing the *mise-en-scène* of any given shot. That said, indexical signs are the most precise of the three types of signs, in that now our photograph of a dog reveals the exact size, breed, and demeanor of one specific dog—the dog who was there when the photograph was taken (see Figure 3.3). One does not think of a beagle when one sees a photograph of a collie. Similarly, the dinosaur bones that scientists have excavated over the years should be

Fig 3.3
Indexical sign: a photograph of an actual dog. Indexical signs are usually the most precise, as "a picture is worth a thousand words."

understood as indexical signs, in that an actual dinosaur had to have lived and died in order for its bones to be rediscovered.

There is another important aspect to indexical signs such as photography, cinematography, or videography. Since there is some version of reality present when indexical signs are produced, it is often easy to mistake them for the things they signify. For example, assume one is shown a photograph of a tree and is asked "What is this?" There is a very good chance that the person asked about the photograph would answer, "It is a tree," which would be wrong. The photograph is an ***indexical sign*** of the tree, not the tree itself. (The real tree has been mechanically converted into a sign of a tree, with photographic properties such as choice of lens, camera distance and angle, lighting, setting, etc. all contributing to subtle inflections of meaning, which might make the tree seem colorful, or menacing, or stoic, or whatever.) This mistaking of the image of reality for reality itself has sometimes been described as one of the more interesting (or perhaps troubling) aspects of **postmodernism** (discussed more fully in Chapter 9). In our hyper-mediated age, it sometimes seems that video and filmic images come to replace reality; events that do not make the nightly news or the daily newspaper may as well not have happened at all. And as our ability to "fake" reality becomes ever greater in the digital age, what are the implications for our understanding of the real world and its inhabitants? Do stereotypes and sound bites alter or even replace our concept of actual human beings? What can we know of reality when it is almost always filtered through various sign systems, each of which distort or shape meanings in different ways? The important thing to remember is that all sign systems—including the indexical signs of film and television—delimit and shape the content they express. As with ideological analysis, one goal of studying semiotics in relation to film and television texts is to make us better "readers"—to encourage audience members to develop the competency to understand how subtle signs like camera angles or costume designs *signify*, that is to say, how they create or add meaning as they are **decoded**.

Putting signs together: Structures of meaning

The idea that signs give rise to other signs in a chain of signification has already been introduced. The cultural theorist **Roland Barthes** explored this phenomenon as the distinction between **denotation** and **connotation**. **Denotation** refers to what we might call "first order" signification—the first thing that the sign suggests in the mind of the reader. **Connotation** refers to all subsequent significations—the second and third and fourth and ultimately infinite number of other signs to which the first sign may give rise. Let us go back to our drawing of Snoopy: on the denotative level this is merely a stylized sketch of a dog. But Snoopy himself can and will set off a plethora of further meanings— connotations—which will necessarily vary from person to person depending on his/her own cultural competence. One person may associate Snoopy with his yellow bird friend Woodstock, which might suggest the music festival from 1969, which might suggest that era's youth movement, which might suggest some detail about the decoder's own youth, and so on and so forth. Another person might start with Snoopy and then think of his fantasies fighting the Red Baron, which suggests something about World War I, which might suggest something about Germany, and so on and so forth. The point to remember is that all connotation is immediately *cultural*, and is determined by the cultural competence of the reader.

To take another example, and one more pertinent to the political world, think of skin color. The color of one's skin may be noted at the denotative level and not really mean anything more than hue: darker or lighter. However, as we move beyond denotative color we encounter an infinite range of cultural connotations about race—its history, its stereotypes, its representations—literally hundreds if not thousands of years of Western cultural artifacts that have suggested the ideological superiority of lighter skinned people and even the bestial qualities of those with darker skins. This is one reason we cannot simply pretend that race or skin color no longer matter in contemporary culture, as some naïve commentators occasionally suggest. While "color blindness" in terms of race may be one desired goal for a more fair and equitable future, how do cultures "erase" the connotations that race and color have accrued over centuries? Perhaps they cannot be erased as much as supplanted by new connotations created by new images and new ideas, which are constantly being created every instant of every day. Thus the election of an African America president or release of a film like *Django Unchained* (2012) both contribute to the ever-changing meanings of race in complex, **overdetermined** ways.

As noted above, these chains of signification are potentially endless. However, these chains can be shut down or stopped in actual processes of communication by invoking a so-called **transcendental signified**. The transcendental signified is a concept or position that stops signification by suggesting all meaning ultimately comes back to one singular source of transcendental meaning. For example, according to some psychoanalytic thinkers, everything in human psychology might be explained by ultimate reference to the idea of sexual difference (the penis/

phallus versus its lack); according to strict Marxists, all the history and workings of the world would necessarily return to the transcendental signified of class struggle. For some conservative Republicans, the thoughts and words of Rush Limbaugh might function as a sort of transcendental signified (his fans do sometimes refer to themselves as "ditto heads" as they are proud never to question the cultural and political assertions of Limbaugh himself). Fundamentalist religions are another good example of social institutions that invoke transcendental signifieds, in this case their holy written screeds which are meant to "set the record straight" and end discussion about controversial human topics. (As one Christian bumper sticker puts it, "The Bible said it—I believe it—that settles it.") However, what most fundamentalists miss is that their holy texts can be and are interpreted by different people in different ways. Who is to say whose interpretations of the Bible or the Koran are the "correct" ones? As contemporary critical cultural theory asserts, all meaning is shaped through specific acts of decoding in specific historical and cultural contexts.

Connotation is one way to think about the possibilities and limits that arise from pondering one single sign. However, we rarely encounter signs as single entities— we are constantly bombarded by signs. Most film, TV, and written languages all consist of multiple signs that are strung together into longer and more complex expressions like sequences, episodes, or sentences. Let us start with language again, and examine the expression "I like dogs." This is a sentence composed of three discrete signs, strung together in a specific order. In semiotic theory, the ordering of signs across time ("I" is followed by "like" which is followed by "dogs") is called a **syntagm** or a text's **syntagmatic axis**. Whether it is a sentence or a motion picture (in which one shot follows another for approximately two hours), many media texts are organized into syntagms in order to tell stories and/or create meanings. The ordering of the signs matters, for the sentence or motion picture might be unintelligible (or give off very different meanings) if the syntagmatic order is changed or disrupted. In classical Hollywood continuity editing, for example, a general syntagm for constructing a "proper" intelligible sequence needs to begin with an establishing shot before cutting into medium and close up shots. If a conversation then occurs, it will probably be ordered according to a shot-reverse-shot editing pattern, which is itself a type of syntagm common to Hollywood (and much televisual) editing.

It is thus a given in semiotics that all words and signs exist in relation to other words and signs, not only along syntagmatic axes, but also in relation to what is called their **paradigm** or **paradigmatic axis**. The paradigm is the set of all possible words (or images) that might be substituted for any given sign at any given spot along the syntagmatic axis. For the sentence "I like dogs," the three paradigms in play are: (1) all the subjects that could replace "I," (2) all the possible verbs that could substitute for "like," and (3) all the possible terms from which the word "dogs" is chosen. Paradigmatic sets contain everything from antonyms (opposite terms) to synonyms (similar terms), and in that way every sign in the paradigmatic set helps to define or give meaning to all the others. This is the way **binary oppositions** (antonyms) tend to function: "masculine" means *not* being "feminine" and vice versa. "Black" is defined as not "white," and "night" is defined as not "day." Similarly, "pink" is defined by and against similar colors represented by words like "red" and "fuchsia" and "purple." The idea of the paradigmatic axis gives rise to the semiotic principle that ultimately all signs are defined against one another—

they do not have meaning in and of themselves, except as we agree that they do. In other words, all meaning is culturally constructed. And when we are born we are **interpellated** into pre-existing language systems, cultures, and ideologies. As **Althusser** suggested about the structural nature of ideology (see Chapter 2) our very identities are subject to the various language systems, cultures, and ideologies that we encounter as we move through our lives.

Applying these semiotic concepts to culture and cultural artifacts (as structuralist and poststructuralist approaches do), one can see that much of the world around us can be expressed or understood in terms of denotation, connotation, paradigm, and syntagm. Human subjects constantly decode meanings from all the signs they encounter, both on denotative and connotative levels. Much in our daily lives can also be structured in terms of paradigm and syntagm. For example, choosing items for a meal from a menu means selecting from paradigmatic sets (appetizers, main courses, desserts) in order to eat in a sequential manner (the syntagmatic structure of the meal). Similarly, getting dressed in the morning in a certain order (syntagm) means selecting specific items from the paradigms of shirts, socks, pants, and so on. Schools and colleges schedule their days into syntagmatic periods in which students opt for different courses selected from paradigms like science, math, art, or history. Choosing what to watch on television is similarly organized: traditionally, television networks program their shows according to a syntagmatic **flow** across time, and at any given moment the viewer chooses what he or she wants to watch from the available paradigm (shows airing on different channels at 8 o'clock, shows airing on different channels at 9 o'clock, etc.). Recently, the time-switching capabilities of new media devices such as Tivo and digital video recorders (DVRs), or streaming video services like Hulu and Netflix, have altered television's usual syntagmatic flows, allowing viewers to create their own syntagms of what to watch and when.

Two other semiotic concepts are useful at this juncture: **langue** and **parole**. **Langue** refers to the language or sign system being "spoken" (or used); **parole** refers to the speech act (utterance) spoken within it. In terms of film and television texts, "the soap opera," "the situation comedy," or "the chick flick" could each be considered individual langues; corresponding paroles (texts spoken within a given langue) might then be *All My Children* (1970–2011), *Friends* (1994–2004), and *Sleepless in Seattle* (1993). In fact, Hollywood narrative filmmaking itself could be considered a langue—a certain sign system used for producing meaning and/or telling stories—thus making all films made in the Hollywood mode examples of paroles. According to this model, *Gone with the Wind* (1939) and *Casablanca* (1943) would both be considered examples of a parole spoken within the Hollywood langue. To relate this model of langue/parole more specifically to the terminology of film studies, one could understand Hollywood **genres** as langues (language systems, structured sign systems), albeit specific subsets of the larger Hollywood narrative filmmaking langue. For example, westerns are part of the larger Hollywood narrative filmmaking langue, but they also contain certain elements and structures that are different from those found in the musical or gangster film. Thus, if the western film genre is thought of as a langue, *Stagecoach* (1939) and *Dances with Wolves* (1990) would both be an example of a parole "spoken" within it. Likewise, if the Hollywood musical genre is thought of as a langue, paroles "spoken" within it would include *Singin' in the Rain* (1952) and *Moulin Rouge* (2001).

As with other approaches to film and television analysis discussed throughout this volume, different theorists sometimes use different terms to discuss similar phenomena. For example, langue might be thought of as similar to a **code**, as well as to a **discourse**. In some usages, a **code** simply refers to the ways in which signs are deployed in an organized way across a single text or a set of texts—thus the examples of langue used in the previous paragraph might also be described as codes: the code of Hollywood narrative filmmaking, the code of the western film genre, and so forth. The concept of langue is also similar to that of **discourse** as theorized by the influential French thinker **Michel Foucault**. As per Foucault, discourse refers to a specific institutionalized way of speaking—a dialect or subset of the larger language system (English, French, etc.) to which it belongs—that shapes and delimits the meanings of the concepts spoken within it. Simple examples of discourses might include "corporate speak," "military speak," or the highly specialized language of almost any academic discipline, from medicine to architecture to even semiotics and structuralism. Some of Foucault's most important writings were on subjects like mental illness and sexuality: he argued that discussing these subjects within (for example) religious discourses versus legal discourses versus medical discourses can and do give rise to very different understandings of the object of discussion (mental illness or sexuality). Applying this concept to film and television analysis, one might say that the discourse of the horror film shapes and delimits a topic like sexuality in ways quite different from those of the musical or romance. In this way, langues, codes, and/or discourses are all inherently ideological, a topic explored in greater detail below.

Side bar: How film and television are un/like languages

This section briefly outlines some of the questions that film theorists have asked about the application of semiotics to the cinema (and by extension television). The name most associated with these ruminations is **Christian Metz**, a French film theorist who also explored ideas pertinent to psychoanalysis and *Screen* theory (discussed in Chapter 7). Much of Metz's early work centered on trying to illuminate the deep structures of the filmic syntagm, the basic ways that filmmakers could and do combine shots to create meaning. This is perhaps the most readily applicable aspect of semiotics to film and television. As we have already seen, both film and television (like language) proceed along syntagmatic axes, selecting shots (words) from different paradigms along the way. Metz called his project "La Grande Syntagmatique," and concluded that there were six (later eight) basic ways that narrative cinema could arrange shots in order to create meaning. Metz's categories included the parallel syntagm (in which shots could be organized as opposing binary motifs), the alternating syntagm (known in Hollywood as **cross-cutting** between two simultaneous lines of action), and the scene (known in Hollywood as **continuity editing**, including shot-reverse-shot structures as in a conversation). Metz's episodic syntagm sounds a lot like a **Hollywood montage sequence**: a series of shots that compress diverse actions in time and space into a short sequence, and held together (usually) by extradiegetic music.

As a very structuralist project—reducing all narrative cinema to six or eight basic building blocks—La Grand Syntagmatique has had a limited impact on contemporary cultural theory as it is practiced now, but it did help to illuminate other differences between film (and television) and language. Among those significant differences is the fact that (unlike language) most human beings do not use film and television to communicate with one another; film and television are generally one-way communication systems (with the recent innovation of the video blog perhaps excepted). Another significant difference is that language is usually thought to be a fairly finite or closed system of signification (although new words are coined every year), whereas the number of signs available in film and television production is infinite. An author may have one hundred words to choose from when describing an apple, but a filmmaker has an infinite number of ways he or she could photograph an apple (based on lighting, lens choice, distance of the camera, etc.). What this means in semiotic terms is that language systems have fairly limited paradigms whereas film and television production have an infinite number of signs to choose from within each paradigmatic stop along the syntagm. Another important difference to note is the symbolic nature of language versus the combined symbolic, iconic, and indexical nature of the filmic or televisual image. Images contain a plethora of detailed information in a way that single words do not; remember: "A picture is worth a thousand words."

Which is not to say that film and television texts as meaning producing systems have no "grammar" or "syntax" at all. A film or television text is best considered a **structured polysemy**, which means that although it is made up of many signs (polysemy) it is nonetheless structured in certain ways in order to create certain meanings. Texts may be structured rather loosely, as with the avant-garde film *Ballet Mécanique* (1924) or rather tightly structured as with the short Disney film *The Flying Mouse* (1934). Loosely structured or more **open** texts tend to give off a range of meanings (their **ideological problematic**), and require a more active effort on the part of the viewer to decode them. More tightly structured or **closed** texts tend to do the opposite—they tell the viewer exactly how s/he is supposed to respond to them. Although film and television arguably have less strict rules than does written language about how syntagm and paradigm can be chosen in order to create meaning or tell stories, audio-visual media nonetheless still have rules and structures, from genre formats, to narrative patterns, lighting codes, and even types of edits, which are perhaps best liked to punctuation and/or conjunctions in written language. For example, a fade to black in film or television production often functions something like a period: it usually signifies the end of a sequence or even the overall film. A dissolve, on the other hand, usually signifies a change in place and time; it might be thought of as a semicolon joining two sequences (sentences) together. A wipe signifies something similar, but the wipe is a more action-oriented device (and is thus used heavily in action-adventure movies like *Star Wars* [1977]). A wipe might best be considered an **iconic sign**, in that it uses graphic qualities to create meaning: in this case "exciting movement" as the scene changes, as opposed to the "lazy tranquility" signified by an extended dissolve between scenes. Much of the rest of this volume explores in greater detail some of the ways that such signs and structures function in film and television analysis.

From structuralism to poststructuralism

The moment semiotics is applied to culture and cultural artifacts, it might be said to become **structuralism**. For example, in the years following World War II, French post/structuralist Roland Barthes applied these methods to magazine covers, wrestling matches, the face of Greta Garbo, and famous French novels, among other texts. In many ways, structuralism (like poststructuralism) is less a set of precise methods and more a set of philosophical outlooks on the goals and means of cultural analysis. Earlier this chapter introduced Claude Lévi-Strauss as the father of structural anthropology, and noted how his attempt to find the deep (binary) structures in human interactions transformed his field from one of Eurocentric observation into something resembling a more objective science. Some structuralist theorists in the wake of Lévi-Strauss continued to focus on underlying structural binaries whose variation and interaction helped to shape (and thus explain) "surface" phenomena, while other poststructuralist thinkers began to question the ideological meanings of such a project itself. For example, while some structuralist thinkers might use "night and day" as a structuring binary opposition common to all human experience, a poststructuralist might reject that simplification, seeing night and day as contiguous overlapping phenomena, not binary opposites. When exactly does day become night, and vice versa? The end point of this poststructuralist logic is that all signs and concepts—even ones we tend to think of as binary oppositions—contain some relation to their alleged opposing term. Furthermore, binaries work to reduce the complexity of the real world into simple and simplified labels (essentialist categories). They also tend to create a hierarchy wherein one term of the binary is privileged over the other. We can thus see how binaries become especially problematic when used to describe complex cultural phenomena such as race. No one on the planet is the color of the ink upon this page nor the paper on which it is printed. So why do we still speak of race in terms of black and white? Therefore, in much poststructuralist thinking, textual binaries exist to be deconstructed and/or problematized in relation to their larger ideological contexts, including language itself.

The work of another scholar, **Vladimir Propp**, illustrates basic structuralist methods and ideas that might be more germane to film and television studies (and Propp's project is also far less dependent on the idea of structuring binaries). Propp was a Russian formalist who studied hundreds of Russian folk-tales in order to discern their underlying structures. He concluded (in his book *Morphology of the Folktale*) that the basic structure of the Russian folk-tale was comprised of seven character types (hero, helper, dispatcher, donor, villain, false hero, and princess), and 31 possible narrative units including departure, struggle, trickery, solution, punishment, and wedding. While this may seem extremely reductive and essentialist—it is after all a structuralist model—it is also most provocative when thinking about much Hollywood narrative filmmaking, which is usually structured around a protagonist (hero), an antagonist (villain), and a love interest (the princess or prize the hero will win). Dispatchers (the ones who send the hero on his quest), donors (the ones who give the hero his special powers), helpers, and false heroes also abound in Hollywood storytelling patterns.

Propp's schema is perhaps even more intriguing if we examine more recent Hollywood blockbusters such as *The Dark Knight*, *Star Wars*, *Harry Potter*, or *The Lord of the Rings* franchises. For the sake of brevity, let us examine Propp's seven character types as they function in the James Bond franchise. Our **hero** is James Bond, agent 007, and the **villain** is the megalomaniac criminal genius who opposes him in any given film, from mad scientist *Dr. No* (1962) in the first Bond film to Silva in *Skyfall* (2012). The **princess** is any number of "Bond girls" throughout the franchise, a female beauty who usually has to be saved by Bond during the climax of the film as he defeats the villain. Bond's **dispatcher**—the person who sends him on his quests—is his boss M, while the **donor** of Bond's special powers is the gadget maker Q. Bond's **helper** might be another friendly agent, while the **false hero** might be an undercover spy who first appears helpful but is revealed to be traitorous. Obviously, many films and TV shows fit less neatly within this paradigm, while still others would need considerable coercion to make them fit. For example, it might be difficult to explain *Sex and the City* (1998–2004) according to this formula, even as the recent *Dark Knight* films fit the formula quite precisely. (I will leave you to debate on your own whether or not all film and TV shows are structured in this fashion, however stringently or loosely!) Nonetheless, Propp's work represents a significant structuralist contribution to the study of narrative, and (as the next two chapters will explore) to the study of auteur and genre theory. A structuralist approach such as Propp's provides a precise and fairly objective model against which other stories may be compared and analyzed for variation or similarities; as such it is a truly structuralist project at heart.

Propp was not alone in trying to find a universal structure of storytelling. Other writers and thinkers have created similar guides to understanding such structures. Among the most well known is Joseph Campbell, who argued that most stories in the world can be reduced to what he termed the "**monomyth**," the story of one ordinary man's journey through an extraordinary world, where he meets and conquers challenges only to bring home a prize or "boon." According to Campbell, there are 17 stages in the hero's narrative, many of which (though fewer) are similar to the ones outlined by Propp. Some Hollywood filmmakers make conscious use of Propp's archetypes and/or Campbell's monomyth, hoping they will ensure box office success, given these models are alleged to be "universal" story structures that should "speak to" all audience members. There are multiple "how-to-write-a-screenplay" guides based on these formulas, and it is well known in Hollywood lore that George Lucas read Campbell's work as a young man, and that he let it influence him as he created the *Star Wars* franchise. However, when a narrative structure like the monomyth purports to be *the* universal way of telling stories, it tends to raise flags of caution (if not outright charges of Eurocentrism) among thinkers more attuned to the nuances of poststructuralist thinking. Do (and did) all human cultures regardless of race, location, climate, nation, development, and era make use of this storytelling structure? And even if they did, poststructuralist thinkers would be more interested in emphasizing how and why they used it *differently*, rather than focusing on its unquestioned and unquestionable centrality. Poststructuralists might also be interested in how the very form of the structure itself marginalizes women and other minorities into prescribed character functions.

Thus while certain filmmakers in Hollywood may be content to script their films according to such structuralist blueprints, many others who work in film and television production (or media scholarship) have critiqued such endeavors as lazy, repetitive, and ideologically problematic in various ways. While the profit motive in the **culture industries** insures that monetarily successful film and television texts will be copied, reworked, sequel-ized, prequel-ized, and remade over and over until the formula is completely worn out, there are other media producers and scholars who do not follow or endorse such methods. They strive to find new ways to tell original stories and to think about cultural texts. Slavishly following a structuralist blueprint like the monomyth arguably hinders or constrains creativity, even as such practice might also give rise to fascinating variations and shifts in structure. In this way, the narrative and ideological structures of film and television—whether they be reality TV or Hollywood cinema—are constantly being hegemonically negotiated. They can be seen to change over time with the industries that produce them and the viewers who consume them.

In summation then, both structuralist and poststructuralist thinking is centered on finding underlying systems (or codes, or structures) that shape and delimit culture-at-large, as well as individual cultural artifacts. But whereas structuralist thinkers tend to find that structure coherent and explanatory in and of itself, poststructuralists look for the incoherence in systems, and explore how multiple social contexts—including social subjectivities like regionality, race, class, gender, sexuality, age, and religion, among others—impact upon the production and reception of media texts. Poststructuralist thinking also insists on the power of language (and more broadly mediated sign systems like film and television) not just to describe the world around us, but actually to constitute it. As later chapters will explore, contemporary poststructuralist scholars who work on gender or race argue that there is no essential quality to either category; instead, they argue that gender and race are only knowable through—are literally constructed by—the languages and images we use to express them. Poststructuralist thinking therefore critiques structuralism as too a-historic, too schematic, and too limiting. Whereas identifying structure is the start *and* finish of some structuralist projects, it is only the beginning of poststructuralist analysis as it is practiced by media scholars today.

Case study: *Palindromes* (2004)

Palindromes is an American independent film made by iconoclastic writer-director Todd Solondz, who also made the cult hits *Welcome to the Dollhouse* (1995) and *Happiness* (1998). Like most of Solondz's films, *Palindromes* is a very black comedy that deals with controversial topics: in this case childhood sexuality, teenage pregnancy, statutory rape, and abortion. The film's syntagmatic story follows the central character of a young (age unknown) girl named Aviva. Early in the film Aviva is willingly impregnated by a dimwitted teenaged boy named Judah, and is forced by her parents into having an abortion which they believe is the best option for her (see Figure 3.4). After a medical

Fig 3.4
In *Palindromes* (2004), Aviva and Judah have awkward sexual intercourse; note the contrasting **phallic** imagery printed on their shirts.

complication that results in an emergency hysterectomy (which Aviva does not know about), she runs away from home. During her journey, Aviva meets and has sex with a much older man, is befriended by the Sunshine family (who are also a Christian singing group), and ultimately becomes involved in a plot—organized by Papa Sunshine—to murder an abortion doctor. *Palindromes* is an interesting film to think about because it directly engages concepts of semiotic and post/structuralist theory, including denotation and connotation, paradigm and syntagm. It is rigorously structured around various binary oppositions that include male/female, blue/pink, child/parent, sex/love, guilt/innocence, east/west, stasis/change, nature/nurture, ability/disability, Christian/Jewish, and many others. Ultimately the film critiques the idea that culture and cultural issues are knowable in terms of such binary oppositions; instead, the film suggests that opposing cultural values are not defined against one another, but actually contain the seeds or roots of their opposing values. In the film's most succinct explication of that point, its anti-abortion activists actually wind up killing a child, which their professed beliefs adamantly oppose and condemn.

While those narrative choices are themselves somewhat provocative, Solondz compounds confusion and invites audiences to question their own "take" on the story by making changes in the film's most significant paradigm: the character of Aviva is played by eight actors of different races, body types, genders, and ages. By changing the actor playing Aviva, Solondz is asking his audience to consider the fact that they may feel differently about Aviva and what happens to her depending upon who is playing the part. Aviva seems like a victim when she is portrayed by a thin white actress, but seems almost mentally challenged when played by an adult (see Figure 3.5). Some viewers make derisive comments when Aviva is played by an obese black woman (and an astute critic might ask why overweight black women are frequently the butt of Hollywood comedies, especially when they are played by men like Tyler Perry, Eddie Murphy, and Martin Lawrence?). We are even encouraged to think about gender during the section of the film labeled "Huckleberry," when Aviva is played by a slight young white boy with longish hair. (Solondz uses pink or blue title cards adorned with gendered objects and names to introduce each change of actor.) The connotations associated with "Huckleberry" recall, of course, Mark Twain's classic nineteenth-century novels about young boys and their adventures; *Palindromes* invites a gendered comparison between Huck Finn, Tom Sawyer,

Fig 3.5
Jennifer Jason Leigh as Aviva towards the end of *Palindromes* (2004). When played by an adult, Aviva seems especially vacuous.

Fig 3.6
Aviva played by a
male actor during the
"Huckleberry" segment of
Palindromes (2004).

and Aviva (see Figure 3.6). Western culture is full of texts that celebrate boys taking such journeys as rites of passage into manhood; the journeys of girls are less celebrated. (*The Wizard of Oz* [1939] is a notable exception to that trend, although Dorothy learns to stay at home whereas most male adventurers eventually claim their home to be the world itself.)

And as for the controversial issues of childhood sexuality, teenage pregnancy, statutory rape, and abortion: the film offers no easy clear cut answers, since these are complex social phenomena that are difficult to reduce to binary sound bites either pro or con. Aviva—whatever her actual age—actively invites and engages in sexual activity with all her partners. When she encounters the Sunshine family, it is apparent that young Peter Paul (who looks about eight) has adult-like sexual feelings for her (see Figure 3.7). (Which relationships are "proper" and which are not?) Aviva has sex as often as she does not for the sake of sex itself (as Judah does) but because she is looking for love, both from her hapless partners but even more so from the baby she imagines she will conceive (perhaps in answer to her own fairly rigid and controlling parents).

Fig 3.7
In *Palindromes* (2004)
fisherman Peter Paul
finds Aviva (played by an
overweight black actor)
asleep by the stream, and
takes her to meet the
Sunshine family.

Director Solondz is careful to show Aviva playing with baby dolls and contemplating possible baby names in color-coded ink in her diary, suggesting the ways that Western culture encourages young girls to "play" at being mothers, even as it also punishes them severely when they get pregnant outside of wedlock or parental approval (see Figure 3.8). Furthermore, Aviva's sexual naivety is only matched by her romantic dreams, which again Solondz implies she has learned from the culture surrounding her. Mouthing platitudes like "Have you ever been in love?" she clearly imagines herself in "love" and in a "relationship" with Bob, the much older man who has been using her to sate his own pedophilic sodomitical desires. (These ironies are also made aurally, as when Solondz layers in lush romantic music by Pyotr Ilyich Tchaikovsky over such images.) These various cultural disconnections in the characters' lives are markedly pronounced throughout the film, as when Bob discovers a baby doll with a beer bottle jammed into its anus in a trash can. Muttering "sickos" under his breath, Bob cannot see his own behavior reflected in the image—instead he projects it onto others, in the process ignoring or absolving his own behaviors (see Figure 3.9).

Fig 3.8
Social conditioning at work: Aviva plays at being a mother in *Palindromes* (2004), only to be punished when she actually gets pregnant.

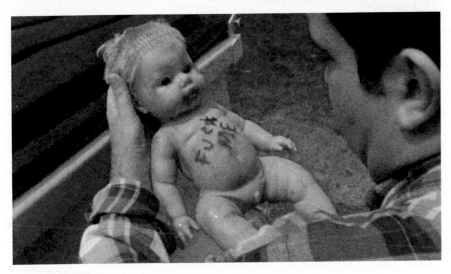

Fig 3.9
In *Palindromes* (2004), Bob finds a baby doll in the trash with a bottle in its anus, but fails to see his own image in the spectacle.

Indeed, one of the central themes of the film surrounds questions of identity and the nature of subjectivity. Aside from its unconventional casting which foregrounds those same issues, the film also seems to suggest—in a semiotic fashion—that we can only know ourselves against a paradigmatic set of others. At the beginning of the film, Aviva (played by a small black girl) worries about whether or not she will grow up like Dawn Weiner (the central character of Solondz's *Welcome to the Dollhouse*) whose funeral opens the film. Dawn has allegedly killed herself after becoming pregnant from a date rape, something Aviva avows she could never do as it would be killing the baby; yet her narrative trajectory is not all that different from Dawn's. Later, at the Sunshine's home, Aviva has the chance to imagine herself as part of a large family whose adoptive children all have various types of birth defects, the types of defects that weigh heavily in some parents' decision to abort a fetus, such as congenital conditions or maternal drug addiction. Director Solondz stages this scene around the family breakfast table as an homage to Tod Browning's classic horror film *Freaks* (1932); however, whereas the older film asked its audience to fear its "freaks" and find them horrific, the attitude in the Sunshine family is unequivocally nurturing and loving (see Figure 3.10). This scene also parallels an earlier one wherein Aviva's mother tries to convince her to get an abortion, noting that many young mothers often give birth to children with physical or mental defects.

Towards the end of the film, Aviva (now played by adult actress Jennifer Jason Leigh) has a discussion with her cousin Mark Weiner (also from *Welcome to the Dollhouse*) about free will versus biological programming. Mark concludes that change (free will) is not possible, that people always remain the same (even when they are played by different actors); the film ends as it began with Aviva once more attempting to get pregnant with a new version of Judah, now calling himself Otto. Earlier, Mark had invoked the metaphor of the palindrome as a model of the human subject—that we all stay the same whether we are seen (or spelled) backwards or forwards. The metaphor also suggests that people (and social issues) are inherently paradoxical and comprised of contradictions. Aviva's parents offer unconditional love and care to her after they learn she is pregnant, but only moments later they threaten to turn her into the street if she insists on keeping her baby. Similarly, the Sunshine family is loving and welcoming but harbors a pedophile and gives cover to a murder plot. In one quick scene wherein the Sunshine children make a poster

Fig 3.10
The Sunshine family around their breakfast table in *Palindromes* (2004); director Todd Solondz stages the scene in reference to a similar scene in Tod Browning's infamous classical Hollywood horror film *Freaks* (1932).

for their singing group, director Solondz points out that you cannot spell "Sunshine Singers" without "Sunshine Sin" (see Figure 3.11).

These complicated social, psychological, and sexual issues find a final form of expression in the film's penultimate scenes at Aviva's welcome home party. Aviva has insisted on inviting Mark Weiner, even though he has been accused by family friend Missy of sexually abusing her daughter. When Aviva tells Mark that she knows he is not a child molester, the prickly and somewhat misanthropic Mark asks her how she can be certain. "Because," she replies, "pedophiles love children" and it is clear that Mark does not. However, a bit of throwaway dialogue in this scene—that Missy too had been molested as a child—suggests another possible culprit in the abuse: Missy herself. (Multiple sources in the fields of social work, counseling, and psychology suggest that people molested as children often repeat the same abusive patterns as adults.) In raising this point and exploring other "hot button" cultural concerns in a similar "deconstructive" fashion, *Palindromes* suggests the need for human understanding to move beyond binary thinking and sound-bite politics, to fully engage with the paradoxes of human experiences in more complex and thoughtful ways.

Fig 3.11
The "Sin" within the "Sunshine Singers," a shot that illustrates one of the central thematic concerns of *Palindromes* (and **poststructuralism**): that every sign or meaning contains (at least) the seed of its opposite sign or meaning.

Questions for discussion

1   Pick a popular TV game show like *Wheel of Fortune* or *Jeopardy*. How can the concepts explored in this chapter—including sign, icon, index, paradigm, syntagm, denotation and connotation—be used to explain how the show works? How important to the functioning of each show is the idea of shared cultural knowledge?

2   Pick a popular Hollywood blockbuster and see how closely it follows the patterns set out by Vladimir Propp in his study of Russian folk-tales. Pick a genre that does not seem to follow Propp's schema, such as the musical or the romance. Do those genres have their own identifiable structures? Are they in any way similar to Propp's?

3   Can you think of any other film or TV shows that foreground their structures in ways similar to *Palindromes*—i.e. in ways that call attention to their formal structures? What do you think those texts are trying to say about the structures of film or television?

References and further reading

Barthes, Roland. *Mythologies*. Trans. Annette Lavers. New York: Hill and Wang, 1972 (1957).

Barthes, Roland. *A Barthes Reader*. Ed. and Intro. by Susan Sontag. New York: Hill and Wang, 1983.

Campbell, Joseph. *The Power of Myth*. New York: Anchor, 1991.

Campbell, Joseph. *The Hero with a Thousand Faces (The Collected Works of Joseph Campbell)* (Third Edition). Novato, CA: New World Library, 2008 (1949).

Chandler, Daniel. *Semiotics: The Basics* (Second Edition). New York and London: Routledge, 2007 (2002).

De Saussure, Ferdinand. *Course in General Linguistics* (Bloomsbury Revelations). Trans. Roy Harris. London: Bloomsbury Academic, 2013 (1916).

Fisk, John and John Hartley. *Reading Television* (New Accents). New York and London: Routledge, 2003 (1978).

Foucault, Michel. *The Foucault Reader*. Ed. Paul Rabinow. New York: Pantheon Books, 1984.

Gordon, W. Terrence. *Saussure for Beginners*. Danbury, CT: Writers & Readers, 1996.

Hall, Sean. *This Means This, This Means That: A User's Guide to Semiotics* (Second Edition). London: Laurence King Publishing, 2012 (2007).

Hodge, Bob and David Tripp. *Children and Television: A Semiotic Approach*. Cambridge: Polity Press, 1987.

Lévi-Strauss, Claude. *Cracking the Code of Culture*. Toronto: University of Toronto Press, 1978.

Lévi-Strauss, Claude. *Structural Anthropology*. New York: Basic Books, 1963.

Metz, Christian. *Film Language: A Semiotics of the Cinema*. Trans. Michael Taylor. Oxford: Oxford University Press, 1974.

Peirce, Charles S. *Peirce on Signs: Writings on Semiotic by Charles Sanders Peirce*. Ed. James Hoopes. Chapel Hill, NC and London: University of North Carolina Press, 1991.

Propp, Valdimir. *Morphology of the Folktale* (Second Edition). Austin, TX: University of Texas Press, 1968.

Roth, Lane. *Film Semiotics, Metz, and Leone's Trilogy*. New York and London: Routledge, 2013 (1983).

Silverman, Kaja. *The Subject of Semiotics*. New York: Oxford University Press, 1983.

Stam, Robert, Robert Burgoyne and Sandy Flitterman-Lewis. *New Vocabularies in Film Semiotics*. New York and London: Routledge, 1992.

CHAPTER 4

Authorship and the auteur theory

One of the most common ways that contemporary filmmakers, filmgoers, and critics think about film—as opposed to television—is via the **auteur theory**. Auteur is the French word for author. As this chapter will explore, the auteur theory is based on the idea that the director of a film should be considered its "author"—the one creative mind or organizing principle behind a film (or an **oeuvre**, another French term that refers to an artist's entire body of work). These ideas might be easily acceded to if we think of films made by single individuals, such as many **avant-garde** or **experimental** films. However, most commercial films are made by groups of individuals who each make artistic and creative contributions to the project. Furthermore, most films already have authors in the literary sense: the men and women who write their screenplays. So why should the director be singled out and given all the credit as the sole author? Simple or basic auteur theory asserts that even though a director is working within industrial contexts with hundreds of other people, it is his or her creative vision that nevertheless leaves its mark on the final film. If a director also writes, produces, scores, edits, and/or appears in his or her film—as did or do directors like Charlie Chaplin, Woody Allen, Sally Potter, and Spike Lee—he or she is sometimes referred to as a **hyphenate auteur**. It might be argued that a hyphenate auteur's creative input increases with each job he/she performs. Yet, in today's Hollywood, and in much historical as well as contemporary thinking about auteurism, a director is not necessarily required to fulfill multiple roles in a film's production in order to be considered its auteur. Today, a film's director might even be considered something of a celebrity or brand, as fans flock to see the latest Quentin Tarantino film or a movie "made by" the Coen Brothers.

And what about television? TV shows are usually written by committees and have a rotating slate of directors throughout their life spans. Who should be considered the author(s) of *Lost* (2004–10): the individuals who created the series, or any one of its multiple directors, writers, designers, special effects technicians, or even actors? Perhaps its network, ABC, should be considered the auteur behind the show, as arguably the industrial and economic concerns of network television production are the most important aspects determining the shape and content of what is produced and aired. As this chapter explores, the auteur theory was originally designed for thinking about films, and its application to television is at best rather strained. When the term auteur *is* invoked in relation to television, it is usually used to describe the writer-producer-creator of a given series, more so than the various writers and directors who might work on the show over the course of several years. (Within the industry, these multiple creative writer-producer-creators are often referred to as **showrunners**.) Thus J. J. Abrams, the man who is credited with creating *Lost*, might be considered its auteur. Other contemporary television auteurs in this **hyphenate** sense of the word include Joss Whedon (creator of *Buffy the Vampire Slayer* [1997–2003], *Angel* [1999–2004], and *Firefly* [2002–3]) and Alan Ball (creator of *Six Feet Under* [2001–5] and *True Blood* [2008–14]). And as with an auteur film director, a hyphenate writer-producer-creator (or showrunner) of a given TV series is thought to imbue each of his or her series with a personalized thematic and stylistic consistency. Thus a Joss Whedon show is probably going to be a playful, self-aware fantasy with romantic and comedic touches, while an Alan Ball series is going to be a darker exploration of contemporary American mores set within morbid or fantastic settings. A new TV show from David Simon may likely be a dark gritty urban serial drama like his previous shows *Homicide: Life on the Street* (1993–9), *The Wire* (2002–8), and *Treme* (2010–11). However, as with the use of all labels or categories, calling someone an auteur or a showrunner is perhaps a limited and limiting way to approach his or her work. However, it does serve as a sort of brief definition of a filmmaker, calling to mind specific directorial approaches and creating certain expectations among viewers.

In the 1960s, the auteur theory was instrumental in helping film be thought of as a legitimate art form, and film studies be thought of as a legitimate academic discipline. As we have seen in previous chapters, many cultural critics (such as the **Frankfurt School**) considered movies to be just so much mass-produced junk, the antithesis of "true art." The auteur theory explicitly challenged those views. By asserting that films could and did have authors, the auteur theory implied that films were creative works like poems or novels, and not just factory-made mass entertainments. The rise of the auteur theory allowed for the creation and recognition of an international art cinema and the canonization of certain filmmakers including Ingmar Bergman, Satyajit Ray, Federico Fellini, Akira Kurosawa, and Jean-Luc Godard as visionary thinkers and undisputed film artists. During the 1970s, however, **structuralist** and **poststructuralist** theorists in/famously declared the "death of the author," and both the auteur theory and the auteur cinema it had helped to create fell into decline. (In corporate Hollywood, filmmakers were increasingly judged on their ability to produce blockbuster hits rather than their creative artistry.) More recent decades have seen the return of the auteur as an important figure in film studies. He or she refuses to go away. **Multiculturalists** argue that a director's social **subjectivity**—including his or her race, class, gender, sexuality, regionality/nationality, etc.—does play an important role in the cultural meaning of any given director's work. Meanwhile, other film scholars are exploring the notion of the auteur as a form of branding, another tool in Hollywood's ever-expanding arsenal of techniques designed to market films to the public. One thing is certain, however. Even after its complex and contested history, people continue to speak about the auteur in relation to cinema, and in some special cases, even in relation to television.

Authorship before the auteur theory

In the earliest years of cinema, the film-going public rarely knew who made the movies, or even the names of those people who appeared in them: movie stars did not emerge until cinema's second decade. At roughly the same time, the names of certain companies and filmmakers began to be recognized via an early form of branding. Some companies (such as Biograph) and film directors (such as D. W. Griffith) started to "sign" their names or initials on their films—primarily on title and intertitle cards—as a way of claiming ownership. It was not unusual at that time for exhibitors to steal others' work and claim it as their own, thus this "signing" was done for legal/financial reasons as much as for self-promotion. When exhibitors realized they could re-title a film without the original owners' signatures, some companies even took to inserting their logos into the *mise-en-scène*! (See Figure 4.1.) Eventually, as the industry consolidated into a powerful oligopoly during the 1920s and 1930s, such practices were no longer needed.

Partly because of his innovations in narrative filmmaking and his extreme prolificacy—Griffith directed approximately 500 short films before he began to make feature films—D. W. Griffith has often been considered one of the first important auteur directors. Other filmmakers and actors of the silent era such as Charlie Chaplin, Mary Pickford, and Douglas Fairbanks also exhibited a great deal of creative control over their projects, and along with Griffith they formed United Artists in 1919 to insure those favorable working conditions (not to mention maximizing profits for themselves). Although movie stars tended to eclipse writers, directors, and producers in the public's eye during the 1920s and 1930s, certain names from behind the screen did become common knowledge to the movie-going public. For example, Walt Disney stood out from the ranks of most Hollywood filmmakers because of his iconoclastic status as a pioneer and innovator in studio animation techniques, not to mention his self-promotion and ancillary marketing of toys related to his films. Nonetheless, animation as practiced at the Disney Studios was an extremely cooperative venture employing hundreds of story men, musicians, "ink and paint girls," editors, and the like; most of those people never received any onscreen credit for their work. Instead, the public recognized

Fig 4.1
Max Linder's *Troubles of a Grass Widower* (1912) was released by Pathé Frères, whose company logo was a rooster: note its inclusion in the *mise-en-scène* on the right side of the door frame.

the name Walt Disney and many may have assumed him to be the sole creative genius behind Mickey Mouse, Donald Duck, and even Disney's first feature length animated film *Snow White and the Seven Dwarfs* (1937).

Other equally independent-minded film producers in the 1930s and 1940s—such as Samuel Goldwyn and David O. Selznick—occasionally rose to public prominence for their quality film productions. Indeed, in these decades it was not unusual to credit film *producers* as the true creative forces behind individual films (even as the term auteur itself had not yet been introduced into the English language). Under the **Hollywood studio system**, actors, screenwriters, and directors were all employees under contract, assigned to certain films on an *ad hoc* or even arbitrary basis. It was the producer who was the most important man on the production, overseeing all aspects of a project and reporting to the studio bosses. One of the most important producers in early Hollywood was Irving Thalberg, a young man sometimes referred to by industry wags as "the boy wonder." Thalberg's clash with film director Erich von Stroheim at Universal Studies in the 1920s exemplifies a producer-director dynamic still in effect in contemporary Hollywood. Von Stroheim was a self-promoting martinet (he passed himself off as a European nobleman when in fact he was a Jewish **working class** immigrant), whose films were renowned for their big budgets, European "decadence," attention to realism, and costly over-budget productions. Stroheim's first few films (including *Blind Husbands* [1919] and *Foolish Wives* [1922]) were box office successes, but when his next film *Merry-Go-Round* (1923) began to go over budget and behind schedule, his producer Irving Thalberg replaced him with a more dependable company man, Rupert Julian. In the confrontation between committed artistry (Von Stroheim) and bottom-line economics (Thalberg), the producer won out. Hollywood history is full of such confrontations. Some of the most innovative American filmmakers, including Buster Keaton and Orson Welles, did their best work outside of the studio system. Even today, the moniker "independent filmmaker" carries a cachet of artistry and creative freedom that is the antithesis of the term "studio hack," a director who supposedly compromises his or her artistry in the name of profitability. That said, Thalberg went on to oversee production at MGM, helping to create numerous Hollywood classics before his untimely death in 1936.

The case of Val Lewton at RKO during World War II is another interesting example of the producer-as-auteur, and demonstrates how what today we might call auteur style is intricately connected to both genre as well as studio. From 1942–46, Val Lewton produced nine remarkably similar B horror films, including *The Cat People* (1942), *I Walked with a Zombie* (1943), *The Body Snatcher* (1945), and *Bedlam* (1946). Despite these films having various directors, screenwriters, and cinematographers (many of whom did admittedly work on more than one of these productions), the films are famous for their consistently eerie tone, understated performances, psychological and artistic allusions, and a chiaroscuro visual style drawn from German expressionist cinema. Thus, in one sense, producer Val Lewton might be considered the auteur filmmaker behind these works, the single artistic force responsible for the creation of a set of very similar (and effective) B horror films. However, one might also consider Val Lewton as just another studio employee who was successfully able to marshal the talent surrounding him at RKO: talent that included directors Jacques Tourneur, Mark Robson, and Robert Wise; screenwriters DeWitt Bodeen and Curt Siodmak; and cinematographers Nicholas

Musuraca and J. Roy Hunt. Together, *all* of these men made use of RKO's considerable studio resources in order to rework and/or embellish the pre-existing conventions of the horror genre. As this example illustrates, creative individuals, a well-financed studio, and a pre-existing genre structure all contributed to the making and meaning of the Val Lewton horror films. Reducing all of those factors into one individual's creative and/or artistic genius is perhaps somewhat reductive and **essentialist**.

In many ways, the underlying assumptions behind early concepts of film authorship (and what would soon be called the auteur theory) were and are deeply connected to broader trends in art and literature: especially nineteenth-century **romanticism** and the rise of **modernism**. As explored in greater detail in Chapter 9, art in the Western world had passed through (and is now frequently classified into) various broad movements or phases. Following the Renaissance and the eighteenth-century's "Age of Enlightenment"—which championed reason, science, and **classical realism** in the arts—a countermovement termed **romanticism** became predominant. As the name implies, romantic poetry, prose, painting, and music were created to express feelings and emotions, not scientific rationality. The romantic artist was prized as someone who had intimate personal contact with non-scientific realms such as aesthetics and perhaps even mysticism. Whereas Age of Enlightenment rationalists approached nature as something to be collected, classified, and controlled, romanticists were more likely to celebrate nature as sublime, unknown, and unknowable. British writers like Lord Byron and Percy Bysshe Shelley (or Edgar Allan Poe and Nathaniel Hawthorne in America) expressed such sentiments in their prose and also helped cultivate the image of the romantic author as someone above the banal normality of everyday perception, someone possessing almost extra-sensory abilities of sensuality and expressivity. This idea of the author as somehow cut off from the quotidian and possessing extraordinary powers of perception and creation, feeds directly into twentieth-century notions of the filmmaker as auteur.

The rise of **modernism** at the end of the nineteenth century also contributed to more contemporary understandings of the cinematic auteur. Modernism proclaimed itself as different from earlier stages of artistic development in many ways, but it held onto the notion that the artist was somehow different from the rest of humanity, brilliantly and sometimes tragically gifted. Some modernists like Vincent van Gogh are today as well known for their personal demons and troubled lives as much as their artworks. As with Edgar Allan Poe in the preceding century, romantic and modernist notions of the artist often conflate madness and genius. Great artists are great—so the logic goes—because they exist outside of normality. Their troubled psyches are the source of their vivid and striking visions. Indeed, modernists challenged traditional classical and realist approaches to art, attempting instead to capture subjective impressions and creative expressions well beyond objective reality. Modernist art is valued more for its artists' creative stylizations— their "take" on objective reality—than for the objects or subjects their works might depict. Unlike classical realist artworks such as the Mona Lisa—which ostensibly looks like its subject—a modernist "portrait" may only barely be recognizable as a human figure. **Impressionism**, **expressionism**, and **surrealism** were three of the leading modernist schools of the early twentieth century, and each movement produced films (as well as paintings and other traditional art forms). For example, compared to American films, the famous German expressionist film *The Cabinet of*

Dr. Caligari (1920) is so bizarrely stylized that it was frequently considered "art" in a way that most Hollywood films were not. Similarly, when surrealists Salvador Dali and Luis Buñuel unleashed *Un Chien Andalou* (1929) on unsuspecting viewers, it was understood as a provocative piece of art made by two radical artists working in the medium of film. Fernand Léger's *Ballet Mécanique* (1924), discussed in Chapters 1 and 2, is usually considered an example of modernist art (as much as it is a film) partly because its creator was an artist who made similar works in other media such as painting and sculpture.

The point of all this is that concepts of cinematic authorship before auteurism were a wide-ranging and not very systematic set of assumptions that allowed some films to be considered art (and their directors and/or producers to be considered artists) while denying that privilege to other films and filmmakers. As the **high–low dichotomy** (discussed in Chapter 1) framed such debates, "real" artists and authors did not produce popular cultural artifacts such as Hollywood films, which would have been considered a low art form—if an art form at all. Filmmakers tied directly to various avant-garde or modernist movements were much more readily understood as artists (and therefore authors) than were the employees of a Hollywood studio. Despite that fact however, we have also seen how some early filmmakers claimed authorship as a brand name for legal and/or economic protection. We have also seen how certain unique and creative individuals were able to emerge out of the supposedly routinized mass produced nature of the Hollywood studio system. It was against these industrial conditions and artistic currents that French critics first seriously began to theorize cinematic authorship.

From "La Politique des Auteurs" to "The Auteur Theory"

Traditional auteur criticism dates back to France in the post-World War II era. Film history sometimes points to Alexandre Astruc's notion of the "**camera-stylo**"—or "camera pen"—as a blueprint for subsequent theorizing about the film author. Writing in 1948, Astruc argued that the filmmaker's camera could be and should be understood as the equivalent of a writer's pen. He argued that all the means of cinematic specificity could be and should be used by a film director in fully artistic and creative ways (as opposed to just setting up the camera and filming a script). But it was the critics of the influential film journal *Cahiers du Cinema* who laid the groundwork for much subsequent theorizing of the auteur. *Cahiers du Cinema* was edited by André Bazin, and the critics writing for him included Claude Chabrol, François Truffaut, Eric Rohmer, Jacques Rivette, and Jean-Luc Godard—men whose names would become synonymous with the **French New Wave** cinema a few years later when they got the chance to make their own films. Bazin himself was a theorist and critic who championed cinematic **realism**: for him, it was cinema's special ability to capture reality through the photographic process that separated it from the other arts. As such, Bazin tended to favor directors like Erich von Stroheim and Orson Welles—directors who used deep space and long takes that captured a sense of real space and time. Still other *Cahiers du Cinema* critics championed certain directors based on other criteria. Eventually, something known as "**La Politique des Auteurs**" (which would later be translated into English as "The Auteur Theory") emerged from the writings of these critics.

One of the most important essays in the development of auteur theory was François Truffaut's 1954 article "A Certain Tendency of the French Cinema." In it,

Truffaut railed against what he found to be the moribund state of French cinema and its so-called "Tradition of Quality," making a distinction between directors he termed **metteurs-en-scène** and those he termed **auteurs**. The former were literary-minded directors who were content to adapt stuffy and stodgy literary classics, composing pretty pictures to accompany a script based on a well-respected novel. The auteur director, on the other hand, was a filmmaker who used all of his or her resources in a far more creative way. In other words, the metteur-en-scène was a director mostly concerned with filming a script, while the auteur should and could be a "man of the cinema," ostensibly more finely tuned to film's specific formal properties. Even more provocatively, as Truffaut and his fellow film critics developed their ideas on auteurism, they began to suggest that auteurs could and did exist even within studio systems such as Hollywood. This was a shocking idea when many critics of the era still thought of Hollywood films as debased cookie-cut products of a mind-numbing **culture industry**. Instead, the *Cahiers du Cinema* critics began to champion the work of John Ford, Nicholas Ray, Howard Hawks, Max Ophuls, Vincente Minnelli, and Alfred Hitchcock (among others), arguing that these directors were true auteurs because they were able to infuse into their films recognizable stylistic elements and thematic concerns in spite of the factory-like structure of the Hollywood studio system. For example, Minnelli's bold color designs, Ophuls's use of the moving camera, and Hitchcock's preoccupation with Catholic guilt and "wrong man" themes all became evidence of their cinematic artistry, not just literary adaptation, or conformity to a studio system that mass produced films.

Intriguingly, the rise of auteur theory appeared against and within various important historical and cultural contexts. On one level (especially in France), it was call for a younger generation of filmmakers to replace an older one. Underlying that call was anger and mistrust directed at some of those older filmmakers, men who had continued to make films under the Nazi-occupied Vichy France government during World War II. The rise of auteur theory was also part of larger post-war cultural movements and intellectual debates over **existentialism**, **phenomenology**, and **medium specificity**. Perhaps most importantly, there was a thriving interest in cinema as an actual art form, which led to the development of myriad film clubs, journals (like *Cahiers du Cinema*), and cinemas that specialized in foreign and American films. The most famous of those cinemas, the **Cinématèque Français**, was located in the heart of Paris and was run by an iconoclast named **Henri Langlois**. Langlois liked to program American films, often in oddly matched double bills. There was also a glut of American films in the marketplace, as Europe was flooded with Hollywood films once the embargoes of the war years were lifted. As such, during those years a very different context for film reception was created in Europe as opposed to the United States. While American critics perhaps saw one new Hitchcock film per year, a new generation of French critics were able to see a handful of Hitchcock films all at once—maybe even in one sitting. It is intriguing to think that these intensified conditions of reception may have enabled critics to notice and remark upon any given director's stylistic and thematic consistencies in a way that a more staggered release pattern did not.

Thinking about the "La Politique des Auteurs" quickly crossed the waters to both England and America. In 1962, the British film journal *Movie* was founded, and it announced its adherence to the tenets of the auteur theory by publishing a ranking of directors in its first issue. That same year in the United States, Andrew

Sarris, then a critic for the avant-garde journal *Film Culture* published his "Notes on the Auteur Theory." Sarris argued that a true auteur filmmaker needed (1) to be talented, (2) to have a "distinguishable personality," and (3) to express in his or her films an "interior meaning" that was to be the result of the director's personal take on the subject matter of the film. Sarris went so far in his 1968 book *The American Cinema* to rank over 200 filmmakers in order of their alleged talent—i.e. their adherence to Sarris's own criteria for an auteur director. Directors were ranked from best to worst in categorical chapters like "The Pantheon" (John Ford, Alfred Hitchcock) to "Less than Meets the Eye" (John Huston, Elia Kazan) to "Oddities, One-Shots and Newcomers" (John Cassavetes, Mike Nichols). While useful as a handy reference book on American film directors up to that era, many of Sarris's rankings seem highly suspect today. Primarily, if a director made many different films in many different styles, as did John Huston, he was ranked lower than someone whose work showed more consistency. (Who is to say that consistency *per se* is what makes an artist great? It might also make him or her merely repetitive.) Sarris's *The American Cinema* is a very judgmental and subjectively evaluative book, ultimately yet another reworking of the old high art ("good") versus low art ("bad") debate, and as such, yet another intervention was needed in the development of auteur theory.

The infusion of semiotics: Structuralist and poststructuralist concepts of the auteur

If someone had asked Andrew Sarris whether or not Ed Wood—a director of 1950s grade Z science fiction horror films—was an auteur, he would have had to answer no, based upon his own subjective criteria of technical competence or talent. Ed Wood is widely recognized as one of the most technically inept directors of all time, and his film *Plan 9 From Outer Space* (1959) has been repeatedly nominated in various polls as "The Worst Film of all Time." But if one actually takes the time to examine Wood's films, as later critics would indeed do, consistent thematic and stylistic motifs can be found, such as his poverty-level budgets, his stock company of Hollywood oddballs, his tendency towards overripe voice-over narration, and his personal predilections for women's garments (and especially angora sweaters). So, if we remove the element of a given director's talent or technical competency from the auteur equation, what are we left with? Are Sarris's categories of "distinguishable personality" giving rise to "interior meaning" still relevant?

One response to these questions came in the form of **auteur-structuralism**, a strain of thinking about auteurism infused with linguistic/semiotic concepts, and most readily associated with Peter Wollen's 1972 book *Signs and Meaning in the Cinema*. This new thinking about the auteur started with the critic and worked its way back through the text to the "idea" of the author. Under auteur-structuralism, the director is understood less as a flesh and blood person (let alone a singular creative genius in the romantic/modernist sense), and more as a set of codes or structures found in his or her films. In a famous turn of phrase, John Ford the man became "John Ford" the linguistic structure—i.e. the consistent thematic and stylistic elements that comprise a John Ford film. To use terms from **semiotics**, auteur-structuralism understands "John Ford" as a **langue** (a specific linguistic subset of Hollywood filmmaking), and each of his films whether *Stagecoach* (1939), *The Searchers* (1956), or *The Man Who Shot Liberty Valance* (1962) as an instance of **parole** (a given speech act or individual text spoken in the language system of "John Ford"). This move from Sarris's version of the auteur theory to auteur-structuralism involved several important theoretical shifts. Perhaps most importantly, it did away with the high/low value judgments associated with earlier auteur theorizing (notably that of Andrew Sarris, but also the *Cahiers du Cinema* critics). Now *any* filmmaker could potentially be considered an auteur, assuming he or she had made more than one film such that their deeper structures could be analyzed and discerned. Auteur-structuralism also challenged the doctrine of intentionality, the idea that only the director can say what his or her film's "true" meaning might be. Instead, under auteur-structuralism, the director is understood as a conscious and unconscious "catalyst" responsible for channeling others' creative work into consistent filmic product.

Auteur-structuralism was part of a trend in critical thinking during the 1960s and 1970s that shifted emphasis away from the writer (filmmaker or auteur director) and onto the reader. **Roland Barthes**'s famous essay "The Death of the Author" argued that—like auteur-structuralism—the author of a text is really only discernable through his or her writings. In effect, the reader constructs an "idea" of the author through the process of reading or decoding the text under consideration—we rarely know the actual author in person. **Michel Foucault**, in his essay "What is an Author?" explored the ideological meanings of authorship, what he called the "author function." Among his findings were that the concept of authorship upheld ideologies of classification, ownership, and control. In other words, the "author function" is a way to identify different types of texts, provide for legal and financial rights (such as copyright), and allegedly fix a text's "true" meaning as the author's intent. The case of *Star Wars*, its fans, and its creator George Lucas may serve to illustrate some of these ideas. From a legal point of view, George Lucas was recognized as the author and owner of the *Star Wars* franchise from its creation in 1977 until its purchase by Disney in 2012. Under copyright law, Lucas had a legal right to control how his films were marketed and distributed, and he sometimes used lawyers to shut down unauthorized uses of his intellectual property. Many fans of the series, however, saw the matter a little differently. As explored in Chapter 11, fans often use ideas and characters from mass-produced media texts in very unusual ways, writing stories or making videos that may alter or expand the original meanings of the mass-produced text. In some cases, fans created sexually explicit texts about *Star Wars* characters that were definitely not part of the PG-rated universe of the official *Star Wars* franchise. Who should be considered the author of such works—the fans or George Lucas? In the past, Lucas used his status as the author and owner of *Star Wars* to try to stop such fan fiction from circulating, probably because he felt it may have tarnished his brand, and changed his original intentions of what *Star Wars* means and expresses. In this way, as Foucault's "author function" suggests, George Lucas-as-author maintains the ability to classify what *Star Wars* "truly" is, and legally pursue others who may try to alter that notion. When he sold his company Lucasfilm to Disney in 2012, he ceded creative control over the franchise to its new owners. And with George Lucas no longer working on the franchise, who should be considered the author of any new *Star Wars* films?

Auteur-structuralism was an important theoretical shift in thinking about the auteur filmmaker, but its ideas rarely reached into the minds of the average filmgoer or journalistic critic. Even to this day most journalistic critics understand auteur theory in terms not all that different from Andrew Sarris's: as a way to judge the quality or artistry of individual films or individual film artists. Other poststructuralist critics critiqued and/or moved beyond auteur-structuralism, understanding it (like all structuralist theories) as too ahistorical and essentialist. Why reduce an entire body of films to a single structure or authorial signature, when there are probably much more interesting differences between them? And what do those different films have to tell us about history, culture, and **ideology**? For many critics, auteur theory in the late 1970s and 1980s ceased to become a productive way to think about film. Declining interest in the auteur director during this era also coincided with the decline of auteur cinema. The filmmakers who had been championed by earlier critics were aging or dying, and in some cases their later works were judged to be (to use Sarris's derogatory term) "Less than Meets the Eye." Celebrated auteur filmmakers of the 1960s like Federico Fellini, Ingmar Bergman, and Akira Kurosawa fell so far out of favor that they increasingly had difficulty raising production funds or getting distribution deals. Hollywood too was changing. It had briefly embraced the concept of the auteur director in the late 1960s and 1970s, allowing distinctive filmmakers like Robert Altman, Hal Ashby, and Martin Scorsese the chance to make some provocative films. But after the success of Steven Spielberg/George Lucas blockbuster franchises like *Jaws*, *Star Wars*, and *Indiana Jones*, a new type of auteur replaced the older one (who represented artistry and innovation). This new Hollywood "corporate auteur" was recognized primarily for making films—and film franchises—that made enormous amounts of money regardless of their quality or artistry. Increasingly, auteurism in Hollywood has become a marketing strategy—just another way to maximize profits by selling not only the film itself, but also the idea of the person who made it.

The return of the auteur

As **structuralism** gave way to **poststructuralism**, interest in authorship declined, while interest in **reception theory** (and more broadly **cultural studies**) began to increase. In general, these schools acknowledged the importance of the author, but not as the beginning or end of cinematic meaning. Instead, more recent media theorists tend to see the author or auteur as but one point of meaning creation in a more complex array of industry, form and style, and audience. The author or producer may **encode** meanings into a text, but readers or audiences also decode meanings, and all of those meanings are situated within multiple contexts of industry, economy, history, and ideology (recall Diagram 1.1). As these more nuanced takes on authorship developed, two main trends in thinking about the author emerged. One centers on examining the social identity of authors, and the other on what has been called "the commerce of auteurism."

With the rise of **multiculturalism** during the last decades of the twentieth century, there was a renewed interest in the idea of the auteur, specifically an author's social subjectivity—his or her race, gender, ethnicity, sexuality, and so forth. Many theorists today do believe that a filmmaker's socio-cultural background is quite important to the meanings that their films (and more rarely TV shows) express. Feminist film theory was among the first disciplines to explore the role of female filmmakers both historically and in contemporary contexts. Feminist film critics pointed out the lack of attention paid to pioneering female filmmakers like Alice Guy-Blaché, Dorothy Arzner, and Ida Lupino, and used auteurist concepts to examine their films for potential feminist import. Other feminist theorists noted that auteurist thinking itself was primarily a male discourse, while still others argued that the very style of Hollywood cinema carried a patriarchal bias (see Chapter 8). Their goal was at first to find a cinematic language that would somehow not carry that patriarchal bias, and many avant-garde and experimental films were made by women and feminist men toward that end. Meanwhile, increasing numbers of black, Hispanic, Asian-American, and gay and lesbian filmmakers were getting the chance to make films from their perspectives. The dominance of white patriarchal capitalism throughout American film history began to be challenged, and by the 1970s and 1980s various minority groups began to make films documenting and dramatizing their own experiences from their own perspectives.

Today, most critics and theorists probably would agree that a director's race, gender, sexuality, nationality, etc. does shape his or her vision of the world, and subsequently his or her filmic vision. Historically, American film was almost always about white people from the point of view of white male filmmakers. People of color were regularly marginalized and stereotyped, women were sexually **objectified**, and gay and lesbian people were censored out of cinematic existence. It has only been in recent decades that members of such minority groups have had the power to depict themselves on screen, implicitly and explicitly challenging the ways they had been represented by white male filmmakers in previous decades. The making of *The Color Purple* (1985) illustrates some of the issues to which these new multicultural discourses have drawn attention. Written in 1982, *The Color Purple* is an award-winning feminist novel about black women, written by a black woman (Alice Walker), and centering on an intimate relationship between two black women. When Hollywood made its film version, it was scripted and directed by two white men: the Dutch-born Menno Meyjes and Jewish American Steven Spielberg. An auteur theory attuned to multicultural thinking might raise questions about the appropriateness of these two men filming *The Color Purple*: what about their backgrounds gives them insight into the historical experiences of black women? Other multicultural auteurists might ask how the film adaptation of the novel may have differed from the Spielberg version had it actually been written and directed by black women? (Of course, it is highly doubtful there were any black female filmmakers on Hollywood's radar when they made *The Color Purple*; even today minority filmmakers tend to have their work more readily funded and distributed through more independent channels.) The point is not that Spielberg should not have made *The Color Purple*—though some critics might still wish to assert that. The point is that a director who is personally closer to the subject matter of any given film may understand it in ways that a director from another cultural group might not. Minority critics and filmmakers are rightfully wary about white Hollywood representing minority characters and communities, because Hollywood did such a biased job of it throughout much of the twentieth century. Many of the formulas and tropes that developed during Hollywood's classical age are still pressed into service when representing minorities in the media today, frequently conveying ideological biases that are not discernable to the average filmgoer.

This is not to assert certain essentialist ideas about social subjectivities. For example, not all black filmmakers are going to have the same take on African American issues. Just like white filmmakers, black filmmakers will express a range of social subjectivities based upon their experiences throughout life. In another example, some women can and do direct male-centered action blockbusters, while others prefer to direct smaller, more overtly feminist films. Gay and lesbian directors tell heterosexual stories all the time, and occasionally make films about their own communities. But the point is to realize that the history of film and television has been littered with stereotypes and formulas—literally ways of seeing and thinking about minorities—that have been shaped by white heterosexual male filmmakers and their ideological positions. Recognizing this fact complicates both historical and contemporary thinking about the auteur, but it is not a call for some sort of quota system in which only Latina filmmakers would be permitted to make films about Latinas. Ideally, any director should be able to make any kind of film he or she desires. However, as in many industries throughout the Western world, access to film and television production in Hollywood is still somewhat limited when it comes to many minorities. One of the goals of what might be called a multicultural auteur theory continues to be the recognition and celebration of minority film and television producers, both historically as well as in the contemporary media environment. The recent publicity surrounding African American female television producer Shonda Rhimes (*Grey's Anatomy* [2005–], *Scandal* [2012–], *How to Get Away with Murder* [2014–]) suggests just how rare it is for women and people of color to reach the status of well-known filmmaker or showrunner, even as it also represents an incremental change in that direction.

Although diversity in the film and TV industry may be one goal of many cultural critics and activists, the industries' goals remain primarily economic. In accordance with those goals, some concepts of auteur theory have become co-opted in new ways. Today, many directors have become like movie stars with their own personas to be maintained and marketed. The idea of "A Steven Spielberg Film" expresses something about artistry, high production values, and lyric romanticism. "A Film by Quentin Tarantino" signifies a hip, violent, and cynical joyride through exploitation cinema(s). A director's entire body of work can be reduced to a sound bite and used to promote his or her newest work. Even films by first time directors are sometimes labeled as "A Film by So-and-So," not because anyone in the audience is expected to know who So-and-So is, but because the "name above the billing" suggests an auteur, and an auteur suggests quality (regardless of the film's actual artistry or lack thereof). In other cases, especially in the horror genre, some directors have allowed their very names to become brands. The low budget horror movie *Hostel* (2005), directed by Eli Roth, was promoted as being "presented by Quentin Tarantino." Similarly, well-known auteur horror directors like Clive Barker and Wes Craven now often allow their names to be attached to (often inferior) horror films that they have not directed. A Wes Craven fan expecting a Wes Craven film might be disappointed to discover that *Dracula 2000* (2000) was actually directed by Patrick Lussier, despite being advertised as "Wes Craven Presents." The very name and "high art aura" of the cinematic auteur—in this case Wes Craven—is used for promotional purposes. Hollywood obviously feels that "Wes Craven Presents" will sell more tickets than would "A Film by Patrick Lussier."

Another issue complicating auteur theory is posed by **postmodernism** (explored in greater detail in Chapter 9). Increasingly, many filmmakers are making films that rely heavily on allusion, quotation, and/or **pastiche** of older films and genres. Brian De Palma, Tim Burton, the Coen Brothers, and perhaps most obviously Quentin Tarantino all have made careers out of recycling previous cinematic modes/styles and even specific directorial flourishes. Likewise, contemporary television **showrunners** like Seth MacFarlane (*Family Guy* [1999–], *American Dad!* [2005–]) create texts whose sole *raison d'etre* seems to be the recycling and repackaging of American popular culture. The existence of such "postmodern auteurs" complicates the "great artistic genius" strain of auteur theory. As the argument goes, Federico Fellini and Ingmar Bergman were considered auteurs in the 1960s because no one had ever seen films quite like theirs before. Today however, some auteurs are celebrated precisely for the ways they copy and quote previous films. Does this reliance on media makers copying other styles (instead of developing their own idiosyncratic styles) compromise their auteur status? (Not according to Hollywood publicity and promotion!) Perhaps there is no such thing as originality in the first place—only the borrowing, copying, and recombination of previous styles, stories, and characters. If so, the romantic and/or modernist notion of the "Great Genius Artist" is further undermined.

And yet, the idea of the "great and talented" auteur refuses to go away, especially in the public's mind. Partly that is because of the way Hollywood promotes directors as stars in and of themselves, as well as the proliferation of DVD commentaries, interviews, and websites all devoted to film directors. These venues help keep the idea of the flesh and blood auteur (as opposed to the auteur as a code as theorized by auteur-structuralism) alive in the minds of the moviegoing public, and help reinforce doctrines of intentionality (Foucault's "author function"). Who would want to argue with the director when s/he tells you on a commentary track exactly what his or her film means? Despite much critical thinking arguing the opposite, the director is still naively understood by many as another version of the voice of God, the ultimate authority on meaning.

Case study 1: Tim Burton (1958–)

Hollywood filmmaker Tim Burton is an excellent example of a contemporary film director most critics and theorists would probably call an auteur, precisely for the ways in which his films express consistent stylistic and thematic motifs, many of which seem tied to his own personal experiences and obsessions. Born in sunny Southern California in 1958, as a child Burton preferred the dark recesses of movie theaters (and especially the morbid thrills of 1960s horror films) to the beaches of Malibu. Interested in graphic design, as a young man he attended the California Institute of the Arts. Subsequently hired by the Walt Disney Company as an animator, Burton worked on the feature film *The Fox and the Hound* (1981) and created two short films of his own: *Vincent* (1982) and *Frankenweenie* (1984). The former was a black-and-white stop-motion animated (and autobiographical) sketch of a boy obsessed with the horror films of Vincent Price. The latter was a live-action riff on classical Hollywood horror films, most notably *Frankenstein* (1931), about a boy who reanimates his dog after it is accidentally run over by a car. (More recently, Burton also produced and directed a full-length animated version of *Frankenweenie* [2012].) Needless to say, neither *Vincent* nor the first *Frankenweenie* film fitted the family-friendly fare that characterized the Walt Disney Company in the 1980s, and the films were rarely screened. However, Burton's feature film debut *Pee-Wee's Big Adventure* (1985) became a cult hit, as did his next film *Beetlejuice* (1988). After successfully rebooting the *Batman* franchise for Warner Brothers in 1989, and following it with the hit sequel *Batman Returns* (1992), Burton

Fig 4.2
A publicity photo of
director Tim Burton reveals
a tall thin man with a
shock of unruly black hair.
Credit: Touchstone / The
Kobal Collection.

became a Hollywood insider. Since then his career has been mostly comprised of films that explore the themes and styles of previous eras' fantasy and horror films. *Edward Scissorhands* (1992) is another reworking of the *Frankenstein* myth, *Ed Wood* (1994) is about the infamous "worst [horror film] director of all time," and *Mars Attacks!* (1996) is a parody of 1950s science fiction invasion films. Similarly, *Sleepy Hollow* (1998), *Charlie and the Chocolate Factory* (2005), *Sweeney Todd* (2007), *Alice in Wonderland* (2010), and *Dark Shadows* (2012) all adapt pre-existing and well-known horror/fantasy texts in new ways.

However, whereas "outsider" figures in traditional horror texts tend to be monstrous (and in need of eradication by the forces of "normality"), in Tim Burton's films, the outsider is the truly heroic character, and is someone with whom Burton almost certainly identifies. Indeed, one clue to the autobiographical nature of Burton's misfit protagonists is their appearance: many are tall, pale young men topped by a shock of unruly black hair—an image that closely corresponds to Burton's own physiognomy (see Figures 4.2 and 4.3). Other consistent aspects of Burton's style include his adaptation of black-and-white **German expressionist** visual designs (the traditional look of classical Hollywood horror films of the 1930s), circus motifs, and use of a stock company of actors including Johnny Depp, Lisa Marie, Helena Bonham Carter, and 1960s horror icons Vincent Price and Christopher Lee (see Figures 4.4 and 4.5). Other consistent collaborators include producer Denise Di Novi and composer Danny Elfman, a musician whose 1980s pop band Oingo Boingo sang songs about old horror movies; their big hit at that time was the bouncy "Dead Man's Party." While he is clearly not the only person involved in making "a Tim Burton movie," Burton nonetheless surrounds himself with like-minded collaborators who know how to create the visual and aural

Fig 4.3
Tim Burton's films often have autobiographic touches. The protagonist of *Vincent* (1982) could be said to resemble director Burton; both character and director were big fans of the 1960s horror movie star Vincent Price.

Fig 4.4 and 4.5
German expressionist visual design in *Vincent* (1982): chiaroscuro lighting, odd angles, and twisted lines.

styles he imagines for his films. Other significant stylistic motifs of the Tim Burton film oeuvre include—although of course not every one of these elements appears in every one of his films—dogs, spiral patterns, and colorful Rube Goldberg-like mechanical contraptions (see Figures 4.6 and 4.7).

Throughout his career, Burton has also repeatedly used stop-motion or 3-D animation techniques to further create his highly stylized worlds, starting with *Vincent* and continuing through *The Nightmare Before Christmas* (1993), *James and the Giant Peach* (1996), *Corpse Bride* (2005), and the latest feature-length version of *Frankenweenie*. Significantly, although Burton was involved as a creative force on each of these films in somewhat different capacities, technically the only ones he directed *by himself* were *Vincent* and *Frankenweenie*. In this case one might suggest that Burton's artistic vision is strong enough to escape the role of the director, and permeate a film even when he might be less directly—or directorially—involved. The fact that each of these films was marketed as "a Tim Burton film" or "presented by Tim Burton" also suggests that his

Fig 4.6
Another Burton motif:
dogs. This one is from
*The Nightmare Before
Christmas* (1993).

Fig 4.7
Another Burton motif:
spirals, also from *The
Nightmare Before
Christmas* (1993).

name serves as a powerful marketing tool—as a logo or brand—within contemporary
Hollywood. For a while (after rebooting *Batman*) Burton was Hollywood's go-to guy when
it wanted to remake or "re-imagine" previously successful film franchises. As early as the
1990s, he was in talks to reboot *Superman*; one imagines he and his Hollywood backers
parted company quite quickly after he announced that he wanted Nicolas Cage to play
the "Man of Steel."

As the previous paragraphs suggest, even Burton's horror films are not exactly horror
films *per se*—arguably, only *Sleepy Hollow* comes close to being a straightforward horror
film. As subsequent chapters will explore, Burton's films might be best considered
baroque or even **postmodern** horror films, in that they allude to the previous themes
and styles of the gothic horror genre but change their *meanings*. In other words, whereas
monsters in classical horror movies are terrible creatures usually meant to be destroyed,

in Burton's films they are often likeable (the "monster" dogs in both *Frankenweenie* films, *Edward Scissorhands*, Jack Skellington in *The Nightmare Before Christmas*), or else they are portrayed as complex characters whose dark natures are somewhat justified by the circumstances in which they find themselves (Batman, Catwoman, and the Penguin in *Batman Returns*, Sweeney Todd, reluctant vampire Barnabas Collins in *Dark Shadows*). Furthermore, in most Burton films, "normality" is presented as banal, venal, and frequently hostile to his misfit protagonists. Sweeney Todd may slit his patrons' throats with a straight razor, but we are meant to root for Sweeney as he carries out his justifiable revenge. In the relatively realist film bio-pic *Ed Wood*, Burton clearly favors director Ed Wood and his band of creative (if none-too-talented) misfit filmmakers over their would-be critics. To be an outsider in Burton's universe is a privileged position. Outsiders, like artists and monsters in general, hold a mirror up to "normality" and frequently judge it to be lacking.

Auteur-structuralist analysis would thus allow us to comprise a list of the elements that make a Tim Burton film a Tim Burton film, much as the previous paragraphs just briefly did. It would allow us to explore how Burton's oeuvre reshapes the ideological meaning of the horror film, and allows us to analyze each new Tim Burton film against all of his previous ones. It might even let us argue that Burton's 2001 rebooting of *Planet of the Apes* was a failure at the box office because it strayed too far from the usual Tim Burton formula. That film's hero was played by action star Mark Wahlberg, a far cry from the usual eccentric Burton antihero played by Johnny Depp. Other contemporary auteur critics might wish to explore how Burton has become a cinematic brand, producing films such as *9* (2009, directed by Shane Acker) or *Abraham Lincoln: Vampire Hunter* (2012, directed by Timur Bekmambetov). Still other critics might note that for all their genre tweaking and wish to celebrate the disadvantaged outsider, most Tim Burton films tow the Hollywood line ideologically, usually centering on straight white male protagonists who serve as metaphorical **Others**. Other less serious critics might wish to investigate the *College Humor* web sketch "Tim Burton's Secret Formula," a skit that humorously suggests Burton does nothing but relentlessly copy his previously successful formulas; in so doing, the skit mounts an important theoretical attack upon the very tenets of classical auteur theory. What is so great (creatively or artistically) about more-or-less making the same movie over and over and over?

Case study 2: Norman Lear (1922–)

Creator, developer, writer, and producer Norman Lear is a good example of someone we might classify as a hyphenate television auteur or **showrunner**, one that flourished in the era of the "Big 3" networks. Lear is chiefly known for a string of hit TV shows during the 1970s that infused countercultural politics into the **sitcom** format, and thus into the living rooms of millions of Americans. Lear began his career as a writer for TV in the 1950s, and quickly branched out into directing, producing, and developing TV shows and movies. A life-long liberal interested in social causes, Lear brought that sensibility to many of his productions, especially his hit sitcoms, whose success made him something of a household name, and altered the history of the sitcom itself. Previously, American sitcoms of the 1960s tended to shy away from politics, and concern themselves with wholesome suburban families (*Leave it to Beaver* [1957–63], *The Andy Griffith Show* [1960–8]) or else derive humor from their fantastic comedic situations (*I Dream of Jeannie* [1965–70], *My Favorite Martian* [1963–6]). Norman Lear's sitcoms took the form in new directions, acknowledging and exploring a range of significant political topics, including racial justice, women's liberation, homosexuality, class mobility (or lack thereof), the Vietnam War, abortion, and rape, just to name a few. And while the sitcom form is hardly the venue for sustained discussions of any of these hot-button topics, Lear's shows did at least raise such issues in an era when many Americans (including TV censors) would have preferred to ignore them.

Lear's first big hit was *All in the Family* (1971–9), a property he had based on a British sitcom entitled *Till Death Us Do Part* (1965–75). The show uses traditional domestic sitcom form but explores political issues through the clash of its characters. Archie Bunker (Carroll O'Connor), the patriarch of the household, is a white, working-class racist who expresses his politically incorrect views in a bellowing voice (see Figure 4.8). His chief adversary is his son-in-law Mike (Rob Reiner) who despite his interest in social justice is just about as blustering and opinionated as is Archie. Thus if Archie represents the reactionary views of the era's older Americans, Mike represents the era's youthful counterculture. Archie's other foils include his long-suffering wife Edith, his daughter Gloria, the Jeffersons (the Bunker's African American neighbors), and Edith's outspoken feminist relation Maude (Bea Arthur). *Maude* was quickly spun off into her own eponymous sitcom (1972–8), and the show was similar to *All in the Family* in that it was a domestic sitcom centered on a very opinionated character. However, whereas Archie was unapologetically conservative, Maude was a firebrand liberal (see Figure 4.9). Both shows milked laughs from their characters' preconceived and/or naïve ideals, and were very popular with audiences.

Lear also created three of the first African American sitcoms since the days of *The Amos 'n Andy Show* (1951–3). *Sanford and Son* (1972–7), starring comedian Redd Foxx, was about a junk dealer and his son. *Good Times* (1974–9) was about an African American family living in the projects, and originated as a spin off from *Maude*. Archie's next door neighbors also got their own TV series with *The Jeffersons* (1975–85), a show that followed an upwardly mobile African American family. Each show significantly expanded the range of black characters on TV, and dealt with the harsh political realities facing African Americans of the era. Lear was also one of the head writers for *One Day at a*

Fig 4.8
Archie Bunker (Carroll O'Connor) in Norman Lear's *All in the Family* (1971–9). In this episode, racist Archie balks at drinking from a glass first used by African American entertainer Sammy Davis, Jr.

Fig 4.9
Norman Lear also created the firebrand liberal character *Maude* (1972–8), played by Bea Arthur, to address social issues of the 1970s.

Time (1975–84), yet another domestic sitcom that broke new ground by focusing on a recently divorced single mother trying to make ends meet while raising her two teenage daughters. While sitcoms in more recent decades have addressed social politics in their own ways—from warm family shows like *The Cosby Show* (1984–92) to animated satires like *The Simpsons* (1989–) and *Family Guy* (1999–)—the auteur television shows of Norman Lear in the 1970s remain important historical antecedents.

Conclusion

Discussions of cinematic and televisual authorship raise many interesting paradoxes and draw upon many different schools of thought, from semiotics and structuralism to identity politics and marketing. As with many of the models or approaches discussed in this book, auteur theory has a complicated and complex history. Although the director is still worshipped almost like a god by some simplistic strands of auteur theory, more sophisticated uses of the theory remain useful to contemporary film and television analysis. However, it is important to remember that there are other forces besides the director that also shape and determine a text: society at large, the institutions under which the film or TV show is made, the money available, etc. These are all seen as various forces or determinants which shape the given author as well as his/her texts. Today, one might say the author is thus a text him or herself, just as is his or her film or TV show.

Questions for discussion

1   Think about your own relationship to film and TV authorship. Do you consciously seek out films from certain directors or TV shows created by certain writer-producers? Who are your favorite auteur filmmakers and/or television showrunners? What are the qualities in their work to which you respond?

2   Think about the work of auteurs or showrunners who are not white men: in what ways does the minority status of people like Spike Lee, Shonda Rhimes, Ang Lee, etc. impact on the texts they create (if it does). What is to be gained by having more people from more diverse backgrounds working in the media industries?

3   Analyze a specific film by Tim Burton or an episode of TV created by Norman Lear. In what ways do they conform to their creator's overall artistic and thematic visions? In what ways do they depart from the same?

References and further reading

Barthes, Roland. "The Death of the Author," in *Image/Music/Text*. Trans. Stephen Heath. New York: Hill & Wang, 1978. Pp. 142–8.

Bazin, André. "On the Politique des Auteurs," *Cahiers du Cinema* 70 (April 1975).

Chris, Cynthia and David A. Gerstner, eds. *Media Authorship* (AFI Film Readers). London and New York: Routledge, 2013.

Corrigan, Timothy. *A Cinema Without Walls: Movies and Culture After Vietnam*. New Brunswick, NJ: Rutgers University Press, 1991.

Foucault, Michel. "What is an Author?," in *The Foucault Reader*. Ed. Paul Rabinow. New York: Pantheon Books, 1984. Pp. 101–19.

Gerstner, David and Janet Staiger. *Authorship and Film*. London and New York: Routledge, 2003.

Grant, Barry Keith, ed. *Auteurs and Authorship: A Film Reader*. London and New York: Wiley-Blackwell, 2008.

Lewis, Jon. *American Film: A History*. New York: W. W. Norton and Company, 2008.

MacCabe, Colin. "The Revenge of the Author," *Critical Quarterly* 31.2 (1989): 3–13.

Sarris, Andrew. "Notes on the Auteur Theory in 1962," *Film Culture* 27 (Winter 1962–63): 1–8.

Sarris, Andrew. *The American Cinema: Directors and Directions (1929–1968)*. New York: Dutton, 1968.

Truffaut, François. "A Certain Tendency of the French Cinema," in *Movies and Methods*, ed. Bill Nichols. Los Angeles: University of California Press, 1976. Pp. 224–37. (Originally published in *Cahiers du Cinema* [January 1954].)

Wexman, Virginia Wright. *Film and Authorship*. New Brunswick, NJ: Rutgers University Press, 2003.

Wollen, Peter. *Signs and Meaning in the Cinema*. Bloomington, IN: Indiana University Press, 1972 (1969).

CHAPTER 5

Film and television genres

As with **auteur theory**, **genre theory** was first developed in regard to film studies, then later expanded and adapted into discussions about television. (And similar to auteur theory, how useful genre theory actually is to the study of television will be explored below.) However, genre theory has been around for millennia, with some historians pointing to Aristotle's *Poetics* as one of the field's founding texts. In it, Aristotle sought to distinguish between different literary forms—such as comedy, tragedy, and various types of poetry—based upon their effect, style, and/or subject matter. Whether it is used to explore literature, film, or TV, genre theory is primarily about labels and labeling: categorizing texts into one group or another. Thus, one of its central tenets is **taxonomy**, or classification, and in this respect genre theory shares much with evolutionary biology, a field that seeks to organize, describe, and label the natural world into discrete categories from kingdom to genus to species. Just as plants and animals can be named and classified according to their shared traits, so too can films and TV shows be named and classified according to their similarities (as well as their differences from one another). The western, the horror film, and the musical are all well known genres that have been explored within film studies; the terms are used by critics, scholars, and everyday movie watchers. Each genre has a specific set of concerns and looks and functions quite distinct from the others.

TV genres are a bit trickier to define. Some arose from film genres (such as the TV western), while others are more specific to television: the news show, the situation comedy, the soap opera, and so on. As this chapter will explore, despite many caveats and conundrums, genre theory is still an important and basic approach to studying film and television, and one that directly involves all three aspects of our larger **cultural studies** model of culture (introduced in Chapter 1 and explored in greater detail in Chapter 10). As such, genre theory ties together **producers**, **texts**, and **readers/audiences**, all of whom/which operate within larger historical spheres of culture and **ideology**. The following chapter explores ideas germane to genre theory as they first evolved in relation to film, and then considers how genre may or may not be usefully applied to the study of television.

Clarifying basic terms and concepts

Broadly, the term **genre** just means type (or kind, or classification, or category). As this chapter will explore, different critics and theorists sometimes use the term in different ways. As with all simplistic labels, there is the need to move beyond possibly reductive uses of the term "genre" and develop more nuanced ideas about how genres work, what they mean, and how they might change over time.

Probably the most common use of the term genre in film studies is to classify different types of Hollywood films—such as the war movie, the gangster film, or the musical. DVD outlets and websites that sell or rent films routinely classify or arrange films according to such commonplace categories. Other critics and theorists have sought to classify documentary as a genre, and experimental film as a genre. The problem with this is that there are different types or genres within the category "documentary" (voice of God, found footage, cinéma-vérité, etc.) and different types or genres within the category "experimental films" (**poetic cinema**, underground film, structuralist/materialist film, etc.). This author prefers not to treat documentary and experimental filmmaking as genres *per se*, but rather as even broader categories of non-fiction filmmaking, within which there are various types or genres, just as within Hollywood filmmaking we find various genres.

Other critics sometimes refer to **blaxploitation film** as a genre. The term refers to the hundreds of American films made circa the early 1970s that centered on African American stories and characters. But blaxploitation filmmaking also contains various identifiable genres within it. Many of the films were action/crime/gangster thrillers (like *Shaft* [1971] or *Super Fly* [1972]), but some were horror films (*Blacula* [1972]), musicals (*Car Wash* [1976]), and even westerns (*Buck and the Preacher* [1972]). In that respect, perhaps blaxploitation is better considered a historical **movement of filmmaking**, as it is limited to a certain time period, and contains within it numerous genres. Similarly, the **French New Wave**, an important group of films made by a new generation of French filmmakers in the 1960s, contains (to name just a few) coming of age stories, gangster films, and musicals. As with blaxploitation filmmaking, the French New Wave is perhaps best considered a movement, in that it occurred in a specific time and place, and contains a variety of previously recognized genres. Still other critics or consumers might use the term genre to describe the slasher film, a type of horror film that is better understood as a **subgenre**, or a subset of the larger genre of horror films.

As is hopefully apparent, many if not most attempts to classify **cultural artifacts** in the material world are fraught with difficulties. Labels are used in different ways by different people, and they are ultimately reductive, as they do not amply account for all the differences that might exist within any given category. Some genre labels are very broad (such as comedy or drama) while others are much more specific (the musical). That is why related concepts such as **movement** and **subgenre** are particularly useful as well as potentially confusing. For example, **spaghetti westerns** are similar-to-but-different-from classical Hollywood westerns. But where do we draw the lines between genre, subgenre, or even movement? This line sometimes seems arbitrary and based on subjective reasoning. Thus, while most critics and fans would probably agree that the spaghetti western shares some similarities with the Hollywood western (the term western is in the label, after all), spaghetti westerns were produced in a specific place and time: southern Europe in the 1960s and 1970s. Should spaghetti westerns be considered a subgenre or a movement? Even if we confine our discussion to western films made in Hollywood, one might further divide the western genre into subgenres like the **singing cowboy film** (prevalent in the 1930s and 1940s), or the **epic western** (prevalent in the 1920s and the 1960s). Genres can also be complicated by auteur criteria: critics often speak of the John Ford western versus the Anthony Mann western.

One could go on classifying westerns (or any other type of film) into smaller and smaller categories until each film comprised its own category, but that would defeat the most basic aspect of genre theory: the classification of multiple texts under group labels based upon their perceived similarities to one another. Some films are so similar to one another, and occur within such close temporal proximity, that they are termed **cycles**. Cycles are formed when a hit film spurs imitations: thus when *Home Alone* (1990) became a big hit at the box office, a brief cycle of films about precocious kids followed, both in terms of official sequels as well as knock-offs like *Curly Sue* (1991). Underscoring the economic dimension of genre formation, if a cycle remains popular with the public it may grow into a genre or subgenre of its own. Roughly speaking, a cycle contains the fewest number of similar films (maybe 10–20), subgenres may contain hundreds of entries, while genres broadly encompass thousands of individual films. Genres are also said to be "leaky" categories, in that genres sometimes blur into one another. Some years ago, theorists pointed out how almost every Hollywood film contains a romance, whether it be a western, a musical, or even science fiction. The element of romance is so ubiquitous in Hollywood movies that it is often taken for granted; however, when a movie is labeled explicitly as a romance, it will probably not contain western, musical, or science fiction elements, instead focusing on contemporary characters who meet and fall in love.

Contemporary Hollywood filmmaking constantly emphasizes the "leakiness" of genres in order to create **genre hybrids** like the musical horror film *Sweeney Todd: The Demon Barber of Fleet Street* (2007) or the self-explanatory *Cowboys & Aliens* (2011). The top-grossing films in the USA for the week of February 4–10, 2013, included the political thrillers *Argo* and *Zero Dark Thirty*, Quentin Tarantino's spaghetti western/slave narrative mash-up *Django Unchained*, the fantasy and old school action films *Hansel and Gretel: Witch Hunters* and *Bullet to the Head*, the horror film *Mama*, the gross out comedy/road movie *Identity Theft*, the science fiction thriller *Side Effects*, and two unusual romantic comedies. *Silver Linings Playbook* tweaks the usual romantic comedy formula by focusing on a somewhat dysfunctional man and woman, while *Warm Bodies* has been described as a "zom-rom-com," a romantic comedy in which the boy who woos the girl just happens to be a flesh-eating zombie.

The point of all this is that genre theory as a system of labeling and classifying is perhaps a useful place to start a film analysis, but it is far from the end of analysis. Thus, in the hopes of creating a more narrow and precise definition of genre, this chapter will define **genre** as *a type of fictional film produced within an industrial context*. This definition thus excludes the broader categories of documentary and experimental film, and focuses our attention onto Hollywood films, the subject of much early genre theory. This definition also works for any film industry around the globe, and it is worth noting here that different national film industries can and do have their own genres—genres both similar to and very different from Hollywood genres. For example, the Japanese film industry is well known for its own version of the gangster genre termed the **yakuza film**, a tradition of giant monster movies like *Godzilla* (1954) and *Mothra* (1961) termed **kiaju eiga**, and Samurai-styled sword fighting films called **chanbara films**. In another example, the mainstream Indian cinema (sometimes called "Bollywood" because of its location near Bombay, now Mumbai) contains some film genres adapted from the West, but it is perhaps best known for its unique **masala films**, films that contain (from a Western perspective) multiple genre elements (including melodrama, crime, history, romance, or even horror) all combined with singing and dancing musical numbers. Masala films offer "something for everyone" in that they contain various generic elements meant to appeal to different sectors of the audience.

Back in Hollywood, even before the advent of film theory, films were often classified by producers and audiences according to their perceived type. Other film genres have been "created" by influential critics: perhaps most famously, **film noir** was the term French critics gave to the bleak and dark mysteries that Hollywood produced during and immediately after World War II. (Once again complicating matters, some critics argue that film noir should not be considered a genre, but rather a *style*.) More recently, the critic David Ehrenstein is said to have coined the term **torture porn** to describe a subgenre of violent horror films that began to appear in the aftermath of 9/11. Generic categories shift over the decades as well. For example, few people would consider the "chase film" a genre today, although some of the earliest filmmakers did. Similarly, the first film version of *The Phantom of the Opera* (1925) was classified as a historical melodrama and/or prestigious literary adaptation upon its initial release; today many critics would probably label it as a horror film.

Many of the genres we still speak of today came into being during Hollywood's classical era (roughly the 1920s–50s). Partly this was due to the way films were made during those years. The so-called **Hollywood studio system** streamlined production into an assembly-line like process. Each studio had separate departments for things like set designing, editing, and scoring, and kept a workforce of ready laborers under contract. Making genre films was thus cheap and easy, because the studios could re-use certain elements (standing sets, costumes, actors under contract, etc.) from film to film. For example, a studio could build a western set and purchase a corral of horses *once*, and then proceed to make a slew of westerns week after week. Only a slight variation in script and casting was needed. As such, some Hollywood studios became associated with certain film genres and subgenres: Universal Studios was known for its horror films, RKO for its lavish and escapist Fred Astaire and Ginger Rogers musicals, and Warner Bros. for its gritty Depression-era backstage musicals (as well as gangster movies, and newspaper pictures, a type of film rarely produced today).

As has been explored in previous chapters, many **high art** critics considered Hollywood genre filmmaking to be a **low art** form, even lower than the usual output of the Hollywood studios. Indeed, the Hollywood industry did itself make distinctions between its classier, more expensive films (often termed **A pictures**) and its cheaper, pulpier fare (termed **B pictures**). While A films were sold via their literary pedigree and/or major stars, B films were often sold via their generic status. B genre films were thus considered of lower artistic standing because of their repetitive nature and lack of complexity. The "complexity" of the B western, for example, could often be reduced to the simplistic visual coding of the good guy wearing a white hat and the bad guy wearing a black one. But even if B genre films were cheaply made and repetitive, they were cost effective for the Hollywood studios (especially during the years of the Great Depression), and they were popular with many different types of audiences.

Partly Hollywood's approach to genre worked because certain types of films quickly developed devoted audiences: people liked seeing similar types of films week after week. Sometimes this facet of genre theory is referred to as its ritualistic aspect: going to a western every week was for some audience members (so the argument goes) almost like going to church every Sunday. The familiar pleasures and messages expressed by western films were obviously something their audiences wanted to experience. (But more on that below.) The point is that genre filmmaking not only streamlined production methods, but it also streamlined audiences' expectations about the types of films they were going to see. Just as many people have favorite movie stars or directors, many people also have favorite genres, or genres they dislike (and sometimes intensely so). As such, genre classification is also a way to market films and maximize profits. Even the worst low-budget horror film will probably still turn a profit at the box office because there is a built-in audience of horror movie fans who will see it no matter what the reviewers say. As the next section will explore in greater detail, film genres provide a sort of "feedback loop," connecting Hollywood producers to texts, texts to audiences, and audiences to Hollywood producers. When a genre thrives, it is because it intrigues a broad section of the audience and makes money at the box office, signaling to producers that they should make more films in the same manner. When a genre "dies" or becomes less popular at the box office, Hollywood looks to cash in on something else, either switching to a new genre, or somehow rebooting or rebranding an old one.

Identifying genres, evolving genres

Like auteur theory, genre theory became more sophisticated when structuralism was added into the mix. The previous *ad hoc* and subjective ways of classifying films (done by filmmakers, critics, and audiences) became a bit more rigorous and theoretical once film scholars applied principles derived from **semiotics** and **structuralism**. For example, genre theorists approached the western as a cultural system and then searched for its opposing and structuring binaries (such as wilderness versus civilization, male versus female, east versus west) that were seen to undergird the genre. Thomas Schatz, in his seminal book *Hollywood Genres: Formulas, Filmmaking, and the Studio System* (1981) expanded that work in many ways. Schatz used the semiotic concepts of **langue** and **parole** to describe (respectively) film genre and the genre film. In other words, a film genre is like a language system (langue), and a genre film is a text written or "spoken" in that langue, i.e. an act of parole. Thus, if science fiction is understood as the genre or langue (a subset of Hollywood filmmaking), *Close Encounters of the Third Kind* (1977) or *E.T.: The Extra-Terrestrial* (1982) are understood as acts of parole— specific films written or "uttered" in the genre or langue of science fiction. This more rigorous approach allowed Schatz and other critics to begin to identify the various elements that make a certain movie part of the western film genre, part of the war movie, or perhaps a hybrid of two or more genres.

As such, it is now commonplace to talk about a genre's **surface structure** as well as its **deep structure**. A genre's deep structure (discussed more fully below) is what the genre is all about—what cultural concerns it is expressing and in what ways. A genre's surface structure is perhaps easier to recognize, and often the term **iconography** is used synonymously with surface structure. (The term's Greek roots literally mean writing ["graphy"] with symbols ["icons"].) Thus, a genre's surface structure or iconography refers to the common signs and symbols, sights and sounds of any given genre. The iconography of the western includes horses, cowboys, Indians, tumbleweeds, and six-shooters. The iconography of the horror film includes old dark houses, rattling chains, screams in the night, blood, and perhaps a monster or maniac. The iconography of the gangster film includes urban spaces, nightclubs, machine guns, and bootleg liquor (or illegal drugs), whereas the iconography of the musical could be said to include characters who spontaneously burst into song and dance, bright colors, and a boy-meets-girl romance. Not every genre film (parole) has to contain every single element common to a film genre (langue), because the latter is the overall system or formula for the genre. But when a film contains a sort of "critical mass" of certain generic elements, it will usually be classified by critics, scholars, and fans alike as belonging to one genre or another.

While iconography is a sort of "window dressing" for a genre, a genre is also defined by its **deep structure**. Some critics refer to a genre's deep structure as its **thematic myth** or **ideological problematic**: what the genre is really "about" on a deeper or more subtle, even subtextual level. A genre's deep structure is how it relates to the culture that surrounds it—the people who made it and the audiences who keep coming back to it again and again. Some people are dedicated fans of certain genres; they like a certain type of film because it conveys certain types of experiences, messages, or myths. For example, the deep structure of the western has often been linked to **manifest destiny**, an American ideology of allegedly God-sanctioned expansionism that was extremely prevalent during the nineteenth and twentieth centuries. According to the precepts of manifest destiny, white Christians had a sacred duty to colonize the western United States; the Native Americans already there had little choice but to be assimilated or destroyed. The deep structure of the western does dovetail nicely with this ideology: westerns assert the right (and "rightness") of a strong and principled white man, standing tall in the saddle and armed with legitimate violence, to bring "civilization" to the west (even if he himself often remains outside of that civilization). Whether or not a given western actually contains Native Americans or not, the overall thematic myth of the genre still figures Native Americans as a force opposing the ideals and aspirations of its white heroes, white heroines, and white civilization in general. In its most blistering formulation, this approach to the thematic myth or deep structure of the western film genre is highly critical: it sees the western film genre as a sort of apologia for Native American genocide—a cinematic reworking of history wherein "the only good Indian is a dead Indian," and the spread of white civilization is an unquestionably good and appropriate thing.

But what about other genres? Genre critics note that the horror film is obsessed with sex and death, which are often conflated in monstrous attacks perpetrated by seductive vampires, lustful werewolves, or maniacs armed with phallic weapons. Some horror critics argue that the appeal of the horror film is both an *approach* towards or desire for such libidinal mayhem, as well as an *avoidance* or **repression** of it—after all, monsters are usually destroyed and normality restored at the end of most Hollywood horror films (at least in their classical form). Similarly, the gangster film genre seems to be about the dark side of the American Dream, and specifically capitalism. The genre asks its viewers: what would you do to become rich and powerful? Traffic in bootleg gin or cocaine? Murder your competitors? Like the horror film, the gangster film tends to thrill audiences with the gangster's violent and sexual excesses, even as it must also work to contain him by the end of the film. The thematic myth of the musical is perhaps more obvious: as a genre, the musical tells its audiences that singing and dancing and heterosexual romancing can and will transform the world into a Technicolor utopia. As discussed below, perhaps musicals are not as popular as they once were because contemporary movie watchers are more cynical about the genre's optimistic and simplistic messages about love and romance.

A few years after Thomas Schatz's important and influential volume on Hollywood film genres was published, scholar Rick Altman revisited basic ideas and assumptions about genre, and proposed what he called his **semantic/syntactic approach** to studying genre. This model refigures Schatz's iconography into what Altman calls a genre's semantic axis: the signs or semes that identify any given genre. A genre's syntactic axis thus refers to how those signs are put together in order to create meaning. Altman was especially interested in how genres were formed, and how they morph or change over time. His semantic/syntactic approach allowed him to theorize, for example, how a western might change into a crime thriller by switching elements of its semantic axis while keeping a very similar syntactic axis. Clint Eastwood's onscreen transformation from spaghetti western antihero in the late 1960s into rogue cop *Dirty Harry* (1971) is a good example of this sort of genre transformation. Although the semantic elements differ between the spaghetti western and the *Dirty Harry* franchise, their syntactic axes—what it is they are saying about American masculinity and its fight against the monstrous Other—are remarkably similar. Some years later Rick Altman added a third axis to his model of genre typology, the **pragmatic axis**. This area of consideration has to do with a genre's use value: what actual audiences *do* with it. People who like to laugh at or make fun of old bad movies (the basis of cult TV shows like *Mystery Science Theater 3000* [1988–99]) upend a film's original genre moorings and place it in a new category—the "bad movie." Such a pragmatic approach allows musicals, horror movies, biker films, *et al.* to be classified not so much upon their semantic or syntactic elements, but in a new way based upon how people actually consume them. Another good example of how a film genre might be defined pragmatically is the drug movie or head film. In the late 1960s, countercultural audiences experimenting with drugs like marijuana and LSD found that films as diverse as *Fantasia* (1940), *Alice in Wonderland* (1951), *The Trip* (1967) and *2001: A Space Odyssey* (1968) were especially enjoyable when watched under the influence of mind-altering substances.

The deep structures or thematic myths of various film genres allow contemporary critics and theorists the chance to study *culture* as well as *film*. Such critics ask questions like: "Why does one subgenre of film suddenly become popular at one point in time and not at another?," "Why do some people like certain genres but avoid all others at any cost?" Or more specifically, "Why are the musical and the western—two genres that thrived throughout the middle of the twentieth century—now only sporadically revived?" The answers lies within the feedback loop that genre filmmaking sets up between audiences and producers. As mentioned above, when a certain type of film (or genre) makes money at the box office, it tells filmmakers to make more of the same kind. When a certain type of film (or genre) fails to make money at the box office, filmmakers know it is time to change the formula or drop it altogether. Many contemporary genre theorists argue that a given film genre falls out of favor when its thematic myth is no longer relevant to its audiences. In this case, we might say that the classical western and the traditional musical—as genres—no longer "speak to" American audiences. Another way of expressing this is to say that American audiences no longer want to hear what a given genre has to say via its deep structure, or thematic myth.

Genre scholar Thomas Schatz was one of the first people to advance the idea that all film genres move or evolve through specific phases of development. Schatz identified these phases as experimental, classical, refined, and baroque. The **experimental** phase occurs before a genre is really formed: films are made with certain elements or themes that will later become important to a given genre, but neither filmmakers nor audiences are yet using a specific label to describe said genre. The **classical** phase (which for many genres coincides with the classical Hollywood studio era of the 1930s) occurs when a genre's formulas become codified and recognized by both filmmakers and audiences. (Recall that most classical genre films were produced within the studio system in an assembly line fashion.) **Refined** genre films, on the other hand, are lavish iterations of the formula that can capture Oscars for Best Picture, transcending the seeming simplicity of classical genre films. The distinction between classical and refined genre films might be likened to that between sausages cranked out by a sausage-making machine (classic genre films produced within the **Hollywood studio system**), versus an elegant five-course dinner prepared by a French chef (refined genre films made by more nuanced artists for more discerning tastes). Finely, Schatz identified a genre's fourth and final phase as its **baroque** phase. Baroque is a term from art history and architecture, and refers to a work that is overly mannered or unnecessarily ornate. In terms of genre theory, the baroque phase occurs when both audiences and filmmakers are so fully aware of a genre's conventions that they can be deliberately played with—mixed and matched, parodied, hybridized, **deconstructed**, etc. In contemporary Hollywood, as we have seen, such baroque play with genre occurs almost as a matter of course.

Schatz's model has been critiqued for being too essentialist, too ahistorical, and heavily dependent on an organic metaphor of growth and decay. Indeed, it is possible to find highly baroque films within a genre's so-called classical phase. For example, the Universal horror film *Bride of Frankenstein* was released in 1935, which by most accounts would situate the film within the genre's classical phase. Yet, upon examining the film, it almost seems to be a complete deconstruction of the classical genre's thematic myth, which asks viewers to fear the monstrous Other until "normality" is restored. In fact, the monsters in *Bride* are probably the most sympathetic characters in the film, and the male creature is even compared to Jesus Christ in several places. *Bride of Frankenstein* was made within the classical era, and looks like a classical Hollywood horror film, but it is actually an elaborate parody or satire of the horror genre, as well as its presumptions about who/what is normal and who/what is not. Thus we might say that it is a baroque horror film produced within the classical era, an intriguing development usually attributed to the film's clever auteur director, James Whale. As usual with film and television artifacts, one needs to examine carefully the texts in question before simply categorizing them according to genre, or according to a stage in a genre's (supposed) evolution.

Case study 1: "Evolution" of the western and the musical

To illustrate some of Schatz's idea about genre evolution (and to point out some of its limitations), let us examine the case of the western. As per Schatz's four-point model, film historians might identify the western's experimental phase as taking place during the earliest years of cinema with films like *The Great Train Robbery* (1903), a film that has many western elements but was not yet readily identified as such. Although it has guns and horses, the film was shot in the east, so the film is missing the usual western landscape. By the early 1910s however, producer Thomas H. Ince was producing westerns on an assembly-line basis in southern California, many starring an early cowboy star, William S. Hart. The western's classical phase, to use Schatz's terminology, had begun, and would last through the 1930s and 1940s until more sophisticated or refined westerns started to be made, such as the "psychological westerns" of Anthony Mann (*Winchester '73* [1950], *Bend of the River* [1952]). By the 1960s however, the genre had entered its baroque phase, becoming elegiac (*The Man Who Shot Liberty Valance* [1962]), cynical (**spaghetti westerns** like *The Good, The Bad, and the Ugly* [1966]), apocalyptic (*The Wild Bunch* [1969]), "drug trippy" (*Zachariah* [1971]), and even homoerotic (*Lonesome Cowboys* [1968]). By the 1970s, there were fewer and fewer westerns being made, and fewer than that succeeding at the box office.

In truth, there are multiple and complex reasons for the decline of the western throughout this period (and its various transformations throughout earlier ones), but the rise of countercultural ideologies that challenged the centrality of manifest destiny is surely one contributing factor. The war in Vietnam also challenged many peoples' thinking about the role of American expansionism, and the civil rights movement fought long and hard battles to show that prejudice and discrimination based on skin color was and is wrong. New histories of the American West and the rise of the American Indian Movement also challenged old myths about "how the west was won" that the classical Hollywood western had tended to promulgate. A few westerns attempted to adapt to the era's new ways of thinking, but in the end, the formula had perhaps run its course. As such, Hollywood westerns in the twenty-first century tend to be few and far between; those that do get made are often nostalgic of earlier eras, or else sound mild critiques of the genre, as with the remake of *True Grit* (2010), whose first version (1969) was itself a film about an aging and outmoded western hero played by John Wayne.

The musical can also be plotted against Schatz's four-phase model of genre evolution. Its experimental phase started in 1927 with the innovation of talking pictures, and the genre quickly entered its classical phase by the late 1920s. Musicals waxed and waned in type and popularity throughout the 1930s and early 1940s, and by the 1950s refined versions of them featured extended ballet sequences (*An American in Paris* [1951], *Singin' in the Rain* [1952]) or social commentary (*South Pacific* [1958], *West Side Story* [1961]) (see Figure 5.1). Arguably, the 1960s represents the musical's baroque phase, after which it too might be said to have "died" as a popular type of Hollywood filmmaking. Partly, the studio system itself was dying during this era, and the lavish sets and talented contract performers of previous generations were no longer available. Popular music was changing, from simple songs about love and romance into social protest anthems, rhythm and blues, and rock and roll—all forms that expressed countercultural ideals and appeals. (The era's films starring pop sensation Elvis Presley were mildly successful at combining traditional notions of love and romance with more modern musical idioms.) But perhaps it was the sexual revolution that changed the way people looked at musicals. While the counterculture was espousing free love and casual sex, musicals were still caught up in courtly romance. Arguably, the public stopped buying the musical's central conceit: that love and romance could transform the world into one big harmonious family.

By the late 1960s, big budget musicals like *Star!* (1968), *Funny Girl* (1968), *Paint Your Wagon* (1969), and *Song of Norway* (1970) were failing to make back their production costs. Hollywood attempted to tweak the formula. *Cabaret* (1972) was critically successful, but with its focus on the rise of Nazism and a ménage-à-trois between its central

Fig 5.1
The "Broadway Ballet"
sequence from the
refined genre film *Singin'
in the Rain* (1952), a
spectacular set piece
designed to show off
the talent of MGM's
performers, designers, and
directors.

characters, it definitely was not a classical musical. A few "rock operas" like *Jesus Christ Superstar* (1973) and *Tommy* (1975) were mildly popular, and even though the nostalgic *Grease* (1978) was a huge success, the musical as a Hollywood staple faded in popularity during the 1980s and 1990s. A few twenty-first-century musicals have been moderately successful, but they do not appear to be heralding a new golden era in screen musicals. Some have been successful by targeting "tween" niche audiences who allegedly are not old enough to be as cynical as their adult counterparts about love and romance: for example, the *High School Musical* franchise (2006, 2007, 2008) or *Jonas Brothers: The 3D Concert Experience* (2009). Others have been adaptations of critically acclaimed Broadway musicals, such as *Chicago* (2002), *Sweeney Todd*, and *Les Misérables* (2012). But here one must also note that the themes of these later musicals—murder and celebrity, revenge and cannibalism, and the suffering souls of the French Revolution—are a far cry from what the classical Hollywood musical espoused about love, romance, and a better world for all.

Genre versus intertextuality

Some critics today suggest that the entire concept of genre is outmoded, partly because so much of what Hollywood produces is hybridized in various ways. The so-called **nostalgic Hollywood blockbuster** that has fueled the Hollywood industry since the 1970s is a type of film that mixes and matches elements as a matter of course. *Star Wars* (1977) for example, is usually considered science fiction, but it also has elements of comedy, romance, sword and sorcery fantasies, the western, World War II dogfight movies, and even documentaries (its ending is often compared to Leni Riefenstahl's famous Nazi documentary *Triumph of the Will* [1935]). The film itself is a postmodern rehash of old movie serials like *Flash Gordon* (1936) and *Buck Rogers* (1939) filtered through numerous other Hollywood epics and several films by Japanese director Akira Kurosawa (most notably *The Hidden Fortress* [1958]). Perhaps *Star Wars*, and most contemporary Hollywood films, are better understood through their **intertextuality**—that is to say a film's various references to other films and filmic systems. Exploring a film's intertextuality is certainly a more nuanced and complex project than simply slapping a generic label on it and leaving it at that. In today's **postmodern** media landscape (see Chapter 9), films and television shows are often recycled and refitted from previously successful films and genres. This is the extended logic of capitalism at work: filmmakers borrow ideas from previously successful films and filmic systems in the hope that those elements will make their new film as successful. One can almost imagine the pitch session for a film like *Deep Rising* (1998), a science fiction action movie about giant snake monsters on a sinking ocean liner—"It'll be great! It'll be just like *Anaconda* meets *Titanic*!"—two very successful films released the year before.

But recall that there always had been an economic motive in producing genre films back in Hollywood's classical era. Within the studio system, producers could reuse sets and props and talent under contract; contemporary Hollywood producers no longer have that particular option, but they can and do re-use ideas and concepts. Films may be cobbled together from other sources as a matter of course, and approaching them as arrays of intertextual references may be one way to think about that process. But it is unlikely that the "short hand" labeling found within basic approaches to genre theory will die away anytime soon. Again, a label like "musical" or "western" may be a starting point for thinking about a given film, but there is much more to say and think about any given film besides what category it falls within. Films (and film genres) have their own aesthetic and formal qualities, ritualistic and pragmatic uses, structures and ideologies. The contemporary **poststructuralist** media scholar needs to keep all of those aspects in mind when analyzing film genres (or genre films) within their various historical and cultural contexts.

TV and genre: An uneasy fit

A precise use of the term genre within television studies is arguably even more problematic than it is within film studies. This is due to many reasons, including different economic and industrial contexts for television—different from channel to channel as well as from Hollywood film—as well as its (arguably) faster changing and more variable history and its (undeniably) broader range of forms and styles. Should **reality television** be considered a TV genre? If so, it would have to include a wide range of **subgenres** like news shows, talk shows, game shows, and voyeuristic "train wreck" shows like *Jersey Shore* (2009–12) and *Toddlers and Tiaras* (2009–13). But, one might reasonably ask, does the *NBC Nightly News* really belong in the same category as *Here Comes Honey Boo Boo* (2012–14)? Perhaps news shows, talk shows, and game shows should each be considered their own TV genre within the larger umbrella category of reality television. But even within a TV genre like game shows we would have to include quite disparate entries like *Survivor* (2000–) and *Jeopardy* (1984–), shows that despite their both being structured around some sort of contest, have vastly different looks, styles, production parameters, and audience appeals. Another way to problematize the adaptation of film genre theory to television scholarship is by recognizing that terms like **iconography** and **thematic myth** may still be relevant to some genres (for example the game show and the police procedural) but less so to others. TV genres also come from disparate places (there was no equivalent of the Hollywood studio system to standardize early television production). Some TV genres arose from pre-existing film genres (like the TV westerns of the 1950s and 1960s), while others arose from radio precursors (the soap opera, the sitcom). What about **infomercials**, strange hybridizations of talk shows and commercials? Is the infomercial a TV genre or is it best described as something else? Is the television commercial itself a genre or something else? Can we even isolate single texts for the process of classification when television offers us an endless **flow** of programming? It is also difficult to talk about television genres (or more broadly the process of classifying television shows) because in today's cable, satellite, or streaming media environment TV consists of at least 500 different channels, each with its own various types of programming. While it may have been easier in the three-network age to categorize the content of television by concepts that resembled those from film genre theory, today the classification of television content is an ongoing and ever-evolving endeavor.

Some scholars and industry insiders today prefer to use the term **format** rather than genre when describing a television show's unique form and style. **Format** differentiates TV categories from those of film genres, while also providing for a more precise labeling category, one tied closely to the economic and industrial parameters of any given television industry. In the case of a game show like *Who Wants to be a Millionaire?* (1999–), its format would consist of its particular rules and processes (including its title, its host, its question format, its set design, etc.) that together comprise the show itself. Formats are like **brands**—copyrighted and corporately owned labels—that can then be sold or licensed to television corporations in other contexts, nations, and/or global **micro-** or **macro-regions** (see Chapter 12). Indeed, *Who Wants to be a Millionaire?* started out as a British game show that premiered in 1998; it was then adapted for American television with host Regis Philbin (1999–2002), and then syndicated with hosts Meredith Vieira and Cedric the Entertainer (2002–). The format of *Who Wants to be a Millionaire?* has now been licensed to and appears within the programming of approximately 100 national or regional television industries. This allows for each national or regional industry to maintain the show's basic premise, while also adapting it to local cultures—most obviously via the amount of prize money available and the languages spoken on the show—but also in terms of the quiz questions themselves, which have to be tailored to each national and regional culture in order for the show to work. Thus, the term format is especially useful when discussing concepts like game shows or talk shows, and how they can be syndicated within national borders or adapted globally. It is perhaps less useful when talking about shows like *Dallas* (1978–91) or *The Cosby Show* (1984–92), shows that were popular globally in their original (albeit subtitled or dubbed) forms, due precisely to their specific formal properties including recognizable actors, urban iconography, and (in the case of *Dallas*) its memorable villain, J. R. Ewing (Larry Hagman).

Still other terms associated with television genre—or more broadly the categorization of TV shows—include the terms **serial** and **series**. These terms represent a broad attempt to categorize all of TV into two categories based on whether or not a certain show contains ongoing story arcs that encompass multiple episodes or seasons (**serial television**), or whether each episode of a show is primarily self-contained (**series television**). The term **series** thus includes shows that usually reach closure at the end of each installment: each episode resolves a "problem of the week" (as in traditional **sitcoms** and police procedurals), pronounces a winner (many game shows), and/or concludes discussions with a given set of guests (the talk show). Each episode of series television is self-contained, and does not require viewers to have a complex understanding of the characters involved. (Indeed, the characters on much series television might even be close to **stereotypes**, as they rarely change or grow over the course of time.) Single episodes of series television shows rarely reference events that have occurred in other episodes; almost like a video game, each episode of a series TV show starts as if it were beginning anew. Series television shows usually have a handful of recurring characters, or sometimes as few as two or three as in the case of the famous police procedural *Dragnet* (1951–9; 1967–70), or even one recurring character, as in the case of many game shows with a single host.

Serial television shows, on the other hand, are characterized by their multitude of characters, ongoing and open narratives that rarely reach closure (if they do at all), and in some cases certain styles of melodramatic acting. Serial television shows arguably allow for greater character development than do series TV shows, as characters grow and change over the course of episodes and seasons. Historically, one of the best examples of serial television has been the afternoon (daytime) **soap opera**. The soap opera—adapted directly from its radio precursors—was a mainstay of daytime networking programming from the 1950s through the 1990s. The term soap opera comes from the fact that many of the early soaps were owned by manufacturers like Procter & Gamble, who used the melodramatic serial form to hook viewers and expose them to their commercials for domestic products (including soap). Unlike film serials—which tended to focus on action adventure or science fiction—television soap operas told personal dramas. Indeed, like the Hollywood **woman's film** genre—sometimes termed the **weepie**—soap operas were aimed at housewives whom advertisers assumed wanted to be entertained by stories of romance, marriage, infidelity, and various other forms of domestic chicanery. Both the woman's film and the soap opera are considered forms of **melodrama**, a (sometimes pejorative) term that connotes an overly mannered or overly emotional drama. For all these reasons—their association with women, their melodramatic form and excess—soap operas were considered a fairly low form of art/culture, at least until television scholars began to study them in the 1970s and 1980s. During those years their fan base also grew to include many men and college students of both sexes, and soap operas like *General Hospital* (1963–) and *Dark Shadows* (1966–71) became more highly produced and narratively elaborate. In more recent years, declining viewership has led to the cancellation of many daytime soap operas, and their replacement by more cost-effective reality programming. For example, ABC's long running soap opera *All My Children* (1970–2011) was replaced with *The Chew* (2011–), a cheaply produced talk/cooking reality show.

Soap operas in America gave rise in the 1970s to the TV **miniseries**, self-contained serial nighttime dramas that extended over several nights, often based on bestselling novels. Popular examples include *Roots* (1977) and *The Thorn Birds* (1983), miniseries that were marketed as important or "high class" media events because of their literary pedigrees, subject matter, and special mode of presentation. The daytime soap opera also gave rise to nighttime serial dramas like *Peyton Place* (1964–9), *Dallas* (1978–91), and *Dynasty* (1981–9). Many other Western nations have long-running never-ending soap operas (such as England's *Coronation Street* [1960–] and *EastEnders* [1985–]), while other regional television industries have soap operas that do eventually come to an end after a set number of episodes; in Latin America this type of serial drama is quite common and is known as the **telenovela**. The Columbian telenovela *Yo soy Betty, la fea* (1999–2001) was so popular it was remade into the American nighttime serial comedy/drama *Ugly Betty* (2006–10). If we consider *Ugly Betty* a **format** based on its serial premise of an "unattractive" young woman working in the world of high fashion design, we can note that as a format it has been sold and adapted into approximately 20 different national and regional contexts (as of this writing).

Like all labels about culture and cultural artifacts, the terms **series television** and **serial television** need to be complicated according to actual television history—not just left as allegedly opposing binary categories. For example, over the last several decades, American television has seen many traditional series forms develop serial elements. Back in the 1970s, series sitcoms like *The Mary Tyler Moore Show* (1970–7) and its spin-off *Rhoda* (1974–8) saw their central characters develop across the years, becoming more independent, earning promotions, or getting married and divorced. (In truth, even some of the earliest sitcoms had serial elements: Lucy and Ricky Ricardo in *I Love Lucy* [1951–7] had a child and moved to Hollywood over the course of their show.) In the 1980s, nighttime dramatic cop and doctor shows like *Hill Street Blues* (1981–7) and *St. Elsewhere* (1982–8) began to include serial storylines in addition to their "crime or case of the week" formulas. By the 1990s, serial elements in what would have formerly been called series television were increasingly common. Shows like *The X Files* (1993–2002) and *Buffy the Vampire Slayer* (1997–2003) introduced season-long narrative arcs (serial elements) into their "monster of the week" (series) formula. Thus Buffy might convincingly put to rest a singing and dancing demon in the episode "Once More, with Feeling," but that episode contains many serial elements that were developed across the entire season, such as Buffy's dissatisfaction with her return to life, Willow's use of a spell to hold on to Tara's love, and Buffy's ongoing love/hate relationship with Spike (see Figure 5.2). Indeed, if one were to attempt to catalog

Fig 5.2
"Once More, With Feeling" was a musical episode of *Buffy The Vampire Slayer* (1997–2003), making the show's blurring of genres even more pronounced than usual.

the various genre elements of this single episode, one would have to include not just series and serial, but also musical, horror, action, and comedy. The series also draws on the martial arts film genre and even the TV sitcom—when they are not fighting monsters, Buffy and her friends tend to sit around a single workplace set trading quips. As with *Star Wars*, perhaps *Buffy the Vampire Slayer* is best approached via its **intertextuality**, not only to the genres and categories just mentioned, but also to other specific shows. Its "monster of the week" formula owes a great deal to *Kolchak: The Night Stalker* (1974–5), its serial narrative and "heroic" monster characters can be traced back to the gothic soap opera *Dark Shadows* (1966–71), and, of course, *Scooby-Doo, Where are You!* (1969–72)—a cartoon show about teenage monster hunters—is repeatedly alluded to within the show as Buffy and friends explicitly refer to themselves as the "Scooby Gang."

Television today is becoming increasingly diverse, with new media outlets that themselves give rise to new genres of viral web videos, YouTube channels, and the like. However, as with film, the concept of genre—the desire to label and categorize—remains a strong one. Television talk shows and news shows are still aired, but now they run alongside parodic and even animated news and talk shows. Series and serials, as well as comedy and drama, continue to blend in nighttime dramas, whether they be police procedurals like *The Closer* (2005–12), fantasy based shows like *Lost* (2004–10) or *Once Upon a Time* (2011–), or even musicals like *Glee* (2009–15) and *Smash* (2012–13). Reality programming—among the most cost-effective form of television production—continues to attract new viewers by showcasing the extremes of human behavior. And despite the overreaching conclusion often heard in the 1990s that the rise of reality programming had killed off the sitcom, sitcoms continue to be produced in ever more diverse and proliferating forms. This chapter concludes with a consideration of the sitcom as a form (or genre, or format), and introduces its complicated history within the media landscape of the United States.

Case study 2: A brief history of the American sitcom

The **situation comedy** or **sitcom** has been around since the earliest days of television and continues to be a staple of network television programming, as well as narrowcast channels like ABC Family, HBO, FX, and Comedy Central. The traditional or classic sitcom is comprised of a number of formal features that mark it as different from other TV genres or formats. First, from its earliest incarnations to many of those produced today, the sitcom has tended to follow a 30-minute **series** format in which each weekly episode presents a self-contained narrative; that is to say, its weekly stories almost always have closure, with little room for character growth from episode to episode. (As noted above however, serial elements are increasingly found in many contemporary sitcoms.) At the start of each week's sitcom episode, there is a specific turn of events (the situation) that gives rise to humor (the comedy). Sitcoms commonly have between four and eight central recurring characters, and are often focused on family units (the so-called **domestic sitcom**) or a group of work friends (the **workplace sitcom**). *The Adventures of Ozzie and Harriet* (1952–66), *Leave it to Beaver* (1957–63), *All in the Family* (1971–9), *The Cosby Show* (1984–92), and *Modern Family* (2009–) are all good examples of domestic sitcoms, and usually take place on a limited number of sets meant to represent their characters' homes. Shows like *Hogan's Heroes* (1965–71), *WKRP in Cincinnati* (1978–82),

Murphy Brown (1988–98), and *The Office* (2005–13) exemplify the workplace sitcom, and take place on sets that reflect the spatial bond that brings the characters together, whether it be a POW camp, a radio station, a television newsroom, or a paper company in Scranton, Pennsylvania. Each central set, whether living room or work space, is used prominently each week, and is generally lit with high key lighting. Of course, many sitcoms did and do combine both domestic and workplace settings.

Traditionally, many sitcoms—especially during the 1970s–90s—were shot live on video tape before actual audiences with multiple cameras, giving them an almost theatrical feel. Before the development of video tape, sitcoms like *Leave it to Beaver* or *Hogan's Heroes* were shot on film in a more cinematic (single camera) style; more recent sitcoms like *Arrested Development* (2003–6; 2013) and *Modern Family* have returned to film style production as a way of differentiating themselves from the run of the mill "taped before a live audience" sitcom. That said, the "shot live on tape" sitcoms were edited in a control booth as they were enacted, as a technician switched between the video feed from three or four cameras, each set-up to record various shots of the action. The live audience's response to the show—laughter—was usually recorded along with the actors' lines, creating a "laugh track" which ostensibly told home viewers when to laugh at the jokes, and how hard. Sitcoms not recorded in front of live audiences tended to layer in laugh tracks on their audio channels, and even shows with actual live audiences often felt the need to "sweeten" the laughter by adding more boisterous pre-recorded chuckles. All of these various diverse elements—character types, settings, lighting, running time, mode of production, laugh track, and "situation of the week"—constitute the overall sitcom form.

As such, the TV sitcom might be said to have its roots in previous comedy fare from other media, such as vaudeville sketches, stand-up comedy, and screwball comedies from Hollywood. But it was radio—TV's closest and most immediate precursor both culturally and technologically—that innovated the form. Along with the soap opera (another staple of radio programming that was easily adapted to television), radio sitcoms were very popular with listeners in the 1930s and 1940s. Many of the first TV sitcoms were adapted directly from their radio antecedents, such as *The Amos 'n Andy Show* (1951–3), which had been a radio show since 1928. *The Amos 'n Andy Show* was a prototypical sitcom in that it featured a recurring cast of characters—in this case a small group of urban African Americans including the titular characters—whose episodic antics provoked humor. (*The Amos 'n Andy Show* had been performed by white actors on the radio, but black actors were cast for the TV version of the show; despite being popular with both white and black audiences, the TV show was ended after only a few years. It survived via syndicated reruns, but became a source of controversy as later generations found its images of African Americans to be offensive.) Other early sitcoms that grew out of previously successful radio shows include *The Goldbergs* (1949–56), *The George Burns and Gracie Allen Show* (1950–8), and *The Jack Benny Program* (1950–65). At least one famous sitcom of the era evolved out of a recurring sketch on Jackie Gleason's variety show *Cavalcade of Stars* (1949–52), before running for a full season under its own name: *The Honeymooners* (1955–6). Probably one of the best known and most beloved sitcoms of the era was *I Love Lucy*, which though shot on film is often said to have invented the multiple-camera sitcom shooting style. One thing that is interesting to note about these first sitcoms was their ethnic and/or racial diversity. *The Goldbergs* were Jewish, *Amos 'n Andy* were black, and Lucy was married to Ricky Ricardo, a Cuban bandleader played by her real life husband Desi Arnaz (see Figure 5.3). One reason these shows were more ethnically diverse than those that immediately followed them was that TV in its infancy was still

Fig 5.3
One of the first sitcoms on television, *The Goldbergs* (1949–56) was created by writer-producer-star Gertrude Berg, and focused on a Jewish family in the Bronx.

a broadcast medium created by urban producers and enjoyed by urban audiences, who tended to be more diverse than rural and suburban audiences.

However, as the suburbs grew throughout the 1950s—as many white middle class families left the more ethnically diverse cities—they and rural America began to receive television transmissions via complex systems of networked broadcast towers connected through wire cables. Perhaps unsurprisingly then, many sitcoms of the mid-1950s and early 1960s centered on white suburban families. These included *The Adventures of Ozzie and Harriet*, *Leave it to Beaver*, *Father Knows Best* (1954–60), *The Donna Reed Show* (1958–66), and *My Three Sons* (1960–72) (see Figure 5.4). These shows were squeaky clean

Fig 5.4
Leave it to Beaver (1957–63) exemplified the white middle class suburban sitcom of the 1950s and 1960s, wherein *Father Knows Best* (itself the title of another **domestic sitcom** that ran from 1954–60).

in their innocence and trifling narrative situations, and they promoted an image of white bread suburban culture where mothers wore pearls to do the vacuuming, and the worst words ever spoken were "darn" or "dang." Perhaps as a response to the bland nature of the white suburban sitcoms, a spate of fantastic family sitcoms also became popular in the early to mid 1960s, including *The Munsters* (1964–6), *The Addams Family* (1964–6), *My Favorite Martian* (1963–6), and the animated sitcoms *The Flintstones* (1960–6) and *The Jetsons* (1962–3) (see Figure 5.5). Although these shows too were cast with mostly white actors, their fantastic differences from their "normal" neighbors hinted that the suburbs might be more diverse than the white bread sitcoms had alleged. *I Dream of Jeannie* (1965–70) and *Bewitched* (1964–72) were also part of this fantastic family trend, deriving humor from powerful women (albeit a genie and witch, respectively) who confounded their bumbling male counterparts, a narrative trope that has led some more recent critics to explore the shows as potentially feminist texts.

One of the more interesting trends in the late 1960s was the popularity of what critics have termed the **rural sitcom**: shows like *The Andy Griffith Show* (1960–8), *Mayberry R.F.D.* (1968–71), *The Beverly Hillbillies* (1962–71), *Green Acres* (1965–71), and *Petticoat Junction* (1963–70) centered on small town southerners, or else the clash of rural and urban sensibilities. These shows too were resolutely white, and even as the struggle for civil rights was accelerating into riots and assassinations, these shows depicted their southerners as mostly good old boys and gals. The rural sitcoms were very popular with audiences, but they were all cancelled by CBS in the early 1970s because although they were watched by many Americans, they were not watched by the *right kind* of Americans: those with disposable income to spend on the products advertised. This shift in programming occurred because the networks began to gauge viewers based on their income demographics, not just as the number of viewers watching what shows. As such, CBS (with ABC and NBC following suit) began to target more urban minded professionals with edgier shows like *All in the Family*, *Maude* (1972–8), *M*A*S*H* (1972–83) and *The Mary Tyler Moore Show*. It may seem ridiculous to call *The Mary Tyler Moore Show* edgy, but it was one of the first TV shows to center on a single working woman, a development

Fig 5.5
1960s sitcoms often featured "odd" people inhabiting the suburbs, such as the vaguely ghoulish members of *The Addams Family* (1964–6).

the network was very nervous about. *M*A*S*H* and *All in the Family* (and other shows developed by "TV auteur" Norman Lear, see Chapter 4) expanded the boundaries of what subject matter the sitcom could contain, dealing with social and political issues like war, sexism, racism, rape, single motherhood, and even (on rare occasion) homosexuality from a leftist/liberal perspective.

In the mid-1970s, nostalgic sitcoms like *Happy Days* (1974–84) and *Laverne and Shirley* (1976–83) became quite popular, and helped ABC capture ratings, as did their "daringly" risqué sitcoms like *Three's Company* (1976–84) and *Soap* (1977–81). As the nation turned more conservative in the 1980s with the election of Ronald Reagan to the Presidency, there was a nostalgic return to warm domestic sitcoms, albeit with a twist. The era's most famous and successful sitcom was *The Cosby Show* (NBC, 1984–92), which centered on an upper middle class African American family (see Figure 5.6). While the show is notable for "crossing over" to white audiences as well as African American audiences, it was not without its controversies. Some critics praised the show for its "positive images," i.e. its financially successful professional couple raising their children with solid "family values" (as the 1980s buzz phrase would have it). Yet other critics took exception to the show's premise as unrealistic and unattainable for the vast majority of African Americans still living in social and economic privation. Some critics argued that *The Cosby Show* worked as a sort of socio-cultural smoke screen, as it generally eschewed the harsh realities of racial discrimination and social stratification in the nation, and suggested that the "American Dream" was just as easily attainable for black Americans as it was for whites. As a sort of African American *Leave it to Beaver*, *The Cosby Show* was perhaps popular with all sorts of audiences precisely because it did not focus too closely on the larger social and economic issues related to race and racial discrimination (as did previous Norman Lear sitcoms such as *Good Times* [1974–9] and *The Jeffersons* [1975–85]). As such, *The Cosby Show* is itself a good example of a text **hegemonically negotiating** with race and racism in 1980s America. It presented African Americans as caring, loving, and "positive" family role models, even as it potentially hid the more egregious and lingering effects of American racism. *The Cosby Show* also demonstrated to television

Fig 5.6
The Cosby Show (1984–92) was the most successful sitcom of the 1980s; despite centering on a black family, it rarely addressed issues related to race or racism.

executives that African American sitcoms, which became a staple of 1990s programming, could be good for business.

The 1990s saw an explosion of diverse and multicultural sitcoms, partly due to changing social demographics as well as new developments in the television industry, including the creation of new networks such as FOX, The WB, and UPN. (The rise of cable television channels, like the Cartoon Network, that were willing and able to produce their own content also contributed to the diversity of the sitcom during this era.) The three new networks often targeted "urban audiences" (a euphemism for black and Latino audiences) because along with being distributed by cable and satellite, they were also aimed at cities via old-style broadcast systems. FOX initially captured audiences with shows that skewered the traditional "white bread" family sitcom, including the caustic live action *Married ... with Children* (1987–97), and the warmer animated sitcom *The Simpsons* (1989–). But they courted urban audiences directly with sketch comedies like *In Living Color* (1990–4) and sitcoms like *Roc* (1991–4), *Martin* (1992–7), and *Living Single* (1993–8). The WB followed suit, targeting African American audiences with shows like *Family Matters* (1989–98), *The Wayans Bros.* (1995–9), *The Parent 'Hood* (1995–9), and *The Jamie Foxx Show* (1996–2001); UPN offered *Moesha* (1996–2001), *Malcolm and Eddie* (1996–2000), and *The Parkers* (1999–2004). The three traditional networks followed the multicultural trend to a lesser extent, with shows like *The Fresh Prince of Bel-Air* (NBC, 1990–6), the *Cosby Show* spinoff *A Different World* (NBC, 1987–93), and *Hangin' with Mr. Cooper* (ABC, 1992–97). Sitcoms grounded in other ethnic or racial milieus have usually not been as successful as those targeted at African American audiences. One of the first sitcoms to feature Hispanic characters and issues was *Chico and the Man* (1974–8); *The George Lopez Show* (2002–7) was a much later success. Sitcoms featuring Asian Americans have been even more difficult to find. *All-American Girl* (1994–5) starring Margaret Cho, lasted for one season. Twenty years later, ABC announced that *Fresh Off the Boat*, a domestic sitcom about a Taiwanese-American family, would be aired in 2015.

1990s sitcoms also offered more diverse images of gender and sexuality. Working women like television journalist *Murphy Brown* (1988–98) and blue collar factory worker *Roseanne* (1988–97) were very popular with viewers, tackling issues like single motherhood and class struggle in ways reminiscent of the 1970s Norman Lear sitcoms. Humor surrounding the changing mores related to gender and sexuality also contributed to the huge popularity of *Seinfeld* (1989–98), which made fun out of four neurotic New Yorkers, and *Friends* (1994–2004), centering on a close-knit group of young urbanites who navigate their personal issues from apartment complexes to coffee houses. TV scholar Ron Becker might describe the casts of both *Seinfeld* and *Friends* as "SLUMPies": Socially Liberal, Urban-Minded Professionals, a type of person the networks were eagerly targeting in the 1990s. In his book *Gay TV and Straight America*, Becker argues that the increasing visibility of gay and lesbian characters and issues on 1990s shows like *Seinfeld*, *Friends*, and *Roseanne* helped the traditional networks differentiate themselves from the new upstarts, and capture upwardly mobile (and white) urban viewers, who had more cash to spend on the shows' advertised products than did their urban peers of color. Eventually ABC allowed Ellen DeGeneres and her eponymous sitcom character *Ellen* (1994–8) to come out as a lesbian, and NBC had a big hit with *Will & Grace* (1998–2006). While many of these shows were met with hostile receptions from some sectors of the nation upon their initial runs, gay and lesbian characters in American sitcoms in the twenty-first century have become increasingly common (if also almost always white and/or upper-middle class).

At the start of the twenty-first century, the American sitcom is more diverse than ever before, both in terms of content and in terms of form. The trend in many of these shows has been towards racial and ethnic diversity, stronger roles for women both behind and in front of the camera, and the inclusion of gay, lesbian, and transgender characters. The traditional networks have reaped success with sitcoms like *The King of Queens* (CBS, 1998–2007), *How I Met Your Mother* (CBS, 2005–14), *The Big Bang Theory* (CBS, 2007–), *30 Rock* (NBC, 2006–13), *Community* (NBC, 2009–), *Parks and Recreation* (NBC, 2009–15), *Modern Family* (ABC, 2009–), and *Brooklyn Nine-Nine* (Fox, 2013–) (see Figure 5.7). Cable and Internet companies continue to produce edgy and original programming such as the reality/sitcom hybrid shows *Curb Your Enthusiasm* (HBO, 1999–), *Louie* (FX, 2010–), and *Arrested Development* (Fox, 2003–6). The latter show is unique in that it returned for a fourth season via Netflix, an on-demand DVD delivery service turned streaming media provider. Netflix has begun to produce and distribute its own content including the final season of *Arrested Development* (2013), as well as serial narratives like *House of Cards* (2013–), *Hemlock Grove* (2013–) and *Orange is the New Black* (2013–). Even more recently, streaming video distributor Amazon Prime has also become a streaming video producer; its domestic sitcom *Transparent* (2014–) won two Golden Globe awards for its first season. Quirky animated sitcoms like *South Park* (1997–), *Family Guy* (1999–), *Aqua Teen Hunger Force* (2000–), *Futurama* (1999–2013), and *BoJack Horseman* (2014–) continue to be popular, and they (like all TV shows and movies) are increasingly being watched via streaming video-on-demand sites like Netflix, Hulu, and Amazon Prime. Whatever the future holds for the distribution of film and television texts in Western or global contexts, it is unlikely that the unique televisual form (or genre) of the situation comedy will disappear for good. Like most long-lived popular cultural artifacts, it will continue to morph in response to the technologies and industries that produce it, and the changing sensibilities of the audiences who consume it.

Fig 5.7
The diverse cast of *Community* (2009–14), even if their "leader" is arguably still a white man, played by Joel McHale.

Questions for discussion

1   Think about your favorite film genre. Why do you like it? What pleasures or experiences does it offer you? Why might other viewers dislike your favorite genre? What is at stake with such varying "tastes"? How do issues of gender, race, or even the high/low dichotomy enter into the ways that people assess film genres?

2   Think about your favorite TV show. How would you describe its "genre"? From the various terms discussed throughout this chapter about televisual forms, how many apply to your chosen text? Is it more appropriate to say it belongs to one format or genre, or is it more intertextually complex?

3   What genres "go better" or hybridize more easily than others? Scholars have noted the success and popularity of "science fiction horror films" from at least the 1950s through today, while something like the "musical western" is much more rarely attempted. Why do some hybrids work while others do not? Is it the clash of iconography? Thematic myths? Both?

References and further reading

Altman, Rick. *Film/Genre*. London: BFI Publishing, 1999.

Becker, Ron. *Gay TV and Straight America*. New Jersey: Rutgers University Press, 2006.

Cawelti, John. *The Six Gun Mystique*. Bowling Green, OH: Bowling Green University Popular Press, 1970.

Davis, Glyn and Kay Dickinson, eds. *Teen TV: Genre, Consumption and Identity*. London: British Film Institute, 2008.

Frayling, Christopher. *Spaghetti Westerns*. London: Routledge, 1981.

Grant, Barry Keith. *Film Genre: From Iconography to Ideology*. London: Wallflower Press, 2007.

Grant, Barry Keith, ed. *Film Genre Reader IV*. Austin, TX: University of Texas Press, 2012.

Gray, Herman. *Watching Race: Television and the Struggle for Blackness*. Minneapolis, MN: University of Minnesota Press, 2004.

Kavka, Misha. *Reality TV*. Edinburgh: Edinburgh University Press, 2012.

Mills, Brett. *The Sitcom*. Edinburgh: Edinburgh University Press, 2009.

Mittell, Jason. *Genre and Television: From Cop Shows to Cartoons in American Culture*. New York and London: Routledge, 2004.

Mittell, Jason. *Television and American Culture*. Oxford: Oxford University Press, 2009.

Neale, Steve. *Genre*. London: BFI Publishing, 1990.

Neale, Steve. *Genre and Contemporary Hollywood*. London: BFI Publishing, 2002.

Rose, Brian Geoffrey. *TV Genres: A Handbook and Reference Guide*. Westport, CT: Greenwood, 1985.

Schatz, Thomas. *Hollywood Genres: Formulas, Filmmaking, and the Studio System*. New York: Random House, 1981.

Turnbull, Sue. *The TV Crime Drama*. Edinburgh: Edinburgh University Press, 2014.

Wright, Will. *Sixguns and Society: A Structural Study of the Western*. Berkeley: University of California Press, 1975.

CHAPTER 6

Psychoanalysis (part one): Basic concepts

Psychoanalysis has been a very important model of cultural analysis since its inception at the end of the nineteenth century. Psychoanalysis is chiefly associated with its founder **Sigmund Freud** (1856–1939), although over the years many other thinkers and theorists have added to the body of thought broadly identified as psychoanalysis, from Carl Jung (who advanced a theory of the "collective unconscious") to many later day film theorists like Christian Metz, Robin Wood, Carol Clover, Barbara Creed, and Linda Williams. Arguably, the modern professions of psychiatry, psychology, social work, and the various forms of psychotherapy associated with them all owe their existence to the innovations made by Freud and other early psychoanalysts. Initially, Freud was interested in treating mental illnesses, and in order to do so he needed to develop a working model of the mind, or psyche. Once that model (or structure) of the healthy mind was inferred or deduced, it could then be used to analyze and treat mental illnesses— diseases or aberrations in a person's affect and/or behavior that seemed not to have organic or physical causes. Psychoanalysis originally referred to these mental illnesses as **neuroses**, a term that broadly describes conditions like depression, hysteria, anxiety, compulsive behaviors, etc. Neuroses are usually less severe than **psychoses**, debilitating mental illnesses like schizophrenia in which the patient has lost touch with objective reality. Today, modern psychology and psychiatry recognize hundreds of mental disorders ranging from the mild to the severe. Modern medicine also has shown that there are biological bases for many of the illnesses that Freud and his followers thought were purely psychological. Today it is common to treat many psychological conditions with medicine, even as various forms of psychotherapy are also still practiced.

Freud's method for treating his patients was the so-called "talking cure," a process that has been featured within and parodied by popular culture ever since. The talking cure occurs as the patient lies on a couch, answering leading questions put to him or her by the psychoanalyst. Through this process, the psychoanalyst comes to understand what is bothering the patient, and hopefully discover the underlying causes of the patient's illness. Freud and his early followers believed that mental disorders could be discerned and treated by analyzing not just what the patient consciously said and did, but also by examining things that the patient might not be aware of at all. According to basic Freudian psychoanalysis, elements of the patient's psyche said to be **unconscious** could be revealed via the patient's dreams, fantasies, free associations, slips of the tongue ("Freudian slips" or **parapraxes**), and the like: it was the psychoanalyst's job to decipher all those hidden clues in order to diagnose a mental illness and then effect a cure.

The application of psychoanalysis to the study of culture—and more specifically film and television—is less interested in curing mental illness in patients and more interested in understanding human behaviors, motivations, and desires. Psychoanalysis thus offers us a model of human identity or **subjectivity**. Who are we? Why are we the way we are? Psychoanalysis attempts to explain how human subjects grow from infants to adults, how they become gendered, how they become sexualized, how they become members of a society (or fail to do so). Similarly, we can use psychoanalysis to study the psychological motivations of characters in film and television texts, or perhaps try to fathom the psyches of film and television makers themselves. Psychoanalysis informs some approaches to star studies, and psychoanalysis also allows us to speak of the deeper unconscious meanings of individual films, or filmic systems like genres. Psychoanalysis has also been important to considerations of narrative patterns: do the ways in which we tell stories relate in some way to our early childhood development? Another very important use of psychoanalysis in film theory attempts to explore the psychic mechanisms involved in the actual processes of watching film and/or television. But before we begin to examine some of those complex topics—covered more extensively in this and the next chapter—it is necessary to understand some of the more basic ideas related to psychoanalysis and human subjectivity.

Psychoanalysis 101: A model of the mind

What is the mind and how does it work? Today many neurobiologists argue that the mind arises from the material functioning of the brain—a somatic organ—but for many people the mind is still an ethereal concept, tied perhaps to religious notions of soul or spirit. Originally, based upon his studies and observations of both patients and Western culture, Freud theorized a two-part model of the human psyche: according to this model the mind is comprised of a **conscious** part and an **unconscious** part. The conscious part of one's mind is aware of what it is doing and thinking, while the unconscious (or **subconscious)** part of one's mind is not accessible or knowable without special intervention and interpretation (provided by the psychoanalyst). Psychoanalysis further theorizes that the unconscious or subconscious mind (and for the purposes of this chapter those two terms will be treated as synonyms) is the site or realm of desires, drives, and/or traumas that the conscious mind cannot or will not tolerate. Those elements within the subconscious are said to be **repressed**, because the subject is not consciously aware of them. Repression is a sort of basic and automatic **defense mechanism** that protects the conscious mind from unacceptable urges, desires, or traumas that may have occurred in the past. Psychoanalysis also posits that there is a certain amount of **basic repression** that is needed for human beings to have culture, identity, and civilization. Without basic repression, so the theory goes, human beings would be like infants or animals—interested only in sensory gratification, feeding, sexuality, etc. The urges and drives associated with this stage of development are referred to within psychoanalysis as **primary processes**. As we grow up and encounter the rules and regulations of the societies in which we live, such urges and desires are channeled into socially acceptable behaviors (through various psychic defense mechanisms), giving rise to the stage or functions of the **secondary processes**.

From this two-part model of the mind, Freud then went on to theorize a three-part model. In this formulation, the conscious mind is now termed the **ego**. Like the conscious mind, the ego is that part of the mind that is self-aware, and regulates its own behaviors. In Freud's three-part model, the unconscious mind is now split between the **id** and the **superego**, two opposing parts of the mind that sort of function in perpetual warfare with one another. The id holds all the drives and desires that are inherited from infancy, as well as any other traumas or unacceptable desires/memories that have been repressed across one's lifetime. Freud suggested that the id also contains two basic conflicting drives: the life drive (**Eros**) and the death drive (**Thanatos**). The life drive is responsible for sexual desire (commonly called **libido**), but also for creation and all aspects of survival, while the death drive supposedly explains our fascination with dangerous activities and risk-taking behaviors. The id and its desires and drives are kept from running amok by the superego, a sort of internalized policeman who keeps one's desires and drives in check. The superego is created as we grow and mature, internalizing the rules of one's given environment; thus the development of the superego is one way we achieve subjectivity within a given family, society, culture, or national body. To take a basic example, if someone angers or hurts us, we may desire to hurt or kill that person in revenge. According to psychoanalysis, that base animalistic desire (primary process) comes from the id, that primitive part of our mind that wants instant gratification and the immediate sating of all of its urges and desires. However, the superego reins those impulses in, reminding the ego that giving in to such retaliation may ultimately cause even more problems (like a jail cell or further escalating violence). It may be helpful to imagine the superego functioning as one's **conscience**—the little voice inside one's head that tells us not to be reckless and impulsive, but instead function according to the rules and laws of the cultures to which we belong. As such, psychoanalysis theorizes human subjectivity as split or divided; what we think of as our "selves" is the unstable result of constantly competing id urges and our superegos' attempts to maintain repression.

Psychoanalytic concepts such as ego, id, and superego are deeply embedded in Western culture at large, often in playful or creative ways. Significantly, the concepts appear in Western culture both before and after they were theorized and labeled by Freud, a fact that lends credence to many of his ideas. For example, Jiminy Cricket in the classic Walt Disney film *Pinocchio* (1940) is a character that functions as the puppet-boy's conscience, or superego. Hollywood films of that era are full of psychoanalytic motifs (Freud's ideas were becoming mainstreamed via popular culture during those years), but the cricket-as-salient-advice-giver was present in the original children's book *The Adventures of Pinocchio*, published in 1883, well before Freud began to publish his thoughts on psychoanalysis. Similarly, Freud's famous formulation of the Oedipus narrative (discussed below), a psychoanalytic model that theorizes the patterns of human (male) subject development, is based on the narrative patterns found in the ancient Greek myth of Oedipus. In a perhaps more obvious example, Robert Louis Stevenson's *The Strange Case of Dr. Jekyll and Mr. Hyde*, published in 1886 and remade as countless films and television shows, is easy to understand as a story about a man (Dr. Jekyll) whose superego fails to keep his id (Mr. Hyde) in check. Stevenson wrote the novel based on his own observations of human behavior, well before Freud published his 1923 treatise *The Ego and the Id*. And as explored below, psychoanalysis has been one of the most important and productive ways of thinking about the **horror genre**, in both film and television.

Another good example of id and superego functioning in American popular culture can be found in old Hollywood cartoons, wherein id and superego sometimes appear (to a confused ego subject) as an imaginary devil and fantasy angel, respectively. For example, in the classic Disney cartoon *Mickey's Pal Pluto* (1933), Pluto's ego (his waking, self-aware mind) must consider whether or not to let some kittens drown in a well. Suddenly, up pops a little devil version of Pluto (representing his id) urging him to go ahead and let the kittens drown. But then a little angel version of Pluto (representing his superego), appeals to Pluto's sense of morality, asking him to save the kittens (see Figure 6.1). Cartoons and popular culture aside, some psychoanalytic theorists have argued that the very concepts of devil and angel, as elements of a larger Western Christian cosmology, might be understood as the outward manifestations or projections of internal psychoanalytic concepts like id and superego. In this way, psychoanalysis has helped shift Western definitions of crime away from a model of external evil ("the Devil made me do it") to an understanding of crime or evil as an internal aspect of the human condition.

To summarize so far, psychoanalysis posits that when disturbing urges or memories of past traumas threaten the stability of the ego, the mind protects itself via defense mechanisms like **repression**, which bury the urges or memories in the unconscious part of the mind. There are a host of defense mechanisms related to repression that work to protect the conscious mind from trauma. Whereas repression is such a thorough mechanism that the ego is not even aware of the unacceptable thoughts or desires being repressed, the related term **suppression** implies a sort of willful forgetting of which the ego is partially aware. (The term **sublimation** is also sometimes used to describe the process of transforming or channeling an unacceptable thought or urge into some sort of more respectable

Fig 6.1
The "Angel and Devil" motif in an early Walt Disney cartoon, *Mickey's Pal Pluto* (1933), representing the psychoanalytic concepts of **superego** and **id**.

behavior.) To take a hypothetical example, let us imagine a man who hates his father, which in Western culture is not supposed to happen: as The Ten Commandments put it, one should "Honor thy Father and thy Mother." If the man in question is not even aware that he harbors negative feelings towards his father, he has completely repressed them. If he knows he harbors ill feelings and worries and frets because he knows he should not, he may consciously work to suppress those thoughts. He may then be said to be sublimating those unacceptable thoughts if, for example, he takes up kick-boxing but only fights against older father figures. In this way, his unacceptable id urges are played out in a sort of culturally sanctioned safety zone.

Denial is another similar defense mechanism—all are based on some relation to repression—in which the conscious subject vociferously attests to the *opposite* of his or her true unconscious desires. In our hypothetical example, the man who hates his father might loudly proclaim how much he actually does love his father. (A psychoanalyst might note the frequency and intensity of such proclamations, and begin to hypothesize the patient's true feelings as the opposite of what he is saying.) Another similar defense mechanism is **disavowal**, in which the subject is aware of some thought or urge but continues to believe its opposite; disavowal depends on a precarious balance of consciously knowing something but also simultaneously repressing/suppressing it. Psychoanalytic film theorists sometimes use the idea of disavowal to explain the "suspension of disbelief" that occurs when people become thoroughly immersed in a film or TV show. We know what we are watching is not really happening, but we react as if it is, feeling fear or delight or desire as if the events depicted were actually happening to us.

Another important aspect of how the subconscious works is called the **return of the repressed**. This idea postulates that repressed urges or desires do not go away when they are repressed (or suppressed, or denied, or disavowed), but that they strive to return in myriad other ways—in dreams, in compulsions, or other types of neurotic behavior therapists label **symptoms**. The term **displacement** is used to describe what happens as such urges strive to return to consciousness: they rarely come out in direct ways (which would be traumatizing to the ego) so they return in hidden or symbolic ways, displaced onto other signifiers (as in dreams) or symptoms (as in neuroses). To return to our example, let us say our father-hating subject has successfully repressed those thoughts to the point that he is not even aware of them. But once repressed, those thoughts become displaced and express themselves in other ways. They might come back in a recurring nightmare wherein the man "kills" the President of the United States (a displaced symbol for the man's actual father). Perhaps our patient visits a psychoanalyst because he has developed the cruel habit of kicking random dogs on the street, a rather disturbing symptom. After many sessions with a psychoanalyst, the doctor brings to consciousness the patient's hostility towards his father and the fact that his father loved dogs. In this example, the man's repressed hatred was displaced onto an aberrant behavior or symptom, in this case the allegedly irrational behavior of kicking dogs. According to classic psychoanalysis, bringing repressed connections such as these into the open and dealing with the issues connected to them will result in the patient's cure. In other words, as our hypothetical patient becomes conscious of his anger towards his father, and begins to deal with it in a healthy way, his disturbing symptoms will begin to fade away, and he will then be cured.

Such repression–displacement is sometimes referred to as **projection**. Projection occurs when someone denies his or her own repressed traits, instead ascribing them to or *projecting* them onto some other person. For example, a man who possesses yet represses same sex desires may go to great lengths to denounce or denigrate openly gay or lesbian people in an attempt to distance himself from his own urges, proving to himself and others that he is not in fact gay. One would say such a man is projecting his own repressed desires onto someone else; whether or not that someone else actually is gay is beside the point. The person onto whom repressed desires are projected is referred to within psychoanalytic theory as the **Other**. In addition to its being a personal psychic phenomenon, projection has also been theorized as a cultural phenomenon. For example, in Western "WASP" cultures (White, Anglo-Saxon, and Protestant), sexuality is often contained and controlled by social and religious institutions as well as personal defense mechanisms like suppression and repression. But WASP culture also has the peculiar habit of believing that *Other* social groups are more promiscuous or wanton: stereotypes of Latin lovers, "oversexed" Africans, and Oriental harems arguably arise from what the West represses in its own culture, i.e. more open or free notions of sexuality. In this case, the repressed sexuality of white Western culture is projected onto the non-white Other (see Chapter 12). Such a dynamic ultimately tells us more about the dominant normative ideologies of Western cultures than it tells us anything meaningful about actual other people, whether they be Middle Easterners, Asian-Americans, gay or lesbian people, or even (within patriarchal systems of thought) the Woman-as-Other.

Still other relevant defense mechanisms (especially relevant in film theory) are **regression** and **screen memory**. Regression occurs when—to escape trauma or unacceptable id urges—the ego reverts to an earlier stage of psychic development. Someone who retreats into childlike behavior in the face of trauma may be said to be regressing, as the character Barbra does in the original *Night of the Living Dead* (1968); after she and her brother are attacked by zombies, Barbra spends the rest of the film in an almost child-like catatonic state (see Figure 6.2). Parents

Fig 6.2
In *Night of the Living Dead* (1968), Barbra (Judith O'Dea) **regresses** to a childlike state after her encounter with flesh-eating zombies.

sometimes see an older child regress when a new baby arrives: threatened by the arrival of a rival, the older child may suddenly start behaving as he or she did in earlier stages of development, perhaps forgetting their toilet training or throwing temper tantrums when they are supposed to be "old enough to know better." The curious defense mechanism known as **screen memory** occurs when an entire new memory is fabricated by the mind in order to hide or cover over a traumatic event. For example, a psychoanalyst working with someone who claims that she was abducted by a UFO might understand that claim as a screen memory hiding some other more realistic trauma that the patient has buried in her unconscious. In treatment, the psychoanalyst and the patient would work to uncover and then process what the real trauma actually was. In facing the real trauma, the need for the screen memory (being abducted by a UFO) would then fade away. Under slightly different circumstances, the young protagonist of *Mysterious Skin* (2004) also learns to come to terms with a past sexual trauma—one he has mistakenly constructed in his memories as an alien abduction.

Infantile sexuality and the Oedipus complex

In addition to theorizing how the mind works in various ways to protect itself from trauma and unacceptable id urges, Freud and his followers also developed a model of how the infant becomes socialized: how it gains **subjectivity**, growing from an undifferentiated extension of its mother into a fully adult (and gendered) human subject. These ideas are expressed in Freud's theory of **infantile sexuality** and his thinking on what has become known as the **Oedipus complex** (or **Oedipal narrative**). Infantile sexuality perhaps sounds like something akin to pedophilia or child molestation, but it actually refers to the idea that the developing child's body has different erogenous zones that respond to sensual (tactile) stimulation. The first or youngest phase of the infant's development is the **oral stage**, wherein most or all of the stimulation that the child receives is centered around its mouth and lips. Feeding or nursing begins almost immediately after the child is born, and thus the child receives all of its stimulation, warmth, and comfort via oral pleasure. We might also say the child comes to know its world through oral exploration: one of the first thing babies do when handed a new object is taste or suck it. The second phase of development is called the **anal stage**, wherein the child learns to control his or her execratory organs. This affords the child a sense of control over his or her body, and control gives rise to further subjectivity and pleasure. (This concept is also at the root of many jokes about psychoanalysis which simplistically reduce all mental dysfunction to "bad toilet training.") The third stage of the child's development is the **phallic stage**, in which the child comes to experience and understand the pleasures associated with touching its (his or her) own sexual organs. Then, according to most accounts, these stages of infantile sexuality are repressed or suppressed, giving rise to the **latency period** (occurring roughly from ages 6–10) during which the child shows very little interest in sexuality. That all changes, of course, as puberty and adolescence set in, flooding young bodies with hormones and sexual urges. Freud labeled this final development as the **genital stage**, wherein young male and female subjects attain their "proper" adult sexual roles.

According to Freud, the most important stage of this developmental model is the phallic stage (ages 3–6), which is also the stage at which the **Oedipus complex** or **Oedipal narrative** plays out. Freud based his model of the Oedipus complex on the Greek myth of Oedipus, who through strange turns of fate, ended up killing his father and marrying his mother. Freud suggests this myth is universal and is what the young male child desires to do during this stage of his development. At the start of the Oedipal narrative, the male child desires the mother because she is the first woman with whom he has a nurturing and physical relationship: she cares for his every whim and desire. But the young boy also fears and resents the father (as he is the boy's rival for the mother); this gives rise to unacceptable urges to murder the father and take his place. Since the desire to kill Dad is unacceptable, it is **repressed** (and perhaps displaced into competition, sports, and war with other men when he is older). The son must give up his mother as his love object, although he will find "her" again later in his life as his wife. (The old adage that everyone ends up marrying someone who reminds them—consciously or unconsciously—of their opposite sex parent plays into this notion.) The point here is that the father is dominant and powerful, and bears both the penis (the anatomical organ) and thus the **phallus** (the symbol of **patriarchal power**), while the mother—who has no penis—presents a troubling **lack**. (Yes, Freud's model was a **sexist** one and will be critiqued in greater detail below.) Thus the male child is plagued with **castration anxiety**: has Mother been castrated? Might he be too? Who might have the power to do so? Assuming that Dad is the powerful and potentially castrating member of the family, the male child begins to identify with him, rejecting or repressing the Mother and the feminine traits that she represents. In this way—through a successful working through of the Oedipal complex, the male child becomes a "proper" adult male (properly masculine and heterosexual) by identifying with his father's patriarchal power, and the patriarchal rules of the society in which they live. Patriarchy and patriarchal power in Western culture is also expressed through (seemingly ubiquitous) **phallic symbols**—things and possessions that suggest both the penis and male strength. Common phallic symbols include items like cigars, skyscrapers, monuments, motorcycles, sports cars, rifles, spears, staffs, rocket ships, oil derricks, trophies, and so on (see Figure 6.3). Visual systems like film and TV often make use of phallic symbols (and occasionally **vaginal symbols**) to underline or comment upon gender (see Figure 6.4).

Fig 6.3
Phallic symbols in Douglas Sirk's *Written on the Wind* (1956); at the end of the film, Marylee must forsake her feminine wiles in order to take over her late father's oil business.

Fig 6.4
Earlier in *Written on the Wind* (1956), Marylee Hadley (Dorothy Malone) is linked to vaginal symbols, such as her curvaceous sports car and red anthuriums.

The scenario for the female child—often referred to as the **Electra complex**—is also fraught with sexist assumptions, and suggests that while the boy at ages 3–6 experiences castration anxiety (because he has a penis that he might lose), the girl at the same age experiences **penis envy** (because she realizes she does not have one). Although the girl's first physical relationship (like the boy's) has been with the Mother, she must learn that like Mom, she too lacks the penis (and the phallus). She then turns to Mom for identification, and turns to Dad for love and nurturance, thus developing into a "proper" adult female, i.e. one who assumes feminine gender traits and heterosexual, opposite sex desires. Allegedly, as the adult female she will desire her own child/baby, which will come to be her own substitute penis/phallus—the object that represents her "proper" place within the heterosexual, patriarchal order. According to Freud and traditional psychoanalysis, problems in resolving the Oedipus and Electra complexes have the potential to result in a host of "dysfunctional" behaviors later in life, such as homosexuality, frigidity, impotence, promiscuity, and confused sex/gender roles. In many cases, as strong-willed Western women struggled across the twentieth century for equal rights with men (see Chapter 8), they were told by the medical profession that they were dysfunctional or even mentally ill because they refused to accept their "proper" (passive, demure, quiet) gender identity. Diagnosed with penis envy and a failure to resolve the Electra complex, their ideas could be dismissed and their bodies even hospitalized or subject to various "treatments." Similarly, homosexual men and women throughout the twentieth century—thought by the official medical profession to be psychosexually abnormal until the 1970s—were also subjected to a range of psychotherapeutic regimes meant to restructure their Oedipal (or Electra) narratives in the hopes of effecting a cure. They were also frequently subjected to less subtle experimental treatments like shock therapy, hormone injections, castration, and even lobotomy.

A Westerner in the twenty-first century might reasonably well ask, how could such a range of beliefs—ones which gave rise to myriad abuses and justifications for bias and prejudice—become so entrenched into dominant medical knowledge and popular cultural discourse? Are these not just a bunch of crazy theories by a doctor who was known to use the psychoactive drug cocaine? What if the child never sees his parents naked, and thus never discovers the penis and the lack? What if a child is raised by two women or two men, as same-sex couples throughout the Western world are increasingly doing? Are male children really afraid of castration? Many of Freud's followers spent their careers modifying his original ideas, seeing some of Freud's initial ideas as more symbolic or mythic, rather than actual. For example, castration does not have to represent the actual severing of genitalia from the male body; perhaps it just refers to the way any male subject might fear the loss of his patriarchal power. (Witness the expression "castrating bitch" as an epithet for an assertive female.) Perhaps—as more recent social psychologists and biologists have argued—children just imprint or model themselves on the parent (or other social agent) who most closely resembles them in terms of temperament, behavior, and gender expression. Nevertheless, many more orthodox psychoanalytic therapists do not dismiss the possibility of the Oedipus or Electra complexes, or their concomitant relationship to Freud's theorization of the stages of infantile sexuality. And as we shall see below, scholars throughout the twentieth century have also used these Freudian approaches in their attempts to think about cultural practices, including film and television.

Whatever one may think of the validity of Freud's thinking, one must concede that many, many of the concepts derived from (or explained by) psychoanalysis are prevalent in Western culture and Western thinking, as they arguably were even before Freud coined the terms he did. When we say someone has an "anal personality," it means he or she is uptight, controlling, rigid, and unyielding: conditions that psychoanalysis might attribute to developmental problems during the anal (toilet training) stage. On the other hand, the term "oral fixation" might be used to describe people who overeat, smoke, binge drink, or even gossip compulsively. Psychoanalysis has yielded very rich traditions within film studies, not the least of them being the seemingly Oedipal nature of classical Hollywood film narratives. Recall that most classical Hollywood narrative centers on a male protagonist who has to overcome some challenge, defeat a male rival, and win the princess or love object. Let us look briefly at the first *Star Wars* films (episodes 4–6). Here we have a young hero, Luke Skywalker, whose parentage is unknown. He battles his arch enemy Darth Vader, who literally does turn out to be his father, in order to win the hand of Princess Leia, whom we could call a substitute for the mother (as a princess she does have more female authority than would other women). Furthermore, as part of the fight between Luke and his father in *The Empire Strikes Back* (1980), Darth Vader uses his lightsaber (an obvious phallic symbol) to symbolically "castrate" his son by cutting off his hand. (In Freudian thought, the loss of any body part or patriarchal privilege is symbolic of castration.) How many other Hollywood films revolve around this central triangle of a young male hero who must defeat a male villain (who initially appears to have superior patriarchal powers) in order to win the female love interest? If we accept this narrative pattern as a basic one within Hollywood filmmaking, then one might conclude that the popularity of Hollywood films could be due to the fact that they fulfill the male spectator's repressed Oedipal desires to kill his father and marry his mother. The idea that mainstream cinema "speaks to" the male spectator's unconscious desires will be explored in greater detail in the following chapters.

But before we leave the Oedipus narrative, there is one more important psychoanalytic concept to be considered: the **fetish**. Generally speaking, the term fetish refers to something overinvested with psychic energy, and especially sexual or libidinal energy. The term can be applied to a range of religious and/ or cultural/anthropological artifacts, but it has a more specific meaning within psychoanalytic thinking. As per Freud, the Oedipus complex gives rise to the idea of the fetish when the male child first sees his mother (or some other woman) naked, realizes she lacks a penis, and is severely traumatized by castration anxiety. In order to shield his ego from the trauma, the child fixates on a nearby object, often a piece of the mother's clothing or a nearby shoe. This object becomes the male child's fetish, and represents (and this is the tricky part) both the *threat of castration* represented by the mother's lack, *as well as the phallus* (the fetish object itself which blocks or covers over the threat of lack). The fetish is thus dependent on the defense mechanisms of **screen memory** (the traumatic memory is replaced with another highly charged one) and **disavowal**: the subject says to himself "I know that there is the possibility of castration or lack, but I have my fetish to focus on and cover over that anxiety." This explains, according to Freudians, why some of the most common sexual fetishes involve women's clothing or footwear: they are allegedly present when the traumatic scene first occurs. Accordingly, this also explains why fetishism is supposedly common in men but less so in women: women cannot experience castration anxiety in the same way that men do, having already been born without a penis and therefore being already symbolically "castrated." As **Christian Metz**, one of the most influential thinkers in psychoanalytic film theory put it: "the fetish signifies the penis as absent. It is its negative signifier; supplementing it, it puts a fullness in place of lack, but in so doing it also affirms that lack. It resumes within itself the structure of disavowal and multiple belief" (1986, 71). As we shall see in subsequent chapters, psychoanalytic cultural critics have adapted the idea of fetishization in multiple ways, especially as it relates to the ways that women and women's bodies are displayed in mainstream film and television texts.

Applying psychoanalysis to film and TV: A text-based approach

The following chapter will examine in greater detail some of the ways film theorists have applied psychoanalytic concepts to the very processes of watching films: they ask questions like "How does the cinematic experience appeal to our unconscious desires? How might that cinematic experience differ from watching television? How might it differ according to gender? What actually happens *psychoanalytically* when we watch films or TV shows?" Those are important questions and during the 1970s much film theory was concerned with thinking about them, leading to the development of what has been called **Screen theory**, or more precisely **apparatus theory**. But before we get to those concerns, there are many other ways to use psychoanalysis to illuminate film and television studies. The remainder of this chapter introduces some of them.

Some of the earliest connections between film and psychoanalysis can be found in early experimental or avant-garde filmmaking. **Modernist** artists in general were often interested in foregrounding **subjective** states and affective responses to the world around them; thus, for example, **expressionist** artists and filmmakers tried to capture visually the psychic states of madness, chaos, and horror they associated with World War I and its aftermath. The famous **German expressionist** film *The Cabinet of Dr. Caligari* (1920) uses bizarre formal and stylistic tropes (such as light and shadow painted on theatrical flats) to depict the disordered states of mind that its mad characters exhibit (see Figure 9.3). Another group of modernists, the **surrealists**, were explicitly fascinated by the concepts of psychoanalysis, and sought to depict or reveal through their artworks the functioning (and the imagery) of the unconscious mind as it was theorized by Freud and his followers. André Breton, the so-called "Father of Surrealism," had studied psychiatry before producing two written manifestoes about the surrealist movement, and his writings (as did Freud's) had a great deal of influence on the work of other surrealists. For example, Salvador Dali and Luis Buñuel collaborated on one of the most famous works of surrealist filmmaking, *Un Chien Andalou* (1929). The film, like most surrealist artifacts, was meant to invoke the unconscious via dreamlike imagery in which sex and gender were confused, lust and violence commingled, and rationality was all but impossible. The film—using highly fragmented narrative vignettes, deliberately cryptic symbolism, discontinuous editing, and shocking visuals that invoke castration anxieties (a severed hand, an eyeball being sliced open with a straight razor)—can still shock and inspire audiences with its hallucinogenic imagery (see Figure 9.4).

Un Chien Andalou, surrealism, and the psychoanalytic tenets that underlie both, have served as inspirations for generations of filmmakers around the world. These filmmakers include avant-garde artists like Maya Deren (*Meshes of the Afternoon* [1943]), but also (somewhat) more narrative filmmakers like David Lynch (*Eraserhead* [1977], *Lost Highway* [1997]); David Cronenberg (*Videodrome* [1983], *eXistenZ* [1999]); Alejandro Jodorowsky (*El Topo* [1970], *The Holy Mountain* [1973]); Dusan Makavejev (*WR: Mysteries of the Organism* [1971], *Sweet Movie* [1974]); Jane Campion (*Sweetie* [1989], *The Piano* [1993]); and Pedro Almodóvar (*All About My Mother* [1999], *The Skin I Live In* [2011]). Psychoanalysis was also central to the work of many of the international "star" directors of the 1950s and 1960s, auteur filmmakers like Federico Fellini, Ingmar Bergman, and Luis Buñuel. Although each of these directors had his own unique style and "take" on psychoanalysis, each was very interested in using film to explore both conscious and unconscious states of mind. For example, Fellini's *8 ½* (1963) hovers between life and death, oscillating between its central character's reality, his fantasies, and his memories. Fellini created many films using this basic structure or technique: films like *Juliet of the Spirits* (1965) and *City of Women* (1980) draw on surrealistic imagery to explore the psychic mindsets of their central characters as well as their hang-ups and neuroses about gender and sexuality. Similarly, Ingmar Bergman created difficult, dense, hallucinogenic, and deeply psychoanalytic films like *Persona* (1966) and *Hour of the Wolf* (1968); even his more accessible films such as *Wild Strawberries* (1957) and *Fanny and Alexander* (1982) are character studies steeped in psychoanalytic concepts and symbolism. Luis Buñuel also had a decades-long career writing and directing films on several continents, most of which engage with psychoanalytic theory on some level, regardless of their national origin or genre. Important films by Luis Buñuel include *El* (1953), *The Exterminating Angel* (1962), *The Discreet Charm of the Bourgeoisie* (1972) and *That Obscure Object of Desire* (1977).

Most, if not all, popular or mainstream films (as opposed to many of those just mentioned that seem directly to invoke psychoanalytic paradigms) can also be approached through and illuminated by psychoanalysis, as the brief exegesis of *Star Wars* above has hopefully demonstrated. In this case, the psychoanalytic media scholar becomes a type of psychoanalytic therapist; he or she deciphers or **decodes** the text under question as if it were a patient lying on the psychoanalyst's couch:

films can thus be "psychoanalyzed" as if they were manifestations of a patient's dreams and symptoms. This suggests that every text has its own sub- or unconscious meaning(s), lying below the surface of its narrative action and/or character development, meanings that are just waiting to be discovered and explored by the psychoanalytic film or TV critic. Similarly, film genres—already seen to contain "deep structures"—might also be illuminated through psychoanalytic criticism. Thus a psychoanalytic reading of the musical might suggest that a utopic longing for sex and sexuality—to merge with the M/Other—is the repressed content of the genre's obsessive singing and dancing. A psychoanalytic reading of the western might reveal white America's guilt over Native American genocide. Still other critics have used psychoanalysis in their approach to auteur studies. Donald Spoto's book *The Dark Side of Genius: The Life of Alfred Hitchcock* is an auteur study that basically posits Hitchcock's films as his personal psychoanalytic symptoms; through close textual analyses of his films, author Spoto creates a psychoanalytic profile of the man Hitchcock might have been.

It is also very common for mainstream film and television texts to contain dream sequences, short hallucinogenic episodes that are meant to illuminate something about the dreamer's character, frequently via some sort of psychoanalytic symbolism. Alfred Hitchcock's *Spellbound* (1945) is (like many Hitchcock films) a psychological thriller about a confused or mis-identified protagonist. In *Spellbound*, a character played by Gregory Peck suffers from amnesia, and when two psychoanalysts (played by Ingrid Bergman and Michael Chekhov) try to help him, they ask him to recount his dreams. As he does, Hitchcock cuts from the onscreen visuals of the psychiatrist's office to those of the protagonist's dream, designed by the surrealist artist Salvador Dali in his unmistakable style. We see a masked man atop a rooftop holding a small "melting" wheel, a nightclub with a giant tapestry filled with eyes, and a male character with a giant pair of scissors cutting away at the tapestry (the eyes and the scissors again invoking castration anxieties) (see Figure 6.5). Through psychoanalysis, the doctors are able to cure not only the protagonist's

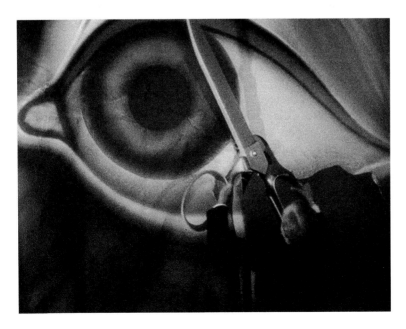

Fig 6.5
The dream sequence in Alfred Hitchcock's *Spellbound* (1945) was designed by surrealist artist Salvador Dali; it contains clues to the protagonist's identity as well as the solution to the murder plot.

amnesia, but also solve the murder that caused the amnesia in the first place. Discovering the murderer depends on solving the psychological puzzle created by Hitchcock's screenwriter Ben Hecht, who, as film history relates, consulted leading psychoanalysts of the day in order to help him construct the screenplay.

As the term psychological thriller indicates, there are entire genres that either invoke directly or lend themselves more than indirectly to psychoanalytic readings. **Film noir**, the hardboiled detective films of the post-World War II years, often give rise to psychoanalytic readings, focusing as they do (like psychological thrillers) on displaced identities, troubled sex and gender relations, and inadequately repressed id urges like murder and lust. The domestic **melodrama** is another genre that has been usefully explored with psychoanalysis, partly because it shares many of the same concerns as does film noir, and partly because it focuses centrally on human emotions, desires, and drives. One of the genres most indebted to psychoanalytic reading protocols is the **horror film**. The usual narrative structure of the horror film is easily read as an eruption of unacceptable id urges, as a sexualized and violent monster runs rampant across the landscape of "normality." Sometimes those monsters literally arise from "below," as when zombies, mummies, and vampires reside in and then emerge from buried tombs, a fact that is again suggestive of their subconscious origins. At other times, as with Dr. Jekyll and Mr. Hyde or any iteration of the werewolf myth, those unacceptable urges—animalistic violence and/or sexual predation—emerge quite literally from within the minds of their central protagonists. Horror films, with their roots in German expressionist cinema, flourished in classical Hollywood cinema (the 1930s), and they have mutated across the decades and across global cultures into all manner of subgenres and cycles; a psychoanalytic critic might argue that they have something basic to say about the operations of the human psyche.

One of the first essays to address horror films (and horror/science fiction film hybrids) from a psychoanalytic perspective was Margaret Tarratt's "Monsters from the Id." In it, she quite eloquently explored how phallic monsters—simultaneously symbolizing fear and desire—tend to "pop up" whenever the romantic couples in horror films begin to get intimate. Other psychoanalytic cultural critics, such as James Twitchell in his book *Dreadful Pleasures*, have suggested that horror films function as allegories of adolescent identity formation; their ongoing popularity with children and teenagers is thus due to the fact that children and teenagers are still developing their own gendered and sexualized identities. Thus the Wolfman myth dramatizes puberty, when strange sexual urges and new hair growth begin; and the Frankenstein myth serves as a proscription against masturbation: men cannot and should not try to create life without heterosexual union. The Frankenstein myth also has a deeply homoerotic and/or homosexual core; repressed same sex desires are present in many versions of the Frankenstein story, even as they are flamboyantly de-repressed in others, such as *The Rocky Horror Picture Show* (1975).

One of the most sustained and influential psychoanalytic approaches to the horror film was created by Canadian film scholar Robin Wood in a series of important articles and essays, most of which are contained in his volume *Hollywood: From Vietnam to Reagan*. Wood brings together psychoanalysis and Marxism (as did many theorists of the **Frankfurt School**, see Chapter 2; and *Screen* **theorists**, see Chapter 7) to explore the ideological functioning of the genre in relation to the cultures that create and consume it. He begins by making a distinction between basic and surplus repression. **Basic repression** (enough repression to organize sustainable communities) is needed in all societies; without basic repression human beings would exist within a murdering, pillaging, and rapacious chaos. **Surplus repression**, on the other hand, is specific to a given type of society. In a matriarchy, for example, men and masculinity would have to be suppressed, repressed, and/or oppressed. (Wood's slippage between these related but different terms, as well as his application of psychoanalysis to culture rather than individual psyches, has been critiqued by later scholars, even as his arguments remain persuasive.) Wood then suggests that in white, heterosexual, patriarchal capitalism—the dominant **ideology** of the Western world—the concepts that undergo surplus repression are those that oppose them: non-white races and ethnicities, non-heteronormative (or **queer**) sexualities including those of women, and systems of political thought that conflict with capitalism.

Then, drawing on the psychoanalytic axiom that states "that which is repressed always strives to return," Wood suggests that those forces that oppose white patriarchal capitalism do return to the culture via its horror films. Wood thus dubs the horror film our culture's "collective nightmare," making explicit the analogy between an individual's dreams and nightmares, and the social functioning of the generic system known as the horror film. There is tremendous amount of textual and cultural data that seems to support Wood's theories: monsters do tend to come from elsewhere (Transylvania, Kong Island, outer space, "Hell"), or else they arise from within the unconscious mind of supposedly normal individuals (as with human psycho-killers). What monsters usually "want" from human society is often some nightmarish amalgamation of human beings' most primitive id urges—to eat, to bite, to seduce, to rape, to devour, to torture, to rule, and ultimately to kill. As such, horror films deal with two of the most heavily charged and heavily repressed topics in Western culture: sex and death. The vampire, whether he be Count Dracula or Edward Cullen from the *Twilight* franchise, is a collection of anxieties about sex and death. The flesh-eating zombies so prevalent in today's media landscape seem even more regressed: they are human corpses with no sense of basic repression, seemingly stuck in an omnivorous oral stage.

Zombies and other monsters have also been explored by feminist theorists like Julia Kristeva and Barbara Creed via the psychoanalytic concept of the **abject**. The abject refers to those aspects of ourselves which are both "of us" and "not of us." Prime examples would be excretory products like urine and feces, and other bodily fluids like tears, saliva, and blood. Within psychoanalysis, these things are abject because they threaten a stable sense of self, by calling attention to that which *is* and that which *is not* us. For Julia Kristeva, one primary example of the abject is the human corpse—the ultimate signifier of a subject who is also no longer a subject. Thus, the living corpses of many horror movie narratives enact the idea of the abject, even as blood, gore, alien ooze, and the monster's wet dripping lair embody the abject in yet other ways. Similarly, Barbara Creed's book *The Monstrous-Feminine: Film, Feminism, Psychoanalysis* argues that in Western patriarchal thought, the abject is centered around and represented by the female—specifically maternal—body, with its border-crossing potentials between self and other, including the processes of birth, menstruation, and lactation. As such, psychoanalysis remains a powerful tool in the cultural critic's tool kit, whether the object of study is the horror film, the classical Hollywood cinema, the avant-garde, or the contemporary Hollywood blockbuster. Although many psychoanalytic theories have been critiqued as outmoded and essentialist (see below), psychoanalysis continues to inform multiple aspects of film and television scholarship, and contemporary cultural studies in general.

Conclusions and critiques

As has been pointed out repeatedly, much psychoanalytic theory is based on forthrightly sexist assumptions—such as the notion that women must always represent the lack. Many feminist theorists in multiple disciplines dismiss psychoanalytic theory forthrightly, and refuse to enter into its allegedly patriarchal **discourses**. That said, psychoanalysis has also been tremendously productive for some feminist scholars, especially feminist film scholars like Barbara Creed, as noted above. So which group of feminist thinkers is correct? Theorists like Creed tend to see psychoanalysis not as a way to uphold patriarchal dominance (as it has often been used), but rather as a model that explains (or at the very least illuminates and critiques) patriarchal dominance. Like any explanatory model or structure, how one approaches psychoanalysis is important, and it is imperative to note its historical dimensions and limitations. In other words, is psychoanalysis some sort of essentialist model that accurately describes human subject formation in all cultures across all eras? Or is it something that perhaps can be tied more precisely to Western thinking about human subject formation at the start of the twentieth century? And even if Freud's ideas do accurately describe certain kinds of gendered and sexualized subject positions that arose in late nineteenth century Europe, does that mean that his ideas are still accurate (let alone useful) in twenty-first-century Iraq, Nigeria, or North Korea? The point here is that while some psychoanalytic theorists and critics may answer that final question with a vociferous "yes," many other cultural theorists and critics remain skeptical about how universal Freud's basic psychoanalytic paradigms truly are. Like any of the other models introduced throughout this volume, psychoanalysis may be useful in answering some questions about film and television (and culture in general), and somewhat less-than-useful when other questions are asked.

One of the most important critiques of psychoanalysis is based on the fact that it is a self-justifying, or unfalsifiable system. In other words, its adherents can use psychoanalysis to answer any critiques that one might raise about it. You say you think castration anxiety is a lot of bunk? An adamant psychoanalyst might suggest that in denying castration anxiety, you are repressing your own deeply rooted fears about castration, therefore "proving" that the psychoanalytic notion of castration anxiety indeed does exist. Let us return to our earlier example of the man who allegedly hates his father. If he insists that he does not hate his father, an adamant psychoanalyst might diagnose him as being in denial. And when it comes to using psychoanalysis to study film and television texts, there is rarely any evidence that can be used to "prove" anything asserted by psychoanalytic critics. There are only speculations—however elegant and/or involved and/or persuasive they may be— that work to greater or lesser degrees in describing certain aspects of certain texts. In this way, psychoanalysis embodies the impetus behind what scholarly writers call the "argumentative essay." The purpose of such an essay is not to identify something as simply true or false; rather, the argumentative essay is either more or less persuasive. It either makes you consider the object of study in new and thoughtful ways—and thus contribute to the creation of knowledge—or it does not.

These important critiques and caveats aside, psychoanalysis continues to be a foundational discourse of Western critical thinking. In many cases, the psychic processes it describes have been prevalent in Western culture and literature for centuries, if not always. One final historical example will suffice to exemplify this point. In Shakespeare's *Macbeth* (1606), Macbeth and his wife murder their rival Duncan by stabbing him in his bed at night. They are then consumed by guilt over their tragic and traumatic act: Macbeth's repressed guilt returns in several visions, including the ghost of Banquo, another rival he has had murdered. Perhaps most famously, Lady Macbeth's repressed guilt and trauma returns in the form of a hallucination: she thinks she sees the blood of Duncan on her hands and resorts to washing them compulsively. Shakespeare was certainly not a psychoanalyst, but this work, like that of so many other Western authors, seems to lend credence to some of the basic ideas that Freud formulated centuries later.

And as the next two chapters will explore, psychoanalysis was incredibly influential to the development of 1970s film theory, helping to open up film studies to highly politicized critiques of dominant cinema and dominant ideologies. More recently, psychoanalysis continues to contribute important ideas to the theorization of gender, race, nation, and sexuality. Each year, new works of theory and criticism appear, refiguring and reformulating psychoanalytic concepts, relating them to the cultures and cultural artifacts that surround us, and helping the cultural critic see the world in new and more nuanced ways.

Case study: *The Machinist* (2004)

The Machinist is a film that would probably be classified (by genre) as a psychological thriller; as such, it can be productively discussed in terms of Freudian psychoanalysis. (In fact, it might seem to make little-to-no sense without Freudian psychoanalysis!) As with Alfred Hitchcock's *Spellbound*, solving the mystery of *The Machinist* depends on deciphering the psychodynamics of its protagonist's mind. The film opens in a dreary nighttime world where a machine shop worker named Trevor Reznik (played by Christian Bale) appears to be disposing of a body wrapped in a heavy rug. He is spotted by an unknown man with a flashlight who asks him "Who are you?"—a highly pointed question in a film about a man's troubled psychic state—and one that remains unanswered as the scene shifts to a new location. The film uses several other motifs to foreground questions of identity, such as reflecting surfaces like mirrors and windows, photographs, and the presence of several **doppelgängers**, imaginary(?) characters who may or may not be reflective of some aspect of Trevor's troubled state of mind. And Trevor clearly is troubled: he is an insomniac who is losing weight faster than he can devour chicken wings, his most significant human relationship appears to be with a prostitute named Stevie (played by Jennifer Jason Leigh), and he constantly washes his hands and scrubs his bathroom with caustic detergents—a motif that recalls the symptomatic behavior of Lady Macbeth. Trevor's only seemingly happy moments are when he flirts with the pretty waitress (and single Mother) Marie (Aitana Sánchez-Gijón) at an all-night airport coffee shop. (Sharp viewers will note that there are multiple parallels in the ways that Trevor treats Stevie and Marie, and that it often seems to be 1:30 a.m. whenever Trevor and Marie have their scenes.)

Trevor's troubles multiply when a new co-worker, Ivan (played by John Sharian), appears in the machine shop. On the floor of the factory, Trevor becomes distracted by Ivan, and accidentally backs into the start button of a machine being serviced by Miller (Michael Ironside). His arm trapped, the machine brutally mutilates Miller's hand and arm. This castration imagery is extended or mirrored in a later scene when Ivan reveals to Trevor a peculiar deformity—several of Ivan's toes have been grafted onto his hand where his fingers should be (see Figure 6.6). Recall that in psychoanalytic theory missing body parts are suggestive of castration and/or loss of phallic power; Ivan further analogizes fingers/hands to the penis when he crudely suggests that his toe-fingers are more than adequate when used to pleasure women sexually. These scenes alert the psychoanalytic critic to Oedipal themes: Ivan (and now Miller) are figures who seem to signify castration anxieties. The phallus-lack dichotomy also plays out in a different register in the film's earlier locker room scene; even before Miller loses his hand, his co-workers tease one another by joking about one of them bringing home a female prostitute who turned out to be a man in drag.

During the official investigation of Miller's accident, Trevor tries to explain to his bosses how the presence of Ivan distracted him, only to learn that there is no such person as Ivan working at the factory. Trevor becomes increasingly confused, and chases Ivan's red sports car through the town, almost causing an accident at a certain intersection marked by an odd-looking water tower. (Trevor careening through this intersection becomes another motif in the film, suggesting its importance to the narrative and a clue to Trevor's mental disintegration.) Meanwhile, Trevor becomes increasingly attached to the waitress Marie and her son Nicholas, and agrees to spend Mother's Day with them at a local amusement park. Passing by the Bumper Cars, Trevor takes the son on a surreal and sexualized automobile-themed "haunted house" ride named Route 666, and near the end of the ride (as the track appears to split into two paths labeled "Highway to Hell" and "Road to Salvation") the boy suffers a seizure. Trevor brings him into the daylight and lays him on the ground, while in the background, another amusement park ride is framed in such a way as to recall the water tower from the driving/chase sequences (see Figures 6.7 and 6.8). This spatial "doubling" is a good example of the film's use of the **uncanny**, as is the fact the film was shot in Spain but purports to be taking place in America: everything looks fairly "normal"—or does it? There is a disturbing sense that "reality" is just a little bit "off." (For Freud, uncanny things remind us of our own repressed desires: they are familiar-seeming but also not quite consciously acknowledged. Dolls, mannequins, lookalikes, aliens, and even apes might be considered common variations of the uncanny: they invite us to project our own frightening desires onto them, which is why they give us the creeps—if indeed they do.)

More bizarre events transpire. Trevor thinks someone is trying to drive him mad, and

Fig 6.6
Phallic and **castration** imagery abounds in *The Machinist* (2004); Ivan "causes" one man to lose an arm, while he himself has had toes surgically grafted onto his hand in place of similarly missing fingers.

Fig 6.7 and 6.8
The strange water tower in *The Machinist* (2004) is graphically matched via editing to the theme park ride behind "Route 666." Which is real and which is hallucination?

continues to find post-it notes (playing the child's game of Hangman) on his refrigerator. When Trevor confronts Miller (thinking that he is tormenting him as a form of revenge for the accident Trevor "caused"), Miller—now associated with overdetermined phallic signifiers like a new sports car and a powerful electric hedge trimmer—socks Trevor in the groin. Trevor immediately spots Ivan and gives chase again (through the odd intersection), but this time he gets Ivan's license plate number, and takes it to the police to be traced. When the police refuse to trace the license unless it has been involved in an accident, Trevor goes into the street and lets himself be hit by a car driven by a woman with a baby (see Figure 6.9). When the police finally do trace the license plate number,

Fig 6.9
In *The Machinist* (2004), Trevor's **repressed** guilt compels him to let himself be run over—by a car containing another mother and her son.

they tell Trevor that the plate is registered to Trevor Reznik himself, *who reported the car missing a year ago*. His mind reeling, Trevor runs from the police station and descends into the passageways beneath the city's public transportation system, a spatial metaphor that suggests a descent into the unconscious. Here Trevor encounters a split in the tunnel system that uncannily recalls the one previously seen on the Route 666 theme park ride.

After a scene with Stevie wherein she states that "hit and run drivers ought to be hanged," Trevor accuses her of conspiring with Ivan against him. Trevor returns to the all-night airport coffee shop only to find that no one named Marie works there. Once again confronting Ivan, Trevor manages to kill him and the film returns to its start, as Trevor tries to dump the body by the shore side. But when the carpet is rolled out, it contains nothing at all. Instead, the "dead" Ivan is seen holding the flashlight and asking the question "Who are you?" Via a flashback, Trevor (and the audience) finally begin to understand what has been going on: Trevor committed a hit and run accident one year ago—killing Marie's son Nicholas—while speeding through the intersection marked by the odd water tower. The "happy" scenes of Marie and Nicholas are thus revealed as a sort of screen memory that Trevor has created to cover over the tragedy he caused. (The doubling of the scene at the fun fair, as Trevor attempts to revive Nicholas in the shadow of the theme park ride [water tower], is thus another version of the "truth" seeping into Trevor's delusions.) The catalyst to discovering this repressed trauma has been Ivan—himself a hallucination of Trevor's creation, the return of Trevor's repressed guilt. Ivan appears to Trevor to provoke him. Ivan causes the accident on the floor of the machine shop, and thus represents Trevor's **repetition compulsion** (another way that repressed guilt or trauma strives to return, literally by repeating itself and causing another terrible accident). As Trevor and the audience members come to realize all this, Trevor finally takes the right fork in the road, heads downtown to the police station, and turns himself in for hit and run. As he is placed in his cell, Trevor is finally able to sleep, no longer plagued by the hallucinations and delusions that were caused by his repressed guilt (see Figure 6.10). By the end of the film, what Trevor had been repressing has been admitted to his conscious mind. In psychoanalytic terms, he has been "cured" of his disintegrating mental (and physical) condition.

However, there is at least one other possible trauma that might be said to be **condensed** onto the hit and run and the accident in the machine shop, a trauma that goes back to a more primal Oedipal narrative, thus enriching and motivating all of the film's castration symbolism. Throughout the course of the film, the audience discovers

Fig 6.10
In *The Machinist* (2004), Trevor finally confesses to his hit and run murder, finding peace and sleep now that justice has been served. (Note the logo on his shirt.)

that Trevor, like Nicholas, was raised by a single mother, creating a doppelgänger or doubling effect between Trevor and Nicholas. This is foreshadowed at the fun fair when Trevor takes a photograph of Marie and Nicholas that duplicates a similar photograph of Trevor and his mother from many years ago. This doubling is concretized when we learn towards the end of the film that all of the "props" contained in Trevor's hallucination of Marie's apartment were actually elements of Trevor's apartment *that belonged to his mother*. Thus Marie and Trevor's mother are condensed into the same character, just as Nicholas and Trevor are similarly condensed. One mother–son dyad suggests the other, and both dyads suggest an Oedipal crisis related to the missing figure of the father. As many psychotherapists would relate, it is not uncommon for children to blame themselves if their parents separate or if one parent dies. Perhaps this is Trevor's ultimate repressed trauma, one stemming from an unresolved Oedipal complex: if little Trevor did wish to kill his father and marry his mother, he may have found that wish suddenly fulfilled when his father left the family. Thus Trevor's original trauma may have been his belief that he somehow did kill his father, a belief so terrible that it would have to be deeply repressed, even as it keeps trying to repeat or reoccur. Thus, in "accidentally" killing Nicholas, Trevor might have been attempting to kill a version of himself, or at least punish himself for symbolically killing his father. (Here it is significant that in Trevor's wishful screen memory he imagines himself to be in love with Marie, a version of his own mother.) Similarly, the nature of the accident with Miller in the machine shop, and the phallic symbols tied to Ivan suggest that Trevor's unconscious mind was either trying to kill off the father figure again (via repetition compulsion), or else perhaps set up another opportunity to be punished not only for the hit and run, but also for the original trauma of "killing" his father.

Questions for discussion

1   Have you witnessed behaviors in real life that might be "evidence" of Freudian paradigms? Common examples might include infants in the oral stage, childhood regression, vehement denial, or aspects of the Oedipal narrative as they play out in actual families.

2   Pick two or three horror films and think about them in psychoanalytic terms. Do the monsters they depict relate to some form of "the return of the repressed"? What ideological markers distinguish the monsters from what the films represent as "normality"? Are the monsters vanquished (re-repressed) at the end of the film or do they continue to run amok?

3   Television is often not discussed in psychoanalytic terms. Why do you think that might be? Are some types of television texts more prone to lend themselves to psychoanalytic readings than others? For example, if long form serial narratives contain more complex characterizations than do sitcoms, are they more likely to engage with psychoanalytical concepts? *Six Feet Under* (2001–5) might be said to be all about repression. What do you think?

References and further reading

Creed, Barbara. *The Monstrous-Feminine: Film, Feminism, Psychoanalysis*. London and New York: Routledge, 1993.

Freud, Sigmund. *Five Lectures on Psycho-Analysis*. Trans. James Strachey New York: W.W. Norton & Company, 1990 (1910).

Freud, Sigmund. *Totem and Taboo*. Trans. James Strachey. New York: W.W. Norton & Company, 1990 (1913).

Freud, Sigmund. *Civilization and its Discontents*. Trans. James Strachey. New York: W.W. Norton & Company, 1961 (1930).

Kristeva, Julia. *Powers of Horror: An Essay on Abjection*. Trans. Leon S. Roudiez. New York: Columbia University Press, 1982.

Metz, Christian. *The Imaginary Signifier: Psychoanalysis and Cinema*. Trans. Ben Brewster. Bloomington, IN: Indiana University Press, 1986, 1973–76.

Spoto, Donald. *The Dark Side of Genius: The Life of Alfred Hitchcock*. Boston, MA: Da Capo Press, 1999 (1983).

Storr, Anthony. *Freud: A Very Short Introduction*. New York: Oxford University Press, 2001.

Tarratt, Margaret. "Monsters from the Id," reprinted in *Film Genre Reader IV*, ed. Barry Keith Grant. Austin, TX: University of Texas Press, 2012.

Twitchell, James. *Dreadful Pleasures: An Anatomy of Modern Horror*. New York: Oxford University Press, 1985.

Wood, Robin. *Hollywood: From Vietnam to Reagan*. New York: Columbia University Press, 1986.

CHAPTER 7

Psychoanalysis (part two): *Screen* and apparatus theory

The preceding chapter explored basic concepts of Freudian psychoanalysis and how they might be used to analyze or explicate cultural artifacts such as individual film and TV texts, or textual systems (genres) like the horror film or the psychological thriller. This chapter explores some of the complex and sometimes contradictory ways psychoanalysis has been used to theorize the very act or process of watching films. (These theories have rarely been applied to television studies for various reasons, not the least of them being that many of them are dependent upon a highly structuralist model of theatrical exhibition, which is no longer the standard for film viewing, and was never the standard for television viewing.) As such, this chapter explores psychoanalysis in terms more global than local. It examines the concepts that developed when theorists began to use psychoanalysis to account for the psychic appeal of cinema, and/or to describe the psychic mechanisms at work when we watch films. These ideas explore how Film with a capital F (and especially a certain kind of film—the **classical realist** text or Hollywood-style film) works in conjunction with our conscious and unconscious desires and drives. And although the concepts explored in this chapter can be and have been used to explore individual film texts (as in the case study that concludes this chapter), they were more regularly used to explore the mental or psychic processes of film viewing in and of itself.

These complicated applications of Marx and Freud were written circa the 1970s, and they were often quite dense and difficult to parse in their original formulations. Even more so than some of the other chapters in this book, this chapter is going to be a (hopefully not too overly) simplified synthesis of a range of ideas associated with thinkers as diverse as Jacques Lacan, Jean-Louis Baudry, Christian Metz, Louis Althusser, Bertolt Brecht, Roland Barthes, Colin MacCabe, Stephen Heath, and Laura Mulvey, among many others. Many of their seminal writings were published in the British film journal *Screen* throughout the 1970s, which is why these ideas are sometimes referred to *en masse* as **Screen** **theory**. (In truth *Screen* theory encompasses a variety of approaches.) Some of these ideas are also commonly referred to as **apparatus theory** (my preferred term) as they attempted to delineate a complex structure or apparatus that its proponents argued was the defining nature of the cinematic experience. Less charitably, these ideas have been referred to as SLAB theory, an acronym for some of the constituent thinkers (the linguist Ferdinand **de Saussure**, the psychoanalyst Jacques **Lacan**, the Marxist philosopher Louis **Althusser**, and post/structuralist thinker Roland **Barthes**) whose myriad ideas helped shape this thing called apparatus theory. While much of apparatus theory was eventually critiqued by **poststructuralist** thinkers (among others) as essentialist and ahistoric, it nonetheless remains a very important moment in the history of thinking about film, and one that gave rise to some of the most important insights about film and gender (explored in greater detail in the following chapters).

The film journal *Screen* and apparatus theory also developed within precise historical and socio-cultural contexts: both arose from European critical thinking and political filmmaking that was caught up in the revolutionary foment of the late 1960s. (Recall that the influx of structuralism into thinking about auteurs and genres also occurred during this era.) Some of the most important ideas related to *Screen* theory first appeared in the influential French film journal *Cahiers du Cinema*, which itself became highly politicized in the wake of the various countercultural and revolutionary movements of the 1960s. (For more on the upheavals of "May '68," see the case study at the end of this chapter.) Drawing on the formulations of Marx and Althusser, the writers and editors of both *Cahiers du Cinema* and *Screen* argued that film itself—and especially the dominant form of cinema—the **classical realist** text—was a powerful political tool for enforcing and replicating the ideological status quo. As such, they argued that *every* film was political in some way or another. Many argued that traditional realist cinema was an ideological sham, that cinema's powerful reality effect was actually a manufactured result of its ideological biases, not reality itself. Roland Barthes's distinction between the **readerly text** versus the **writerly text** was also theorized around this time, and subsequently drawn into *Screen* theory. The readerly text—like classical realist cinema—is easy to consume and offers the simplified pleasures of hero versus villain and a happy ending; the writerly text—which is purposely difficult or ambiguous—forces its readers to think about its meanings and means of production. Thus, like the Frankfurt School and Brechtian theorists who preceded them by several decades, many of the *Screen* and *Cahiers du Cinema* critics argued that only "difficult" art could shake spectators free from the ideological hold of dominant cinema. In this way, much of this thinking upholds the old "high art/low art" dichotomy of Western culture.

Such a critique of film form is evident in "Cinema/Ideology/Criticism," first published in *Screen* in 1971. In it, authors Jean-Louis Comolli and Jean Narboni suggested a five point political classification system for fictional films, including (a) films whose content expresses **dominant ideologies** in dominant (i.e. classical realist, Hollywood) ways. Type (b) films, on the other hand, are the exact opposite of type (a) films: their content attacks or challenges dominant ideology and they do so in radically experimental (non-dominant) forms. Type (b) films are thus highly indebted to Brecht's ideas about Epic theater and the **alienation effect**; the films made by Jean-Luc Godard in the late 1960s and early 1970s are often cited as good examples of type (b) films. Type (c) films do not appear to be about political issues, but their form is experimental and is thus challenging to the cinematic status quo; type (d) films are overtly political films that use classical realist style, such as *Reds* (1981) or *Syriana* (2005). More intriguingly perhaps, type (e) films are those that appear to be type (a) films, but whose political agenda becomes more obvious upon closer examination. In this case, some films produced within the **classical realist film** industry might be recouped as important political films, based upon a critic's bravura reading (or **deconstruction**) of that film's deeper, or submerged political messages. As this brief précis seems to suggest, classifying films in this way is a very **structuralist** project, even as type (e) films seem to point forward to **poststructuralist** thinking: the classification of type (e) films—like poststructuralism in general—is dependent upon and stresses the importance of critical reading (**exegesis**). Furthermore, analyses of type (e) films will inherently explore the contradictions, ambiguities, and multiple meanings to which any single film text may give rise.

Another very important—and more forthrightly poststructuralist—essay appeared one year earlier in *Cahiers du Cinema*; it was translated and published in *Screen* in 1972. Written by the Editors of *Cahiers du Cinema*, "John Ford's *Young Mr. Lincoln*" is exemplary in its poststructuralist approach to cinema. In it, the authors first examine the various historical contexts—industrial, economic, authorial, etc.—surrounding the production of this famous 1939 Hollywood film. They then proceed to explore the ideological meanings of the film through close textual analysis, revealing **structuring absences** and hidden agendas. Although published a year before Comolli and Narboni's "Cinema/Ideology/Criticism," "John Ford's *Young Mr. Lincoln*" might best be described as a thorough critical exploration of a type (e) text, a type of poststructuralist criticism that is still often practiced in the twenty-first century. However, for better or worse, *Screen* theory also became known for its more essentialist, structuralist accounts of cinema and the cinematic apparatus, with its allegedly monolithic effect upon its subjects. What follows will be a necessarily simplified account of apparatus theory, beginning with Lacan's rewriting of Freud in linguistic and imagistic terms, and then exploring the nature of the cinematic apparatus itself as described by Jean-Louis Baudry, Christian Metz, and others.

Lacanian psychoanalysis: Rewriting Freud

Just as Sigmund Freud was central to the concepts explored in the last chapter, so too is French psychoanalyst **Jacques Lacan** (1901–81) central to this chapter. While Lacan's writings are often difficult to read (because of their theoretical nuance and arcane prose style, not to mention translation issues), it could be said broadly that his greatest innovation was the application of semiotics to psychoanalysis. As we shall see, he rewrote Freud's Oedipal model of subject formation by shifting its emphasis away from individual fathers and mothers, and more towards a larger social model in which the child attains subjectivity via the acquisition of language—his/her entry into the realm of the **Symbolic**. The Symbolic realm of language, however, is still associated with or even constituted by the phallus (patriarchal power), as its most common spokesmen are fathers, politicians, policemen, governments, and even God (presumed to be male in most Western thought). Language may thus be described as **phallogocentric**, a term that underscores the patriarchal nature of linguistic sign systems. Lacan also challenged Freud's earlier model of the unconscious mind being a wild, primitive, chaotic, and unstructured realm: Lacan argued that even the unconscious mind is a product of language and culture. One of his more famous aphorisms, "The unconscious is structured like a language," stresses that point. If the unconscious is made up of things that are repressed from the realm of consciousness (the ego), they must have direct ties to that conscious realm, the phallogocentric realm that Lacan termed the Symbolic.

Opposing and predating the Symbolic (in the child's development) is the **Imaginary**, somewhat analogous to Freud's pre-Oedipal period of infantile development (just as the Symbolic is somewhat analogous to Freud's post-Oedipal). The **Imaginary** is a world of maternal plenitude originally centered around the mother's body and especially the mother's breast. The Imaginary is an almost utopic stage before the infant acquires language and attains subjectivity. The Imaginary is the realm of the senses, of taste, touch, sound, and image. In the Imaginary stage, the child has no identity of his/her own; he/she is not aware of where s/he stops and the mother begins. Lacan sometimes used the punning term *l'hommelette* (which means "the little man") to refer to this aspect of the Imaginary—like eggs in an omelet, it is hard to tell where the infant's sense of self begins and where it ends. Mother and infant are commingled, mixed together without a clear sense of boundaries. (Lacan also theorized the **Real**, but as in Louis Althusser's formulations about the pervasive nature of **ideology**, the Real is not actually accessible to the human subject; we can only know the world through Symbolic sign systems.)

Lacan thus rewrote Freud's ideas about the Oedipal narrative into a theory about how the child acquires (patriarchal) language. As the child develops, he (or she) finds his (or her) place within the pre-existing linguistic and cultural structures into which s/he is born. This part of Lacan's theories are somewhat analogous to Althusser's notion of **interpellation**: we discover our own subjectivities when we accede to a place in the ideological structures that surround and hail us. For Lacan, we become subjects when we learn to recognize our place within the phallogocentric realms of culture and language: i.e. the Symbolic. Most importantly for film theory, Lacan also theorized the acquisition of subjectivity in visual terms, in a series of narrative events called the **mirror stage**, occurring at approximately 6–18 months in the child's development. The mirror stage is what allows the child to realize that he/she is a separate entity from the mother, moving him or her from the Imaginary realm and into the Symbolic. Recall that during the Imaginary stage, the child cannot perceive of itself as distinct from the mother. The child's visual powers also outstrip its actual motor abilities at this point. But through the act of looking into the mirror (with or without the mother), the child comes to realize his/her own status as a separate entity, by identifying with the image in the mirror. Lacan dubs this image in the mirror the child's **ego ideal**, for the child allegedly imagines its image to be better than s/he truly is—more whole, more competent, more capable, more mobile. The image in the mirror is also—importantly—not the child itself, but *an image* of the child. (To be precise, we could classify the child's mirror image as an **indexical sign** of the child, as he or she has to be there to produce it; see Chapter 3.) Lacan thus suggests that this recognition in the mirror is actually a **mis-recognition**. This sets up a confusing split in the child's ego, as its self (its subjectivity) is predicated on an image that both *is and is not* "me."

Furthermore, in entering the Symbolic in this divided way, the child still retains a sense of lack, having lost its sense of wholeness tied to the mother during the Imaginary stage. Lacan suggests that human subjects are constantly in a search for something that will fulfill that childhood experience of lack—i.e. the loss of an Imaginary oneness associated with the mother—and Lacan called the object of that (metaphorical) search *l'objet petit a* ("the little object a"). This suggests that although we exist primarily with the Symbolic throughout most of our lives, we are constantly searching for some object or experience that might overcome (or fill) our initial sense of lack. In this way the human subject is a divided subject, one that is dependent upon relations both Symbolic and Imaginary. Self and Other—which might be traditionally thought of as opposing binaristic terms—are thus deeply imbricated in one another, as we search out in other people (friends, lovers, enemies) and in other things (possessions, wealth, fame) the things that might allow us to overcome this primordial sense of lack. The very act of sex itself might also be considered in these terms (especially for the male heterosexual subject), as sexuality involves the loss of personal physical boundaries and a sense of merging into a unified oneness (however fleeting those sensations might be). The important thing is this: the Symbolic order allows us to think of ourselves as whole and unified (and not fragmented and contradictory) through static, pre-existing linguistic constructs such as "I" and "You," or imagistic cultural productions like photography, film, and video: processes that seem to "fix" a stable identity that Lacan and other psychoanalytic thinkers would suggest is an impossibility. (Compare this to Althusser's notion of the human subject in flux, rather than the static individual.)

So what does all this have to do with the cinematic apparatus? According to apparatus theorists, cinema is meaningful and appealing to us, because it restages this narrative of subject acquisition via the mirror stage over and over again for its spectators. In this model, the screen of the cinema functions as a kind of mirror, inviting us to mis-recognize ourselves in the characters and actions depicted on screen. In other words, we identify with our ego-ideals, whether they be Indiana Jones or Bridget Jones. Part of the way classical realist texts work is by hiding their means of production, affording spectators the chance to form close identifications with the characters and the events unreeling on the screen. Broadly speaking, the term **suture** has been used to describe how the very form of classical realist cinema works to pull spectators into the diegetic world of the film. When the classical realist text is "firing on all cylinders," its spectators might be said to be seated in an auditorium, but they are also somehow *not* in the auditorium—they are somehow transported, literally sutured or stitched into the world of the film. In this way, spectators are interpellated into the form of classical realist cinema (in general) and into the ideological structures of any given text. And for proponents of apparatus theory, it does not matter if that given text is *Die Hard* (1988) or *Thelma and Louise* (1991). Because both texts are made in the classical realist style, both ultimately situate their spectators within the same ideological structures. The following section explores in greater detail how various scholars have theorized the cinematic apparatus and its concomitant ideological functioning.

The cinematographic apparatus: Baudry and Metz

This section attempts to synthesize some of the most complex ideas of apparatus theory into a rudimentary interlocking four-part model or structure. As such, we might say that the cinematic apparatus is composed of (1) its **technical base** (camera, lighting, film stock, choice of lenses, etc.); (2) its **conditions of projection** (spectators sit passively in the dark, with projection occurring from behind); (3) **classical realist film** style; and (4) the **mental machinery of spectatorship** (the psychoanalytic processes that allow for regression and identification). Apparatus theory quite literally imagines a physical, psychoanalytic, and ideological structure that surrounds and engulfs filmgoers, placing them within (interpellating them into) an almost machine-like environment. One of the most important parts of this model is to recognize the crucial difference between the **spectator** and the "actual" reader, filmgoer, or audience member. The latter three terms refer to flesh and blood people who are said to inhabit the spectator position within the apparatus. Thus, while the term spectator is sometimes used interchangeably with the other three terms, in apparatus theory it refers to *a specific slot in the machine*, into which actual readers willingly place themselves. Apparatus theorists are not interested in the divergent subjectivities that actual readers bring to the cinema (one aspect of Cultural Studies; see Chapters 10-12). Rather they are interested in exploring how all humans are allegedly subjected to the ideological effects of the apparatus. The next few paragraphs explore some basic aspects of each of the four parts of the cinematic apparatus as outlined above.

The **technical base** of the cinematic apparatus would include things like lighting, film stock, choice of lenses, and camera work—and specifically how those various technical elements create a version of reality (but not reality itself). The camera is monocular, for instance, when human beings are binocular. The camera and its lenses also create spatial relationships based on **Renaissance perspective**, a system of representing three-dimensional reality within two-dimensional media that became central to Western "ways of seeing." The acts of lighting, focusing, and framing also tend to create a unified, centered vision and expression of meaning, one that the spectator is encouraged to share (again, via Renaissance perspective that situates the spectator at the precise site of seeing and understanding). The term **conditions of projection** refers to the ways in which the cinematic apparatus encourages a passive audience, sitting the dark, to figuratively "dream" the images on the screen: the images in front of us are projected from behind, seemingly emerging—like dreams—from the recesses of our minds' unconscious states. These same conditions also encourage **regression**—the psychic defense mechanism in which the ego retreats to an earlier state of development. In this case, regression in the movie house is said to recall or facilitate the spectator's recollection of the mirror stage, when he or she was also less mobile and more acutely visual. The **classical realist film** text, as has been stressed throughout this chapter and this book, hides the work that it takes to create it, and presents a seamless diegetic world into which the spectator is sutured.

In his seminal essay, "Ideological Effects of the Basic Cinematographic Apparatus," **Jean-Louis Baudry** suggests these aspects of the cinema produce a **transcendental spectator position**—an omniscient, all-seeing, all-knowing subject position. The cinematic apparatus centralizes and spoon feeds to the spectator all the information he or she needs to know to follow the story and emotionally engage with it, all the while hiding edits, smoothing over ellipses, and masking the actual work that went into the production of the film. Baudry therefore suggests that the cinematic apparatus creates an **idealist ideology**, through which the spectator is encouraged to see the world in rose-colored and idealistic ways (as opposed to pragmatic or material ways). As he concludes, "The cinema can thus appear as a sort of psychic apparatus of substitution, corresponding to the model defined by the dominant ideology" (540). In this way, the cinema's "reality" or "truth" is anything but—it is instead a reflection of the dominant institutions, forces, and ideologies that produce it.

The **mental machinery of spectatorship** is perhaps the most complicated part of the cinematic apparatus, and has been the aspect most thoroughly explored by psychoanalytic thinkers. Much of this thinking is tied to **Christian Metz**, whose essays on the subject were published throughout the 1970s and then collected in his book *The Imaginary Signifier: Psychoanalysis and Cinema* (not published in English until 1986). The title refers to Metz's theorization of cinema's unique aesthetic and perceptual qualities, which as critics have pointed out down through the decades, seem to encompass just about all of the other arts: painting, dance, drama, music, *et al*. Metz compares cinema to the legitimate theater most directly, noting that when in the theatrical space, the audience watches actors and sets (signifiers) who really are on stage in front of them. That is to say, they have a material quality. Cinema, on the other hand, only shows its spectators *images* of what was once recorded in front of the camera, images that constantly suggest their lack of materiality. It is in this sense that the cinema's signifier is imaginary, and Metz argues that it is this specific quality of cinema that allows it to appeal to spectators in a variety of psychoanalytically meaningful ways. As such, he and later thinkers elaborated on psychoanalytic concepts related to **scopophilia**, simply the love of looking or watching, which has libidinal (sexual) implications in many cases.

Following on Baudry's thinking, Metz wrote about the cinematic apparatus's ability to invoke or create identifications. Baudry's transcendental subject position— produced by the first three aspects of the apparatus—becomes for Metz the process of **primary identification**, the spectator's identification with the *very act of cinematic perception*. Metz then classifies the spectator's identification with the film's characters as **secondary identifications**. Both of these forms of identification are tied back to the mirror stage, in which the infant first attains his/her subjectivity by mis-recognizing him/herself in the mirror. In the case of primary identification, the spectator is placed in an all-knowing, all-seeing subject position (that of the cinematic apparatus itself) that then allows or permits secondary identifications (with the characters) to occur. It is easy to see how the mirror stage analogy fits into this model: spectators are encouraged to mis-recognize themselves in their cinematic ego ideals (who are more handsome, more mobile, more powerful, etc.) who appear before them on the screen. In this way, the pleasures of looking are tied up with our own primordial memory of the mirror stage; at the cinema we reenact our own entrance into subjectivity, albeit in highly fantasized ways. And as these aspects of identification have to do with the subject's ego functioning, they are sometimes labeled the **narcissistic** aspect of scopophilia (after the Greek myth of Narcissus, a young dreamer who fell in love with his own reflection in a pool of water). Broadly speaking, in psychoanalytic terms **narcissism** refers to an unhealthy fixation on oneself; in apparatus theory it refers to those processes whereby classical realist texts invoke and/or allow for identification with both the cinematic apparatus and the ideal characters it depicts.

Another important aspect of cinematic scopophilia is **voyeurism**. A **voyeur** (someone who might colloquially be called a "Peeping Tom") is a person (usually male) who derives sexual pleasure from spying on people as they undress, become sexual, or otherwise engage in private, personal matters. Voyeurism is thus more a function of **libido** than is narcissistic identification, which is more an aspect of ego. It should come as no surprise that the cinema affords more than ample opportunities for voyeuristic pleasure, from the scantily clad chorus girl of the classical Hollywood musical to the muscle-bound Greek hero of the nostalgic action film—not to mention the entire industry of film and video pornography. Acts of voyeurism are ubiquitous in teen comedies like *Porkies* (1982) and *American*

Pie (1999), while some of the most famous films in Western film history have thematized and explored the issues surrounding voyeurism in quite direct and serious ways. Alfred Hitchcock's *Rear Window* (1954) and *Vertigo* (1958) are about men obsessed with spying on people, while the infamous British horror film *Peeping Tom* (1960) equates the gaze of the male voyeur directly with violence against women (and perhaps more audaciously, the cinematic institution itself) (see Figures 7.1 and 7.2). In this way, voyeurism is often linked to **sadism**, a term that refers to sexualized pleasure derived from inflicting pain or humiliation on someone else. Sadism is also expressed through domination, and/or the need to control other people and things. The "opposite" or complementary term to voyeurism is **exhibitionism**, in which the subject derives pleasure from showing off his or her

Fig 7.1
Voyeurism is a central theme of many of Alfred Hitchcock's films, and especially *Rear Window* (1954).

Fig 7.2
In *Peeping Tom* (1960), a murderer films his victims as he kills them; the film is arguably an indictment of the sadistic impulses that lie at the heart of cinema.

body in a sexualized way. And while it might be cynical to suggest that all actors are exhibitionists, they do have to be willing to display their bodies (in more or less sexualized ways) for the camera, and by extension, the spectators who sit in movie houses like anxious Peeping Toms.

The third (and possibly most complicated) aspect of scopophilia is referred to as **fetishization**. Recall from the previous chapter that a fetish object is something overinvested with libidinal energy, one that represents both the phallus *as well as* the threat of castration. The fetish is thus dependent on the defense mechanism of **disavowal**, which involves a dual belief, or the "denial of perception," as in the statement "I know very well, but all the same…" In *The Imaginary Signifier*, Christian Metz describes this primordial process of disavowal as:

> the lasting matrix, the affective prototype of all the splitting of belief which man can henceforth be capable of in the most varied domains, of all the infinitely complex unconscious and occasionally conscious interactions which he will allow himself between "believing" and "not believing."
>
> (70)

Metz then goes on to describe the cinema itself as a fetish:

> the cinema as a technical performance, as prowess, as an *exploit*, an exploit that underlines and denounces the lack on which the whole arrangement is based (the absence of the object, replaced by its reflection), an exploit which consists at the same time of making this absence forgotten.
>
> (74)

In other words, the various lacks that cinema is comprised of—its lack of material signifiers (as opposed to the live theater), or even its cuts and ellipses and plot holes—is "papered over" by the functioning of the classical realist text. In these passages, Metz is using psychoanalytic theory to explain the processes that occur when watching mainstream movies, processes that more colloquial commentators have called the "suspension of disbelief." The phrase "suspension of disbelief" refers to how spectators know—on one level—that the film they are watching is not "really" happening, but they nonetheless become psychically invested in it as if it were real.

Metz also points to film buffs who fetishize cinematic technique and/or specific directors as basic aspects of cinema's fetishistic appeal. Other theorists have noted the fetishistic appeal of movie stars, and an entire industry of *paparazzi*, tabloid magazines, and tell-all TV shows exists to appeal to film fans' voyeuristic and fetishistic desires. Ultimately, Metz theorizes the cinema itself as a sort of "a generalized strip-tease," as it dares to show us something we want to see onscreen while it simultaneously denies us seeing what is offscreen (or in the next shot). Then the next shot does appear, and again the spectator feels momentarily fulfilled, only to start sensing lack again (from the views that are again being withheld). In this way, the spectator is **sutured** into the film for its duration. For Metz and like-minded thinkers, this oscillation between onscreen and offscreen, between phallus and lack, between the Symbolic and the Imaginary is what makes cinema so psychoanalytically meaningful. Politically, the classical realist text thus uses the primordial appeal of the Imaginary to attract moviegoers and give them pleasure, even as it narrates that experience via Symbolic (phallogocentric) structures, i.e. classical Hollywood narrative form and its idealist reality effect. In a slightly different formulation, one might say that film makes us aware of lack/absence/ separation/passivity (which is discomforting to the ego), but that it also constantly attempts to cover over that sense of lack via classical realist style which gives us the illusion of unity, meaning, and truth.

Conclusions and critiques

As the next chapter explores in greater detail, apparatus theory became very important to feminist thinking about gender in relationship to mainstream cinema: the various aspects of the cinematic apparatus are themselves gendered in various ways. (As will be argued, the cinematic apparatus creates a male subject position that arguably speaks to that subject's unconscious desires.) However, basic apparatus theory has also been critiqued on many levels, and is—in and of itself—less important to film studies in the twenty-first century than it was in the 1970s. Perhaps the most important reason for this is that so few people experience cinema in the ways that apparatus theory suggests: projected in an actual darkened movie house. With the rise of home theaters, new media, DVRs, and Internet streaming services, etc., more and more people are watching films on mobile devices and computer screens rather than seeing them projected in a cinema. Similarly, apparatus theory has rarely been of interest to television scholars, precisely for the same reasons. How do concepts like regression, voyeurism, and suture work—if they even do—for a distracted viewer watching a reality game show on TV? Each new innovation in film and television distribution and exhibition potentially creates brand new apparatuses for the experience of audio-visual signals. Today, the cinematic apparatus is but one of many different ways that people experience film and television texts.

Another important critique of apparatus theory, like psychoanalysis in general, is that apparatus theory cannot be proved or disproved, and is thus unfalsifiable. These various psychoanalytic dynamics might be occurring when spectators watch classical realist texts, but then again they might not. Furthermore, like most structuralist models, apparatus theory has been critiqued as essentialist, ahistoric, and **Eurocentric**. It attempts to explain everything about cinema in one monolithic way; even before the rise of digital media, apparatus theory overlooked different cinematic exhibition practices that can and do vary from place to place and time to time. Rarely do (or did) movie houses function in the orderly fashion asserted by apparatus theory; in some cultures a highly vocal, interactive, and even mobile audience is more the norm. For example, silent cinema in Japan was usually accompanied by a *benshi*, a live narrator who explained the story. Federico Fellini's *Roma* (1972) and *Amarcord* (1973) depict the movie houses of the director's youth as almost anarchic spaces, filled with noise and boisterous behaviors often unrelated to the images on the screen. Perhaps only Western cinephiles (discussed further in the case study) place themselves in a passive, regressed, and almost somnambulistic state when attending the cinema.

Apparatus theory's assertion that all classical realist texts create the same ideological effect(s) is also highly problematic, as is its insistence (shared by the Frankfurt School) that only radically formalist works can express politics in any meaningful ways. To return to the ideas of Jean-Louis Comolli and Jean Narboni that were introduced at the start of this chapter, apparatus theory suggests that only one type of film practice is worth pursuing—the type (b) political film made in a radically formalist (and therefore political) style. All other filmic styles are somewhat demonized by this approach as insufficiently political, when in fact films can and do make political statements in a multitude of styles. For example, some audiences respond to the soft-pedaled political messages of Hollywood **social problems films** much more readily than difficult, deconstructive avant-garde texts. Such films use classical realist style to reach audiences with liberal messages about social issues like anti-Semitism (*Focus* [2001]), racism (*42* [2013]), or other social issues including AIDS (*Philadelphia* [1993]) or environmentalism (*Erin Brockovich* [2000]). It seems mistaken to discount the **ideological messages** or political effects of those films, as some *Screen* and/or apparatus theorists might have us do. Contemporary cultural criticism finds those texts as worthy of study as any others.

As we shall see in the following chapters, 1970s apparatus theory was slowly supplanted in the following decades by poststructuralist and cultural studies approaches that were highly skeptical of essentialist structures like "the cinematic apparatus." Both poststructuralist and cultural studies approaches also eschew the high–low, good–bad dichotomy which was still so prevalent in much *Screen* theory. Today, it is much more important to think about all the multiple parameters of film and television texts. It may still be important to theorize how texts are experienced via certain apparatuses, but one also needs to take into account their complicated modes of production, their explicit and implicit textual meanings, as well as their multifarious reception contexts (within and across actual human beings with differing and intersecting social subjectivities). Some of the dynamics of apparatus theory—and especially as they are gendered—are still quite relevant to contemporary film and television criticism. However, they are but one part of more nuanced cultural criticism: one tool among many in the cultural critic's tool box.

Case study: *The Dreamers* (2003)

The Dreamers is an allegorical drama directed by Bernardo Bertolucci, an Italian filmmaker best known for films such as *The Conformist* (1970), *Last Tango in Paris* (1972), *1900* (1976), *The Last Emperor* (1987), and *The Sheltering Sky* (1990). Many of Bertolucci's best films are about sex, politics, and sexual politics; *The Dreamers* is certainly no exception. By focusing on three young Parisian *cinephiles* (movie lovers)—Isabelle (Eva Green), her twin brother Theo (Louis Garrel), and an American student studying abroad named Matthew (Michael Pitt)—the film dramatizes the connections between the personal and the political, knowingly drawing on the Lacanian concepts of the Imaginary and the Symbolic. Based on the 1988 novel *The Holy Innocents* by poet and film critic Gilbert Adair, *The Dreamers* is perhaps a deceptively simple film on the surface of things—but it is steeped in film history and film theory, specifically the ideas and concepts raised by Lacanian, *Screen*, and/or apparatus theory as introduced in this chapter. Drawing on real life events related to film culture and the countercultural (leftist) social movement that practically brought the French government to a standstill in May of 1968, *The Dreamers* explores the various relationships between film, culture, politics, **ideology**, desire, identity, and structure— just as that generation of film and cultural critics was beginning to do. *The Dreamers* takes place during the historical moment in which modern cultural criticism was invented and politicized, even as it also suggests the limits and blind spots of much structuralist theorizing of history and culture.

1968 was a year of turmoil in many Western nations: young people, the **working class**, women, anti-war protestors, and civil rights advocates of multiple varieties were making their voices heard, often for the first time. Sit-ins, strikes, boycotts, "zaps," and protest marches were calling attention to the outmoded (and for some people immoral) politics of the older generation. There was a youthful exuberance that thought itself capable of changing the world, even as those same young people rarely agreed on how to make that happen, or what the world might actually look like should some form of revolution actually be accomplished. Informing many leftist ideals of the era was the *Little Red Book*, more officially known as *Quotations from Chairman Mao Tse-Tung*, a book originally meant to propagandize for Communist (Red) China's internal political goals, including the so-called Great Proletarian Cultural Revolution. However, the book also became the center of debate in Western nations after it began to be translated in the mid-1960s, and many leftists of the era agreed with its basic Marxist-Leninist philosophies. (The more nuanced forms of Marxist thinking associated with theorists like Althusser and **Gramsci** had yet to be considered.) In *The Dreamers*, Matthew and Theo have a discussion about the *Little Red Book* that allegorizes their attitudes about social change. Theo—like a structuralist— believes in the book's revolutionary plan, but Matthew—more like a poststructuralist—is skeptical that any single book can provide answers to such complicated questions. Spring of 1968 was especially important to film culture in France. Recall (from Chapter 4) that in the post-World War II years, film clubs and film journals like *Cahiers du Cinema* proliferated, with most of these institutions professing the importance of new methodologies like **auteur** and **genre theory**. But in the late 1960s, film studies was taking a sharp turn into more ideological and structuralist thinking, with critics, *cinephiles*, and filmmakers starting to think of themselves as oppressed workers at the beck and call of totalizing governmental (and cinematic) apparatuses. Much of this thinking began during and in response to the so-called "Langlois Affair," which occurred in February of 1968 when Minister of Cultural Affairs André Malraux fired the much-beloved **Henri Langlois** from his post as founder and director of the Cinémathèque Française, Paris's premiere repertory cinema (see Figure 7.3). In protest of Malraux's decision to remove Langlois, thousands of film fans, critics, directors, and

Fig 7.3
The Dreamers (2003) uses documentary footage of Henri Langlois to establish the time and place of the film, as well as its thematic interest in spectatorship.

actors rebelled, holding demonstrations at the Cinémathèque and other venues around Paris that eventually forced Malraux to reinstate Langlois. The Langlois Affair did not just politicize film culture in France (and elsewhere), it was also important in predating or foreshadowing the wider nation-wide demonstrations that would sweep across France just a few months later in May. It is within this milieu that *The Dreamers* takes place; filmmakers Bertolucci and Adair knowingly comment on these events as well as theorize them through that era's developing methods of cultural criticism.

For example, *The Dreamers* begins with a credit sequence played out and through a politically overdetermined symbol of the state—the Eiffel Tower—awash in the shifting national colors of blue, white, and red. As the camera moves down the length of this giant phallic symbol, the names of the cast and filmmakers appear from within the tower's ornate "Victorian Structural Expressionist" style, only to be absorbed back into it (see Figure 7.4). A better visualization of **phallogocentrism** is hard to imagine: language is patriarchal (phallic) and structural, and it delineates our experience of the world (and this film) from start to finish. In case the importance of these types of structures to the meaning of the film is missed, Bertolucci and Adair insert an entire scene with Isabelle and Theo's parents where Matthew literally measures the dining room table with his cigarette lighter, pointing out the prevalence of underlying patterns (ideological structures) that comprise our world (see Figure 7.5). But the most interesting structural component of the film is the design of the apartment where Isabelle and Theo live with their parents. The parents' portion of the apartment is fairly normal, ordered, and filled with familiar bourgeois furnishings of neutral green and brown shades (see Figure 7.6). Conversely, the younger generation occupies a maze-like wing of the apartment bathed in womblike pink lighting and covered with movie memorabilia, reflecting Isabelle and Theo's intense desire to merge with the cinema. These two spaces in the apartment are highly suggestive of Lacan's Symbolic and Imaginary stages. The parents' (Symbolic) zone is that of the adult world and patriarchal language—Papa is a poet, after all—it represents the properly socialized **heteronormative** family structure. The youngsters' (Imaginary) zone is all about cinematic images, games, and undefined sexualities (see Figure 7.7). The real drama of the film is how these two zones (and what they represent) interact, once the parents leave town for an extended stay elsewhere and Matthew moves into the apartment with Isabelle and Theo.

Fig 7.4
Phallogocentrism
exemplified: the title
credits for *The Dreamers*
(2003) materialize from
within the structure of the
Eiffel Tower, only to be
absorbed back into it.

Fig 7.5
In *The Dreamers* (2003) Matthew points out the invisible structures that surround all of us as we move through our lives.

Fig 7.6
In *The Dreamers* (2003), the parents' part of the apartment represents their **Symbolic** space ...

At first, Matthew is happy to be drawn into the Imaginary world of Isabelle and Theo, a world in which they watch films at the Cinémathèque and obsessively try to recreate or relive them in their "real" lives. For example, as Isabelle moves around a room in imitation of Greta Garbo in *Queen Christina* (1933), or as the three youths race through the Louvre recreating a scene from Jean-Luc Godard's *Bande à part* (1964), director Bertolucci cuts between Matthew, Isabelle, and Theo and footage from the actual films they are mimicking, suggesting the blur between self and M/Other that is one aspect of the Imaginary stage of development. Even in the Cinémathèque, the goal of watching films is to merge with the Imaginary: thus Matthew's description of *cinephiles* as insatiable, sitting in the first rows of the theater in attempt to encounter the images before anyone else in the theater. Things start to turn a little awkward for Matthew when he observes how physically as well as mentally close to one another Isabelle and Theo are: they sleep naked in bed together and share a bathroom with little concern for privacy. There is even the intimation that they were conjoined twins in the womb. Furthering the idea of the Imaginary as it plays out across these characters' actions is the film's focus on—

Fig 7.7
... while the maze-like
pink hallways and
bedrooms associated
with Isabelle and Theo
represent the **Imaginary**.

and its characters' disregard for—taboos around the **abject**—here signified by bodily
excretions such as blood, saliva, semen, tears, urine, and even "sleepy dirt" which Isabelle
licks out of a bewildered Matthew's eyes. In psychoanalytic theory, the term **abject** is
used to define those aspects of the self that become "not self" the minute they are
extruded from the body; learning to distance oneself from the abject is thus part of the
subject's move from the Imaginary stage to the Symbolic, whose phallogocentric laws
and prohibitions define what is and is not self and other, normal and abnormal. The point
of all this is that Matthew, Isabelle, and Theo are attempting to avoid the Symbolic (the
political world around them) by regressing into the Imaginary, blurring into the cinema,
and merging into one another. The sequence that shows Theo masturbating and then
ejaculating onto a photo of Marlene Dietrich in *Blonde Venus* (1932) draws all of these
aspects of the Imaginary together: fantasy, desire, cinema, and the abject. Another scene
in which the three dreamers share a bathtub situated under three mirrors—two of
which reflect across the tub to show someone else's face—also visualizes this sense of
pre-Oedipal, Imaginary, not-yet defined or free floating subjectivity. The dreamers could
be undifferentiated fetuses in the womb (see Figure 7.8).

Fig 7.8
Bathtub mirror scene: the
identities of *The Dreamers*
(2003) blur and merge.

But the Symbolic eventually begins to intrude on the three dreamer's Imaginary idyll, as the Imaginary fusion of the three characters starts to take on aspects of a socialized Symbolic—that is to say "properly" heterosexual and dyadic—nature. (This "three versus two" motif also appears in the scenes of the three dreamers sharing two sandwiches and a single banana.) The Symbolic begins to intrude as the childlike sex games the characters play become increasingly cruel and tinged with petty jealousies. Significantly, when Matthew is coerced into having sexual intercourse with the virginal Isabelle on the kitchen floor, Theo opens a window that lets in the sounds of street fighting and police sirens. A bit later Matthew tells Isabelle and Theo that their childlike sex games have to come to an end—that they need to grow up. Part of that process involves Matthew taking Isabelle on a "proper" date to the movies, but now the couple sit in the back of the theater finding pleasure in one another and not the images on the screen. (Bertolucci underscores the normative and even clichéd nature of their date by using an iris-in shot of Matthew and Isabelle sipping one soda with two straws) (see Figure 7.9). Over the course of the film, the dreamers' childlike world becomes increasingly untenable, as when they run out of money and are reduced to sorting through the garbage for something to eat. (Rotting food is another good example of the abject, something that once was whole and healthy that then becomes grotesque and vile) (see Figure 7.10). Theo is increasingly isolated from the trio as Isabelle and Matthew develop a normative sexual relationship; when Theo brings home a girl of his own, Isabelle suffers a jealous breakdown. Matthew and Theo have a conversation about the nature of the war in Vietnam and the leftist revolutions occurring around the globe: their disagreements have changed significantly from whether Charlie Chaplin is a better filmmaker than Buster Keaton, or whether Eric Clapton is a better guitar player than Jimi Hendrix. Matthew chides Theo for believing that revolutionary violence can change the world, and suggests that Theo may be somewhat selfish—expressing his love for mankind as a kind of private privileged experience within the (Imaginary) world of the apartment, rather than in the real (Symbolic) world.

All of these themes come to fruition in the film's final sequence. As a sort of last ditch effort to hold their Imaginary closeness together, Isabelle constructs an almost **Orientalist** tent-like structure out of pillows and blankets, and invites Matthew and Theo to join her in that sensuous space (along with several bottles of wine). But Isabelle's mistake is constructing her tent within the parent's zone of the apartment; her efforts are

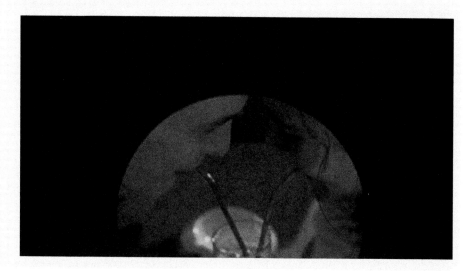

Fig 7.9
When Isabelle and Matthew go out on a "proper date," director Bernardo Bertolucci comments upon its clichéd nature with an "iris in" on the two sipping a drink.

Fig 7.10
More of the abject in *The Dreamers* (2003): what was once healthy food is now repulsive garbage.

doomed to fail because she is trying to recreate the Imaginary within her parents' always-already Symbolic zone (see Figure 7.11). The parents do return to the apartment the very next morning and see their children and Matthew passed out in the tent in various stages of undress; rather curiously, they write another check and tiptoe out of the apartment without waking the dreamers. Do they feel a certain nostalgia for their own younger selves? For the long lost pleasures of their own Imaginary desires? Or are their actions another comment on how that era's youthful counterculture (as represented by Matthew, Isabelle, and Theo) was often still dependent upon—and still a product of—white bourgeois privilege? Did that generation have the pleasure of rebelling and regressing—of dreaming of the Imaginary—only because their parents were paying for it? However one reads this scene, what happens next again underscores how the conditioning of the Symbolic is always-already inescapable. When Isabelle realizes her parents have discovered them, she retreats into shame and guilt—learned aspects of the Symbolic and not the Imaginary order. She turns on the gas and prepares to die in her tent, alongside Matthew and Theo, until the outside world once again comes crashing into the apartment:

Fig 7.11
In a last ditch effort to preserve the **Imaginary**, Isabelle builds a "pillow fort" for *The Dreamers* (2003); however, her quest is doomed since she builds it within her parents' **Symbolic** part of the apartment.

quite literally, a rock from the street fighting below is thrown through the window waking Matthew and Theo and ending Isabelle's suicide (and murder) attempt. All three dreamers take to the streets, and despite Matthew's efforts to coerce Theo and Isabelle away from fighting violence with violence, Theo and Isabelle succumb to the urge to fight fire with fire. Despite their attempts to find new (Imaginary) ways of relating to the world, they end up trapped in the Symbolic, using its own weapons, words, and structures against it.

The final shot of the film, as the credits roll, is a slow motion long shot of the rampaging riot squad headed straight towards the camera as they beat back the protestors (see Figure 7.12). The shot begs the spectator to consider the following questions: if the screen of the cinema is indeed a mirror of sorts, then are we expected to see ourselves in the jackbooted, patriarchal, violent police force? Do we have any other choice *but* to see ourselves in these images, if we (as members of civilized society) are always-already caught up in the Symbolic order? Regression to the Imaginary may be a necessary precursor for a dream of a better tomorrow, but is it really possible to change the world once one has become so thoroughly interpellated into it? Will the new revolutionary order truly be any different from the old oppressive one, especially if the old oppressive order is one that we have always-already internalized? Is social change even possible, and if it is, how does it happen? The British rock band The Who addressed many of these questions in their famous 1971 song "Won't Get Fooled Again," which concludes rather cynically with the line "Meet the New Boss—Same as the Old Boss." In other words, it may be somewhat easy to change the *names* of the people (or political parties) in charge of any given society, but changing the *hearts and minds* of people and parties—that is to say the ideologies and structures of dominance and meaning that give cohesion to any given society—may be a lot harder to accomplish.

Fig 7.12
The final shot of *The Dreamers* (2003): if the screen is in fact a mirror, have we all internalized our own marauding policemen?

Questions for discussion

1   What narrative feature films would you classify as overtly political? What sort of filmic style(s) do they make use of? Are they more formalist or realist? Are realist styles privileged by some filmmakers when trying to tell "serious" stories about political issues? Can you name some other films that could be classified as type (b)

films, *a la* Comolli and Narboni? What kind of filmic styles do you think are most effective for conveying political messages?

2   Think about the ways you yourself watch film and television. Do the different devices on which you watch—computers, cell phones, tablets, home theaters, etc.— significantly change your experience of a given text?

3   Contemporary cultural critics would agree with at least one aspect of *Screen* theory—namely that *all* film and television texts are political, even if they do not appear to be so on the surface of things. Pick several film and TV shows that many people might feel are apolitical, and discuss the political (ideological) messages they express.

References and further reading

Baudry, Jean-Louis. "Ideological Effects of the Basic Cinematographic Apparatus," in Bill Nichols, ed. *Movies and Methods Volume II*. Los Angeles: University of California Press, 1985 (1974). Pp. 531–42.

Cahiers du Cinema editors. "John Ford's *Young Mr. Lincoln*," *Cahiers du Cinema* 223 (1970).

Comolli, Jean-Louis and Jean Narboni. "Cinema/Ideology/Criticism," *Screen* 12:1 (Spring 1971), 27–36.

Dor, Joel. *Introduction to the Reading of Lacan: The Unconscious Structured like a Language*. New York: Other Press, 1998 (1985).

Easthope, Anthony, ed. *Contemporary Film Theory*. New York: Longman, 1993.

Harvey, Sylvia. *May '68 and Film Culture*. London: BFI Publishing, 1980.

Hill, Philip. *Lacan for Beginners*. Danbury, CT: For Beginners LLC, 1999 (1997).

Lacan, Jacques. *Ecrits: a Selection*. Trans. by Alan Sheridan. London: Routledge, 1989.

Lapsley, Robert and Michael Westlake. *Film Theory: An Introduction*. Manchester: Manchester University Press, 1988.

Metz, Christian. *The Imaginary Signifier: Psychoanalysis and the Cinema*. Bloomington, IN: Indiana University Press, 1986.

Rosen, Philip. *Narrative, Apparatus, Ideology*. New York: Columbia University Press, 1986.

Rushton, Richard and Gary Bettinson. *What is Film Theory?* New York: Open University Press, 2010.

Silverman, Kaja. *The Subject of Semiotics*. New York: Oxford University Press, 1983.

CHAPTER 8

Feminist approaches to film and television

Like many of the other concepts explored in this volume, **feminism** is a much-discussed and much-contested term. To put it simply, feminism means different things to different people in different times and places. For some (like this author) it means the basic idea that men and women ought to be treated equally in all aspects of culture. A more theoretical approach might be to say that feminism is a critique of inequality based on one's biological **sex** or **gender** expression; in most places in the world today, men have more opportunities, more rights and privileges, and more freedoms than do women. Feminism is thus a critique of **patriarchy**, literally "rule by the father." Patriarchy is a term used broadly in feminist theory to describe the various **overdetermined ideologies** that keep men in socially dominant positions. That said, for some people feminism represents a challenge (or even a threat) to traditional ways of thinking about men and women, sex and sexuality, the structure of the family, and the structure of the work place.

The feminism that most Westerners are probably somewhat familiar with arose in the 1960s and 1970s. Following that, many scholars and critics saw a period of cultural reaction to the women's movement, a reaction most famously described as a "backlash" by Susan Faludi in her book of the same name. What that meant was that during the 1980s and 1990s, many conservative critics and pundits began to demonize the women's movement, coining inflammatory terms such as "Femi-Nazi" and "National Organization of Witches" (instead of the National Organization of Women). In the United States, the ERA (Equal Rights Amendment)—which had been written to insure federal equality regardless of an individual's sex—had been passed by both houses of Congress in 1972, but by the 1980s it failed to be ratified by the requisite number of state legislatures. Clearly, in ten years the national mood had changed significantly. In general, the 1980s did see a rise in more conservative cultural politics across many different sectors of society; indeed, the backlash to the idea of women deserving equal rights with men was even successful enough to make many people wary of using the term "feminism" itself. Feminism had been rebranded from a movement meant to open up and equalize opportunities for everyone (whether male or female), into something that many people saw as "man hating," "male bashing," or destructive of traditional "family values." When the term was co-opted, the ideas that it signified were similarly co-opted, or even silenced, and many people refused even to speak the word let alone self-identify as feminists.

Feminism is also a tricky topic for many people because sex roles are so intimate to our daily lives: **sex** (that is to say, whether one is male or female) has a biological basis, and is central to very personal concepts of identity, sexuality, and one's place in society. Indeed, one of the more famous slogans of **second wave feminism** was "the personal is the political," which means that discrimination based on sex is perhaps more subtle and private than that based on race or ethnicity or class. For example, bias based on sex was and still is pervasive in the work place, in politics, in schools, and in the media, but it also takes place within allegedly private or interpersonal spheres, such as marriage, the family, and religious belief systems. Furthermore, the ideas and ideals of feminism have much more impact upon our daily lives than do concepts of **auteur theory** or **genre theory**. As such, many more people have some understanding of what feminism means than they do **poststructuralism**, primarily because it has become such a pervasive personal, public, and politicized issue in recent decades. Another way of saying this is that ideological biases based on sex or gender expression are heavily **overdetermined** in Western nations and Western cultural artifacts. Arguably, they are embedded in every single cultural institution in which human subjects—as distinct entities termed men and women—participate. And since bias based on sex permeates so many different ideological structures and social institutions, it may be "harder" for some people to see and acknowledge than other forms of discrimination.

Most of us live intimately (if not unconsciously) with dominant notions of sex and **gender** (see below), having been assigned one of two possible sex identities at a very early age. Even individuals who have one of the many biological conditions that can cause ambiguous sexual characteristics (conditions broadly termed as **intersex** syndromes), usually find themselves forced to accede in daily life to one of two strikingly different sex/gender categories. Similarly, people who identify as **transsexual** or **transgender** often face a great amount of psychic and often physical violence in many cultures, a fact that suggests how overly charged the issue of sex and/or gender is for many people. Indeed, sex is one of the most fundamental structuring binaries of Western culture (if not all global cultures), and as such it is one of the hardest to pull apart or **deconstruct**. Like all linguistic and structural binaries, the allegedly opposite terms of sex and/or gender (male/female, masculinity/femininity) are defined against one another, and one term is culturally privileged (in this case male/masculinity is more culturally valued than is female/femininity). Even when these terms can be shown to overlap—whether in biological cases of intersex conditions or the simple observation that men can have (what are thought to be) feminine qualities and women can have (what are thought to be) masculine qualities—Western culture continually asserts an opposing (and to a great extent mutually exclusive) definition of sex and gender. If being masculine is thought to entail strength, stoicism, and aggression (as in the common phrase "boys don't cry"), being feminine is defined in opposing terms: delicacy, emotionality, and passivity.

Further complicating feminist studies (let alone feminist media studies) is the number of diverse ways feminists themselves have sought to label, classify, and define the movement. For example, it is now common to speak of three different "waves" of feminism, and over the years the broad movement has given rise to myriad approaches variously labeled radical feminism, cultural feminism, bourgeois feminism, Marxist feminism, **womanism**, and poststructuralist feminism, among many, many more. Feminism also means different things dependent upon nation or region. One of the goals of contemporary Western feminism might be attaining equal pay for equal work, while in other regions of the globe feminism might be about trying to end the legal beating and rape (or even murder) of women by their own family members. As such, feminism really ought to be considered *feminisms*. And as we shall see, even within film and television studies, there are different approaches to and applications of feminist theory—some of them are firmly rooted in cultural studies methodologies, while one particularly rich vein of feminist film theory has drawn on various psychoanalytic and structuralist approaches associated with **apparatus theory**. Additionally, feminism intersects with just about every other issue discussed in this volume, from the study of authorship (**auteur theory**), to genre, to fandom/reception practices, and to thinking about race and nation. This chapter explores ideas and concepts germane to **second wave feminism** and the rise of feminist film and television theory during those same decades, roughly the 1960s–1980s. Chapter 12 will explore in greater detail some of the theoretical shifts in thinking about gender and sexuality that have come to be defined more recently as **third wave feminism**.

Basic terms and concepts

At its basis—whichever variation we choose to single out and focus on—**feminism** might best be described as a critique of the diverse inequities created and maintained in various human cultures based on biological sex. As such, feminism is an ideological critique, and owes a great deal to concepts first developed within Marxism. Recall that **Marxism** sought to expose and challenge social inequities created and maintained by class; feminism seeks to expose and challenge social inequities created and maintained by sex and/or gender. However, the cultural critic is immediately faced with a series of essentialist dilemmas that the use of the terms **sex** and/or **gender** create. In popular usage, sex and gender are used somewhat interchangeably, but feminist theory has attempted to clarify matters by assigning sex and gender different (but related) definitions. Thus, the term **sex** is used to refer to the differing biological characteristics of men and women, whether they be chromosomal, hormonal, and/or physical. Biologists define sex (or sexual) characteristics as either **primary** (based on sexual organs and their reproductive functions) or **secondary** (based on other physical features such as breast development or facial hair). **Gender**, on the other hand, is emphatically not biological—it is social and cultural. Gender refers to the complex and diverse ways that people are treated (or choose to behave) based on their biological sex. In many places throughout recent Western culture, individuals of the female sex were expected to express their gender by being demure and passive, speaking softly, freely expressing emotion and sentiment, all the while maintaining a (private) home and raising children. At the same time, individuals of the male sex were expected to express their gender by being strong, assertive, stoic, and to earn a good living in a (public) venue, in order to support the wife and kids back home.

The tricky issue then becomes: where does one draw the line between sex and gender? Which aspects of **masculinity** and **femininity** (terms usually descriptive of gender rather than sex) are biologically determined, and which are purely social constructs? We might agree that lactation and nursing babies have a basis in biological sex, whereas the fact that Western women are expected to wear make-up and high heels is a facet of their playing a social role, that is to say gender. But what about a quality like leadership? Leadership is usually linked to traditionally masculine gender roles: is there something biological in male humans (and allegedly lacking in human females) that gives rise to superior leadership skills? People who believe there is something biological about leadership skills (or the lack thereof) might be best described as **gender essentialists**. An **essentialist** approach to gender suggests that since there are significant differences between male and female biology, those differences "naturally" give rise to the social roles (or genders) enacted by men and women. There are many men (and even women) who fall into this gender essentialist camp, people who believe that biology is destiny, that qualities such as aggression and/or passivity are linked primarily (if not solely) to one's biological make up. However, there are also many men and women who support an opposing, more socially-determined view of gender: these people might be broadly termed **gender anti-essentialists**, or more commonly **anti-essentialist feminists.** The anti-essentialist approach to gender suggests that even if there are biological differences between men and women, they are insignificant compared to the social, linguistic, and structural conditioning that each human being receives about gender from the moment they are born. Thus, while an essentialist feminist might argue that (biological) sex gives rise to (socio-cultural) gender expressions, an anti-essentialist feminist might argue the reverse: that it is the gender roles we enact socially and culturally that determine what sex we are perceived as being.

Recent feminist approaches have also shifted their emphases away from what might be termed "Women's Studies" and towards a more inclusive area of research termed "Gender Studies." The newer terminology suggests that masculinity is just as culturally constructed as is femininity, and that although the roles men are expected to play within most given cultures usually privilege them over female roles, such masculine roles might in their own way be constrictive and even unhealthy. For example, men in Western cultures tend to die at earlier ages than do women; but is that because of biological differences (sex) or the social roles they are expected to perform (gender)? According to traditional Western gender roles, men are expected to be aggressive (and even violent) risk takers. Is reckless behavior something encoded into male DNA (a biologically essentialist belief), or is it something that men in Western societies learn to enact as part of being masculine (a more social-constructionist, anti-essentialist belief)? These questions are important ones to ask, and some cultural critics today would probably argue that they require a "both/and" answer rather than an "either/or" approach. In other words, some scholars argue that biology does contribute to certain aspects of our sexual and/or gendered identity, but so do the complex cultural environments within which we exist.

Furthermore, it is patently obvious that genders are expressed in many different ways depending on a multitude of cultural variables. History, nation, region, class, religion, etc. all impact on how a given individual's sex (male or female) is expressed through his/her gender role (masculinity or femininity); this basic observation lends considerable credence to the anti-essentialist model of gender. To give a few brief examples, women who follow Judeo-Christian religious traditions rarely wear *burqas*, the enveloping head-to-toe garment that women in certain Islamic communities are expected to wear as a matter of course. Similarly, some masculinities in the Middle East allow for heterosexual men to hold hands, a sign of gender expression that would probably be interpreted in the West as homosexual. In yet another example, in the United States it is usually considered important for women to shave their legs and under their arms before they present themselves publically; this is less the case in Europe and other regions of the world. Masculinity in the West has also undergone various changes in recent decades: many young men now sport unshaven faces and tattoos, expressions of gender for which their fathers and grandfathers rarely opted (unless they were **working class** sailors).

It is self-evident that gender roles fluctuate: they differ in various historical eras, and they differ from region to region, nation to nation, community to community, family to family, father to son, and mother to daughter. The ideal Western gender roles of the 1950s—briefly sketched above with the (private) stay-at-home Mom and the (public) working Dad—are for many people today an economic impossibility, even as they may still be considered desirable goals by some people. However, such an ideal was out of reach even in the 1950s for many American families, based on other social factors such as class or race. For example, the racism of pre-civil rights America caused many white business owners to deny jobs to black men (who would also have had a very hard time attaining the education necessary for white collar jobs), forcing many black women to become the breadwinners of their families. In a famous bit of racial/racist "science" reflecting this history, sociologist Daniel Patrick Moynihan's 1965 report *The Negro Family: The Case for National Action* (also known as the Moynihan Report) more or less blamed the lower class status and outright poverty of many African American families not on the socioeconomic impact of the era's institutionalized racism, but rather on black families' allegedly disordered gender relations. The point to remember here is that gender does not exist as a discrete category: in any given society it is deeply intertwined with other social factors like class, race, ethnicity, regionality, sexuality, and so forth.

To return to another basic feminist critique, across much of the globe human societies have tended to be male dominated, or patriarchal. Most Judeo-Christian religions proscribe different roles for men and women, allowing men positions of leadership denied to women. The traditional Western nuclear family, as described above, also sets out different tasks for men and women, and places the male as the head of the family. Because most white middle-class men worked outside the home (while white women were contained within), men were expected to become involved in social organizations like politics and business associations—to lead local, state, and federal governments. Because men as a group were perceived as stronger and more aggressive than women, they led state militias and staffed most of the Armed Services. They also comprised most of the sports teams and much of the audience for spectator sports. And as is also historically apparent, the film and television industries were mostly staffed by male producers, directors, agents, and studio moguls; the images of men and women they constructed in their media texts tended to reflect their eras' patriarchal assumptions about sex and gender. Classical Hollywood narrative form itself is usually structured around an active male protagonist and a more passive female love interest. Television genres and formats are perhaps less proscriptive when it comes to gender (because they are more diverse than Hollywood narrative filmmaking), but TV too finds ways to differentiate between men and women and suggest what type of gender expressions are possible for each. Again, it is important to remember that film and television are **ideological state apparatuses** that work to maintain the status quo of dominant ideology; in the case of gender, much film and television tends to uphold the dominance of patriarchy, interlocking with other ideological state institutions like religion, sports, and the government that do the same. To quote feminist and anti-racist cultural critic bell hooks's famous turn of phrase, "Patriarchy has no gender." To critique patriarchy is not to attack men. Patriarchy is instead an **overdetermined** ideological structure that pervades most global cultures, shaping—some might say deforming—the many ways we think about men and women.

First and second wave feminism: Impact on film and television

As noted above, it is commonplace (albeit overly simplistic) to speak of three broad historical eras or "waves" of feminism in the West. Partly this is because feminist activism has been thought to wax and wane according to other social forces, such as the Great Depression and World War II, both of which occurred between the first and second waves of feminism, somewhat "interrupting" the development of feminist thought as more pressing struggles were met. (Of course, World War II greatly contributed to the feminist movement in its own way, as women were encouraged to enter the work force in unprecedented numbers in order to bolster the war effort.) **First wave feminism** refers to the struggles surrounding sex and/or gender inequities that occurred in the late nineteenth and early twentieth centuries, actions and struggles centered on issues such as women's rights to vote, to enter professional careers, frequent public spaces, receive birth control information, and even smoke cigarettes. (In the United States, many first wave feminists were also involved in the temperance movement which led to the era of Prohibition [1920–33].) **Second wave feminism** describes the feminist actions and struggles of the 1960s and 1970s; in many ways, second wave feminism was part of the broader countercultural and civil rights movements of that era, and its goals included freeing up access to birth control, legalizing abortion, and continuing to fight for equal access to education and jobs. **Third wave feminism** arose roughly in the 1990s, and is primarily a shift in ways scholars think about gender and sexuality. Third wave feminism is perceived as moving beyond the (frequently) essentialist, bourgeois, white, and heterosexual shortsightedness of much second wave feminism. Incorporating concepts drawn from structuralist and poststructuralist theory, such as the social and linguistic construction of gender, third wave feminism suggests that all qualities of gender (like female passivity and male aggression) are creations of the linguistic and mediated structures within which we are born. While many second wave feminists may have accepted an essentialist, biological explanation for female passivity and/or male aggression, third wave feminists do not. Their position is that the culture and media that surrounds us teaches us to be masculine or feminine, that being male or female really has very little to do with biology. Third wave feminism is thus considered an **anti-essentialist feminism**.

Obviously, there was very little scholarship about film and television during feminism's first wave; after all, TV would not be an important cultural artifact until the late 1940s/early 1950s, and films were seen by many as nothing but a cultural curiosity. However, feminist thinking about media was an integral part of film studies as it matured or came of age in the 1960s; the feminist scholarship about television that soon followed helped expand "film studies" into "film and television studies" more generally. As such, feminist approaches to film and TV were vital to the expansion of the discipline throughout the 1970s, and multiple books, journals, conferences, and film festivals were increasingly devoted to topics exploring gender in the media. Recall that much early film theory was comprised of basic auteur and genre approaches; as such, a generation of second wave feminist film scholars began to explore gender in connection to those approaches. Pioneering female film directors like Lois Weber, Alice Guy-Blaché, Dorothy Arzner, and Ida Lupino were rescued from the dustbin of (male-written) film history, as feminist film theorists began to ask questions like "What does it mean to be a female auteur?" Female screenwriters (Anita Loos, Frances Marion), actresses (Mae West, Katharine Hepburn), and actress/moguls (Mary Pickford) were reclaimed as important feminists, women who worked within—and frequently challenged—the male dominated world of classical (and pre-classical) Hollywood cinema. One of the central goals of this earlier feminist film scholarship was to rewrite the canon of film history, to go in search of women's voices throughout the history of the medium, in order to investigate and explore their (previously overlooked) importance. And as film studies became film and television studies, scholars focused on other powerful women in the media industries. A small sampling might include Lucille Ball (who with her husband Desi Arnaz owned her own TV studio, Desilu Studios) as well as Irna Phillips and Agnes Nixon, who, respectively, created the long-running soap operas *As the World Turns* (1956–2010) and *All My Children* (1970–2011). Other more recent figures of feminist inquiry have included Mary Tyler Moore (a force in 1970s television production via her MTM Enterprises), and Roseanne Barr, whose "unruly woman" persona challenged patriarchal assumptions about femaleness and femininity in the 1990s.

Other second wave feminists turned their analytical tools towards Hollywood film genres, noting how most film genres were (and still are) centered on men: the war film, the western, the gangster film, comedy, science fiction, horror, film noir, etc. On the other hand, female genres in Hollywood are so rare they have to be singled out and named as such: the classical era's **woman's film** or **melodrama**, a format that has more or less evolved into today's **chick flick**. It is a given (even today) that most Hollywood films center on a male protagonist and relegate women to the roles of love/sex interest (or occasionally the villain). As such, women's stereotyped roles in Hollywood film can often be easily described in terms of the **virgin/whore dichotomy** (also known as the **Madonna/whore dichotomy**). As the later term suggests, this split is central to Western culture and Christianity in general; it tends to reduce a woman's subjectivity onto a singular aspect of her being—her sexuality. As this virgin/whore discourse frames and shapes femininity, women are either "good girls" who abstain from sex (the virgin, the Madonna, or the Mother whose sexuality is contained and controlled by patriarchal structures like the church and the family), or they are the "bad girls" who are sexually active (the whore, the femme fatale, the "tragic **mulatto**"). In Hollywood genre filmmaking, virgins range from the sheriff's wife or farmer's daughter in the western to the just-married heroine of the classical horror film. The whores in both of those genres, respectively, are the saloon keeper with a heart of gold (a Hollywood euphemism for prostitute), or else countless sexualized monsters like those found in *The Vampire Lovers* (1970) or *Species* (1995). It is easy to find remnants of the virgin–whore dichotomy configuring representations of women in multiple Hollywood genres, as well as in specific filmic contexts. For example, the trope also lingers in the formula of the slasher film—wherein sexually active teenage girls are killed for their transgressions while the asexual "final girl" defeats the killer.

Perhaps unsurprisingly, second wave feminist film theorists focused on the ways that the so-called **woman's film** (or Hollywood **melodrama)** did or did not offer up spaces for feminist critique. Do the films inure women to their status as suffering and sacrificial second class citizens, cathartically allowing them a good cry at the movies even as they must then return home to less-than-blissful marriages? Or do the films present a critique of the patriarchal structures (marriage, family, lack of work opportunities) that so entrap and enclose women? Do today's chick flicks embrace and celebrate female bonding and independence, or do they merely chronicle the proper way for a young woman to find her Mr. Right? (Those questions might best be answered on a film by film basis, although even today it is difficult for most feminist critics—myself included—to label most mainstream films or TV shows as in any way feminist. Instead, most popular culture seems to negotiate nervously with patriarchy in **hegemonic** ways, perhaps lightly tweaking patriarchal assumptions while simultaneously shoring up its dominance.) Film noir was also a topic of interest for second wave feminist film scholars, as its images of femme fatales ("spider women") seemed both stereotypical—villainous women using their sexuality to lure men to their doom—as well as potentially empowering. Important work on TV soon followed the film scholarship: for example, Tania Modleski's *Loving With a Vengeance: Mass Produced Fantasies for Women* was among the first feminist works of scholarship to take seriously Harlequin romances and the TV soap opera, "low art" forms deemed by most to be unworthy of consideration. The work of Modleski (and many others in this mode) helped mount a critique of the "high art" bias still found in much of the era's film and television scholarship; it helped open up a broader range of film and TV texts for scholarly study, as did cultural studies in general.

Among the most important work of second wave film critics and scholars— partly because much of it was widely distributed via mass market paperback books—partakes of what has been called basic **image** (or **stereotype) analysis**, a form of structuralist content analysis designed to reveal persistent patterns and character motifs within Hollywood filmmaking. As such, image analysis can be and has been performed on many different filmic subgroups, such as Irish Americans, Native Americans, gay men and lesbians, etc. The scholarship mentioned above focusing on the virgin–whore dichotomy is a good example of second wave feminist image analysis. Other important image analyses of women from this era include Marjorie Rosen's *Popcorn Venus: Women, Movies & the American Dream* and Molly Haskell's *From Reverence to Rape: The Treatment of Women in the Movies*. Each book reviewed hundreds of Hollywood films and revealed a cinematic history of vamps, princesses, long-suffering mothers, and mad women—each often some variation of the virgin or the whore. Haskell's book also celebrated the strong female characters of the classical Hollywood cinema (those played by Mae West, Barbara Stanwyck, Bette Davis, Joan Crawford, etc.) but noted how they were co-opted or contained by the generic imperatives of film noir or the woman's film. Haskell lamented the mid-1960s demise of the Hollywood Production Code because she felt it had been useful in the creation of complex female characters. When the Code fell, she argued, male producers simply opted for more sex and violence, replacing the strong women found in previous eras' musicals, screwball comedies, and women's films with nubile actress-models whose chief attribute was their pneumatic sexuality. Haskell further argued that despite the rise of second wave feminism, Hollywood in the 1960s and 1970s had failed to keep up; instead, they tended to offer images suggestive of first wave feminism, as in the period musicals *Mary Poppins* (1964), *Funny Girl* (1968), and *Star!* (1968). (Compare this to the somewhat analogous Hollywood films *The Butler* [2013] and *Selma* [2014], released some sixty years after the civil rights movement occurred.) Haskell went so far as to accuse male Hollywood of not knowing how to create realistic or complex female characters at all, citing a slew of buddy movies (or male-male love stories, as she called them) such as *Butch Cassidy and the Sundance Kid* (1969), *Midnight Cowboy* (1969), and *The Sting* (1973): in those films women are relegated to marginal female love interests, or absent all together.

Throughout the 1970s and 1980s, feminist film and television scholars continued to explore gender in relation to a wide range of texts and industrial contexts. Lynn Spigel explored how television became a ubiquitous household appliance in the 1950s, and what that development had to tell us about gender during the postwar era. By the 1990s, it was not unusual to find feminist work being done on any and all manner of film and TV shows, from "quality television" to *I Dream of Jeannie* (1965–70), and from the Home Shopping Network to the nightly news. Shows that seem skewed toward women in their approach (such as *Cagney & Lacey* [1981–8]) also came in for close scrutiny, as did the rise of music videos and the phenomenal popularity of the pop singer Madonna. In short, there is no area of film and television studies that cannot be investigated in terms of gender and sexuality. And as third wave feminism arose in the academy in the 1990s, it began to redress some of the shortcomings it perceived in second wave feminism, primarily by acknowledging the diversity of women's experiences. Today it is not good enough to assume that all women respond to the same texts in the same way, a naïve and (essentialist) assumption of some second wave feminist thinking. Today feminist media theorists including bell hooks, Gloria Anzaldua, Cherríe Moraga, B. Ruby Rich, Diane Negra, Mary Kearney and many others insist on the diversity of women's experiences of and representation within film and television texts, specifically seeing gender as imbricated in other forms of social difference such as class, race/ethnicity, regionality, nation, age, and sexuality. But before we return to those concerns (in Chapter 12), we must first examine the incredible impact psychoanalysis had upon second wave feminist film theory.

Laura Mulvey: Psychoanalysis, apparatus theory, and gender

One of the most important feminist interventions in film studies occurred in 1975, when Laura Mulvey published her landmark essay "Visual Pleasure and Narrative Cinema" within the pages of *Screen* magazine. While much feminist media scholarship up to that time (like Molly Haskell's) had been focused on the *content* of Hollywood films (and to a lesser extent the content of European art cinema), Mulvey's essay focused on the patriarchal nature of Hollywood *form* itself. Mulvey's essay shifted the scholarly discussion away from how Hollywood films represented gender, by arguing that Hollywood form itself can be thought of as gendered, and more precisely gendered male. Drawing on then-prevalent theories of the cinematic apparatus (see Chapter 7), including its use of psychoanalysis to theorize the pleasures of looking (**scopophilia**) and the construction of the cinematic spectator, Mulvey persuasively argued that Hollywood form was designed to speak to and/

or appease the male unconscious. She examined the different pleasurable looks that Hollywood cinema affords its spectators, and concluded that they were all male. For example, Mulvey argued that the **narcissistic gaze** encourages the spectator to identify with the central male character on screen. The **voyeuristic gaze**, which looks at human bodies on screen in an erotic or libidinal way, is also male, since it is the female body that is usually **objectified** or put on sexualized display for the male (character, camera, and audience member). As Mulvey puts it,

> As the spectator identifies with the main male protagonist, he projects his look on to that of his like, his screen surrogate, so that the power of the male protagonist as he controls events coincides with the active power of the erotic look, both giving a satisfying sense if omnipotence.
>
> (720)

Regardless of the genre or individual film text, Mulvey suggests that Hollywood narrative form (its storytelling mechanisms as well as its editing, lighting, framing, etc.) creates a situation in which man is the bearer of the look, and woman is that object to-be-looked-at. As such, Hollywood cinema constructs and facilitates a specifically patriarchal way of seeing, a way of seeing that has come to be called the **male gaze**.

Mulvey's essay pointed out how Hollywood cinema is comprised of three specific "types of looks" that make up the working mechanism of cinema: (1) the look of the camera on the sound stage that records the actors as they perform their characters, (2) the looks of the diegetic characters at other diegetic characters and things, and (3) the look of the spectator in the audience watching the screen. Noting that much of classical Hollywood cinema was shot by men (look 1), and that male protagonists are more likely to be given point-of-view shots than are female characters (look 2), Mulvey argued that in classical Hollywood syntax the spectator is also assumed to be male, regardless of his or her actual gender (look 3). Indeed, each of these three looks is exactly the same when a male protagonist is given a point of view shot: the male camera's look (1) is the same as the male character's look (2), forcing the spectator's look (3) to be aligned quite literally with that of the (male) camera and (male) character. (Recall that within *Screen* or **apparatus theory**, the spectator refers more to a place in the cinematic machinery than an actual human being) (see Figures 8.1 and 8.2). As such, even "real" women in the audience are forced to look through the eyes of the male filmmakers and male characters, especially as the men (filmmakers and characters) look at other women with desire. In a later article, Mulvey suggests that women in the audience have only two very limited choices when confronted with the dynamics of the male gaze: either to identify against her own gender (aligning her gaze with the male camera and characters), or else to identify with the women on screen who are presented as less than human subjects—literally sexual objects of the libidinal male gaze.

But that is not the end of the story for Mulvey, because even as Hollywood form and the male gaze work to frame women as glamorous, sexualized, and on display, "in psychoanalytic terms the female figure poses a deeper problem. She also connotes something that the look continually circles around but disavows: her lack of penis, implying a threat of castration and hence unpleasure" (721). Mulvey suggests this threat is dealt with in two ways within classical Hollywood cinema:

Fig 8.1
In *I Am a Fugitive From a Chain Gang* (1932)—or almost any classical
Hollywood film—an objective shot of the protagonist looking ...

Fig 8.2
... is immediately followed by a subjective shot of what he is looking at,
suturing everyone in the audience into the "male gaze" at the female body.

either through narratives which sadistically investigate and punish women (and
the mystery they represent), or through **fetishistic scopophilia**, in which the
onscreen woman is literally turned into a collection of objectified and fetishized
body parts that work to cover over the threat of castration caused by an actual
female subject. Mulvey cites the generic narratives of film noir and the work of
Alfred Hitchcock as prime examples of the first mechanism. Many mysteries and
hard-boiled detective fictions, as well as Hitchcock films like *Vertigo* (1958) and
Marnie (1964), are about little more than a male protagonist's obsessive drive to
investigate and observe (through the male gaze) the enigmatic mystery of a woman.
And as far as **fetishization** goes, just about any classical Hollywood musical
number or more recent music video contains fetishized close up shots of women's
body parts, part of a sexualized male fantasy world constructed by (usually male)
singers/songwriters and film and video makers. Laura Mulvey's ideas about the
male gaze have been tremendously influential in film studies; her "Visual Pleasure
and Narrative Cinema" became one of the most frequently anthologized essays
within the discipline. That said, her ideas—like much of apparatus theory itself—
have also been critiqued as essentialist and reductive. One of the first problems
that arises is how monolithic and overwhelming the idea of the male gaze is (or
became) for some theorists. Based upon the proposition that all Hollywood films—
Screen theory's **classical realist texts**—inherently construct a male subject position,
every Hollywood narrative film whether it be *Rambo: First Blood Part II* (1985) or
Norma Rae (1979) automatically exploits and reinscribes the male gaze. Because
of this assertion, Mulvey's essay called for an end to narrative (Hollywood) cinema
and challenged filmmakers to find new ways of making films that would not speak
(solely) to the male unconscious. As such, her essay did spur a vibrant feminist
avant-garde film culture throughout the 1970s and 1980s, of which Mulvey's own
film *Riddles of the Sphinx* (1979) remains exemplary. Other important feminist films
that were created in response to the essay (either in whole or in part) include Sally
Potter's *Thriller* (1979), Michelle Citron's *Daughter Rite* (1979), Lizzie Borden's *Born
in Flames* (1983), as well as works by Barbara Hammer, Ulrike Ottinger, Chantal
Akerman, and Yvonne Rainer.

Indeed, Mulvey's essay arguably inspired a generation of experimental filmmakers (both men and women) to seek out new ways to tell stories and make films. Like some experimental writers before them, some of those filmmakers went in search of what has been called **écriture féminine**, a practice of female writing (or female filmmaking) meant to transcend or exist outside of **phallogocentric** language systems (like Hollywood narrative form). While many fascinating films and videos were made in this tradition, their experimental nature foreclosed the possibility of their crossing over into a larger, more mainstream audience. Furthermore, the whole project of creating or defining a female language (or **discourse**) rests upon questionably essentialist assumptions: do men and women really make films (or write novels) differently, based on their biological and/or social conditioning? If so, is there one proper form or style of female writing (or female filmmaking) to which all women are supposed to adhere? And perhaps more problematically, if we are already always caught up in phallogocentric language systems from the moment we are born, is it even possible to "get outside" of that system and imagine something new?

The case of a more popular female filmmaker like Sofia Coppola may be somewhat illuminating in these respects. Coppola's films—including *The Virgin Suicides* (1999), *Lost in Translation* (2003), *Marie Antoinette* (2006), *Somewhere* (2010), and *The Bling Ring* (2013)—do seem to mount a challenge to usual Hollywood style: they often feature dream-like and/or anachronistic elements, and often center less on narrative occurrences and more on aimless or "lost" characters as they struggle to make sense of the world around them. But should Coppola's auteur signature necessarily be considered a feminine or female auteur signature? It might be somewhat different from normative Hollywood style—and that different style may open up spaces to express new types of ideas, including feminist ones— but clearly male directors can and do make films in styles similar to Coppola's. Similarly, there are female directors in Hollywood who make mainstream action films that are indistinguishable from those directed by men. In a perfect world, filmmakers of all genders and races could make films and videos about whatever subject matter they wanted, in whatever styles they chose. However, trying to find and classify a female film and video aesthetic, or an African American or Chicano film and video aesthetic, or even a **New Queer** aesthetic is a problematic and potentially reductive project, reducing the complexity of any given filmmaker to one essentialized element of his or her race, gender, or sexuality.

Laura Mulvey's landmark essay had far less impact on mainstream Hollywood film practice—let alone television, which her essay did not address—than it did on media scholarship and experimental filmmaking. If anything, films that play to an overtly libidinal male unconscious are arguably more prevalent today than they were during the classical era, while everything from "soups to nuts" is advertised with images of near-naked young women used to entice the heterosexual male gaze. Mulvey's thinking may have also fallen out of favor somewhat as the essentialist aspects of apparatus theory were more generally replaced by poststructuralist and cultural studies approaches in the 1980s and 1990s. However, Mulvey's thoughts on the dynamics of **objectification** (if not her revolutionary call for a women's experimental cinema that would challenge Hollywood's dominance) can and do continue to illuminate thinking about gender in film and television texts. This dynamic remains an important one to consider when analyzing film and television texts, but there is also the need to look at texts and contexts more carefully.

Some of the more interesting scholarship to follow after Mulvey's explores the objectification of *male* bodies on screen. The display of the male body onscreen was far less common during the classical era of Hollywood than it is today; in that era, male bodies were usually meant to signify strength and stoicism, especially during action and/or torture sequences (unlike female bodies, which were usually presented as sexualized spectacle, unimportant to the narrative information). However, since the 1980s, men's bodies have become increasingly objectified in Western cultures, in both advertising and in film and television. Some films, like *300* (2006), use CGI to fetishize their male characters' bodies, but do so mostly in accordance with earlier Hollywood practices that showcase the male body in order to dramatize its power and virility (and thus uphold its patriarchal privilege). Other films like *Magic Mike* (2012) present the dancing male body as more of a sexualized spectacle, without the narrative action sequences as "camouflage." One even earlier film that subverted (by inverting) the dynamics of the male gaze was *Thelma & Louise* (1991), during the scene in which a shirtless J. D. (Brad Pitt) poses seductively for Thelma (Geena Davis). Shot as a series of shot-reverse-shots exchanges from Thelma's point of view, the film sutures its audience into Thelma's libidinal gaze at J. D., just as a Hollywood film might have sutured a libidinal gaze at Marilyn Monroe into that of her male co-star (and by extension the male spectator) (see Figures 8.3 and 8.4). Some feminist theorists insist that this example of objectification should still be considered an example of the male gaze in action,

Fig 8.3
In *Thelma & Louise* (1991), the dynamics of the male gaze are reversed, with Thelma (Geena Davis) doing the looking ...

Fig 8.4
... at the objectified body of J. D. (Brad Pitt).

even though it is a woman gazing at a man; if so, this then creates a homosexual or homoerotic effect that can be potentially threatening to a heterosexual male spectator, now forced to gaze with desire at the body of another man. But why can it not also be a female heterosexual gaze, which is clearly what is occurring within the diegesis?

Rather than claiming that any sexually objectifying gaze is necessarily male, some scholars suggest that it is the camera which does the objectifying, and that the sex of the person holding the camera, or doing the looking within the diegesis, does make a difference. The gaze might be better thought of as multiple and varied, depending upon who is doing the photographing, the sexes of the characters involved in the scene, and the actual audience members watching it. In the example above from *Thelma & Louise*, reversing the genders involved in the traditional voyeuristic gaze has the ability to unseat and destabilize it, not merely replicate it. The editing patterns of classical Hollywood style that create and encourage spectators' gazes—whether they be narcissistic, voyeuristic or fetishistic— have been endemic to Western visual cultures for over one hundred years (if not longer). John Berger's important volume *Ways of Seeing* documents these tropes as far back as the work of Renaissance figure painters. They are probably not going to go away in the near future. The point is to be aware of them, and like any aspect of film or televisual style, continue to find new ways of working with them, tweaking them, amending them, if not forthrightly replacing them. As the people making film and television texts continue to diversify in terms of gender, so will the stories they tell hopefully diversify, as well as the ways in which those stories are told. And feminist cultural critics will be there to observe, comment, and critique.

Case Study 1: *The Magdalene Sisters* (2002)

Different critics and scholars often have different interpretations of what exactly might constitute a "feminist film" or a "feminist TV" show. Today, many texts appear to speak to certain feminist issues but ultimately still seem to support dominant patriarchal ideologies in various ways (as in an actual episode of *The View* [1997–] devoted to breast augmentation strategies). Perhaps a better question to ask rather than the (quite essentialist) question "Is this a feminist text or not?" is "In what ways does this text negotiate with dominant patriarchal ideologies about sex roles?" Or: "What does this text reveal about social inequities based on gender?" When asking those types of questions, film and TV analysis becomes more nuanced and more productive, and allows the cultural critic to examine a wider range of texts than those only written and directed by women, or those made within a self-proclaimed feminist avant-garde movement. Of course it is important to have "Women Make Movies," as the name of one feminist film/video distribution outlet would have it. However, women can make movies in line with dominant patriarchal ideologies just as men can; likewise, it is more than possible for a man to make a film that has important things to say about gender and female oppression. *The Magdalene Sisters*—though written and directed by Peter Mullan, and centering on the victimization of women—is exactly that sort of film.

The Magdalene Sisters is an independent film made in Scotland but set in County Dublin, Ireland during the mid-1960s. Though a work of fiction, the film is based on the actual accounts of women who were incarcerated in that era's Magdalene asylums, a sort of social refuge/convent/workhouse system created by and controlled by the Catholic church. (The more recent film *Philomena* [2013] is also about the abuses women suffered within the Magdalene asylum system.) Peter Mullan's film dramatizes the brutal mistreatment that many young women suffered in those places, and how that era's patriarchal institutions (including the family, religion, business, and local community governance) worked together in ideologically **overdetermined** ways to maintain and legitimate a system of remarkable cruelty to young women. In exposing the specifically gendered and sexualized dynamics of one historical place and time, *The Magdalene Sisters* might be said to be doing **queer** work (see Chapter 12). In other words, the film demonstrates that gender and sexuality are far from fixed entities, that how they are understood by a community or culture varies from place to place and time to time. Furthermore, the film dramatizes how particular socio-cultural institutions shape and construct specific views of gender and sexuality, and in the case of Catholic Ireland in the mid-1960s, how those specific views led to the persecution of over 30,000 women.

The Magdalene Sisters centers on three young women who are introduced in three short vignettes at the start of the film. Margaret (Anne-Marie Duff) is introduced at a community wedding celebration, where she is drawn aside and raped by a cousin. When the men of the family discover this, they usher the perpetrator out of the room (his fate is left uncertain), but Margaret's father, in collusion with his local Catholic priest, sends Margaret off to a Magdalene laundry, as she is now considered a disgrace to her family, having been sexually violated. The adolescent orphan Bernadette (Nora-Jane Noone) is similarly transported to the Magdalene laundry after the people who run the orphanage see (and fear) the sexual attraction she holds for the local teenage boys. Rose (Dorothy Duffy) is introduced as a young woman who has just given birth out of wedlock; her parents force her to give up her "bastard child" for adoption and ship her off to the Magdalene asylum as well. Once there, the girls are expected to work in the laundry without pay, and maintain a convent-like regimen of silence and prayer. They are also subjected to various forms of psychological and physical abuse at the hands of the nuns who run the institution. Instead of expressing compassion for the young women they oversee, the nuns have internalized the patriarchal belief system of the Catholic church, with its gendered hierarchies and inherent violence.

The head of the laundry/convent is Sister Bridget (Geraldine McEwan), a sadistic older woman who rules the asylum with an iron hand. As do her fellow nuns, sister Bridget constantly belittles and harasses her charges, calling them stupid and sinful. But Sister Bridget also knows these young women comprise her workforce, allowing her to earn the money which keeps her in power as leader of the institution. Mullan underscores the overdetermined connections between capitalism and Catholicism during Sister Bridget's initial interview with her three new charges: while the audio track features Sister Bridget extolling Catholic dogma about hard work being the way to heavenly salvation, the visual track shows her greedily counting and packaging the money she earns by exploiting her incarcerated workforce (Figure 8.5). Thus, in addition to the young women's persecution based on their alleged religious crimes (for Catholics of the era, unwed sexuality was a mortal sin tantamount to murder), and their persecution by their families and especially their fathers (who send them away out of shame), there is also a capitalist motive for the brutal and oppressive system. At another point in the film, Mullan again underscores the connections between capitalism and patriarchal Catholicism when he represents the laundry as a cogwheel-filled industrial space, or when he depicts a priest blessing a new washing machine (see Figure 8.6).

Fig 8.5
A close up of Sister Bridget counting money in *The Magdalene Sisters* (2002) suggests the real reason so many young women are incarcerated in the laundry.

Fig 8.6
Money and religion are again intertwined in *The Magdalene Sisters* (2002) when the priest blesses the new washing and drying machines.

Much of the film depicts the cruel treatment the young women receive at the hands of their "benefactors." Rose suffers in silence from mastitis, a painful inflammation of the breasts that can occur after pregnancy; her baby and proper medical care are nowhere to be seen. Margaret prepares for an escape, only to witness the runaway Una (Mary Murray) brought back to the asylum by her father who violently beats her in front of all the other young women (as well as Sister Bridget who does nothing to stop the attack). Bernadette's failed escape results in a gruesome and bloody head-shaving at the hands of Sister Bridget and her nuns, a fate also meted out to Una (see Figure 8.7). In another scene, the girls are made to stand naked in front of two nuns who play a humiliating "game" with them, mocking their bodies based on their sizes, shapes, and amount of body hair. Unlike the usual objectifying and fetishizing ways women's bodies are portrayed on screen, there is nothing sexy or titillating about this scene, and the spectator is not invited to find it erotic. The women's bodies are plain and varied, without fetishizing make-up, costumes, hairstyles, lighting (or airbrushing, as is commonly done with photographs of women in fashion magazines). The gaze that these

Fig 8.7
In *The Magdalene Sisters* (2002), the penalty for trying to escape the workhouse is a brutal and bloody head-shaving from Sister Bridget.

women are subjected to—in this case from the leering nuns—is shown to be cruel, demeaning, and controlling (see Figure 8.8). Even at the end of the film after Bernadette has escaped the asylum, Bernadette reacts with anxiety when she sees two nuns watching her.

Perhaps the most tragic character in the film is Crispina (Eileen Walsh), a seemingly mentally challenged young woman who has been placed with the nuns for having had a child out of wedlock, as was Rose. Crispina's soul survives on the rare glimpses of her son, brought to the gate of the asylum by a kindly family member, even as she is forbidden to speak to him or even acknowledge his existence. Psychologically immersed in the very ideological institution that is abusing her, Crispina believes she can communicate with her son through a matching set of Saint Christopher medals—one belonging to her son and one that she wears around her neck. When the medal goes missing, Crispina fears she is being punished by God and attempts to kill herself, first by sleeping in a wet nightgown to bring on the flu (which she believes is not quite the sin of suicide), and then by taking more drastic measures by attempting to hang herself. Crispina is

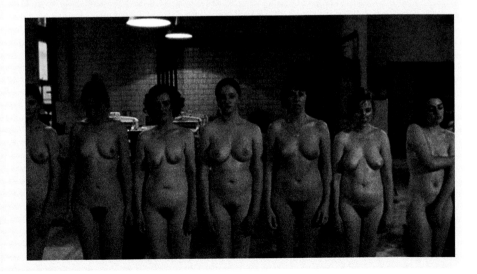

Fig 8.8
In *The Magdalene Sisters* (2002), nuns taunt and humiliate their nude charges as part of a sadistic game. Compare the shot of these women with how popular media usually represents the female form.

also being sexually abused by Father Fitzroy, the local priest who oversees the asylum. Margaret secretly avenges Crispina by putting a poisonous plant into the priest's clothes as they are processed in the laundry, and a public spectacle ensues: in front of the gathered community, the priest rips off his clothing to reveal the itching fiery lesions covering his body caused by the poisonous plant. At the same moment, Crispina also acknowledges an itching in her groin and has a complete breakdown, screaming over and over at the priest "You are not a man of God!"

Silence is a powerful theme throughout *The Magdalene Sisters*, used to symbolize not just the repression of gender and sexuality in this place and time, but also how silence tacitly gives approval to the heinous deeds and immoral practices represented. In the case of Margaret and Rose, their mothers remain silent even as their daughters are mistreated. Is this because as patriarchal wives they are not allowed to express an opinion? Or is it that they are *afraid* to express an opinion, when the men in their lives are shown giving in to such violent behaviors? Or do they share their husbands' points of view, having internalized the church's patriarchal teachings about the sinfulness of women? Clearly, not only the nuns who run the asylum but also the older women who have spent their entire lives incarcerated within it have done the latter. Silence is also powerfully invoked during Crispina's public denunciation of the predatory priest. All the inhabitants of the laundry as well as the gathered townspeople (including policemen and public officials who should suspect something "wrong" has been going on) remain silent in response to Crispina's allegations; in this way writer-director Mullan indicts their complicity in the abusive Magdalene asylum system, which they refuse to see for what it really is.

While the abuses against women depicted in *The Magdalene Sisters* may seem totally of another era and unrelated to today's feminist struggles, it is perhaps surprising to note that the last Magdalene laundry closed in 1996. The film reminds us that even in a decade (the 1960s) celebrated for its countercultural ideals and feminist consciousness raising (at least in some areas of the West), such abuses against women and women's sexuality could be and were still being perpetrated on such a massive scale. The film may also ask us to think beyond Western borders, and to acknowledge the abuses that women are still suffering around the globe at the hands of repressive doctrines expressed through families, churches, communities, and even capitalism itself. Today, wealthy Western white women may take for granted their rights to an education, a career, and a closet full of designer shoes, but there are millions of women the world over who are still struggling for basic human rights. Contemporary feminist film and media production, theory, and scholarship is still dedicated to addressing those inequities.

Case study 2: *Masters of Sex* ("Pilot," 2013)

The Showtime serial *Masters of Sex* is another good example of a film or TV text that engages with and explores issues related to historical constructions of gender and sexuality from a potentially feminist point of view. Created by writer and producer Michelle Ashford (*The Pacific* [2008]), the show is one of the few contemporary on-air television dramas to have a female **showrunner**. The vast majority of television producers and showrunners are still male, as are the vast majority of Hollywood film directors. However, recent years have seen the rise of a number of significant female film directors and showrunners. Among the latter are Jill Soloway, who started writing and producing for shows like *Six Feet Under* (2001–5) and *United States of Tara* (2009–11); most recently she created the critically acclaimed and award-winning Amazon Prime **sitcom** *Transparent* (2014–). African American female showrunner Shonda Rhimes has garnered considerable buzz with her shows *Scandal* (2012–) and *How to Get Away with Murder* (2014–), while the Netflix hit *Orange is the New Black* (2013–) was created by Jenji Kohan. Ilene Chaiken was one of the creators of the lesbian serial drama *The L Word* (2004–9) and now produces for *Empire* (2015–). Similarly, Lena Dunham (*Girls* [2012–]) and Mindy Kaling (*The Mindy Project* [2012–]) seem to be as successful behind the camera as well as in front of it, both starring in hit shows that they either created or produced. It seems that TV—and especially cable and streaming TV—are affording women more chances than are feature films to be creative executives, to tell different types of stories from female (and hopefully feminist) points of view.

Showtime's *Masters of Sex* dramatizes the life and work Dr. Bill Masters and Virginia Johnson, two real life sex researchers of the postwar era who revolutionized the ways in which medical doctors—if not entire Western populations—think about gender, sex, and sexuality. Before their laboratory work with actual human subjects, knowledge about sexuality had been gained either through interviews and questionnaires (the basis for Alfred Kinsey's two best-selling books *Sexual Behavior in the Human Male* [1948] and *Sexual Behavior in the Human Female* [1953]), or theorized in mostly abstract ways by armchair psychoanalysts building on Sigmund Freud's notions of the **Oedipal complex**. Masters and Johnson documented that human sexual response goes through four phases: arousal, plateau, orgasm, and resolution (see Figure 8.9). They also showed that some women can be multi-orgasmic, and that clitoral stimulation was central to a woman's sexual pleasure. Masters and Johnson helped to demystify human sexuality, and contributed to a major shift in the culture's understanding of women and women's sexuality. Whereas many previous theorists considered that women's pleasure in sexuality was either unimportant or even impossible, Masters and Johnson's work contributed to the sexual revolution, insisting on the importance of pleasure, intimacy, and healthy sexuality to both men and women. Their work was thus highly significant to **second wave feminism**, as it suggested that women as well as men could and should have equal access to sexual pleasure.

Masters of Sex dramatizes a time in American history when sexuality was often

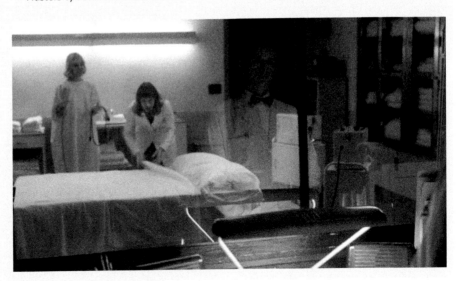

Fig 8.9
Showrunner Michelle Ashford's *Masters of Sex* (2013–) dramatizes the sex research undertaken by Dr. Bill Masters and Virginia Johnson that gave substantial impetus to **second wave feminism**.

thought of as a (at times onerous) marital duty. In the show's pilot episode, Bill Masters (Michael Sheen) and his wife Libby (Caitlin Fitzgerald) are trying to have a baby. They have rather passionless and even somewhat painful sex—not for pleasure, desire, or love—but for the sole purpose of trying to get pregnant. Libby blames herself because she cannot fulfill her prescribed function as a wife—to give birth to children—even as Masters withholds from her the knowledge of his own low sperm count. (Masters' initial professional work as a fertility expert was soon eclipsed by his sex research.) The pilot episode contrasts their cold sex scene with one between Virginia Masters (Lizzy Caplan) and a young intern, Dr. Ethan Haas (Nicholas D'Agosto). Whereas Bill mechanically enters Libby from behind (because he believes that is the best position to ensure conception), Virginia and Ethan run through a series of sexual acts and positions from which they derive considerable pleasure. The rights to female empowerment and female sexual pleasure (literally embodied in Virginia) are major themes throughout the series. The show also plays frequently with Western society's expectations about gender roles: in the pilot episode Virginia tells Ethan that she is content to be his friend (albeit with "benefits"); it is Ethan who is emotionally besotted with Virginia, and he even strikes her in the face and calls her a "whore" out of his felt rejection. An autonomous female partner is seemingly more than he can handle.

Virginia Johnson is portrayed as a strong, capable, and compassionate person. She is a single mother raising two kids and holding down a job, in an era when such an arrangement was frowned upon by many people, including women themselves (in the pilot episode Virginia is berated by a snippy female registrar who thinks Virginia belongs at home with her family). The terse and cold-hearted Bill Masters quickly realizes he needs Virginia's help with the human side of his research—especially with his female subjects (see Figure 8.10). She explains to him why a woman might fake an orgasm, and recruits new women to take part in the study. Although Virginia technically works for Masters, she finds ways to empower herself in the sexist world of the research hospital, and eventually becomes co-author of Masters' study. Throughout the first season she also is instrumental in helping a female doctor research ways to prevent cervical cancer. The serial nature of *Masters of Sex* is itself important, as it allows for complexity and nuance in both character development and the range of ideas that the show can address. Over the two seasons produced (so far), *Masters of Sex* has explored a host of issues related to

Fig 8.10
In *Masters of Sex* (2013–), Dr. Bill Masters (Michael Sheen) quickly realizes he needs Virginia Johnson (Lizzy Caplan) to help him with his study.

women and sexuality in complex and thoughtful ways, including prostitution, male and female impotence and sexual dysfunction in general, racism and interracial relationships, male and female homosexuality, and even the question of what should be done when a child is born with an intersex syndrome, i.e. with ambiguous genitalia. As they did in real life, Masters and Johnson themselves eventually become sexually intimate; he deludes himself that their sex is only for the "good of the study," while Virginia has a much more knowing and self-aware take on what is really going on.

Masters of Sex plays like a more feminist version of *Mad Men* (2007–15), in that both focus on women in the workplace during an era when men still called most of the shots—if not all of them. However, *Masters of Sex*'s critique of postwar American gender roles is sounded much more strongly than in *Mad Men*. Some viewers of *Mad Men* apparently decode it not as a critique of outmoded gender norms, but as a nostalgic wish for the "good old days" wherein the workplace was filled with booze, cigarettes, and subservient women. *Masters of Sex*—perhaps due to its female showrunner, its multiple female writers, and occasional female directors—each week makes much more forceful assertions about the limits placed on women in the postwar era. In so doing, it invites us to compare and contrast the limits our contemporary cultures may still be placing on women in the twenty-first century.

Conclusion

Although we end our chapter on "Feminist Approaches to Film and Television" at this point, that is not to say that this form of criticism has come to an end, any more than auteur, genre, or psychoanalytic criticism has come to an end. Feminism continues to be an integral part of contemporary cultural criticism, especially within various and varied cultural studies approaches (Chapters 10–12). Indeed, Chapter 12 introduces ideas germane to **third wave feminism**, and especially how those approaches can and do differ from those of **second wave feminism**. Feminist approaches to film and TV now regularly include considerations of men and masculinities on screen as well as women and femininities on screen. Contemporary approaches also tend to pay more attention to related discourses of class, race, regionality, sexuality, etc. than did second wave approaches. However, we might also note from a contemporary perspective that while some cable and streaming television services are increasingly giving women *and women of color* the chance to create and produce television, the Hollywood film industry seems a bit more reticent to offer those opportunities. That said, Disney's *Frozen* (2013) and *Maleficent* (2014) are two recent films that rewrite classic fairy tales from more feminist perspectives. Both became surprise blockbuster hits, and especially the former, written by Jennifer Lee; *Frozen* has broken all sorts of national and international box office records and become a cultural phenomenon. As with the **hegemonic negotiation** of any cultural issue, one can say that these films (and other film and TV shows like them) suggest new and emergent forms of gendered relations in the West. How we represent and understand men and women, and masculinity and femininity, continues to change as both men and women begin to confront (and respond to) the critiques of gender inequity sounded by feminist scholars, theorists, and media producers alike.

Questions for discussion

1 Identify some films or TV shows that you might consider feminist. In what ways do the texts hegemonically negotiate with patriarchy? Are women's issues, strengths, and/or autonomy undercut in any ways by male characters, narrative events, costuming, etc.?

2 What was the last film or TV show you watched that sexually objectified a male body (or bodies)? Was the male body "doing things" or was it merely a spectacle that stopped the narrative (as Mulvey argues women's bodies do)? Who was the text "aimed at": women, men, teenagers, kids, or some sort of general or mixed audience? How do genres influence the way male and female bodies are depicted on screen?

3 Try to become aware of how mainstream media habitually depicts women as sexualized objects and/or fetishizes their body parts. Besides film and television, where else does this occur? Try to find some recent fan art on the Internet that calls attention to those dynamics by reversing them, as did the recent mock-poster for *The Avengers* (2013), found at http://www.comicbookmovie.com/images/users/uploads/33503/Official%20Avengers%20Promo%20Poster_parody.jpg.

References and further reading:

Anzaldua, Gloria. *Borderlands/La Frontera: The New Mestiza*. San Francisco: Aunt Lute Books, 2012 (1987).

Bean, Jennifer M., Diane Negra, Amelie Hastie, and Jane Gaines, eds. *A Feminist Reader in Early Cinema*. Durham, NC: Duke University Press Books, 2002.

Berger, John. *Ways of Seeing*. New York: Penguin Group 2009 (1972).

Brundson, Charlotte, Julie D'Acci, and Lynn Spigel, eds. *Feminist Television Criticism: A Reader*. Oxford: Clarendon Press, 1997.

Carson, Diane, Linda Dittmar, and Janice R. Welsch, eds. *Multiple Voices in Feminist Film Criticism*. Minneapolis, MN: University of Minnesota Press, 1994.

Cohan, Steven. *Masked Men: Masculinity and the Movies in the Fifties*. Indianapolis, IN: Indiana University Press, 1997.

Faludi, Susan. *Backlash: The Undeclared War Against American Women*. New York: Doubleday, 1991.

Haskell, Molly. *From Reverence to Rape: The Treatment of Women in the Movies*. Chicago: The University of Chicago Press, 1987 [1973].

hooks, bell. *Teaching Critical Thinking: Practical Wisdom*. New York and London: Routledge, 2010.

Kaplan, E. Ann, ed. *Women in Film Noir*. London: British Film Institute, 1978.

Kaplan, E. Ann. *Women and Film: Both Sides of the Camera*. New York: Methuen, 1983.

Kearney, Mary Celeste, ed. *The Gender and Media Reader*. New York and London: Routledge, 2011.

Kinsey, Alfred Charles, Pomeroy, Wardell B., and Martin, Clyde E. *Sexual Behavior in the Human Male*. Philadelphia: W. B. Saunders, 1948.

Kinsey, Alfred Charles, Pomeroy, Wardell B., Martin, Clyde E., and Gebhard, Paul H. *Sexual Behavior in the Human Female*. Philadelphia: W. B. Saunders, 1953.

Kuhn, Annette. *Women's Pictures: Feminism and Cinema*, Second Edition. New York: Verso, 1994 (1982).

Modleski, Tania. *Loving With a Vengeance: Mass Produced Fantasies for Women*. New York: Methuen, 1984 (1982).

Modleski. Tania. *The Women Who Knew Too Much: Hitchcock and Feminist Theory*. New York: Methuen, 1988.

Moraga, Cherrie, and Gloria Anzaldua, eds. *This Bridge Called my Back: Writings by Radical Women of Color*. New York: Kitchen Table/Women of Color Press, 1984.

Moynihan, David Patrick. *The Negro Family: The Case for National Action* (the Moynihan Report). Washington, DC: Office of Policy Planning and Research, U.S. Department of Labor, 1965. Detroit, MI: Gale, 2010.

Mulvey, Laura. "Visual Pleasure and Narrative Cinema," in Timothy Corrigan, Patricia White, and Meta Mazaj, eds. *Critical Visions in Film Theory: Classic and Contemporary Readings*. Boston and New York, Bedford/St. Martin's Press, 2011 (1975). Pp. 715–25.

Rich, B. Ruby. *Chick Flicks: Theories and Memories of the Feminist Film Movement*. Durham, NC: Duke University Press Books, 2002.

Rosen, Marjorie. *Popcorn Venus: Women, Movies & the American Dream*. New York: Coward, McCann & Geoghegan, 1973.

Spigel, Lynn. *Make Room for TV: Television and the Family Ideal in Postwar America*. Chicago: University of Chicago Press, 1992.

Tasker, Yvonne. *Spectacular Bodies: Gender, Genre, and the Action Cinema*. New York and London: Routledge, 1993.

CHAPTER 9

Film, television, and the postmodern

There are many terms in critical-cultural studies that have varied and/or ambiguous meanings (and/or are *used* in various and/or ambiguous ways), and **postmodernism** is certainly one of them. It is also a term—like many of the others—that is charged with political and ideological ramifications. For some people, postmodernism suggests a new world order of equal access to media technologies and unfettered participation in the public sphere, primarily due to new communication protocols to which everyone allegedly has access (at least in the West). Conversely, other critics and theorists see it as the ultimate triumph of Western capitalism and its stranglehold on meaning, culture, and the political process. How one feels about postmodernism is often based on how one feels about **modernism**. For example, some critics of postmodernism see it as the debasement of serious, high-minded artistic modernism: the terms "vulgar modernism" or "modernism for the masses" tap into those sorts of feelings. Yet other critics see postmodernism as *freedom from* the **Eurocentric** elitism allegedly at the core of modernism. Still others feel that postmodernism is basically a meaningless buzz word, and that it really contributes little to our ongoing understanding of culture, politics, and mass media forms. This chapter does not share that sentiment, seeing postmodernism as a term that encompasses interesting shifts in how we think about history, about aesthetics, about philosophy, about capitalism, and about **ideology**: in other words, how we think about and theorize culture. Like the other models/ theories/methodologies introduced throughout this book, postmodernism can be thought of as another form of aesthetic or cultural analysis applicable to film and TV (and cultural artifacts in general).

Because there are various (contested) aspects about what postmodernism means, it is very hard to come up with a "25 words or less" definition of it. But before we examine the many interrelated meanings of the term, we can try to map out some of the various ways we might think about postmodernism, even as these ways are themselves highly imbricated with one another. Briefly, postmodernism can be used to describe an aesthetic or formal *style*; much of the latter part of this chapter will attempt to to do just that. Postmodernism also represents a *period* in art and culture that comes after **modernism** (roughly 1870s–1940s in the West). Where modernism ends and postmodernism begins (if indeed it does) varies from discipline to discipline, but most critics would probably agree that postmodernism was firmly in place by the 1980s. Postmodernism also represents a *philosophical change* in the way we understand the world around us, the ways and means we come to know what we know (a very short definition of **epistemology**). For some critics this change represents a significant *epistemological break* in ways of thinking about art and culture and politics, while others see these changes as more tentative and overlapping. Postmodernism has also been tied to *economics*, and specifically the rise of the West's present form of capitalism, **global corporate** and/or **consumer capitalism**. This stage of capitalism follows the dominance of **industrial capitalism** which was prevalent during the age of modernity and modernism. Most famously, postmodern theorist **Fredric Jameson** has termed postmodernism "The Cultural Logic of Late Capitalism," meaning it is a state of sociocultural affairs that arises from the dominance of global corporate capitalism and its emphasis on a consumer economy.

If we are talking about capitalism, then a discussion of ideology cannot be far behind, and the *theorization* of culture and ideology is another important aspect of understanding postmodernism. While postmodernism and **poststructuralism** share many overlapping suppositions (and sound like they might be similar), they are not necessarily the same thing. Recall from Chapter 3 that poststructuralism generally still finds some value and meaning in structure, but rather than seeing structure as explanatory in an essentialist sense, poststructuralism stresses the incoherence of systems and structures, attempting to explore or illuminate the "wiggle room" in cultural meanings. This is one aspect postmodernism shares with poststructuralism: many postmodern theorists posit a decentered universe, where understanding and meaning are not top-down and stable. Instead, meanings need to be understood from multiple (and potentially infinite) perspectives. Taken to its extreme, this tenet suggests that even moral absolutes are relative and culturally determined, a facet of postmodernist thinking that has caused it to be attacked by religious fundamentalists of all types. Indeed, some critics have theorized the global rise of religious fundamentalism as a sort of backlash to the rise of postmodernism. Thus, while the rise of the postmodern condition suggests that all truths are relative, various fundamentalisms may have arisen as a way of asserting a compensatory and comforting certainty based on strict adherence to religious tenets of one sort or another. (Of course what usually escapes the notice of most fundamentalists is that even within a given religious tradition—whether Christian or Muslim, for example—there are different ways to interpret their given holy texts. Who is to say whose reading of the Bible or the Koran is the absolutely correct one?)

Questions of interpretation are addressed within poststructuralist and postmodernist thinking, as well as within cultural studies, explored in the next chapter in greater detail. Recall that poststructuralists emphasize how language and other cultural systems construct meaning—that meaning only exists in the play of **signifiers**. Some postmodernist thinkers also share this assumption, and argue that any sense of the real is subsumed by language and representations. In the terms of influential postmodern thinker **Jean Baudrillard**, the final stage of the postmodern condition is reached when representation of the real is replaced by its **simulation**. That is to say, the image of something has replaced its **referent**; the **signifier** has replaced its **signified**, and meaning is nothing but a free floating play of signifiers. Poststructuralism and postmodernism also share the impulse to question any and all essentialisms, the so-called **master narratives** of the West which construct certain ways of thinking about the self, about the Other, about history, about progress, etc. As explored in Chapter 12, many of the newer ways of thinking about issues of identity (including **third wave feminism**, **critical race theory**, and **queer**

theory) are indebted to concepts found in poststructuralist and postmodernist thought.

One of the difficult things about thinking about postmodernism today is that for students born after the 1980s—the era when postmodernism as a concept might be said to have entered mainstream consciousness (as a buzz word at the very least)—is that what it attempts to describe is a state of affairs within which younger generations have been raised. As such, it may be difficult for younger generations "to see the forest for the trees." Like an ideological structure into which one is thoroughly **interpellated**, it may be difficult for young people to recognize that culture *was* different before the advent of this thing called postmodernism, just as culture in the 2010s is different than it was in the 1980s. (Various ideas about post-postmodernist movements will not be discussed in this chapter!) However, many of the concepts theorized in that former decade seem to resonate in the contemporary era; if anything, the rise of new media technologies has made much postmodern thinking seem quite prescient and still relevant. This chapter is primarily concerned with how a postmodern aesthetic differs from a classical or modernist one, and how this aesthetic is today the essence of most (if not all) film and television texts. Postmodernism challenges the ways we think about basic cinematic theories like authorship and genre, and raises vexing questions about ideology and representation (especially the representation of minority groups). But before we turn to those concerns, it is important to understand more thoroughly the eras and forms of classicism and modernism, as well as the various historical-aesthetic and cultural-theoretical forces that helped to shape and define this shift in consciousness, or "cultural logic."

From classicism to modernism

Western art history (and more broadly Western history as a whole) is often defined retrospectively in terms of period or eras. Two of the most important eras for understanding postmodernism are the **classical era**, and the **modernist era**. When speaking of the arts and other cultural formations, the terms classicism and modernism refer to broad trends within all of that era's art forms, including theater, literature, painting, sculpture, music, etc. The classical era comes first in Western history, and is associated with the philosophical, political, and artistic ideals of the so-called **Age of Enlightenment** (or Age of Reason), roughly demarcated as the seventeenth and eighteenth centuries. Age of Enlightenment thinking championed reason and science over religion and superstition; historical figures like Benjamin Franklin and Thomas Jefferson are good examples of thinkers within the Enlightenment tradition: pragmatic, rational, egalitarian, and scientific. As such, the arts of this era stressed themes that harkened back to Greco-Roman ideals. In part, classical art can be defined as being **mimetic** or realist—that is to say the artistic creation should mimic or look as closely like the subject who sat for it as possible. For example, ancient Greek sculptures closely resemble the nude models that posed for them, representing what was thought to be the ideal form of the human body. Michelangelo's *David* or Da Vinci's *Mona Lisa* (although created in the early sixteenth century) are also good examples of mimetic or classical art, as is Thomas Gainsborough's *The Blue Boy* (circa 1770), thought to be a portrait of a son of a wealthy merchant (see Figure 9.1). The goal of a classical painter (regardless of his or her era) would be to make art that conveys as closely as possible

Fig 9.1
Thomas Gainsborough's famous painting *The Blue Boy* (circa 1770) is thought to be a portrait of the son of a wealthy merchant. One goal of **classical art** is **mimesis**—to depict "reality" as closely as possible. Credit: The Art Archive/Huntington Library/Superstock.

the "real" or "true" image of the artist's chosen subject: thus the era's penchant for portraiture, landscapes, and "still life" paintings. Classicism also implies ideal forms of beauty and truth, and was often created to honor the **ruling class** (noble men and women, wealthy businessmen, the Catholic church, etc.), who also paid for much of it. Indeed, only those people and institutions with money could and did commission artworks during this era. Artists worked under a system of **patronage** and they were expected to exalt the ideals and beliefs (and possessions) of the powerful people who employed them.

Classical art shares other broad traits, such as an emphasis on unity, harmony, and balance. In other words, classical art conveys a unified impression—the painting or sculpture presents a single perspective on its subject, usually posed in the center of the canvas, with the other elements of the scene creating a balanced composition in depth—the so called **Renaissance perspective**. A classical book, poem, play, or concerto is precisely structured with a beginning, middle, and end—each section of a work relates to the others and all "add up" to a unified and coherent expression of meaning or feeling. (It is in this sense that we often refer to Hollywood films of the 1930s and 1940s as **classical Hollywood cinema**.) What we think of today as classical music—for example the preludes and fugues of Johann Sebastian Bach—are harmonic wholes; even when his fugues meticulously and mathematically rearrange musical motifs in every possible permutation, they still add up to a unified, harmonic, and balanced whole. Bach's works are so complex that music historians often label him as a **baroque** composer, a phase which heralds the start of the classical era of music. More truly classical composers (according to the historical and formal rubrics constructed by Western thinkers) include Wolfgang Amadeus Mozart and Ludwig van Beethoven. The point of all this is that such labeling, classification, or **taxonomy** (as critiqued in earlier chapters) is itself a bit reductive.

Periods and labels (including those of classical and modernist) are reflective of broad trends across complex terrains. Examples and exceptions surely abound when simplistic labels are examined more closely. But for now, realize that classicism broadly implies works of art that express formal concepts like realism, mimesis, unity, harmony, and balance.

Things started to change throughout the nineteenth century. As Age of Enlightenment thinking gave rise to industrial capitalism (via the era's so-called **Industrial Revolution**), art and culture begin to shift in certain ways—often in directions away from the ideals of the Enlightenment. Waves of **romanticism** and **gothicism** in literature started to privilege emotion, sensation, and the sublime over scientific rationality. Musical composition began to get more romantic (as with Pyotr Ilyich Tchaikovsky), or more self-ware, abstract, and/or minimalist (as with Erik Satie). The visual arts also started to become more abstract and experimental. Some theorists like André Bazin suggest that the innovation and dissemination of photographic technologies throughout the nineteenth century fundamentally altered the meaning of (or need for) classical painting and sculpture. Photography could now achieve the mimetic, realistic goals of classical painting and sculpture better than any painter or sculptor could. As such, the visual arts were "freed up" to become more experimental in their methods and execution. All of these developments in the arts coincided with the ongoing rise in industrialization and urbanization throughout the Western world, and came to be known as **modernism**. The similar term **modernity** is related to modernism, but refers more to the ways that life was experienced during this era, rather than explicit developments in the arts. Modernism might best be thought of as a philosophy or cultural practice (or cultural logic, to borrow from Jameson) that attempted to represent and make sense of the various challenges created by modernity, such as urbanity, factory life, class struggle, and eventually World War I. Modernists in general wanted to critique the world they saw around them, and challenge basic assumptions about art and culture; they did so by transforming the way people experienced art, primarily by calling attention to art-making in a number of self-aware and **self-reflexive** ways. As such, modernist art is **medium specific**, in that it calls attention to the medium it is created in, either by (for example) producing atonal sounds, emphasizing brushstrokes or chisel marks, and/or by becoming increasingly abstract.

Modernist artists felt in some basic way that the new world of modernity needed new means of expression. Classicism was outmoded. New scientific and sociological paradigms were emerging that significantly challenged centuries-old beliefs and practices. The theory of evolution, proposed by Charles Darwin in his 1859 treatise *On the Origin of Species*, directly challenged Christian cosmogony and its creation myths. It challenged the idea of humankind as a divine creation, much as the discovery (centuries earlier) that the earth revolves around the sun (and not vice versa) displaced humankind from the center of the universe (as it was then theorized). Similarly, the writings and philosophies of Karl Marx and Friedrich Engels also informed and critiqued the age of modernity, laying the groundwork for the rights of the **working classes** and exposing the ideologies of the ruling class (including the church) as a form of false consciousness. Also highly significant was Sigmund Freud's development of **psychoanalysis**, a system of thought that suggested everything we thought we knew about ourselves as moral civilized human beings could be (and in fact probably was) wrong. Freud's theories also challenged the divinity of man, and suggested that angels and demons were not external forces of a moral and balanced Christian universe that shaped our individual lives, but rather the outward projection of our own **superegos** (angels) and **ids** (demons) at war within ourselves.

When we think of modernism today, we often think of the various schools or movements that existed within it. One of the first movements to emerge (around the 1870s) was **impressionism**, which as its name implies, was interested in creating art that conveyed the artist's *impressions* of reality, not merely slavishly mimicking reality (as did classical art and photography). Impressionist paintings, like those produced by Claude Monet, Édouard Manet, Mary Cassatt, and Pierre-Auguste Renoir, focused on everyday subjects, and can be characterized by their pastel colors, attention to shifting patterns of light, and often visible brushwork. Impressionism started mainly in France but quickly spread throughout Europe. Likewise, **expressionism** began in Germany around the end of the nineteenth century and lasted well into the 1920s. Expressionist artists presented a distorted (and almost hostile) view of their worlds in an attempt to express their critique of modernity: one of the best known examples of expressionist painting is Edvard Munch's *The Scream*, which features a seemingly angst-ridden wraith of a human being howling at the universe in existential despair (see Figure 9.2). **Surrealism,** popularized by painters like Salvador Dali and Max Ernst, was another modernist school of art innovated in the early twentieth century. The surrealists were inspired by Freud and often created dream-like work that was meant to express the unconscious mind. **Cubism**—associated primarily with Pablo Picasso—attempts to break up the unified wholeness of things and represent them from different perspectives, in the process turning the human form into an almost abstract concept. **Dada** was one of the more politically committed movements of 1920s modernism; it was anti-war, anti-bourgeois, and ultimately anti-art. Its goal was to create abstract and nonsensical images in a sort of **culture jamming**

Fig 9.2
Edvard Munch's
expressionist painting
The Scream (1893); unlike
The Blue Boy, modernist
art moved away from
mimesis towards more
artistic license. Credit:
The Art Archive/Nasjonal
Galleriet Oslo.

technique, forcing people to confront what was meant by art in the first place. For example, the dadaist Marcel Duchamp championed the idea of the "ready-made," any old common object that he insisted was art if it was hung on the wall of a gallery and was treated as such. Most famously, his piece *Fountain* is a men's room urinal which he signed "R. Mutt" and then exhibited (or at least tried to exhibit) in a New York City art gallery.

Obviously, many modernist artists set out to shock and awe bourgeois society with their scandalous art, fervent manifestos, and outrageous antics. Modernist provocations and artistic explorations spread across various art forms (as had classicism), including literature, theater, music, painting, sculpture, and the nascent medium of cinema. Indeed, cinema is itself a product of the age of modernity, a mechanized and urban wonder that transformed the ways its spectators saw and understood the world. Innovated in France and America in the mid-1890s as first a novelty and then as an entertainment business, cinema was also an art form deeply connected to various modernist movements. **German expressionist** cinema is perhaps the best known of these movements today, as represented by films like *The Cabinet of Dr. Caligari* (1920), *Nosferatu* (1922), and *Metropolis* (1927) (see Figure 9.3). These films created stark nightmare worlds filled with distorted *mise-en-scène* reflective of their twisted characters' delicate and abnormal psychic states. German expressionist style would be imported to America for the look of the classical Hollywood horror film (in the early 1930s) as well as **film noir** (throughout the 1940s). The movement of **French impressionist** cinema contains filmmakers like Germaine Dulac and Abel Gance who made (respectively) *The Smiling Madame Beudet* (1923) and *Napoleon* (1927); their filmmaking was an attempt to use the formal properties of cinema—distorting lenses, off-kilter framing, soft lighting and filters, rapid montage, etc.—to approximate the visual style of impressionist painting. **Surrealist** cinema's most famous film is Salvador Dali and Luis Buñuel's *Un Chien Andalou/An Andalusian Dog* (1929), a film that still maintains its power to shock audiences, especially in its scene of a straight razor slicing open (what appears to be—via clever editing) a living human's eyeball (see Figure 9.4). The image—

Fig 9.3
The famous **German expressionist** film *The Cabinet of Dr. Caligari* (1920) used stark contrasts in light and dark, painted sets, and a highly artificial style of performance to achieve many of its effects.

Fig 9.4
In *Un Chien Andalou* (1929), a razor blade slices open an eyeball, an act of shocking violence that also invites audience members to open up their eyes and see in a new way.

like much modernist art in general—is an attack on the bourgoisie's usual ways of seeing, and a literal exhortation for the audience to open its eyes and see things in a new way. *Ballet Mécanique* (1924), discussed in Chapters 1 and 2, is considered to be a dadaist or cubist film, one that is expressly about the concerns of modernity, including urbanization and mechanization.

Modernism in the arts flourished in Europe throughout the decades before and after World War I, only to be challenged by the rise of fascist regimes during the 1930s. Those regimes attempted to enforce their own modes of state sanctioned **classical realism**, and often discredited modernism as Jewish and primitive (as did the Nazis in their 1937 propaganda exhibit "Degenerate Art"). As the fascists in Germany, Italy, and Spain came to power, many European modernists fled to America and elsewhere; many found refuge in the bohemian communities of New York City, Boston, and Chicago, and some filmmakers were absorbed into Hollywood. More purely modernist filmmaking in America survived in the form of **poetic cinema**, a movement that drew upon psychoanalysis to explore personal psychic landscapes, as in films like Maya Deren's *Meshes of the Afternoon* (1943) and Kenneth Anger's *Fireworks* (1947). The modernist impulse remained alive in filmmaking well into the 1960s, ranging from the minimalism of Andy Warhol's *Eat* (1963) and the *Screen Tests* (1964–6) to the excessive visual provocations of underground filmmakers like Jack Smith and Stan Brakhage. Modernist filmmaking probably reached its apex with an avant-garde movement known as **structural/ materialist filmmaking**. These films perhaps represent one end point of cinematic modernism and its medium specificity: they are largely devoid of content and are instead "about" the material form of cinema itself. Examples include Michael Snow's *Wavelength* (1967)—which simulates a 45-minute zoom shot—and Ernie Gehr's *Serene Velocity* (1970), a view of an empty hallway that nonetheless oscillates back and forth as the filmmaker adjusts the camera's focal length from shot to shot. Structural/materialist films are "about" cinema in the way that **abstract expressionist** paintings (like Jackson Pollock's "action paintings") are "about" their medium: paint and its multiple qualities like color and texture. But once modernist art had been reduced to its very basic media-specific forms—whether paint blobs or the very grain of the cinematographic image (as in Ernie Gehr's *History* [1970])— where was the movement to go?

From modernism to postmodernism

Modernist styles, like classical styles, have not really disappeared: artists can still paint, sculpt, or compose music in any style they choose. Similarly, filmmakers are often still described in ways that refer to their use of classical or modernist styles. However, for many critics, theorists, and cultural commentators, the term postmodernism is useful when describing the broad shifts in art, commerce, and culture that have occurred throughout recent decades (roughly the latter half of the twentieth century and on into the twenty-first). As suggested in the introduction to this chapter, postmodernism arose from within and alongside modernism due to broad socio-economic and cultural factors, as much as (if not more so than) any outright changes in aesthetic form. One might say that the very meaning of art changed or shifted in this new era, having become increasingly commercialized, institutionalized, and mass produced. As Fredric Jameson succinctly put it in his groundbreaking essay "Postmodernism, or the Cultural Logic of Late Capitalism," "aesthetic production today has become integrated into commodity production generally" (1991, 4). When we think of TV and film, for example, we are dealing with art forms (if we deign to call them art forms) that are first and foremost created for economic profit, by large numbers of people working within ever-larger corporate structures. Yes, a single individual may still write a poem, or paint a painting, or even make an experimental film, but those modes of production are distinctly of another generation (or even of another century). While classical artists made art for the ruling classes under systems of patronage, and modernist artists made art in order to shock a blasé middle class into new spheres of social awareness, most postmodern artists (like those in the film, television, or the publishing industries) make art to make money, to earn a living (if they can) by selling their talents to the **culture industries**.

Although some filmmakers and TV producers do stand out as **auteurs** in this era (see Chapter 4), almost every film or television show produced today is the collaborative effort of hundreds if not thousands of different people. As such, film and TV might be thought of as postmodern phenomena in their own right. And although we still use the terms classical Hollywood film and/or modernist film at times, what constitutes classical or modernist television? For many critics, the rise of television culture (and now cyber culture) is one of the defining aspects of the postmodern condition in and of itself. The innovation and dissemination of television arose generally during the same years that postmodernism did. Television was not something that was affected by the rise of postmodernism (as were most pre-existing art forms); rather it is more of a historical and technological phenomenon that indicates or lies at the heart of the shift from modernism to postmodernism in the other arts. In fact, the shift in cultural theory from a focus on "art" to a focus on "cultural artifacts" is also reflective of this shift. What is the meaning of "art" in the postmodern, digital era? It would take many volumes to begin to answer that question, but perhaps we can at least agree that it means something different than it did during the classical or modernist era.

The meaning of art also changed throughout the twentieth century as many of the previously radical aspects of modernist art became "tamed" by their assimilation into culture, specifically through their institutionalization into museum culture (and other pop culture artifacts). Modernist texts that once caused riots (like Duchamp's *Fountain*) are now found in stately museums; the surrealist film *Un Chien Andalou* has played on MTV. Somewhere between the start and end of the twentieth century, modernist art lost its power to shock and scandalize the middle classes ("épater la bourgeoisie" as the French have phrased it). Similarly, what was once considered "high art" has now become merely another element of "low art." It is not uncommon for commercial artists who create popular culture (filmmakers, musicians, television producers) to "cannibalize" or quote from famous modernist texts as matter of course (a key aspect of the postmodern aesthetic, explored below). One very early example of this tendency might be the climatic ballet sequence in the Oscar-winning MGM musical *An American in Paris* (1951), a sequence that was designed by director Vincente Minnelli to evoke the specific styles of several French impressionist painters, including Pierre-Auguste Renoir, Maurice Utrillo, and Henri de Toulouse-Lautrec (see Figure 9.5). Herein, forms once considered "high art"—ballet and French impressionism—were now used to "dress up" a mass produced, mass marketed Hollywood film musical. The art forms being quoted may have been modernist, but their placement within a mass

Fig 9.5
A scene from the climactic ballet in *An American in Paris* (1951) recreates the visual style of modernist artist Toulouse-Lautrec.

produced artifact suggests their postmodernist usage. Walt Disney's *Fantasia* (1940) is a similar early mash-up of high and low art forms, in this case classical music and cel animation; although the film scandalized high art aficionados upon its initial release, it is difficult to imagine anyone today being upset by its blurring of high and low art forms. (Indeed, Disney's "sequel" *Fantasia 2000* (1999) hardly raised any eyebrows among the cultural cognoscenti.) By the 1980s, film, TV, and especially music videos were routinely quoting modernist (as well as classical) works in order to create highly stylized and unique texts (albeit still commercial, mass produced, and postmodern ones). For example, Madonna sang and danced in "Express Yourself," a music video explicitly designed in the style of Fritz Lang's German expressionist science fiction epic *Metropolis* (1927) (see Figures 9.6 and 9.7).

A key figure in the move from modernism to postmodernism is the graphic artist Andy Warhol. Significantly, Warhol began his career as a commercial artist and became famous for turning everyday household items into artworks through painting and silk screening. The dadaist Marcel Duchamp had hung a urinal on the wall and insisted it was art; Warhol painted Campbell's Soup cans and Brillo Pad boxes and insisted the same. Warhol (as did many other artists of the 1960s Pop Art movement) frequently took American popular culture as his subject matter, turning photos of Hollywood stars like Marilyn Monroe, Elizabeth Taylor, or Elvis Presley into brightly colored series of silk screens. Importantly, these were works created by what might be called "industrial methods" that blurred the artistic impulse (Warhol's creativity) with commercial imperatives (the mechanical reproduction of photography and the serial production of prints for sale). Indeed, Warhol's work space was nicknamed "The Factory" by the people who inhabited it, and who in many cases were the ones actually making the silk screen prints that Warhol would

Fig 9.6
The German expressionist science fiction classic *Metropolis* (1927) ...

Fig 9.7
... is refigured in the postmodern era within the Madonna video "Express Yourself."

then sign. Besides blurring the boundaries between high and low (serious and commercial) art, and questioning issues around authorship and authenticity, Warhol himself became a sort of postmodern celebrity, famous for being an eccentric character as much as for being an important artist. His 1968 quip "In the future, everyone will be world-famous for 15 minutes," describes postmodern media culture as it was then evolving: well before the rise of reality TV, Warhol predicted the shallow celebrity culture to which it would give rise. By the end of his career, Warhol insisted (ironically or not), that art was making money and that "good business is the best art."

As a cultural text himself, "Andy Warhol" was emblematic of the flamboyant 1960s counterculture and all that it represented, even as Warhol (the man) was a rather shy and retiring individual. But Warhol surrounded himself with hipsters and hippies, would-be artists and musicians, wealthy socialites, drag queens, hustlers, and drug addicts—all of whom moved in and out of "The Factory" and many of whom also appeared in Warhol's films and videos of the era. (These films themselves confound and blur boundaries in a postmodern way. Are they portraiture? Documentary? Performance art? Exploitation? Pornography? All of the above?) Warhol's "Superstars" reflected the growing interest in socio-cultural diversity expressed by many people during that era, when protests, marches, and demonstrations began to undermine the pervasive idea that American culture was somehow represented solely by squeaky clean white suburban patriarchal families (as seen on countless TV **sitcoms** of the era). And although the era's countercultural movement may have died out or become increasingly insular by the 1970s, it was nonetheless effective in destabilizing baseline assumptions about America as primarily white, patriarchal, and middle class. The unified subject of "America" had now to be acknowledged as a highly fragmented (and inherently unequal) culture of men and women, straight and gay, white and non-white, rich and poor, and so on. This move away from unity and emphasis on fragmentation is a key aspect of the postmodern aesthetic (discussed below).

The rise of the advertising industries, TV cultures, and now cyber cultures, is another important aspect in the development of postmodernism. Television (and to a lesser extent photography and film) created a new mediated world of live instantaneous transmission, helping to create a sense of culture wherein the image of something is more significant than the thing itself (as it might exist in the "real," unmediated world). French theorist Guy Debord in his 1967 book *Society of the Spectacle* was one of the first to analyze this state of affairs, which he felt was dehumanizing and degrading to the human beings living within it. He argued that under advanced capitalism (Jameson's "late capitalism," or global corporate consumer capitalism), actual interactions between real live human beings—expressive of real live human concerns—were being systematically replaced by mediated interactions that distorted reality in the pursuit of profits. If one fast-forwards 40 or 50 years, Debord's thinking seems especially prescient: new media technologies are increasingly creating virtual worlds for us to inhabit, (arguably) isolating us ever further from the "real."

Debord's thinking looks back to that of the **Frankfurt School** (who saw the culture industries as colonizing us with mindless commands to conform and consume) and forward to that of postmodern philosopher Jean Baudrillard, whose 1981 book *Simulacra and Simulation* theorized four stages in how representation was changing in the postmodern era, due to advances in technology and global capitalism (among other factors). In the first phase, signs and images (like those found in classical art) are thought to represent something that actually exists in the world. In the second phase, the image (or sign of an alleged reality) has become perverted, distorted into something that only hints at the real. The third phase is the phase of the **simulacrum**, an image that purports to be a copy of something that no longer exists in reality (or never did exist in reality). The fourth phase in Baudrillard's model is the phase of pure **simulation**, in which signs and images function (represent the world) purely in relation to one another, with no connection to reality whatsoever. For Baudrillard and other postmodern thinkers, these final two phases describe the very condition of postmodernity, creating a sense of **hyperreality**, where images and signs have become untethered from the material world. The blur between the *image of reality* and *reality itself* is sometimes considered a key "crisis" of the postmodern condition.

Simulacra and simulation are theoretical concepts whose meanings are sometimes difficult to grasp. Both Fredric Jameson and Italian semiotician Umberto Eco refer to various aspects of the Disney theme parks as good examples of postmodern **simulacrum**: a copy of something that does not exist in actual reality. The area of Disneyland known as Main Street USA, for example, purports to be a copy of a middle-American small town street at the turn of the twentieth century. However, there never was a Main Street precisely like the one constructed in Disneyland (with its false fronts and forced perspectives). Main Street USA is the *copy of something that never actually existed*, or rather it is the *copy of an idea* of Main Street, not an actual Main Street. In postmodern exchanges, signs themselves—not reality—give rise to other signs and meanings (this is what is meant by simulation). Main Street USA functions similarly to how Fredric Jameson theorizes **nostalgia**, the overly sentimental feelings one might have for a previous era, feelings often based on mediated and/or even false images and memories. In this sense, nostalgia is also a simulacrum—the fond remembrance of an *idea of the past, not the past itself.* For many people, feeling nostalgic about the 1950s may invoke peaceful suburban family lives, white picket fences, and two-car garages. But those are images of the era that many of us conjure up based on the era's *representations* in films and TV shows (like domestic sitcoms), and not on any actual lived experience in that decade. Under these conditions of postmodernity, the image or idea of something—in this case the past—has come to be represented through free-floating signs without a clear connection to any lived referent. Thinking that the 1950s was like it was represented on *Leave it to Beaver* (1957–63) may seem naïve; but in our televisual, cyber-mediated, postmodern world, those images are arguably much more constitutive of our common understanding of the era than are any number of history books.

At their very basic levels, all film and TV texts—even those that are not forthrightly nostalgic—are simulacra, copies of things that are not real. Hollywood filmmakers have always created sets and costumes that were then meant to represent the "real" world of the film (its **diegesis**). In other words, Hollywood movies (and most TV shows) create "pretend" realities, set them up for the camera, and then film and edit them together in order to create a sense of the real for the viewer who willingly suspends his or her disbelief. There is no "real" Jurassic Park, and the film *Jurassic Park* (1993) can only present its idea of such a place. Even documentaries or reality TV shows are highly mediated versions of some pre-arranged, pre-lit, scripted, and edited "reality." However, we laugh, we cry, we fear, or we feel sad at the movies because we react to the unreal worlds that Hollywood asks us to experience as real. In this sense, when we watch film and/or TV we are always/already reacting to simulacra and simulations. And the more we consume such texts, the further immersed in postmodernist sensibilities we may become. For Jameson, these postmodern experiences, texts, and sensations have created a sense of cultural **ahistoricity**, or a culturally schizophrenic state in which actual history and reality (if they ever were knowable) have been replaced by ever-multiplying and competing images/signs of history and reality, all of which exist simultaneously in our contemporary era thanks to cinematic, televisual, and now computer-mediated culture. How these and various other aspects of postmodern theory manifest themselves in film and television texts formally or aesthetically is the subject to which we now turn.

Towards a postmodern aesthetic

The previous section discussed some of the historical factors and theoretical interventions that led to the development of this thing called postmodernism. And again, while the term may be used to describe those sociocultural shifts and/or the historical era during which they occurred, it can also be used to describe an aesthetic. As such, this section explores four "cluster areas" of related formal traits (as well as their theoretical ramifications) that could be said to define a postmodern aesthetic, especially as it relates to film and television texts. This section draws heavily on Jim Collins's much reprinted essay "Television and Postmodernism" (1992), expanding upon his thoughts also to include a consideration of how postmodernism functions in relation to contemporary film texts. These four (related and intertwining) cluster areas of traits that might describe this postmodern aesthetic are: (1) **fragmentation**, (2) **semiotic excess**, (3) the **blurring of boundaries**, and (4) **hyperreality** or **hyperconsciousness**.

Fragmentation is a formal trait that postmodernism shares with modernism; recall how modernists wanted to break up unity and wholeness by foregrounding formal techniques like brushstrokes, or by splitting their subjects into different perspectives (as in cubism). Contemporary film and television texts are increasingly fragmented in a number of ways, especially in terms of their formal construction. First, compared to classical Hollywood filmmaking or early (pre-1970s) television, contemporary films and TV shows are cut into ever-smaller shot lengths and narrative sequences. (On television this fragmentation is exacerbated each year by more and more commercial interruptions, station breaks, and public service announcements, leading theorists like Raymond Williams to approach TV as an endless **flow** of fragments rather than a discrete set of texts.) Partly the speed of editing in film and television texts has gotten faster since the 1980s due to the development of digital technologies, and especially non-linear (computerized) editing systems that make the selection and combination of individual shots much easier to accomplish than ever before. In earlier decades, a film editor actually had to work with strips of film, painstakingly cutting shots into certain lengths, gluing (or splicing) them together, then seeing how they played together on a bench-top monitor. If he or she did not like the edit, the pieces of film would have to be split apart again and a new combination tried. Today, those functions can be accomplished in milliseconds via computerized editing systems, and editing in general in both film and TV has gotten not only quicker, but also more complex. Similarly, many older TV shows were either shot live or "live on tape" and edited in real time—as they transpired—by switching between cameras as the action occurred. Although some television is still shot that way today (especially talk shows and game shows that want to preserve a sense of "liveness"), more and more television is created using cinematic technologies and techniques, including non-linear, computerized editing systems.

The fragmentation of media texts in the 1980s is also related to the development of a new (to that era) kind of media text—the music video. While musical sequences had existed in film and television before the advent of the music video, they usually consisted of a single performance, captured for the camera with continuity editing (or even a single long take). The music video was something new, quickly intercutting images of the performer with related images that either told a short narrative or reflected on the song in thematic ways. The wholeness and unity associated with classical art (or someone like Frank Sinatra singing a song in a film or on a television special), was broken up into shorter and shorter fragments. Some music videos suggest avant-garde or experimental forms, while others try simply to be colorful eye-candy with little narrative coherence. These new ways of editing quickly influenced other TV texts and Hollywood films in the 1980s: *Miami Vice* (1985–90) became famous for its "MTV editing" and music video aesthetic, and musicals like the Prince vehicle *Purple Rain* (1984) looked more like the music videos they were based on rather than classical Hollywood film musicals. And while montage sequences had always existed within the grammar of classical Hollywood filmmaking, during the 1980s montage sequences set to pop songs were increasingly integrated into films like *Risky Business* (1983), *The Breakfast Club* (1985), and *Top Gun* (1986). That era's "training montage" sequence became such a cliché that later postmodern texts like *Buffy the Vampire Slayer* (1997–2003) could copy and comment upon them in self-reflexive ways. (See the Season 6 episode "Once More, with Feeling.")

Fragmentation also exists on the level of film and television narratives. Media scholars have noted a shift from classical Hollywood-style storytelling (with a beginning, middle, and end that all link up into a whole narrative experience), to one based on a more episodic approach. The case of the contemporary postmodern horror film is especially egregious in this regard: narrative or thematic coherence is often sacrificed for a series of interchangeable blood-letting episodes that may or may not contribute to the narrative in any significant way. Similarly, many contemporary Hollywood blockbusters are either based on video games or written to feel like one: their narratives move from set piece to set piece, episode to episode, without significant development of character or theme (things that classical Hollywood screenwriting usually tried to do). For example, movies like *Silent Hill* (2006), *Prince of Persia* (2010), or *The Hobbit* (2012) all feature underdeveloped characters who must vanquish one monster or narrative obstacle before they move onto the next episode, wherein they encounter a similar challenge. Likewise, in much contemporary film and TV, there is less emphasis on narrative closure, and more emphasis on breaking up one potential text into multiple installments of texts. In the film business, this is referred to as **franchising** (the creation of one ongoing story across multiple film texts) and on TV it is called serialization (the presentation of ongoing stories that develop from week to week). It is no secret that contemporary corporate Hollywood now seeks to create highly lucrative film franchises (*Harry Potter*, *Twilight*, *Pirates of the Caribbean*, *X-Men*, et al.) because a successful film franchise can create exponential returns at the box office, far more than a string of unrelated films. On TV, the popularity of serial dramas like *The Wire* (2002–8), *True Blood* (2008–14), and *Game of Thrones* (2011–) is also indicative of this shift; as discussed in Chapter 5, since the 1980s narrative television shows have increasingly been moving from the single unified (**series**) format into larger ongoing (**serial**) meta-narratives that potentially have no end. Both film and TV texts are also increasingly broken up across multiple distribution platforms, creating what scholars like Henry Jenkins refer to as **transmedia storytelling**: many movies and TV shows are no longer just movies or TV shows, but instead branded franchises that can and do expand across multiple films, TV shows, comic books, websites, video games, theme parks, and the like.

Fragmentation is closely linked to (2) **semiotic excess**—a term that refers to the literal "bombardment of signs" that exists in postmodern culture and within postmodern media texts. Once the world—mediated or otherwise—has been fragmented, postmodern media culture takes those fragments and hurls them at us in unending streams of images. In the "real" world we are increasingly bombarded by advertising pitches and ever-changing digital billboards; surfing the web is a point-and-click onslaught of words, images, pop-up ads, and sound bites, a state of affairs that has been described as the "information explosion." (That term— coined as it was in the 1960s—seems almost quaint today, compared to the semiotic excesses of contemporary culture.) Likewise, the increasing quality of digital video technologies in recent decades has allowed film and TV images to become much more densely packed with information, creating a much "busier" frame than could be captured by earlier film and TV technologies. New technologies have given rise to new and multiple forms of audio and visual excess, expressed through the overly-cluttered *mise-en-scènes* and sound mixes that comprise much contemporary film and television. In blockbuster filmmaking, **CGI (computer generated imagery)** creates thousands of extra signs, whether they be armies of Orcs, giant fleets of starships, or marauding zombies. Taking advantage of such new technologies, George Lucas went back and added images and sounds to his original *Star Wars* films (1977, 1980, 1983) when he rereleased them in the 1990s. John Caldwell, in his book of the same name, describes similar technical and formal developments in 1980s television aesthetics as **televisuality**; contemporary TV looks very different than it did in the 1950s or 1960s. Even a relatively simple form like the local or national nightly newscast has been transformed by postmodern technologies and aesthetics. In earlier decades, the nightly newscast featured a single man sitting in a plain studio, at a plain desk, reading the news off a teleprompter or a script. Comparatively, today's newscasts are awash in semiotic excess—the host has become several hosts and hostesses, or else he/she has been pushed to one side to allow for multiple graphics, crawls, updates, advertising logos, flashing lights, and swooping camera movements.

The opening sequence of *The Colbert Report* (2005–14) brilliantly captures and satirizes the semiotic excess of today's television news/commentary shows. In a little over 15 seconds, the credit sequence contains at least ten complex shots or images. (Given the amount of CGI involved in the sequence it is difficult to tell where shots begin and end, as CGI can be used to hide a cut.) In the first image (1), a red, white, and blue bald eagle soars against a red, white, and blue night sky. The eagle "wipes" into (2) a zoom-in on anchorman Stephen Colbert, who faces the camera and raises an eyebrow. Another fly-by "wipe" (3) of the eagle gives way to (4) a longer shot of Colbert running towards the camera. Colbert (5) grabs a United States flag from a flag pole and leaps into the air; after flying downwards like a superhero (6), Colbert aggressively plants the flag in the ground, which creates a circular "seal" that contains the shows logo (7). As the camera moves in and then back out, the planting of the flag gives rise to (8) a CGI stadium-like background. The next image (9) is the title logo for "The Colbert Report," which moves down over the previous image. This is followed by (10) another aggressive "eagle wipe" out along the z-axis, in which the bird seems to be attacking the viewer. The eagle's mouth opens and the first shot of the show itself commences—a wide-angle boom camera shot that swirls around the studio in a dizzying manner. And if that is not enough semiotic information to process in 15 seconds, images 2–7 are set against a background of words swirling in space (such as "strong," "patriot," and "star-spangled"); similar words and phrases ("kingmaker") are also part of the stadium graphic. The images also contain (in each of three corners) a TV ratings logo, a "closed captioning" logo, and the Comedy Central logo; a sponsor banner also appears across the bottom of the screen. Meanwhile, the sound track is filled with the show's synthesized brass and guitar-riffing theme song, eagle screeches, and finally the applause of the studio audience (who have been coached to stand and cheer excessively).

In the context of *The Colbert Show*'s larger project, this opening sequence is meant to satirize the empty "smoke and mirrors" grandstanding of much contemporary television news commentary (such as that found on CNN and Fox News), and more generally, on the excessive flash and emptiness of postmodern media culture itself. For a viewer "in on" the satire, the credit sequence reads ironically, critiquing the self-centered and self-aggrandizing Colbert persona as a shameless huckster who wraps himself in the flag of patriotism. However, some viewers might decode the sequence less ironically, seeing it as just red, white, and blue eye-candy. Other viewers may miss the satire altogether and mistake the Colbert persona for "real." The creation of this dual or multiple reading position is another hallmark of the postmodern aesthetic, as is **irony** in general. In much postmodern media, there is the sense that signs and texts are always being presented in qualified ways—as if in "quotation marks." In other words, the same signs and texts can either be taken at face value (seriously and straightforwardly), or as a joke, satire, or comment upon those same values. Postmodern meanings themselves are excessive—they multiply in various ways among various audiences. For example, when a character in a Hollywood film makes a humorously disparaging remark about someone in a wheelchair, are we supposed to laugh at the cruel joke or laugh at the boorishness of the character? In this case, some theorists suggest that film and TV sign systems are operating on their own, untethered from the reality of their referents (such as actual disability, sensitivity to other people or lack thereof), in yet another version of postmodern simulation. Increasingly, we see the signs we want to see and make the sense we want to "know" out of them. Stephen Colbert's neologism "truthiness" alludes to this precarious and highly mediated state of "knowing," wherein logic, facts, and scientific evidence are trumped by political spin that speaks to viewers' preconceived ideas about the world around them. Again, this notion—that images have replaced the real—or at least become more important than the real—is central to postmodern thought and politics.

As this example demonstrates, fragmentation and semiotic excess emphasize the surface "flash" or "spin" of a text more so than its deeper structures or subtexts. Fragmentation and semiotic excess create a (media) world where exciting images are more important than substances, and where everything can supposedly be defined, described, and/or categorized by a catchy sound bite or colorful graphic. In the postmodern horror film, one excessive gore effect quickly gives rise to another, while on the contemporary TV newscast, one brief sound bite or "news story" quickly gives rise to another in an unending stream of signs (unending at least on 24-hour news channels). Today, even a so-called "in-depth report" on most newscasts lasts for barely a minute or two, and within that time the report engages multiple reporters, experts, witnesses, and graphics. Connecting the horror film and the nightly newscast is the old adage of journalism, "if it bleeds, it leads," meaning that the most sensational stories or violent footage should be showcased at the top of the show. Underlying the surface flash of such postmodern media one senses a great deal of cynicism about the nature of the audience: do producers really assume that the attention span of their viewers is truly that short? For better or worse, postmodern film and TV tends to be fragmented and semiotically excessive because producers, advertisers, and programmers believe that viewers who are not immediately—and continuously—entertained by sensationalized situations or eye-popping graphics may switch the channel or stop watching the film.

Another way that texts become semiotically excessive is through (3) the **blurring of boundaries**, a common postmodern trope that might include the hybridization of film genres and television formats, the mixing of tropes from high and low arts, classical and modernist, and even historical eras. Consider a film like *The Rocky Horror Picture Show* (1975), which is (at least) a horror-science fiction-musical-comedy whose set design contains (unexplained) copies of famous art works like Michelangelo's *David*, the ceiling of the Sistine Chapel, and Grant Wood's *American Gothic*. The latter work is "quoted" within the text at least three times: first in the opening wedding sequence when the church caretakers strike the painting's iconic pose, second when the painting itself appears in the foyer of Dr. Frankenfurters's castle, and third when Riff Raff and Magenta (who struck the pose in the first instance) appear as their "true" alien selves brandishing a pitchfork-shaped space gun. Are these "quotations" meant to contribute to the deeper meanings of *The Rocky Horror Picture Show*—perhaps suggesting how horror lies just below the surface of (mid)western American culture—or are they just playful allusions that might amuse a bored spectator familiar with art history? Contemporary postmodern films mix and match historical eras as well as genres, as in the science fiction westerns *Wild Wild West* (1999) and *Cowboys & Aliens* (2011), or the science fiction-film noir thriller *Blade Runner* (1982). David Lynch's *Blue Velvet* (1986) has been hailed as postmodern not only for its excessively stylized performances, but for the way its *mise-en-scène* suggests both the 1950s and the 1980s. (This might be another good example of Fredric Jameson's concept of **ahistoricity**: such films seem literally unstuck in time.) TV of course, has also become increasingly hybridized, not just as serial and series forms have merged, but as producers try to mix and match previously successful genre elements. The musical police show *Cop Rock* (1990) may have died a quick death several decades ago, but the musical-comedy-drama *Glee* (2009–15) was a big hit, as is *Empire* (2015–), a musical-family drama *à la Dynasty* (1981–9) with violent "gangsta" elements. Similarly, how many (non-musical) TV series in the last decade have had special musical episodes wherein their characters sang and danced?

The postmodern concept of **bricolage** is a special type of border or boundary crossing. Bricolage refers to the postmodern penchant for combining (sometimes highly) disparate elements from previous texts into a new text. The term might be used to refer to the **textual poaching** that media fans commit when they take disparate elements from their favorite texts and recombine them into something new (see Chapter 11), or it might be used to refer to the way that many postmodern texts are a combination of different stylistic and generic elements. Bricolage in this case is similar to **collage**, an art form that assembles together different elements from diverse sources. All of the films and TV shows mentioned in the previous paragraph could be seen as examples of bricolage. Critics have noted how the first *Star Wars* movie (1977) is a bricolage of generic elements from the western, the war movie, the samurai film, the swashbuckler, and even Leni Riefenstahl's Nazi propaganda film *Triumph of the Will* (1935). Some postmodern texts seem to be nothing but extreme bricolage, such as the TV show *Aqua Teen Hunger Force* (2000–) discussed in Chapters 1 and 2. With little classical narrative or thematic consistency, the show is nothing but a series of elements and references to other texts of popular culture, from McDonald's "Happy Meals," to cinematic vampires, to tourism, to Nashville, to Elvis, to rap music, to comic books, to detective shows, to cloning, to the *Alien* films, and so on and so forth. This is yet another example of how postmodern media texts have moved away from being grounded in reality (even *The Brady Bunch* [1969–74] suggested some form of "real" familial relations), relying instead on the free play of signs and signifiers culled from pop culture.

Fragmentation, semiotic excess, and the blurring of borders or boundaries all help to create what postmodern theorists call (4) **hyperreality**, or what Jim Collins defines as **hyperconsciousness**: "a hyperawareness on the part of the text itself of its cultural status, function, and history, as well as of the conditions of its circulation and reception" (1992, 335). This postmodern self-awareness is very different from high modernist self-reflexivity, which was meant to challenge audiences by revealing the means of production (*à la* **Bertolt Brecht** or Jean-Luc Godard); rather it is "a hyperconscious rearticulation of media culture by media culture" in which the viewer is expected to find pleasure in the intertextual, meta-textual nature of much film and television (Collins 1992, 335). Hyperconsciousness thus arises from postmodern media's collusion with the viewer. In the case of the TV show *Buffy the Vampire Slayer*, the characters can refer to themselves as the "Scooby Gang" because they know their media literate audience will get the reference to the cartoon show *Scooby-Doo, Where are You!* (1969–72). Likewise, the show's musical episode ("Once More, with Feeling") contains multiple hyperconscious remarks about the kinds of songs the characters are singing, and even a throw away reference ("respect the cruller … tame the donut") to the sexist motivational speaker played by Tom Cruise in P. T. Anderson's film *Magnolia* (1999) (see Figure 9.8). (Note also the multiple sexualized meanings of the pastries in question!) Getting all the in-jokes, allusions, and references in postmodern media texts can have the effect of making the viewer feel smarter: he or she may feel rewarded for catching the reference(s). Postmodern media culture seems to imply that if a viewer does not catch the reference, he or she probably needs to consume more film and TV until one is able to do so. If the apparatus theorists who published in *Screen* magazine during the 1970s theorized that Hollywood film worked to suture spectators into a single filmic experience, postmodern media culture expects its viewers to suture into the entirety of postmodern media culture.

Another key aspect of postmodern theory and hyperreality is **pastiche**. Pastiche is best understood as "blank parody," or the copying of a style or element of culture, not to make fun of it or to find humor in it, but simply for the sake of quoting a distinctive style. (Works constructed via bricolage may therefore make stylistic use of pastiche.) This may give the newer text a patina of high art (as with the "German expressionist" Madonna video "Express Yourself" mentioned above), or it may simply be another way to allude to previous pop culture texts, blurring the borders between one text and another, one style and another, or one genre and another. Pastiche thus blends into the media industries' penchant for recycling and remaking previously successful formulas; here the profit motive runs counter to creativity and/or originality. The film and television industries are always ready to green light a new project that is based significantly on an older, previously successful one. Thus the *Star Wars* franchise looks back upon and copies elements of 1930s science fiction serials (like *Flash Gordon* [1936] and *Buck Rogers* [1939]),

Fig 9.8
A tossed-off intertextual reference in *Buffy the Vampire Slayer* (1997–2003): Xander paraphrases Paul Thomas Anderson's *Magnolia* (1999), stating the need to "respect the cruller [and] tame the donut."

while the *Indiana Jones* franchise can be understood as a pastiche of Hollywood's action-adventure serials of the 1940s. Such recycling and remaking may activate **nostalgia** in older filmgoers, while younger viewers unfamiliar with the original texts can see them as "originals" (yet another example of how postmodern texts may speak to multiple audiences in different ways).

This state of affairs has led some to describe postmodernism as a state of **cultural exhaustion**, wherein all originality is supposedly dead, wherein all the great ideas have already been thought, and all the great film and TV shows have already been made. According to this scenario, all current media makers can hope to do is recycle, remake, repackage, and reprocess all that has come before. In truth, Hollywood and the media industries have always copied and repackaged their previous successes, even as the degree to which sequels and remakes get made appears to have increased greatly during the postmodern era. As the media industries become increasingly integrated both vertically and horizontally, ever-increasing profits depend on the synergistic production, promotion, and distribution of similar pre-packaged or pre-sold properties like comic books, successful novels, popular TV shows and/or films. The media industries have an economic incentive to repeat their successful formulas, but other distribution outlets allow for a wider range of product to be produced, whether it be the independent film scene, straight-to-DVD production, or new Internet channels devoted to short films and independent video. And perhaps there is no such thing as originality anyway, as many postmodern theorists have suggested. Shakespeare borrowed from previous authors, classical Hollywood films were often based on novels and theatrical melodramas, just as more recently they are based on popular novels and comic books. Perhaps creativity has *always* been about the recycling and recombining of previous forms into something new. The trick is to do it in new and interesting ways.

Case study: *Pee-Wee's Playhouse Christmas Special* (1988)

From the moment it premiered on CBS's Saturday morning television lineup, *Pee-Wee's Playhouse* (1986–91) was an instant hit with children, but it also garnered quite a few adult fans, thanks to its *double entendre* jokes and perverse pop culture sensibility. Indeed, the Pee-Wee Herman character began his life in a distinctly adult nightclub act that satirized children's TV shows. From its inception then, *Pee-Wee's Playhouse* simultaneously addressed two if not multiple audiences: it was both a straightforward kid's TV show as well as *satire* of a kid's TV show. Noting this multiple appeal, and its balance of high and low art forms, *The Hollywood Reporter* once opined that *Pee-wee's Playhouse* was "TV gone Dada ... skillfully balanc[ing] the distinction between low-camp and high performance art." *Pee-Wee's Playhouse* also captured the attention of its era's film and television scholars: an entire issue of the media journal *camera obscura* (May 1988) was devoted to analyses of the show from feminist, **queer**, consumerist, and above all postmodern perspectives. As this case study will sketch out, the multiple addresses and appeals of *Pee-Wee's Playhouse* are but one factor of its overall postmodern aesthetic: the series is a highly fragmented, hyper-self-conscious, boundary-blurring text of semiotic excess, as was *Pee-Wee's Playhouse Christmas Special*, a single hour-long prime time episode of the show that aired during the holiday season in 1988.

To begin with, *Pee-Wee's Playhouse Christmas Special* not only addresses a multiple and fragmented audience, but its formal composition is also highly segmented and semiotically excessive. As did the regular weekly series, the 49-minute *Christmas Special* incorporates a barrage of short sequences made up of vintage cartoons, old educational films, newly produced stop-motion animation, Claymation, nascent computer animation, hand puppets, marionettes, and skits featuring a large cast of endearingly eccentric characters (the talking and animated denizens of the Playhouse). In charge of all this chaos is the gray-suited and red-bow-tied Pee-Wee Herman himself, played by the adult actor Paul Reubens as a greedy man-child. Pee-Wee's (gargantuan) wish list of toys that he wants Santa Claus to bring him is matched by his (gargantuan) set of guest stars who appear on the *Christmas Special*, including Charo, Cher, Grace Jones, Zsa Zsa Gábor, Magic Johnson, Little Richard, k. d. lang, Dinah Shore, Whoopi Goldberg, Joan Rivers, Frankie Avalon, Annette Funicello, Oprah Winfrey, and a (faux) Marine Corps men's choir. Many of these guest stars are mostly famous for being famous "personalities," or else they are there to invoke **nostalgia**, as with the appearance of Frankie and Annette, the stars of a slew of *Beach Party* musicals in the 1960s. And although the guest star singers do get to sing (briefly) on the *Christmas Special*, many of the other guest appearances consist of little more than one- or two-line walk-on appearances. Things move so quickly at the Playhouse that when the group settles down to sing Christmas carols towards the end of the show, they only sing each song's title refrain before moving on to the next one.

Semiotic excess defines many aspects of the show, from its *mise-en-scène* to its performance aesthetics. The Playhouse is cluttered with kitschy retro furniture, including a talking chair, a talking globe, and talking flowers. Beyond the plethora of characters that inhabit the Playhouse, every possible wall or floor space is covered with some sort of fantastic mosaic design or geometric pattern. Indeed, some of the Playhouse walls are constructed as vertically beveled surfaces, such that they reveal one image from one perspective and another image from a different point of view. This visual confusion gets even busier after Jambi the Genie (himself only a fragmented head in a bejeweled box) magically decorates the Playhouse with scads of Christmas garlands and other assorted accoutrements of the season. Similarly excessive, Pee-Wee forces Frankie and Annette to make one thousand Christmas cards (plus envelopes), and serves Santa from a tray overflowing with cookies. Pee-Wee receives so many fruitcakes for Christmas that he uses them as bricks to build a new wing to the Playhouse. In another amusing use of excess, the (seemingly) never-ending Christmas carol "The Twelve Days of Christmas" is sung by Dinah Shore to Pee-Wee via his tin-can video telephone booth; Pee-Wee gets bored after a few moments and substitutes a mannequin copy of himself (a **simulacrum**) inside the booth. Later in the show we hear that the song is still being sung by its hapless and abandoned singer, its original verses now expanded to include "18 bags of nachos" and "17 body builders." In another register of excess, most of the human characters on the show are performed in campy or excessive manners (perhaps most conspicuously k. d. lang who sings "Jingle Bell Rock" as if she were on amphetamines), while Pee-Wee's "Secret Word of the Day" routine is answered by the entire Playhouse following Pee-Wee's exhortation to "Scream Real Loud!"

The show continually blurs boundaries in multiple ways as well, from the Pee-Wee character's man-boy status, to its historical schizophrenia: the Playhouse's TV screens and much of its décor appear to be from the 1950s, even as the show's formal aesthetic is a good example of 1980s **televisuality**. *Pee-Wee's Playhouse Christmas Special* partakes heavily of a **bricolage aesthetic**, not just in terms of its wide array of guest stars, musical performances, and animated sequences, but also in terms of its set design. The exterior of the Playhouse is comprised of an Egyptian sphinx, lava lamps, and a barber pole, among other elements (see Figure 9.9). The inside of the playhouse contains Greek

Fig 9.9
Pee-Wee's Playhouse
is itself an example of
bricolage, made up
of multiple disparate
elements including a
sphinx and lava lamps.

statuary, a Tiki totem, and sculptural wall art of a giant can opener that just might be
a winking reference to Andy Warhol's Campbell soup cans. (The fact that Frankie and
Annette are mass producing their Christmas cards via stencils and a reusable "potato"
printer may also be a nod to Warhol's serialized Pop Art productions.) At another point
in the *Special*, a highly condensed (two-minute) Hollywood studio cartoon is presented
by The King of Cartoons: the short film itself dramatizes the concept of bricolage as a
Santa-like figure reassembles broken and discarded household objects into workable toys
for orphaned children (see Figure 9.10). The cartoon itself is notable for its incorporation
of an actual "live action" Christmas tree model within its otherwise two-dimensional
cel-animated milieu (a technique practiced by the Fleischer Brothers at Paramount
Studios, who created the original eight-minute short, *Christmas Comes but Once a Year*
[1936]). Pee-Wee's robot Conky is also a work of bricolage, comprised of an old boom
box, various electronic radio parts, and old-fashioned camera flash bulbs that serve
as his "eyes." Similarly, Pee-Wee's Christmas tree is assembled from various pieces of
neighborhood detritus, including what appears to be an old outdoor grill. Even the
show's opening musical number combines two different musical idioms: it begins as
a solemn chorale sung by what appear to be members of the US Marine Corps, until
it bursts into a funky 1960s girl group sound. At that moment, lead singer Pee-Wee is
instantly flanked by two female African American backup singers in gold lamé gowns.
Here the allusion and pastiche is suggestive of Diana Ross and The Supremes, or any
number of 1960s girl groups (see Figure 9.11).

Indeed, allusions and references appear throughout the show in multiple ways,
contributing to the show's **hyperreality** or **hyperconsciousness**—that is to say its
self-conscious irony, and hyperawareness of its own textuality. For example, the Marines
are choreographed at one point in a signature Busby Berkeley array, the "Penny" cartoon
alludes to Bob Hope and Bing Crosby's 1940s "Road pictures," and the secret code to
Pee-Wee's toy box sounds suspiciously like the five-note theme used to communicate
with the extraterrestrials in *Close Encounters of the Third Kind* (1977). As a **pastiche** of a
children's show, *Pee-Wee's Playhouse* invokes *Mr. Rogers' Neighborhood, Captain Kangaroo,*

Fig 9.10
More **bricolage** in *Pee-Wee's Playhouse Christmas Special* (1988): a cartoon from the 1930s features a Santa-like figure building new toys out of discarded household items.

Fig 9.11
Pastiche in *Pee-Wee's Playhouse Christmas Special* (1988): Pee-Wee is flanked by two African American back-up singers suggesting the girl groups of the 1960s.

and *Sesame Street*. As a pastiche of televised holiday shows, *Pee-Wee's Playhouse Christmas Special* invokes hundreds of such texts, with their routinized guest stars, musical performances, comedy sketches, and moral lessons. However, Pee-Wee's big lesson in his *Christmas Special*—"Christmas is a time we should be thinking about others" (and not merely being greedy for desiring an excessive amount of presents)—is rendered as possibly parodic via its clichéd presentation as an echo-filled flashback sequence. Is the show asserting an actual moral lesson, or making fun of the usual Christmas special's felt need to do so? That self-conscious dynamic also informs the *Special*'s take on holiday diversity, as Mrs. Rene (Suzanne Kent) proudly announces that she is Jewish, and turns to the camera to exclaim "Come on everybody! It's the Hanukkah portion of the Show!" before leading the Playhouse in a rousing version of "The Dreidel Song" (complete with a bouncing Jambi head bobbing along to the superimposed lyrics).

Pee-Wee's Playhouse Christmas Special also creates hyperreality or hyperconsciousness through its self-conscious acknowledgement of its own status as a TV show. Not only does Mrs. Rene break the diegetic space of the Playhouse when she addresses the camera during the Hanukkah portion of the show, but at another point Pee-Wee asks the televisual audience what they think of the show so far. ("Well, same to you!" he responds snarkily.) At another point, Pee-Wee's ice skating prowess (and televisual trickery in general) is revealed to be the work of a stunt double named Hans (a reference to the famous children's story *Hans Brinker; or, the Silver Skates*). And while self-reflexively talking to the home audience may not seem extraordinarily out of place in a children's TV show or a televised Christmas special, at one point *Pee-Wee's Playhouse Christmas Special* directly alludes to a famous self-reflexive moment in cinematic high modernism. In the climax to Orson Welles's famous **film noir** *The Lady from Shanghai* (1948), a shoot-out taking place in a hall of mirrors ends when even the "lens" of the camera (that is to say the frame presented to the spectator) appears to become cracked itself. In the *Playhouse Christmas Special*, a similar moment occurs when Pee-Wee's reckless yo-yo-ing seemingly breaks the lens of the camera recording his actions (see Figure 9.12). As with many similar examples discussed within the body of this chapter, this quoting of a specific high modernist trope within a popular film or TV text is a key trope of postmodern aesthetics.

Fig 9.12
In *Pee-Wee's Playhouse
Christmas Special* (1988),
Pee-Wee's yoyo "breaks the
lens" of the camera filming
him, a self-reflexive device
more common to high
modernist filmmaking than
a children's TV show.

While it is perhaps easy to see a postmodern aesthetic at work in *Pee-Wee's Playhouse
Christmas Special*, what can we say about its political or ideological meanings? As with
many postmodern texts, its excessive irony and bricolage aesthetic make it hard to get
a bead on any single meaning arising from the show. What does the show have to say
about Christmas and consumerism? Pee-Wee's bratty marionette friend Randy sounds like
a junior Marxist when he asserts that "Christmas is just a commercial exploitation for big
business trying to capitalize on consumer guilt!" In response, Pee-Wee's friend Magic Screen
says that the "true meaning" of Christmas is "the celebration of the birthday of the Christ
child," but that meaning is problematized by how Magic Screen visualizes the traditional
Christmas narrative. As he (she?) speaks, Magic Screen shows what appears to be someone's
old home movie footage of a tacky children's Christmas pageant, performed inside a church
for what looks like the edification of Japanese school girls. In this way, *Pee-Wee's Playhouse
Christmas Special* pays lip service to the standard Christian meaning(s) of Christmas, while
also raising issues about the spread and meaning of Christianity within global contexts,
where it has been used to aid in colonization and economic exploitation (see Chapter 12).

A similar ideological conundrum arises over the portrayal of social difference on the
show. On one level, the show's collage of oddball characters and guest stars is definitely
multi-cultural, but the show's main character is male and white (albeit infantile and
greedy). More problematic is that since some of the multicultural characters are on
screen for only moments at a time, some of them (like Mrs. Rene) feel like stereotypical
caricatures. On the other hand, sometimes the Playhouse seems more queerly
multicultural. Pee-Wee's mail "man" is Reba, an African-American mail lady (played by
S. Epatha Merkerson) who brings the dance club diva Grace Jones to the Playhouse.
Latino soccer player Ricardo (Vic Trevino) tries to teach Pee-Wee how to pronounce the
name of the Spanish-language Christmas song "Feliz Navidad," which Charo then sings,
accompanying herself on the classical guitar. And if one cares to analyze it, Cowboy
Curtis, decked out in pink and purple cowboy garb (and played by Laurence Fishburne)
suggests the forgotten histories of black and/or gay cowboys in the Old West. The show
also contains another subtle but extended gay in-joke, as Pee-Wee's new wing of the

Playhouse is being built with fruitcakes (a slang term for gay men in previous eras) by two hunky construction workers, one of whom is shirtless (see Figure 9.13). Furthermore, the doorway to the new wing features a reproduction of Thomas Gainsborough's famous portrait *The Blue Boy*; *Blueboy* was the name of a gay men's magazine during the 1980s (see Figure 9.14). While not all contemporary films and TV shows partake of a postmodern aesthetic quite as vehemently as does *Pee-Wee's Playhouse Christmas Special*, it remains a good example of what that aesthetic looks like and how it operates ideologically.

Fig 9.13
An elaborate gay joke in *Pee-Wee's Playhouse Christmas Special* (1988): a secret new wing of the playhouse is being built entirely out of fruitcakes by hunky construction workers …

Fig 9.14
… note how the new wing is positioned behind a copy of Gainsborough's *The Blue Boy*, referencing a gay male magazine of the era.

Conclusion: (Some) politics of postmodernism

For many of the reasons explored in this chapter (and in the case study), it is often hard to make a coherent ideological "reading" of many postmodern texts. Being fragmentary and cobbled together from disparate sources (as in the bricolage aesthetic), many postmodern texts are made up of widely varying if not contradictory elements and ideologies. In those cases, such postmodern texts might be said to be ideologically incoherent, in that it is very hard to get a bead on what sorts of **ideological messages** they are actually expressing. The multiple addresses (or reading positions) that many postmodern media texts create also compound their ideological incoherence, forcing the cultural critic into closer analyses of such texts' reception (see Chapters 10 and 11). Unlike more unified classical or modernist texts where ideological meaning is perhaps more straightforwardly expressed, the use of the term **ideological problematic** may be more useful for many postmodern texts. As Chapter 2 suggested, just what sort of ideological work is a show like *Aqua Teen Hunger Force* doing? It may depend more on the viewers' use of the text than anything related to its actual content.

Some theorists of the postmodern, including Hal Foster and Linda Hutcheon, have made a useful distinction between what might be called **co-opted** or **commercialized postmodernism**, and a more **critical** or **deconstructive postmodernism**. These terms refer to the ways that postmodern media texts either conform to the dominant ideologies of Western capitalism and thinking (thus becoming co-opted or commercialized postmodern texts) or whether they tend to oppose them (thus becoming critical or deconstructive postmodernist texts). Like all binaries, however, these labels should be approached with caution, and understood as opposing trends within postmodern media, and not **essentialist** labels or categories. As noted above, many postmodern texts have ideologically incoherent or diffuse messages, and this aspect probably places them more in line with a co-opted or commercialized postmodernism. The majority of contemporary film and TV texts could probably be described in this manner, as they are often constructed to have multiple appeals to varying segments of the population, and they are definitely made with the intent of making a profit.

Perhaps more egregiously, the recycling and remaking of texts from previous eras runs the risk of recycling and reinscribing the earlier era's ideological messages. For example, *Indiana Jones and the Kingdom of the Crystal Skulls* (2008) contains monstrous dark-skinned Others more common to Hollywood serials of the 1930s and 1940s; would they not be considered politically incorrect by twenty-first-century standards? The Indiana Jones films might best be considered **nostalgic Hollywood blockbusters**. Not only are they set in previous eras, but they are also pastiches of a previous era's cinematic format and style. Unwittingly or not, they recirculate and reinscribe racist and sexist stereotypes common in those previous eras. Similarly, Jar Jar Binks from the *Star Wars* franchise may come from the city of Gunga on the planet of Naboo, but his comedic antics reminded many critics of stereotypical **coon** roles played by African American men in Hollywood films of the 1930s and 1940s (see Chapter 12). Most of the Hollywood blockbusters that play throughout the year in multiplex theaters across the globe tend to be these commercial or co-opted postmodern texts, nostalgically reinscribing the character types, narrative tropes, and ideological assumptions of previous decades. (Generations of filmmakers who attended film schools rather than studying "real world" issues have perhaps exacerbated this situation.) Rather than addressing current realities (and current ideologies), nostalgic Hollywood blockbusters recall escapist entertainment formats from the past, and continue to reinscribe the **dominant ideologies** of white, Western, patriarchal, and imperialist capitalism.

Texts that fall within the range of more critical or deconstructive postmodernism tend to be fewer in number and reach fewer audiences. Perhaps a documentary/ experimental film hybrid like Errol Morris's *Fast, Cheap & Out of Control* (1997) comes close to being a postmodern text with a deconstructive edge. In a highly fragmented and excessively stylized manner, the film centers on a topiary gardener, a robot scientist, a mole rat expert, and a lion tamer. Shots and scenes of these four men are intercut with one another as well as seemingly random shots from pop culture history, and especially an old movie serial (of the type that *Indiana Jones* pastiches). But rather than being simply incoherent eye-candy or hollow musings, through the processes of comparison that the (dialectical) editing sets up, the film presents a thoughtful take on what it means to be human. It explores topics including the role of the individual versus the collective, mortality, war, risk, evolution, and ultimately asks us to question the meaning(s) of (our) existence. What does the future hold for humankind? As an independent film, *Fast, Cheap & Out of Control* perhaps has the ability to express things other more commercialized postmodern texts cannot. Nonetheless, it still circulates within and as a product of the culture industries. Perhaps a better place to look for critical or deconstructive postmodernist texts would be in art galleries and museums. As was discussed in Chapter 5, openly critical or deconstructive texts do not often do well at the Hollywood box office.

Questions for discussion

1   Compare and contrast an episode of a sitcom from the 1950s (such as *Leave it to Beaver* or *I Love Lucy*) with one from the twenty-first century (such as *Community* or *Modern Family*). Can you identify aspects of the four postmodern "cluster traits" in the newer texts? What can you say about the ideological messages of each text? Are those messages coherent or not?

2   Films like *Frozen* (2013) and *Guardians of the Galaxy* (2014) have been very popular recently. In what ways may these texts be considered postmodern? How do they appropriate or pastiche previous films or film genres? What are the ideological ramifications of the ways they do so?

3   Try to identify some postmodern texts—like *Fast, Cheap & Out of Control*—that you would consider to be critical or deconstructive. How do they achieve their effects? Are they more mainstream texts, or more independent/artisanal texts?

References and further reading

Baudrillard, Jean. *Simulacra and Simulation*. Trans. Sheila Faria Glaser. Ann Arbor: University of Michigan Press, 1994.

Caldwell, John Thornton. *Televisuality: Style, Crisis, and Authority in American Television*. New Brunswick, NJ: Rutgers University Press, 1995.

Collins, Jim. *Uncommon Cultures: Popular Culture and Post-Modernism*. New York and London: Routledge, 1989.

Collins, Jim. "Postmodernism and Television," in *Channels of Discourse, Reassembled: Television and Contemporary Criticism*, Second Edition, ed. Robert C. Allen. Chapel Hill and London: The University of North Carolina Press, 1992 (1987). Pp. 327–53.

Debord, Guy. *Society of the Spectacle*. Trans. Ken Knabb. Oakland, CA: AKPress, 2006 (1967).

Eco, Umberto. *Travels in Hyperreality: Essays*. San Diego, CA: Harcourt Brace Jovanovich, 1986.

Foster, Hal, ed. *The Anti-Aesthetic: Essays on Postmodern Culture*. Port Townsend, WA: The Bay Press, 1983.

Hutcheon, Linda. *The Politics of Postmodernism*. New York and London: Routledge, 1989.

Jameson, Fredric. *Postmodernism, or The Cultural Logic of Late Capitalism*. Durham, NC: Duke University Press, 1991.

Jameson, Fredric. *The Cultural Turn: Selected Writings on Postmodernism, 1983–1998*. London: Verso, 1998.

Jenkins, Henry. *Convergence Culture: Where Old and New Media Collide*. New York: NYU Press, 2008.

Lyotard, Jean-Francois. *The Postmodern Condition: A Report on Knowledge*. Trans.

Geoff Bennington and Brian Massumi. Minneapolis, MN: University of Minnesota Press, 1984 (1979).

Sarup, Madan. *An Introductory Guide to Post-Structuralism and Postmodernism*, Second Edition. Athens, GA: The University of Georgia Press, 1993 (1988).

Williams, Raymond. *Television: Technology and Cultural Form*. London and New York: Routledge, 2003 (1974).

CHAPTER 10

Cultural studies and reception

Many of the ideas already introduced in this book—especially those focused on **ideology**, representation, and audio-visual form, are central to **cultural studies**, an interdisciplinary field that (broadly) seeks to understand various aspects of human cultures via the **texts** they produce and consume. In *Cultural Studies: Theory and Practice*, author Chris Barker suggests that the "intellectual strands of cultural studies" include ideas drawn from **Marxism** and ideology, **structuralism** and **poststructuralism**, psychoanalysis and subjectivity, and "the politics of difference: feminism, race, and postcolonial theory" (12). As such, cultural studies might be thought of as a synthesis of many different Western, twentieth-century ways of thinking about culture and cultural artifacts. And cultural studies understands "culture" in its broadest possible terms, addressing topics as diverse as human biology and emotion, space and nation, globalization, urbanization, history, digital media, various types of social difference, the relationships between dominant cultures and subcultures, and for the explicit purposes of this chapter, film and television texts (as well as their industries and audiences). As such, some of this chapter may seem like a review of certain ideas already presented in previous chapters—and expanded upon in later ones—but herein they are synthesized into a more comprehensive portrait of this thing called cultural studies, especially as it relates to film and TV. To a great extent, because of cultural studies' integrated approach to understanding texts within and against their cultural contexts, much contemporary film and television scholarship might be considered to be in the "cultural studies" mode. Such work often draws upon one or more of the various methodologies explored throughout this book, but it also seeks to place its analyses (auteur, genre, psychoanalytic, etc.) within their specific socio-cultural, historical, and industrial contexts. Broadly, that is the central goal of cultural studies scholarship: relating texts to contexts. In this way, cultural studies explores what texts tell us about the cultures that produce and consume them, and *vice versa*, how texts are produced within specific cultural contexts.

Cultural studies arose in Great Britain in the mid-1960s, quietly revolutionizing multiple disciplines including anthropology, sociology, history, philosophy, ethnography, and literary studies. Recall that during those years, film and television studies were in their infancy—**auteur** and **genre theory** were first introduced in the postwar era and then more finely nuanced with the addition of semiotic and structuralist concepts in the 1960s and 1970s. The **structuralist** turn in film theory became most pronounced by the mid-1970s, when *Screen* or **apparatus**

theory was in vogue. Apparatus theory had little-to-nothing to say about television and/or its contexts, and as such the first generation of television scholars often turned to cultural studies as a broad set of ideas that could be used to study TV (and its viewers). To a certain extent, the rise of cultural studies facilitated the development of television studies: cultural studies insists it is important to study *all* aspects of culture, not just those deemed to be "high art." In the same way auteur and genre theory helped establish film studies as a serious scholarly endeavor in the 1960s, so too did cultural studies legitimate the study of TV in the 1970s and 1980s. Cultural studies has also legitimated the scholarly study of any number of other "low brow" cultural artifacts and genres, including comic books, graffiti, exploitation films, horror films, reality TV, and pornography. If one can be permitted a vampiric metaphor, cultural studies firmly drove a stake into the heart of the notion that only "high art" was worthy of serious study. The shift in nomenclature from talking about "art" to talking about texts or **cultural artifacts** (introduced back at the start of Chapter 1) has been a result of the rise of cultural studies.

As an introduction to these seismic shifts in thinking about culture, one can draw several important distinctions between *Screen*/apparatus theory and the cultural studies model that has supplanted it since then. (1) *Screen*/apparatus theory spoke of the **spectator** as a slot or position in the cinematic machine, into which the flesh-and-blood human agent was **interpellated**. This notion of the passive and undifferentiated "ideal viewer" is replaced in cultural studies by the study of actual human beings (and subcultures) whose race, class, gender, nationality, etc., render them—and their viewing practices—diverse, multiple, and perhaps most importantly, *active*. (2) Drawing on poststructuralist ideas, cultural studies scholars understand human beings not as static biologically essentialist entities but as complex ever-transforming **subjects** comprised of the multiple social forces, institutions, and ideologies in which they have been (and continue to be) forged. The cinematic apparatus is but one of many ideological structures that subjects encounter throughout their lives—and in the twenty-first century many people no longer even encounter the cinematic apparatus, instead consuming media on televisions, computers, tablets, and even cell phones. (3) *Screen* theory has been critiqued by poststructuralists as too monolithic, essentialist, and/or ahistorical. In response, cultural studies emphasizes the particularities of history and reception: different people make sense of the same media artifacts in different ways, based upon their own socio-historical positionings. Cultural studies is thus anti-essentialist, a trait it shares with most **postmodern** and **poststructuralist** thinking. Perhaps most importantly, (4) cultural studies views popular culture as a *site of struggle and contestation* between competing cultural groups or classes, not just economic classes but also social classes based on other markers of social difference such as race, ethnicity, gender, and sexuality.

Cultural studies thus theorizes that ideological control over human beings is dependent upon the control of meaning, and that meaning is always being shaped and reshaped by the popular culture that expresses it. Whoever controls the *meaning(s)* of certain ideas or terms controls the debate, and shapes public understanding in accordance with their political aims. In perhaps the best (if most simplified) example of this point, viewers of Fox News versus those of MSNBC experience and come to understand two very different worlds based upon those networks' ideological biases. For example, are "illegal aliens" criminal threats to the American way of life (as they might be presented on Fox News), or are "undocumented workers" central to the US economy and (as the Statue of Liberty would have it) the nation's mission to accept "tired … poor … huddled masses yearning to breathe free"? In reality, they are the very same people, but notice how language and rhetoric plays a crucial part in framing the differences between "illegal aliens" and "undocumented workers." What is important to remember is that how a given culture defines the terms and meanings of social identities (or more broadly social issues) directly impacts on the ways it writes its social policies and laws, elects politicians, and even starts or ends wars. Images matter—perhaps more than "reality" itself does in our postmodern, hyper-mediated world. In the end, human lives are often at stake in these struggles over meaning.

Examples from TV news shows or highly politicized debates are perhaps easier to understand as ideological battlegrounds than is the alleged "mere entertainment" of most popular culture, including TV and Hollywood. Using terms like "enhanced interrogation" versus "torture" has clear political biases, meant either to justify or decry the harsh treatment of suspected criminals. Likewise, debates over the display of the Confederate flag in the contemporary United States often devolve into simplistic "conservative versus liberal" sentiments: those who support the flag claim they are honoring and supporting their "Southern heritage," while critics see the flag as representing slavery and racism. The latest Hollywood movie or **sitcom** might not be so politically charged, but recall from Chapter 2 that all texts convey ideology: either overtly as in a Michael Moore documentary or TV newscast, or perhaps more subtly in the ways that Hollywood blockbusters or network sitcoms shape perceptions about race, gender, class, nation, religion, and so forth. It therefore becomes the goal of the cultural studies critic to tease apart these film and television texts—via critical formal analysis—to reveal what it is they are saying about social and political issues. Why this text, at this time, from these producers? How did or do audiences make sense of them? These are important questions that film and television scholars working within the cultural studies tradition try to answer.

To sum up this introduction then, cultural studies is a series of interrelated concepts exploring cultural texts and contexts more than a divine method or essentialized approach. It is a highly interdisciplinary field, drawing from and giving back to fields as diverse as mass communications, literary studies, sociology, anthropology, **ethnography**, history, art, visual culture, as well as more recent fields devoted to thinking about race, ethnicity, gender, and sexuality in more complex ways (the topic of Chapter 12). Cultural studies has thoroughly penetrated academia, even influencing fields such as medicine, law, and psychology. Cultural studies examines cultural artifacts (texts) as a way of exploring cultural issues, whether those texts be an episode of *Duck Dynasty* (2012–) or a Shakespeare play. The goal of cultural studies scholarship is not to pronounce any given text as good or bad, or high or low art, but to explore how specific texts represent and create meanings, how they negotiate with the ideological assumptions of their given contexts. In its broadest sense, cultural studies research focuses on relating the semiotic analysis of a text to its historical and socio-cultural contexts. In so doing, it attempts to provide a "thick description" of both texts and contexts, illuminating not only texts themselves, but also the cultures that produce and consume them.

A brief history of the rise of cultural studies

It is significant that cultural studies first arose in Great Britain in the years following World War II. Great Britain has a long history of class consciousness—meaning that its society has long been deeply divided by socio-economic factors, wherein some people are born to rule while others are born to serve. Popular British TV shows like *Upstairs Downstairs* (1971–5) and *Downton Abbey* (2010–)—which dramatize the social stratifications that existed in England in the years before and after World War I—continue to fascinate Western audiences (even in the United States where we like to believe we live in a "classless" nation). Socio-economic class remains an important structuring ideology in Great Britain (as in all nations), but the nature of those classes has been observed to shift and transform over time. For example, the end of World War II signaled the end of the British Empire (see Chapter 12), and British society became less rigidly class-based. New social institutions arose to afford opportunities for a growing middle class, even as the aristocracy was losing its baronial estates and imperialist fortunes. One of those not-so-new institutions was the University of Birmingham, one of the six so-called "red brick universities" chartered in the first part of the twentieth century to provide educational opportunities for everyday working people, regardless of their class standing. These **working class** universities were created to counter the elitism of centuries-old universities such as Cambridge and Oxford, schools to which only the wealthy and titled had regular access. Thus, from its very inception the University of Birmingham was a scholarly institution given to addressing issues of class and culture, so perhaps it is unsurprising that it nurtured many of the scholars whose ideas would give rise to the field we now call cultural studies.

Several diverse scholars influenced the development of cultural studies during the postwar era. All of them helped to broaden the definition of culture from that of "high culture" to include the culture of everyday life, and they understood culture itself to be a site of class struggle. In order to understand culture better they began to apply the tools of textual analysis—previously relegated only to the study of literature—to the texts of everyday life. One of the most important of these early scholars was Richard Hoggart, who also founded the Centre for Contemporary Cultural Studies at the University of Birmingham in 1964. Hoggart was raised in poverty, trained in literary studies at the University of Leeds (another "red brick university"), and made a splash with his 1957 book *The Uses of Literacy*, which applied textual analyses to both mass produced cultural artifacts as well as folk cultural ones. Hoggart clearly preferred everyday working class folk cultures (including things like pub songs, local rituals and celebrations) to what he called the "massification" of popular culture, i.e. the rise of pulp fiction, tabloid newspapers, the cinema, the radio, etc. Similar to the work of the **Frankfurt School** theorists (who also decried the mass culture produced by the "**culture industries**"), Hoggart's book lamented the loss of "authentic" everyday culture in favor of mass produced consumer diversions he felt were imposed on the working class from above. In addition to re-sounding the Frankfurt School's similar critique, Hoggart's book also served as a model for how everyday activities—going to the pub, organizing a union meeting, family relations—could be (and should be) studied as texts in and of themselves.

Another important thinker to contribute to the rise of cultural studies was E. P. Thompson, a Marxist scholar best known for his work on the history of eighteenth- and nineteenth-century radical movements, and particularly their importance to *The Making of the English Working Class*, the title of his 1963 book. Thompson's work framed culture as a struggle between competing ways of life, and argued for the importance of human agency. *The Making of the English Working Class* also helped shift the very meaning of history—from merely the chronicling of Kings and Queens and who went to war with whom—to the history of everyday lives and everyday people. This form of personal or social history has grown into an important subset of history in general, and today's historians often work to explore the marginalized and/or forgotten histories of not just the working classes, but also those of women, various ethnic and racial groups, and sexual minorities.

The writings of Raymond Williams, including *Culture and Society 1780–1950* (1958), *The Long Revolution* (1961), *Television: Technology and Cultural Form* (1974) and *Marxism and Literature* (1977) might be said to exemplify—in microcosm—the maturing of cultural studies during these decades. Indeed, Williams's *Keywords: A Vocabulary of Culture and Society*, first published in 1976, became a dictionary of the discipline's most important ideas up to that date. Like Hoggart, Williams was trained in literary analysis, and became interested in applying those methods to the study of culture. Williams's famous definition (in his first book) of culture as a "whole way of life, material, intellectual, and spiritual" (1958, xvi) was refined in his second: "culture is a description of a particular way of life, which expresses certain meanings and values not only in art and learning but also in institutions and ordinary behavior" (1961, 57). The analysis of culture, Williams declared, "is the clarification of the meanings and values implicit and explicit in a particular way of life" (1961, 57). Although he did not have access to the vocabulary of the French Marxists at that time, Williams's phrase "the meanings and values implicit and explicit in a particular way of life" could be describing ideology as theorized by **Louis Althusser**. Recall from Chapter 2 that Althusser theorized ideology as structural and pervasive, arguing that there was no "outside" of ideology. Unlike the basic Marxist "ideology-as-false-consciousness" model that suggested ideology could be "unlearned," Althusser and the cultural studies scholars who would later draw upon his work understood ideology to be expressed in and through culture and cultural artifacts, what Althusser termed **ideological state apparatuses**.

Williams's career also mirrored the work of many scholars at the Birmingham Centre for Contemporary Cultural Studies throughout these years. Initially centered on everyday and working class cultures, the cultural analyses produced by these scholars soon turned to other venues: youth subcultures (Dick Hebdige, Angela McRobbie), television news and serial dramas (David Morley, Dorothy Hobson, Charlotte Brundson), race and colonialism (Paul Gilroy, Stuart Hall), feminism and pop culture (Angela McRobbie, Celia Lury), childhood and youth cultures (Debbie Epstein, Chris Griffin), and even science and medicine (Jackie Stacey, Sarah Franklin). Even quintessential British icons like James Bond and Doctor Who have been scrutinized as significant cultural artifacts by Tony Bennett and Janet Woollacott (James Bond) and John Tulloch (Doctor Who). More generally, John Fiske's *Television Culture* has become a canonical textbook in the field of TV Studies. Drawing on semiotic and (post)structuralist notions, the book examines TV in relation to realism, ideology, subjectivity, audiences, intertextuality, narrative, and character, and devotes special chapters to the cultural meanings and functioning(s) of music videos, TV quiz shows, and news programming. By 1992, with the publication of the massive edited volume *Cultural Studies*, the field had come to encompass not only the topics just mentioned, but also portraits of people with AIDS, popular music, *Hustler* magazine, "Book of the Month clubs," Shakespeare, gender and ethnicity in England in the 1830s and 1840s, new age "technoculture," and the Hungarian uprising of 1956. Cultural studies opened up new ways of writing and thinking about history, the body, the politics of difference, and of course, film and TV.

"Encoding/decoding" and Gramscian hegemony

One of the most significant founding figures and scholars of cultural studies was **Stuart Hall**. Hall was born in Jamaica where he lived until he won a scholarship to study English at Oxford University in 1951. In England, Hall became increasingly interested in leftist politics (including the Campaign for Nuclear Disarmament), and worked for various leftist journals; in 1960 he became the founding editor of the *New Left Review*, one of the most prestigious journals covering world politics and culture both then and now. Soon after, he was invited to become a member of the Birmingham Centre for Contemporary Cultural Studies, and he led the center as its director from 1968–79. Hall's work often centered on issues of class and race, but he is perhaps best known for formulating a model of communication that has become central to film and television criticism. First presented in a 1973 working paper entitled "Encoding and Decoding in the Television Discourse," the essay was later anthologized as "Encoding/Decoding" in the 1980 volume *Culture, Media, Language: Working Papers in Cultural Studies, 1972–79*. Since then it has been reprinted many times over, and has become a touchstone of cultural criticism in general.

This book introduced some of the basic ideas associated with Hall's famous essay "Encoding/Decoding" in its very first chapter, precisely because it is so significant to much (if not most) of the film and television criticism that takes place today. (It is also a model that does not necessarily negate most of the other approaches explored in this book—the notable exception being **apparatus theory**—and thus might be seen as a useful overall framework for doing film and TV criticism.) The various aspects of Hall's "Encoding/Decoding" model still allow for (and encourage) a consideration of auteurs and showrunners, the media industries, formal textual analyses, genres and formats, and even psychoanalysis. It is especially useful in theorizing reception and audiences, as this and the next chapter will explore. Recall that Hall's model reworked the more traditional communication studies paradigm of "sender-message-receiver" into a more nuanced and active model. For Hall, the idea of "senders" now becomes a complex set of parameters that influence media production including "frameworks of knowledge," "relations of production," and "technical infrastructure." In other words, media producers produce texts from certain points of view, and within varying economic and technical structures such as a TV studio or an independent film shoot, all of which exert pressure on or contribute to the final form of the **text** (formerly the "message"). Hall uses the term **encoding** to refer to this complex and ideological process of textual production. Encoding includes what the producers consciously want to say within their text, but it also takes into consideration complex factors of production, ideology, genres and formats, etc. that go well beyond simply the author's intent. (As such, cultural studies has been instrumental in the rise of newer forms of industry studies.) Similarly, **audiences** or **readers** (formerly "receivers") **decode** the text from their own cultural positions, as well as their own understandings of a text's economic and technical infrastructure—i.e. their relations to "frameworks of knowledge," "relations of production," and "technical infrastructure." One of Hall's key points is that the meanings encoded into a text by its producers ("meaning structures 1") may not be (and probably are not) the same as the meanings that readers decode from the text ("meaning structures 2"). Hall's model also insists that decoding is an active process: audiences and readers must "do work" to understand texts, something the passive term "receivers" does not emphasize (see Diagram 10.1).

Hall's essay then proposes "*three* hypothetical positions from which decodings of a televisual discourse may be constructed" (2011, 85). Those three possible reading positions are (1) the **dominant-hegemonic** or **preferred** position, (2) the **negotiated** position, and (3) the **oppositional** position. When a reader performs a **dominant** or **preferred** reading, he or she decodes the text according to how the producers encoded it. He or she understands the text in the way that its producers designed it to be understood, perhaps because he or she shares many of the same cultural positions and ideological understandings as do the producers. An **oppositional** reading means that an audience member resists the meanings that were encoded by the producers. As Hall puts it, the reader "detotalizes the message in the preferred code in order to retotalize the message within some alternative framework of reference" (2011, 87). This may occur because the audience member's own socio-cultural positionings or ideologies differ from those of the producers. In the middle of these two positions lies the **negotiated reading** position, which "contains a mixture of adaptive and oppositional elements," that is to say a position that allows the reader to accept some portions of the text as it was encoded while resisting others (2011, 87). In actual practice, it is best to think of preferred readings and oppositional readings as opposing ends of a continuum. In this sense all readings are negotiated readings; indeed, we sometimes describe the act of watching a film or television text as the act of individual readers negotiating with a text, drawing from it (decoding) meanings based upon his or her personal subjectivity.

The term negotiation also refers to **hegemonic negotiation** as theorized by **Antonio Gramsci**. Recall from Chapter 2 that the neo-Marxist thinking of Louis Althusser and Antonio Gramsci became central to contemporary cultural studies in the 1970s. Althusser's ideas about the structural nature of ideology

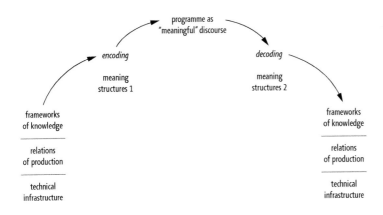

Diag 10.1
Stuart Hall's "Encoding/
Decoding" model as he
originally described it.

and **interpellation** became important to *Screen* and **apparatus theory**, while Gramsci's ideas about hegemony became central to cultural studies—the work done by scholars working at the Birmingham Centre but also throughout the soon-to-be burgeoning field. In truth, both Althusserian and Gramscian concepts are important to contemporary cultural studies. Althusserian ideas such as **overdetermination**, **uneven development**, and **relative autonomy** contribute to a complex model of how ideologies, texts, and institutions circulate and impact upon one another. Gramsci's concept of **cultural hegemony** also affords us a more nuanced model of how rule is maintained in Western nations through cultural institutions and ideologies. As one later scholar sums it up, "Gramsci's theory of hegemony holds that cultural domination or, more accurately cultural leadership is not achieved by force or coercion, but is secured through the consent of those it will ultimately subordinate" (Turner, 1990, 66–7). Subordinated groups consent because they are convinced the ideological positions offered to them serve their interests (whether or not they actually do). Thus, rule over any nation or population is not assured or static, but must be won and re-won in an ongoing struggle, one that occurs by constantly **negotiating** with subcultural artifacts, ideas, and/or social movements that may be in opposition to dominant ideologies. Another way to picture cultural hegemony might be to think of it as a constantly evolving and fluctuating **dominant ideology**.

Gramsci's model allows cultural theorists to understand rule and domination in the Western world as evolving processes, not static or unchanging inevitabilities. It theorizes how culture can and does change—through hegemonic negotiation. (The rise of cultural studies itself might be understood as a hegemonic shift in how Western thinkers understand the concept of culture.) Building on Gramsci's model, Raymond Williams identified three kinds of co-existing cultural forces—*dominant*, *residual*, and *emergent*—to theorize how various aspects of culture can and do change. At any moment in history all three forces are present; dominant forces are those that are most prevalent, while residual forces look backwards to previous eras and ways of thinking. Emergent forces are those that are just beginning to enter the culture. We can look at a specific historical era and a specific cultural issue to exemplify these ideas: race and racism in America during the 1950s and 1960s. At the start of the era, most *dominant* social forces, institutions, and discourses still endorsed segregation and white supremacy. The ingrained racism expressed in centuries of slavery and decades of separate-but-equal "Jim Crow" laws were likewise *dominant*, but they became increasingly *residual* as the 1950s became the 1960s, and laws and attitudes changed. Things changed because the *emergent* forces and voices of the Civil Rights movement became more and more dominant. Does this mean that racism and discrimination against African Americans suddenly came to an end? Certainly not, but cultural attitudes on race and racism shifted in dramatic ways, resulting in Civil Rights legislation, increased access to education, more and more visibility within the public and media sphere, etc. The *dominant* ideologies of white supremacy negotiated with the *emergent* ideologies of civil rights thinking and organizing; racism and white privilege still exist in the United States sixty years later, but it is not the same form of racism and white privilege that existed in 1950. That form has now become *residual*.

As noted in Chapter 2, the theory of hegemonic negotiation allows for a more dynamic (and for some more optimistic) view of culture and cultural change. It holds out hope that currently non-dominant ideologies might eventually become dominant ones. Perhaps most importantly, hegemonic negotiation suggests that all areas of culture—including film and television—can and do contribute to such social and cultural changes. Whether or not those negotiations will eventually undo the supremacy of whiteness, or patriarchy, or unchecked capitalism, or any other dominant Western system rooted in social inequity remains to be seen. But film and television can be part of the process of undoing such systems (or conversely, reinforcing such systems). To return to the example of the Civil Rights movement, it might be said that in many ways, popular culture is still playing "catch up" vis-à-vis the politics of race in that era. Recent films like *The Butler* (2013) and *Selma* (2014)—which could never have been produced and released in the 1960s (the era in which they are set) because of the volatility of race at that time—nonetheless recall that history and share it with contemporary audiences. The optimistic cultural critic might argue that films like those are part of the nation's ongoing march towards understanding and ending racism. The pessimistic cultural critic might look at those same films as commercial exercises in nostalgia, placing racism safely in the past, while ignoring or obscuring the ongoing racism in the nation today. Contemporary cultural studies overall might understand the films to be doing both of those things simultaneously.

Related concepts of texts and discourses

Stuart Hall's model of "Encoding/Decoding" asks us to think about the production and reception of media texts in complex and complicated ways, but it also calls attention to the text itself as a complex **structured polysemy**. The term refers to the ways that all texts are made up of many signs (polysemy), but that those signs are then structured or ordered in some way to create certain kinds of meanings. In this way, textual structures themselves (and their usage) help shape certain meanings, a topic to which we now turn. Some of the ideas discussed in this section were introduced in Chapter 3, "Semiotics, structuralism and beyond," while others developed from them in various ways. Chapter 3 introduced basic ideas such as **syntagm** (the way that texts can be and are structured across time) and **paradigm** (how images, words, and signs take their meanings only by comparison against other images, words, and signs). Also recall the concepts of **denotation** (the first order of meaning any given sign expresses) and **connotation**, the potentially infinite number of meanings (beyond the first denotative one) that images, words, and signs can express as they enter and circulate in culture. The terms langue and parole are also important to recall at this point: **langue** is a subset of speech or text-making (such as a TV sitcom or Hollywood film genre that organizes signs in certain ways). **Parole** refers to the utterance spoken within a langue or the production of a text within a given langue (again our media example might be "*Modern Family* is an act of parole spoken in the langue of the twenty-first-century domestic sitcom"). The point of reviewing these terms here is to underscore how texts can and do give off multiple meanings and create multiple reading positions (up to a point), and that it matters who is producing or "speaking" them, as that can and does also contribute to their meaning(s).

The terms **multi-accentuality** and **uni-accentuality**, first theorized by Soviet linguist **Valentin Voloshinov** in the early twentieth century, refer to how signs and texts can be inflected with different meanings based on who is using them (or "speaking" them). Like cultural studies in general, Voloshinov understood language and other textual systems as ideological, as they are all socially constructed. He argued that acts of parole matter: different speakers might use the same term but it could mean different things to different groups of listeners. This is an example of **multi-accentuality**: one term can be spoken in different accents—given different inflections—by the people and the groups speaking it. A good historical example might be the use of the term "black" when referring to people with dark skin tones. For some people in the 1950s, the term was derogatory and abusive. Then some younger African Americans **reappropriated** the term as a source of pride and power, as in the 1960s slogan "Black is Beautiful!" Other terms referring to various social groups are often sites of struggle over meaning. They are given different meanings (accents, inflections) depending on who is using them: in a more contemporary example, a right-wing male radio host is probably going to give the term "feminism" a different inflection than a left-wing college professor. For Voloshinov and contemporary cultural theorists, this struggle over meaning was and is an element of class struggle. The interests of the dominant class tend to be served when the possible meanings of words are reduced to a single meaning (the definition of **uni-accentuality**). When words or texts have only one meaning—defined by the dominant class—they are taken out of struggle or contestation, and potentially voided of their significance. If "feminist" is derided as something negative that no one would want to call themselves, the issues and challenges it raises would be likewise silenced.

Similar to uni-accentuality and multi-accentuality are **Mikhail Bakhtin**'s concepts of **monoglossia** and **heteroglossia**. Cultural studies tends to understand uni-accentuality and multi-accentuality as qualities of speech or speaking while monoglossia and heteroglossia refer more to the nature of texts. The etymological roots of the terms mean single tongued (or voiced) and different or multiple tongued (or voiced); the words are somewhat analogous to the terms "closed" and "open" when describing the degree of structure versus polysemy a given text exhibits. A **monoglossic** text tends to be more closed in meaning, as it is spoken with one unified voice. A **heteroglossic** text, on the other hand, tends to be a more open text, because it contains various elements or voices, and can be interpreted in more diverse ways. (Some critics also use the terms centripetal and centrifugal in a like manner: closed, monoglossic texts might be described as centripetal as they force meaning towards one central point, while open, heteroglossic texts throw off multiple meanings from the central source.) Examples of such texts were discussed in Chapters 1 and 2; the Disney cartoon *The Flying Mouse* (1934), with its linear narrative and stated moral lesson could be described as closed, monoglossic, or centripetal. Likewise, the modernist art film *Ballet Mécanique* (1924) and the Adult Swim cartoon *Aqua Teen Hunger Force* (2000–) could be described as open, heteroglossic, or centrifugal. In a more contemporary example, the various voices who make up a panel on a talk show like *The View* (1997–) quite literally make it a heteroglossic text, while the single voice of syndicated radio host Sean Hannity constructs a strictly monoglossic text. (Note his show airs on the radio network WORD and advertises itself as "The Word"—not words!) Following from these ideas, cultural theorists should expect the audience to express a wider range of readings when dealing with open, heteroglossic, or centrifugal texts. Monoglossic texts, similar to the uni-accentual use of language—close down the "play" of meaning and seek to concretize a single perspective as "*the*" truth or proper meaning.

There is also the notion that different texts engage us, speak to us, and invite us to see ourselves in them in different ways—this is why textual analysis is still central to cultural studies. Comedies versus horror films suggest and invite a different kind of reader—someone who wants to laugh versus being scared. An art film versus a "dumb white guy" comedy also suggests varying modes of reception, perhaps still tied to the expectations of high versus low art. Fictional film and fictional television also differ from much of the rest of television, which operates in what TV scholar Robert C. Allen calls the **rhetorical mode**. Talk shows, chat shows, the news, game shows, religious shows, home and garden shows, etc. are all constructed in the rhetorical mode, simulating a "face-to-face encounter by directly addressing the viewer and, what is more important, acknowledging both the performer's role as addresser and the viewer's role as addressee" (1992, 118). Such TV shows invoke the *appearance* of two-way communication, and many even have on-camera studio audiences meant to mirror the audience watching at home. This mode situates the viewer as a friend to the performers, or perhaps even a member of the team, as in local news shows or chat/news shows like *Fox and Friends* (1998–). In many instances, phone calls, emails, texts, and tweets connect the home viewer even more directly to the on-air performers, creating an aura of connectivity (and shared positionality) in the home viewer. In this way, the rhetorical mode of TV hails viewers as potential friends, helpmates, and/or ideologues. Such shows also make use of what Robert Stam has named the "Regime of the Fictive We," a rhetorical device used by news anchors and television commentators to suggest or imply that everyone agrees with their positions, whether they do or not.

Finally, the concept of **discourse** was also introduced in Chapter 3 and it remains central to cultural studies thinking about texts and cultural meanings. Associated with the ideas of French historian **Michel Foucault**, discourse refers to the way that meanings (and especially the meanings of identities) are socially constructed through languages and other sign systems. Like the other thinkers in this section—and cultural studies scholars in general—Foucault saw language and meaning as sites of struggle between classes or other social formations. Foucault was interested in how the power of the **ruling class** was not simply a top-down phenomenon, but was actually embedded within and circulated through all aspects of culture and language (what he called its "capillary" nature). Foucault also helped change the meanings and methods of historical inquiry, often focusing his work on "forgotten" or overlooked subjects like prisons, mental illness, and sexuality. (This is perhaps somewhat analogous to the ways that Hoggart, Thompson, and Williams changed the focus of culture to include various elements of daily life.)

For our purposes in film and television studies, the concept of discourse allows us to speak of how various institutional forms shape and delimit the meanings spoken within them. Hollywood narrative form might be thought of as a certain kind of discourse, as might the format of a game show. In this way, we might also say that hegemonic negotiation is discursive: **decoding** is what happens when the discourses of the text intersect with the discourses of the reader.

Reception studies

One very important area of inquiry to arise from within cultural studies overall is **reception studies**. The study of reception overlaps with and is sometimes used synonymously with **audience studies** (covered in more detail in the next chapter), but there are differences in emphasis. While both fields focus on the text-reader portion of Stuart Hall's "Encoding/Decoding" model, reception studies tends to refer to how texts are positioned by the media industry to be read by audiences via things like publicity, promotion, reviews, patterns of distribution, etc. Audience studies focuses more on what audiences actually do with texts—what meanings they actually take away from them and what they might then creatively do with those meanings. Audience studies more often involves **ethnographic** techniques like interviewing readers, attending fan conventions, or analyzing user-generated comments about film and television texts as significant cultural artifacts in and of themselves. The case study at the end of this chapter combines both approaches to examine what *Brokeback Mountain* (2005) meant to audiences in north Texas upon its original release; the media frenzy the film engendered allowed cultural studies scholars to examine attitudes about social issues like masculinity and male homosexuality. Ultimately, the goal of much reception or audience study is less about textual analysis of any given film or TV show and more about using that film or TV show to study the *cultural issues* it raises.

Broadly, reception studies is a field within or subset of **phenomenology**, a broad philosophical discipline that studies how individual subjects perceive the world around them—how they make sense of their own experiences. (In philosophical terms, **phenomenology** is a theory of **ontology**—a theory about the nature of being or existing.) For a phenomenologist, reality is not some objective thing that exists outside of human perception; instead, phenomenologists emphasize that we can only know reality through our given perceptual organs and reasoning. The old brain teaser—"if a tree falls in the forest and no one is there to hear it, did it make a sound?"—is perhaps a good pop culture example of what phenomenology is all about. To take another example, some species and some people are color blind. How does that affect their understanding of reality? In movies and television, sometimes subjective point of view shots are used to emphasize how certain characters see the world differently than do others: think of science fiction films like *Predator* (1987) that use special effects technology to create an alien monster's point of view (see Figure 10.1). All of which is to say that reception studies or audience studies focus on the ways individual human subjects

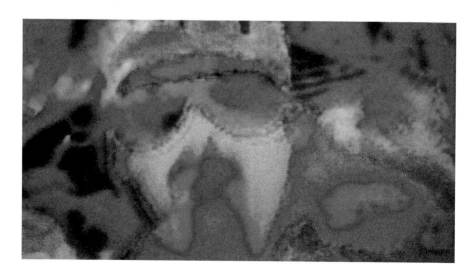

Fig 10.1
"Alien vision" from *Predator* (1987), suggesting a subjective point of view different from that of human beings.

see their worlds, and how they can and do make (sometimes quite divergent) readings of the same film or TV show.

As mentioned earlier in this chapter, scholars at the Birmingham Centre for Contemporary Cultural Studies began to do this type of reception work in the 1970s, often focusing on how people watched television. For example, David Morley used focus groups and open-ended questionnaires to explore what different subjects thought of a single episode of the newsmagazine show *Nationwide* (1969–83). Dorothy Hobson studied the early-evening soap opera *Crossroads* (1964–88), concentrating not only on its industrial context and its textual parameters, but also its audiences. Hobson watched the show with her subjects, interviewed them extensively, and let them talk about what the show meant to them in personal terms. Similarly, Ien Ang explored what the popular American evening serial drama *Dallas* (1978–91) meant to Dutch viewers by studying the written correspondence of 42 regular viewers. The important thing to note about these seminal reception/audience studies is that they all demonstrated that TV shows can and do mean different things to different viewers. They all analyzed viewers' responses as cultural texts in and of themselves, and tried to understand the deeper social and intertextual contexts involved in watching television. Unlike **quantitative audience studies**, which usually ask audience members precise questions that can then be numerically analyzed, cultural studies reception or audience studies use open-ended **qualitative approaches** to get to their subjects' experiences of watching texts. In so doing, they create scholarship that might be called "thick description," a term coined by the anthropologist and ethnographer Clifford Geertz to refer to the need to understand behaviors and/or texts within all of their multiple cultural contexts, including their reception. This approach to doing film and TV scholarship has arguably become one of the most central ways that scholars do their work. One good contemporary example of such work is Wayne State University Press's *TV Milestones* series of books. As their website explains it, "Each book offers a comprehensive account of a particular television show, placing it in the context of the history of television and broader cultural history, as well as discussing representative episodes of the show in detail." Most also include a consideration of how the show was received when it first aired, and in some cases, how and why a given show continues to attract new viewers perhaps decades later.

Today, contemporary reception or audience studies can be relatively easy to do, due to the world wide web and new social media technologies, whereon actual viewers share their thoughts on films and TV shows in various online forums. It gets much trickier when trying to do a **historical reception study**, but it can be (and is) done by cultural studies media scholars. Such a study might want to explore what a given film or TV show meant to audiences upon its initial release, asking questions such as "How was *King Kong* (1933) received and understood by audiences during the Great Depression?" (This is indeed one question explored by Cynthia Erb in her book *Tracking* King Kong, *a Hollywood Icon in World Culture*.) A cultural studies scholar can ask present-day viewers what they think of the original *King Kong*, but those responses might be very different from ones that may have been expressed in the 1930s. So how does one do a historical reception study? (See Figure 10.2.)

As mentioned above, historical reception requires a "thick description" approach, and scholars usually focus on three central things: (1) the text under consideration, (2) all of its multiple socio-historical contexts, and finally, (3) any

Fig 10.2
Images we would today consider racist appear throughout *King Kong* (1933). A **historical reception study** might explore how those images were understood at the time of the film's initial release.

and all **primary materials** related to the text on its initial release, such as film reviews, commentaries, and publicity. The first object of study—the film or TV show itself—can be more or less readily available to contemporary media scholars, depending on what text one is looking to study. In today's age, films and TV shows are arguably more available for study than ever before. However, many, many more film and TV texts have been lost over the decades. Some films only exist in tattered faded negatives, while some TV shows only exist as **kinescopes** (filmic records made of live TV broadcasts before the advent of video tape). In using poor quality prints or duped video tapes, the media scholar would need to acknowledge the possibility of missing footage and/or decreased image clarity, which might affect the study. That said, prints of films and TV shows might also have been censored or edited over the years, just as today some films exist in multiple editions or "director's cuts." To return to *King Kong*, the film as it was originally seen in 1933 is not the same film that one generation of scholars grew up watching on TV: certain scenes had been deleted after the enforcement of the Hollywood Production Code in 1934, resulting in a truncated text. Fortunately, with the arrival of the digital age, film and TV restoration is becoming more common—missing scenes are tracked down and reinserted, and faded fuzzy prints are made crispy and like new. Both physical and digital archives (such as those associated with The Academy of Motion Picture Arts and Sciences, the Museum of Broadcast Communications, and the Paley Center for Media) collect, collate, and preserve as much film and TV history as they can, and they are often incredibly useful when doing historical reception studies.

The second thing the reception studies scholar needs to focus on is the multiple contexts surrounding and permeating his or her chosen text. (To explore a text within its historical context in this manner is often referred to as **historicizing** the text.) Scholars might draw on social, political, and/or industrial histories of the era (**secondary sources** written at a later time) to begin to understand the period in a "thick" way. Again, in our example of *King Kong*, one would want to research and understand the various contexts surrounding it, from its studio and production history, to the people involved in its production, to its patterns of release, distribution, and censorship. The cultural studies scholar would also need to research the broader issues of the era, including political trends, the impact of the Great Depression, and the era's most dominant understandings of race, gender, class, etc. All of this research then helps the scholar construct a reading of the text in a more historically accurate way—as it might have been made in 1933.

The third thing needed for a historical reception study are actual **primary materials** related to the text, and for these one usually has to go back to the archive. One good source of primary materials that shed direct light on a film's reception are film reviews from the era, which used to be collected in archived volumes and now can often be accessed online. Major newspapers like *The New York Times* or *The Los Angeles Times*, and industry publications like *Variety* and *The Hollywood Reporter* can tell the researcher what the era's journalists thought about the film, but what about the responses of more general or specific audience members? What if the scholar wanted to know how *King Kong* was received by African American audiences? One might be lucky enough to find old community-based newspapers that mentioned the film and covered it from an African American perspective. Or not. Oftentimes, smaller community-based journalism was not considered worth saving by some archives. In that case, a visit to a community-based library or history project could be helpful. Another way to collect primary data on reception might be through personal interviews, assuming there are people still around who might recall their experience of seeing a particular film or TV show. However, memories can be fuzzy, or even manufactured. Diaries, journals, and/or interviews conducted closer to the time of the primary text's actual reception might be of more use.

The scholar doing historical reception work is something like an archeologist; he or she starts digging and hopes to find things that will be relevant to the study. All sorts of things collected in archives or found online might be useful, including a consideration of the text's previous source material: was the text adapted from a preexisting play or novel? If so, how was it changed, and how might that impact possible readings of it? Perhaps memoirs of those involved in the text's production could be useful if located, or even biographies about a text's star(s) or director. If the text was controversial in some way, there may be op-ed columns and letters to the editors to be found in the historical record. Were their censorship struggles? (The Academy of Motion Picture Arts and Sciences' Margaret Herrick library has all the correspondence files from the Hollywood Production Code Administration in its archive.) Censorship struggles can reveal quite a lot about what was considered proper or improper in the era's films or TV shows.

Finally, one might also examine the ways the film or TV show was advertised: how did its producers position the film to be received? For a TV show, where was it placed on the daily or weekly schedule? Who were its sponsors? The products being advertised on the show might reveal something about who its intended audience was thought to be. For individual films, posters, newspaper advertisements, "ballyhoo" gimmicks, books and music tie-ins, etc. could all help the scholar understand how the text was meant to be received by its makers, as might its coverage in industry-sanctioned fan magazines like *Modern Screen* and *Photoplay*. The possible sources of data are potentially endless, but all of them contribute to a more thorough understanding of how the text was originally positioned in popular culture, affording the historical reception scholar clues to how it may have been understood at the time of its release. That said, if the scholar is working at the time of the text's initial release (as with the following Case study), trips to the archive become less relevant. Data can be collected (or generated) at the spatial and temporal source.

Case study: The reception of *Brokeback Mountain* (2005) in northern Texas[1]

By almost anyone's calculations, *Brokeback Mountain* was *the* movie event of 2005/2006. And as one of the few popular movies dealing with issues surrounding male homosexual desire and questions of identity, its reception makes for an interesting case study. Not only does its reception support various concepts of contemporary cultural theory (such as the necessarily negotiated decodings of **polysemic**, **heteroglossic** media texts), it also underscores the many interpretive meanings of (male) homosexuality that exist within contemporary culture-at-large. As do many reception and/or audience studies, this case study draws on personal experiences, conversations, film reviews, op-ed pieces, letters to the editors, and an anonymous voluntary survey of people who had seen the film. It exposes and explores the fear, anger, delight, disappointment, and moral outrage that was generated in northern Texas by the film's release. Its reception created an important public space for discourse on the place and meaning of men and masculinity in contemporary America, even as much of that discourse attempted to reduce complex **queer** concepts about sexuality (see Chapter 12) into easily dismissed factoids about "gay cowboys." While the film deliberately blurs the lines between male **homosocial desire** and male **homosexual desire**, and dramatizes the traumatic effects of "the closet," the study of its reception in northern Texas revealed a great amount of personal and societal **homophobia** (see Figure 10.3).

One of the more intriguing aspects of the *Brokeback Mountain* phenomenon was the number of straight men who admitted that they were "afraid" to see the film. Some pundits felt that straight men might be "grossed out" by the film's portrayal of homosexual intimacy—the fundamentalist Christian lobby group the American Family Association

Fig 10.3
Brokeback Mountain (2005) repeatedly blurs the line between homosocial horseplay and homosexual desire, an aspect that troubled some viewers.

did claim that the film would make patrons vomit in the aisles.[2] Other respondents to the anonymous survey suggested that straight men were avoiding the film out of fear "that they might be 'stimulated' by the gay sex scenes," forcing them "to think about the certainty of [their] own sexual preferences." Obviously, titillation and repulsion are not mutually exclusive, and are perhaps more deeply conjoined than is commonly acknowledged. According to data on the conflicted sexuality of gay bashers, many homophobic people do have ego-dystonic homosexual desires—same sex desires that they find highly disturbing to their sense of self.[3] Fear of *Brokeback Mountain* even extended to going to the theater itself. Some straight men worried what their friends would think if they were seen going into the movie; some wives reported that their husbands refused to accompany them to the film. One straight male student recounted this tale:

> When I went to see the film with a friend who is also a heterosexual male I was bombarded with questions and accusations from friends and colleagues. Friends snickered and joked, saying that [I] was now a homosexual for simply seeing the movie with another male. A few co-workers asked if we had held hands in the theater. One female co-worker was so disgusted when she discovered that I had seen the film that she no longer speaks to me.

Among the local people most disturbed by *Brokeback Mountain* were the area's cowboy poets, men probably used to defending their masculinity against the feminizing effects of poetry. In a special *Dallas Morning News* story, rather pointedly entitled "Protecting Their View: Cowboy Poets Gather to Preserve a Culture—and Keep Out Pretenders," cowboy poets lamented the fact that Hollywood had "finally taken the last American hero and pulled him down a notch."[4] One cowboy poet "was saddened that the agenda-driven Hollywood crowd's movie, *Humpback Mountain*—you may laugh at that if you like—disparages the way of my life." Of course, *Humpback Mountain* was but one of many homophobic puns—including *Buttback Mountain*, *Bareback Mountain*, *Brokebutt Mountain*, and *Backdoor Mounting*—that circulated during and after the film's release. These puns seemingly attest to the general public's fascination with anal sexuality. Although statistics show that approximately 35–40 per cent of heterosexual couples engage in anal sex, the very idea of anal sex is almost always displaced onto gay men.[5] This fixation on anal sexuality—and *Brokeback Mountain* as a signifier thereof—was evidenced by many commentators and survey respondents. One such respondent chose to fill out his questionnaire "comically." Giving his age as "69" and his profession/occupation as "butt lover," this individual wrote that the message of the film was "butt sex *good*" and that watching it "made me want to be a cowboy and want to screw a horse." As in much residual discourse about male homosexuality, human same-sex intimacy is associated with bestiality.

Perhaps unsurprisingly, many fundamentalist Christians in north Texas used *Brokeback Mountain* as a chance to proselytize, citing the Bible to condemn the film as an example of contemporary culture's moral depravity. After local secular critics lauded the film, one such person wrote to the *Dallas Morning News* to express her concern:

> I am both saddened and outraged at the results of the Dallas-Fort Worth Film Critics Association pick of *Brokeback Mountain* for best picture. As a Christian, I believe we need to take a stand when biblical truths are being trampled by society's push toward tolerance and acceptance of a lifestyle that is blatantly against God's standard.[6]

Another letter continued in the same vein, drawing upon the religious and medical discourses of previous decades: "There is no way abomination can be called love. It is filth and nothing else. All two male perverts can give life to is AIDS. The film, *Brokeback Mountain*, is not a love story. It is pornography. Why does the media promote perversion?"[7] The idea of a pro-gay Christianity is largely beyond the scope of such people, even though Dallas is home to the Cathedral of Hope, one of the largest gay Christian churches in the world. The comments also reveal the oft-heard trope that "Hollywood elites" are trying to promote some sort of "homosexual agenda."

Other more professional and moderate Christian commentators decoded (and even recommended) *Brokeback Mountain* as a film about the wages of sin (see Figure 10.4). Local talk radio host Mark Davis felt the need to come out of the closet with his editorial "I'm a Conservative, and I liked *Brokeback Mountain*."[8] Although his main point was to defend his decision to even see the film, he also used his essay to further his right-wing agenda, speaking out against domestic partner benefits, gay marriage, and adoption. Davis's fellow conservative Christian editorialist at the *Dallas Morning News*, Rod Dreher, took another approach to containing the film's dangerous ideas, suggesting that it was OK to see it because it was genuine "art."[9] As Dreher saw it, the film is clearly not "about the need to normalize homosexuality, or 'about' anything other than the tragic human condition." Typical of many of these conservative op-ed pieces, the writer does realize to some extent what the film is about: "True, the men begin their doomed affair in a time and place where homosexuality was viciously suppressed, and so they suffer from social constrictions that make it difficult to master their own fates." But he then goes on to suggest that Jack (Jake Gyllenhaal) and Ennis (Heath Ledger) are not "real" men because they have failed to rise above such constraints: "both men are overgrown boys who waste their lives searching for something they've lost, and which might be irrecoverable. They are boys who refuse to become men." Dreher realizes that homophobia and heterosexism create a tragic state of affairs for LGBT (Lesbian, Gay, Bisexual and Transgender) people, yet he fails to see his own complicity in propagating such attitudes. He mistakes the socially constructed effects of **heteronormative patriarchy** for the "tragic human condition" (see Figure 10.5).

Reaction to the film varied among local LGBT people, although a majority of them seemed to like it, decoding it mostly as a love story between characters with whom

Fig 10.4
Some conservative critics read this scene in *Brokeback Mountain* (2005) as "proof" that Jack and Ennis had failed at their job and failed as men.

Fig 10.5
In *Brokeback Mountain* (2005), Ennis as a child was forced to witness the aftermath of a gay man's mutilation and murder, memories of which have left him scarred and fearful.

they could empathize and identify. Most understood the film to be as much about the closet as it was the love affair between Jack and Ennis. However, a small but vocal minority of gay men were *very* disappointed with the film, seeing it as more of the usual Hollywood approach to matters homosexual. Some argued that Jack and Ennis were far from "positive role models," and were angry that Hollywood had served up yet another tragic tale about being gay (see Figure 10.6). As one such critique expressed it, "*Brokeback Mountain* had a wonderful opportunity to provide a history of the struggles faced by gay men during this period. The movie accomplished that. What it didn't do was take advantage of the chance to provide hope and a sense that gay men can overcome these struggles and social adversities."[10] Letters by other gay men sounded similar themes, calling *Brokeback Mountain* "another film that portrays male homosexual love as ultimately just a tragedy and betrayal against women ... The only way mainstream society can deal with gay love is to portray it as a tragedy, and this film is no different."[11]

One of the more provocative debates surrounding the release of *Brokeback Mountain* was its relation to reality. Several locals went on record saying that gay cowboys simply

Fig 10.6
"The Closet" is a central thematic issue in *Brokeback Mountain* (2005); is it part of the "tragic human condition," or a manifestation of socially constructed biases and prejudices?

did not and could not possibly exist. One man asserted that he and his ranching friend Buck "have about 120 years of experience between us, and we have never seen a gay cowboy."[12] In one manner the speaker is correct, since "gay" is a specific type of late twentieth-century urban male homosexual identity, and many cowboys with same sex desires—like Jack and Ennis—would probably not use that term to self-identify (especially if they knew their colleagues were homophobic). In actuality, the Dallas area is home to many LGBT rodeos and cowboys who do self-identify as gay. Perhaps in response to assertions that there are no such people as gay cowboys, area newspapers ran several extended stories about real life "gay cowboys." The day of the Academy Awards, the *Dallas Morning News* ran a long, full-page story about two real life cowboys and the injustices they suffered at the hands of the legal system.[13] Caught in a legal *Catch-22*, the men were unable to argue that they were a committed gay couple, since that would have been admitting to a felony crime in Oklahoma. Thus they lost their property when their wills were contested by hostile relatives. Despite many appeals (even after the federal Supreme Court voided such state laws in 2003), the surviving cowboy was booted off his ranch and driven into bankruptcy. Other stories about "real life" gay cowboys were less heart-wrenching, but still effective in asserting the existence of homosexuals in the Wild West. When Willie Nelson released his song "Cowboys are Secretly Fond of Each Other," the *Dallas Morning News* featured a story on it, complete with a picture of cowboys dancing together at The Round Up, a local country and western gay bar.[14]

Intriguingly, when pundits could no longer rationally argue that no lesbian or gay people could conceivably be cowboys, a few turned to arguing that *Brokeback Mountain* was really not all that significant anyway. Iconoclastic blogger Mickey Kaus, who apparently self-identifies as a neo-liberal but often sounds more like a neo-conservative, wrote a long jumbled editorial in which he argued that "The Heartland Breakout Meme"— his expression for the idea that *Brokeback Mountain* was doing good business in the so-called red states—was itself liberal propaganda. Kaus argued that people in red-state America were in fact avoiding *Brokeback Mountain* because of their understandable homophobia. He argued that it would be a bad mistake for liberals to ignore "the depth of cultural antipathy to homosexuality." (Commentators like Kaus often find ways to avoid the term "homophobia," unless they are using it as an example of a nasty epithet the Left unfairly hurls at the Right.) Unable to address the film's more unsettling destabilizations of masculinity and sexuality, pundits such as Kaus attempted to contain the very meaning of the film's popularity, reassuring readers that their justifiably homophobic belief systems will ultimately triumph over gay marriage, just as they allegedly triumphed over the release of *Brokeback Mountain*. Ten years later, with gay and lesbian marriages legally occurring throughout much of the Western world, we might say that such hostile thinking about LGBT people is becoming more and more *residual*. The *emergent* forces of LGBT equality continue to become more and more *dominant* (albeit not without some hegemonic backlash). The reception of TV shows and films like *Brokeback Mountain* not only demonstrate the ways that society can and does change in relation to social issues, they themselves actively contribute to those changes as well.

Questions for discussion

1   Write a short reception study: pick a recent film that deals with a social issue like race, gender, class, or sexuality, and then research its reception online. What do the

comments you found tell us about the contemporary meaning(s) of the social issue you chose?

2   Similarly, organize a screening of a TV show or movie that deals with some socio-cultural issue for a handful of friends or colleagues. After the screening, compare your various responses to it.

3   Culture is continually changing, as dominant discourses hegemonically negotiate with emergent social forces. Can you see in your own extended family how those processes may have played out? Talk to your parents and grandparents about things like their gender, race, and class. Did they experience those aspects of identity any differently when they were younger, compared to today?

Notes

1   This case study is adapted from a longer essay originally published in *Jump Cut* 50 (Spring 2008) which can be accessed at www.ejumpcut.org/archive/jc50.2008/BrokbkMtn.

2   Reported in Leonard Pitts, "Why *Brokeback Mountain* is so Frightening," *Denton Record-Chronicle*, 17 January 2006: 10A.

3   Overviews of homophobia can be found in Byrne Fone, *Homophobia: A History* (New York: Metropolitan Books, 2000) and David Plummer, *One of the Boys: Masculinity, Homophobia, and Modern Manhood* (New York: Harrington Park Press, 1999). See also Gregory M. Herek, "Beyond 'Homophobia': A Social Psychological Perspective on Attitudes Towards Lesbians and Gay Men," in *Bashers, Baiters, and Bigots: Homophobia in American Society*, ed. John P. De Cecco (New York: Harrington Park Press, 1985). The study that proved that homophobia is positively correlated with same-sex feelings is reported in Henry E. Adams, Lester W. Wright, Jr., and Bethany A. Lohr, "Is Homophobia Associated with Homosexual Arousal?" *Journal of Abnormal Psychology* 105:3 (1996): 440–5.

4   Bryan Woolley, "Protecting Their View: Cowboy Poets Gather to Preserve a Culture—and Keep Out Pretenders." *Dallas Morning News*, 26 March 2006: 13–15.

5   See, for example, the CDC report online at www.cdc.gov/nchs/data/ad/ad362.pdf.

6   Paige Mayhew, letter, *Dallas Morning News*, 1 January 2006: 2G.

7   Alvin H. Roeder, letter, *Denton Record-Chronicle*, 3 February 2006: 8A.

8   Mark Davis, "I'm a conservative, and I liked *Brokeback Mountain*," *Dallas Morning News*, 1 February 2006: 17A.

9   Rod Dreher, "The Real Message in *Brokeback*," *Dallas Morning News*, 29 December 2005: 25A.

10 Mike Henley, letter, *Txt Newsmagazine*, 23 December 2005: 13.

11 Steve Lindsey, letter, *Dallas Morning News*, 1 January 2006: 2G.

12 Dwight Crawford, letter, *Denton Record-Chronicle*, 9 January 2006: 8A.

13 Adam Pitluk, "Only Memories Left of 24 Years Together," *Dallas Morning News*, 5 March 2006: 26A.

14 Mario Tarradell, "Willie Opens the Closet with 'Cowboys'," *Dallas Morning News*, 14 February 2006: 1G, 4G.

References and further reading

Allen, Robert C., ed. *Channels of Discourse, Reassembled*. Chapel Hill, NC: The University of North Carolina Press, 1992 (1987).

Ang, Ien. *Watching Dallas*. London and New York: Routledge, 1985 (1982).

Barker, Chris. *Cultural Studies: Theory and Practice*, Third Edition. London: Sage Publications, Inc., 2008 (2000).

Barthes, Roland. *Mythologies*. Trans. Annette Lavers. New York: The Noonday Press, 1972 (1957).

Bennett, Tony, Colin Mercer, and Janet Woollacott, eds. *Popular Culture and Social Relations*. Maidenhead: Open University Press, 1986.

Brundson, Charlotte. "*Crossroads*: Notes on Soap Opera," *Screen* 22:4 (1981).

Erb, Cynthia. *Tracking* King Kong*, a Hollywood Icon in World Culture*, Second Edition. Detroit, MI: Wayne State University Press, 2009.

Fiske, John. *Television Culture*. London and New York: Routledge, 1987.

Foucault, Michel. *The History of Sexuality, Vol. 1: An Introduction*. Trans. Robert Hurley. New York: Vintage Books, 1990 (1978).

Geertz, Clifford. *The Interpretation of Cultures: Selected Essays*. New York: Basic Books, 1973.

Gray, Ann and Jim McGuigan. *Studying Culture: An Introductory Reader*, Second Edition. London and New York: Arnold, 1997 (1993).

Grossberg, Lawrence, Cary Nelson, and Paula Treichler, eds. *Cultural Studies*. New York and London: Routledge, 1992.

Gurevitch, Michael, Tony Bennett, James Curran, and Janet Woollacott, eds. *Culture, Society and the Media*. New York: Methuen, 1982.

Hall, Stuart. "Encoding/Decoding," in *Critical Visions in Film Theory: Classic and Contemporary Readings*, eds. Timothy Corrigan, Patricia White, with Meta Mazaj. Boston and New York: Bedford/St. Martin's 2011. Pp. 77–88.

Hall, Stuart, Dorothy Hobson, Andrew Lowe, and James Curran, eds. *Culture, Media, Language*. London: Hutchinson, 1980.

Hobson, Dorothy. "*Crossroads*": *Drama of a Soap Opera*. London: Methuen, 1982.

Hoggart, Richard. *The Uses of Literacy: Aspects of Working-Class Life*. London: Penguin Classics, 2009 (1957).

Morley, David. *The Nationwide Audience: Structure and Decoding*. London: British Film Institute, 1980.

Morley, David. *Television, Audiences, and Cultural Studies*. London and New York: Routledge, 1992.

Morley, David and Kuan-Hsing Chen. *Stuart Hall: Critical Dialogues in Cultural Studies*. London and New York: Routledge, 1996.

Staiger, Janet. *Media Reception Studies*. New York and London: New York University Press, 2005.

Stam, Robert. "Television News and it Spectator," in *Regarding Television—Critical Approaches: An Anthology*, ed. E. Ann Kaplan. Frederick, MD: University Publications of America, 1983.

Thompson, E. P. *The Making of the English Working Class*. New York: Vintage Books, 1966 (1963).

Turner, Graeme. *British Cultural Studies: An Introduction*. Boston: Unwin Hyman, 1990.

Turner, Graeme. *Film as Social Practice IV*. London and New York: Routledge, 2009 (1988).

TV Milestones series of books: http://www.wsupress.wayne.edu/books/series-and-imprints/tv-milestones-series

Williams, Raymond. *Marxism and Literature*. Oxford: Oxford University Press, 1977.

Williams, Raymond. *Culture and Society 1780–1950*. New York: Columbia University Press, 1983, 1958.

Williams, Raymond. *The Long Revolution*. Peterborough, Ont.: Broadview Press, 2001, 1961.

Williams, Raymond. *Television: Technology and Cultural Form*. New York and London: Routledge, 2003, 1974.

Williams, Raymond. *Keywords: A Vocabulary of Culture and Society*. Oxford: Oxford University Press, 2014, 1976.

Audiences and fandoms

The last chapter introduced some of the basic ideas germane to cultural studies, including (historical) **reception studies**. This chapter will explore in further detail the idea of audiences and **audience studies**, and focus on the contemporary phenomenon of **media fandoms**, and especially how they relate to gender and other forms of social difference. Recall that reception studies and audience studies are similar and/or overlapping projects, but that reception studies tend to emphasize how a film or TV text is positioned by the media industries to be received by readers, while audience studies tend to emphasize the behaviors and actual responses of readers. Oftentimes audience studies are called **reader-response studies** or **reader-response criticism**, especially in literary fields, where people actually encounter texts quite literally *through reading words on a page*. Audience studies is the preferred term in media studies, however; for although we still use the terms "reader" and "reading," reading media involves **decoding** complex audio-visual signals, and not just words on a page.

That said, along with the early work done on television audiences noted in the last chapter (by Morley, Brundson, Ang, *et al.*), one of the first important audience studies was written about reading books: Janice Radway's *Reading the Romance: Women, Patriarchy, and Popular Literature*. In it, Radway sets out to challenge the basic assertion that reading romance novels can only serve to keep female readers firmly ensconced within patriarchal ideologies. Romance novels—with their emphasis on women finding and transforming men into suitable lovers and husbands—have long been critiqued for reinscribing patriarchal attitudes about gender. But Radway explored what *the experience of reading romance novels meant* to women, and she investigated that question by talking to the actual women who read them. She interviewed women about their reading habits, what they read, how they responded to it, and what was at stake in it. She argued that her readers did engage with (negotiate with) the ideological meaning of the romances they read, rather than passively assimilate those meanings as some social critics (following the **Frankfurt School**) might suggest. Importantly, Radway argued that the very act of reading itself was an act of resistance to the patriarchal structures most of the women lived within: in reading their favorite novels, they carved out a space and time for their own fantasies, their relaxation and pleasure, and their own social interactions (discussing the novels with other readers). Concluding that a simple ideological text-based approach to romance novels would miss the way(s) that the very act of reading itself could be resistant to dominant ideologies, Radway's work helped to legitimate the field of audience studies within literature and multiple other disciplines.

Radway's work, like that of Morley, Brundson, Ang, *et al.*, is based on the

principles and practices of **ethnography**. Derived from the ancient Greek, the term literally means writing (graphy) about social groups (ethnos). Ethnography as its own academic method is closely linked to **anthropology** and **sociology**, two related fields devoted to studying human cultures. Ethnography might thus be thought about as the practice of writing about (or making media about) certain cultural groups, whether they be Trobriand Islanders, **working class** youths, women who read romance novels, or *Supernatural* (2005–) fans. Two central tenets of ethnographic research are **participation** and **observation** or (**P and O**). The first term refers to the fact that the ethnographic researcher needs to participate in the culture she or he is exploring or studying; while partaking of and sharing in a culture, the researcher also observes its practices. By both participating *and* observing, the researcher hopes to minimize biases and obtain an accurate understanding of the culture and its practices. Problems can arise if the researcher only observes a culture from outside of it, especially if that culture is markedly different from his/her own. In this case, the researcher's own biases might influence the interpretations of what s/he records. (Indeed, this was one of the central problems of much nineteenth- and twentieth-century anthropology, which was increasingly critiqued as **Eurocentric** for the ways in which Western explorers and anthropologists represented "primitive" non-white cultures.) On the other hand, if the ethnographic researcher becomes too much of participant in a given culture, he or she may lose critical distance on it.

Contemporary (literary) ethnographers, like ethnographic filmmakers, or people doing audience studies, thus strive to be aware of and balance out their own participation and observation as they create their studies. They also try to give their subjects as much opportunity as possible to communicate about their cultures in their own ways, which is a major way that cultural studies and audience studies differ from audience studies in quantitative fields like mass communication or media economics (where precise questionnaire answers are then numerically evaluated). However, even cultural studies ethnographers, filmmakers, or audience studies researchers still create and organize the final form that presents their research—whether it be a book, film, or a journal entry. To try to overcome or at least acknowledge that fact, it has become common in contemporary cultural studies for audience researchers to announce their own subjectivity—to tell their readers who they are, how they did their research, and what their explicit relationship to the culture being studied might be. This trend is also observable in contemporary documentary filmmaking, wherein a filmmaker might place him/herself within the film, and/or document his/her participation with the culture being explored. Whatever one thinks of the documentaries of Michael Moore, there is no way he can be faulted for trying to hide behind his images, or presenting them as if they were a version of objective "truth" via "Voice of God" extra-diegetic narration. For example, Moore's documentary *Roger & Me* (1989)—on the decline of the American auto industry in Flint, Michigan—begins with an autobiographical segment covering Moore's youth spent in Flint, and his relationship to the people of the city. In this way, he positions himself vis-à-vis his subject matter: this trait is also shared by most scholars doing film and television reception and/or audience studies.

One of the more interesting and dynamic areas of recent film and television audience studies explores the diverse ways people **decode** ever-expanding media **franchises** like *Star Trek*, *Star Wars*, *Harry Potter*, or *Lord of the Rings*. Each of these franchises represents a large number of professionally-produced media texts that may encompass films, TV shows, books, video games, and so on. Audiences passionate about these large franchises are often termed **fans** or said to be members of a **fandom**, due to the ways that they relate in oftentimes intensely personal ways to particular TV shows, films, or franchises. The term "fan" derives from "fanatic," a person who overinvests in something emotionally, often to a pathological degree. When the study of media fandoms began in earnest in the 1980s, scholars often had to combat a preconceived notion that media fans were indeed crazy or lacked a meaningful connection to the real world. The media industry itself made movies about dangerously psychotic fans (*Fade to Black* [1980], *Misery* [1990]), and fans were often stereotyped as lonely single women or nerdy men. Unlike sports fans (and the sports-entertainment industries)—who are arguably closer to dominant forms of patriarchal capitalism—media fans were often shunned and ostracized within the public sphere, often told (most famously on a *Saturday Night Live* skit featuring *Star Trek*'s William Shatner from 1987) that they needed to "Get a Life!" Such thinking reveals a **binary opposition** prevalent in that era between the terms "fan" and "normal viewer," wherein the former is devalued and/or pathologized vis-à-vis the latter, supposedly those people who do "have a life" outside of media fandom. Even though more and more people consider themselves fans in today's media-saturated environment, traces of the binary can still be found in individual attitudes, as in people (for example) who collect everything connected to the *Harry Potter* franchise but refuse the nomenclature "fan," or in *Star Trek* fans who argue over the terms "Trekkie" versus "Trekker." Like most binaries, the "fan/normal viewer" dichotomy can be easily **deconstructed**, and shown to be dependent on highly subjective value judgments. For example, a sports fan who dresses up in his team's uniform is rarely remarked upon, but a Harry Potter fan dressed in wizard robes is still likely to be singled out as odd by journalists and other cultural commentators. We probably all tend to view our own fannish practices as "normal," defining ourselves against **Others** who we think perhaps go a bit "too far" in their fannish adorations.

For a variety of reasons (some of which are explored below) media fans are no longer seen as a nutty fringe culture. More and more people identify themselves as fans of some film or television show, or even more regularly a media franchise. A brief personal anecdote exemplifies this shift: when I first began to teach about media fandoms in the mid-1990s, I would often ask students if they considered themselves to be fans of some media text or another. Usually, only a few students would sheepishly raise their hands. When I ask the same question in 2015, almost every student raises his or her hand. What has changed, and why? The following section explores some of the ways that media fandoms first developed and then evolved over the years, in the process becoming a major phenomenon studied by media scholars, and courted by the media industries.

A brief history of media fans

The phenomenon of the film and TV fan is not as recent as one might think. It actually dates back at least to the first decades of film history, when Hollywood began to create and publicize movie stars, exploiting fan's preferences for certain performers in order to sell tickets and differentiate their products. (Before that there were also fans of theater and opera stars.) Studio-backed or studio-sanctioned fan magazines like *Photoplay* and *Modern Screen* arose in the 1910s and lasted well into the 1960s, each issue purporting to reveal "behind the scenes" stories and "the secrets" of the public's favorite stars. In truth, these magazines were just another form of Hollywood promotion and publicity, even as they would occasionally carry feedback from actual fans in the form of letters to the editor. Also during this era, fan clubs often arose around certain movie personalities and/or popular singers, but they were loosely organized and rarely centralized aside from an occasional fan contest or Hollywood visit arranged by one of the magazines. By the 1970s and 1980s, movie fan magazines had morphed into more generalized and better-selling staples such as *People* and *Us Weekly*; these magazines (still) cover film and TV stars, and various aspects of pop culture as well as more "human interest" stories. Also in the 1970s and 1980s, fan magazines devoted to soap operas, such as *Soap Opera Digest*, arose to meet the era's growing fascination with daytime and nighttime serial narratives. Today, fan magazines are often studied by contemporary cultural studies scholars in order to explore how and why certain movie stars were popular when they were, and what that popularity might have to tell us about historical constructions of gender, race, class, etc. Today a good portion of the media industry is still serving up the scandals and sex lives of stars and celebrities, as on TV shows like *Entertainment Tonight* (1981–), *Access Hollywood* (1996–) or *TMZ* (2007–), shows that themselves are becoming the object of cultural studies scholarship.

In the post-World War II era, fan magazines began to arise for specific film **genres**, especially horror and science fiction. (The pulp magazine *Amazing Stories* was devoted to *literary* science fiction and its fans since its inception in 1926.) These new genre-based magazines were often aimed at more juvenile audiences than *Photoplay* or *Modern Screen*, whose gossipy stories about Hollywood romances were aimed mostly at women. Publications like *Famous Monsters of Filmland* (1958–83) and *Castle of Frankenstein* (1962–75) celebrated classical Hollywood horror films. Those films were finding a new audience at that time due to their sale to television; the magazines also promoted new horror releases and featured fan feedback in the form of letters to the editor. More adult or cerebral versions of those genre-based publications soon emerged: *Cinefantastique* (1970–) and *Cinefex* (1980–) appealed to adult fans of horror and science fiction, and often focused on the business of special effects technology, perhaps a more traditionally "masculine" area of interest as opposed to romance or monsters. By the 1980s, the glossy *Fangoria* (1979–) had supplanted *Famous Monsters of Filmland* as the leading horror fan magazine: as its name implies, *Fangoria* focused on the newer and gorier horror films of the 1980s, and especially the special effects techniques used to create them.

Arguably, it was the original *Star Trek* series (1966–9) and the first three *Star Wars* films (1977, 1980, 1983) that led to the creation of more modern day fandoms. *Star Trek* (discussed more fully in the case study below) had been a mildly popular weekly prime-time TV show in the late 1960s, but it found an ever-growing audience of fans during the 1970s as the series entered **strip syndication**. Strip syndication is a model of television programming that broadcasts re-runs of a weekly series in a consistent daily (usually Monday–Friday) time slot. Thus, many *Star Trek* fans of the 1970s watched it every weekday after school or work, rather than once a week in the evening. *Star Trek* fans (as well as fans of other cult 1960s shows like the gothic soap opera *Dark Shadows* [1966–71]) soon coalesced into local fan clubs and many fans began creating their own

homemade magazines, often termed **fanzines** (or just **zines**) to differentiate them
from the slicker, industry-sanctioned fan magazines. The fanzines of this era were
difficult to produce and disseminate, as they had to rely on mimeograph and Xerox
machines as well as the United States Postal Service. Some fanzines were devoted
to updates on meetings, conventions, and star appearances in other related texts,
while other fanzines printed original stories, poems, songs, drawings, and so forth
made by the fans themselves. In so doing, fans were creating new adventures for
beloved characters, expanding and perhaps reworking the diegetic universes those
characters inhabited.

One of the reasons media fandoms have grown so rapidly in the ensuing decades
is technology. VCRs and DVDs (and now Netflix, Hulu, and Amazon Prime)
allow fans to collect and watch their favorite movies and TV shows on their
own terms, decreasing the importance of strip syndication (even as many local
TV channels still package re-runs in this way). Collecting film or video before
the VCR/DVD-era was an expensive and arduous task, involving bulky 16mm
film prints or grainy video copies made from (sometimes bootlegged) master
tapes. Today however, media fans can purchase or watch their favorite texts at the
push of a button. Contemporary video technology also allows fans to re-edit or
"mash-up" characters and texts in unique and creative ways, and then share them
with one another via the Internet. Indeed, computers and cyberspace have made
it much easier for fans to network with one another, and most fan productions
now appear on the web rather than in homemade magazines printed and circulated
among a small group of friends. Furthermore, the contemporary media industry
has finally recognized that fans are not crazy outsiders to dominant cultural trends,
but important and consistent consumers of their products. Today, most film and
TV shows come with a "built-in" web presence that encourages (or even creates
and controls) fandoms, a process that some more independently minded fans find
manipulative or even exploitative.

Another reason fan culture has increased over the last few decades is perhaps
due to changing notions of masculinity in Western cultures. As many critics have
discerned, twenty-first-century Western masculinities are somewhat different than
those of previous generations. For example, the 1980s was an era of "hard bodied"
masculinity exemplified by Hollywood action stars like Sylvester Stallone (*Rocky*,
Rambo) and Arnold Schwarzenegger (*Terminator*, *Predator*). Similarly, President
Ronald Reagan drew upon his former roles in Hollywood westerns and war
films to create a "tough-talking" masculine persona that won votes and inspired
confidence. However, as mentioned at the start of this chapter, the era's nascent
science-fiction fandoms were often represented as feminine or feminizing spaces—
as sites of "failed" masculinity. The men who participated in science fiction media
fandoms were often considered nerds, wimps, or geeks; women were likewise
stereotyped as not living up to traditional gendered ideals, being thought of as
unattractive, overweight "lonely hearts" who couldn't get a date with a "real man."
In truth, women of all sorts, differently abled people, racial and ethnic minorities,
and lesbian and gay people did belong to a lot of early science fiction fandoms,
partly because they felt welcome in them (and still do). Science fiction and fantasy
genres invoke and celebrate the non-normative, especially in comparison to
other types of fandoms, such as sports fandoms, which are more closely tied to
the practices and beliefs of patriarchal capitalism such as competition, aggression,
and material success. Anything can happen in science fiction and fantasy genres,

whereas in sports there is a pretty rigid structure for how the games must be played and consumed. Perhaps in response to being stereotyped, some media fans of the era started to use the derogatory term "mundane" (which means everyday, common, or ordinary) to refer to non-fans. A variation of "mundane" is found within *Harry Potter* fandoms, wherein fans refer to non-fans as "Muggles," a term from the *Harry Potter* lexicon used to describe people without any special magical powers. As the use of these terms suggest, many fans take a fierce pride in what they do and what they create.

So what has become of 1980s "hard body" masculinity? Yes, there are still muscle-bound cinematic characters like *Thor* and *Captain America* (the latter of whom notably began life as a scrawny young man), but the aging Stallone and Schwarzenegger types have been relegated to nostalgic kitsch like the *Expendables* films (2010, 2012, 2014). Increasingly in the twenty-first century, our new blockbuster heroes tend to be younger or smaller men like Harry Potter (Daniel Radcliffe), Edward Cullen in *Twilight* (Robert Pattinson), The Amazing Spiderman (Tobey Maguire and Andrew Garfield), and Frodo (Elijah Wood) and Bilbo (Martin Freeman) from Peter Jackson's *Lord of the Rings* and *Hobbit* franchises. The rise of female action heroes in franchises like *The Hunger Games* (2012–15) and *Divergent* (2014–) also speak to this trend. Whereas Stallone and Schwarzenegger used their big muscles and even bigger guns to save the day, our newer, kinder, gentler action movie heroes are more likely to have intelligence and/or magical powers that help them complete their quests. This trend is certainly tied to the rise of films and TV shows based on Marvel comic books, in many cases texts from the 1960s that often centered on ordinary or outcast figures thrust into heroic situations via the acquisition of special powers. All of which is to say that twenty-first-century media culture has seen the rise of—as some waggish pundits have named it—a "nerd chic" aesthetic. In addition to the movies just mentioned, the popularity of the **sitcom** *The Big Bang Theory* (2007–)—which centers on geeky scientists who are also rabid science fiction and fantasy fans—attests to this phenomenon, as do the characters Troy and Abed on *Community* (2009–).

Perhaps another factor contributing to the changing dimensions of Western masculinity is the ever-amazing and ever-increasing technology that currently pervades our lives. In this sense one might suggest (only partially in jest) that computers and smart phones are our new "magic wands": men and women can do things with these special devices that Stallone and Schwarzenegger could never hope to do with guns and muscles. It might also be noted that many of these newer, younger, and smaller male action heroes tend to work with or in relation to others like them. Whereas Stallone and Schwarzenegger only needed themselves to take down entire armies and/or assorted evil empires (making them examples of traditional American individualism and exceptionalism), in our more recent media franchises, it takes almost a village to defeat Voldemort or return the "One Ring" to Mount Doom.

Manufacturing fandoms?

While any cultural text can become the object of a fan's devotion, over the last few decades media producers and scholars alike have figured out some of the textual qualities that might engender a healthy fandom (and likewise healthy profits based on franchising). The first of these is (1) genre, and specifically the science-fiction/fantasy genres. As mentioned above these genres—unlike the western or the war film—are non-realist in design and narrative: they invite spectators into an imaginative world where anything can and could happen. Although the horror genre can also be the basis of a healthy fandom, it is worth noting that when that happens the more graphic or violent nature of the genre is played down, as in the *Dark Shadows* (1966–2012), *Twilight* (2008–12), or *Supernatural* (2005–) franchises. If outright horror and social realism are muted in fandoms, what is stressed? The next characteristic of a succesful franchise likely to give rise to a fandom might be identified as (2) a handful of complex characters who relate to one another in complex ways. Cult TV scholar Matt Hills has further suggested that at the heart of these complex characters there should be (3) a heterosexual romance that is unresolved and/or unconsummated. Earlier examples of this trait can be found in TV shows like *Beauty and the Beast* (1987–90), and it is arguably the entire basis of the *Twilight* franchise. In this way, fans are invited to project themselves into the romance (which never seems to resolve itself, or at least not until the end of the series or franchise). But even in texts without a strong heterosexual romance in the narrative (like *Star Trek*, *The Lord of the Rings*, or *Supernatural*), the relationships between the **homosocial** male characters need to be complex, often verging on almost romantic dynamics. And as explored below, some media fans have found ways to deepen and even eroticize those diegetic homosocial bonds, rewriting original texts to appeal to their own desires.

One of the most important characteristics of a franchise-that-gives-rise-to-a-fandom is its (4) textual openness or **serial** form. It is rare that a single Hollywood film will engender a passionate fan following (films like *The Wizard of Oz* [1939], *Casablanca* [1942], and *The Rocky Horror Picture Show* [1975] notwithstanding). Especially since the advent of cable television and the proliferation of niche TV channels, serial narrative form has been important in creating franchises and fandoms. Certainly a series sitcom like *The Simpsons* has its fans, but shows that combine **series** and **serial** elements (see Chapter 5) like *Buffy the Vampire Slayer* (1997–2003) and *The X-Files* (1993–2002) have been much more likely to generate intense fandoms. (These shows also exemplify traits 1–3, and especially the troubled or unconsummated heterosexual romance.) Opened-ended serial forms allow for characters to morph and change across episodes and across seasons (making them more complex). Like the soap operas from which they derive, serial narratives might feature a villainous character in one season who becomes a trusted confidant in the next. Closely related to this aspect of textual openness is (5) a multi-textual form: most of these franchise fandoms exist across multiple and varying platforms, encompassing movies, TV shows, cartoon spin offs, books, graphic novels, toys, videogames, websites, etc. Henry Jenkins (2008) refers to this development as **transmedia storytelling**, in that the entire story of a given franchise can only be known by exploring it across its multiple distribution platforms. As with genre and textual openness, these multi-platforming texts encourage different "takes" or "rewrites" of the original texts, almost to the point where it becomes impossible to single out one text as original or separate from the others. All of these formal features create (6) an ever-expanding diegetic universe that fans are invited to explore across different platforms, including their own fannish productions, explored below.

There may be at least one other important quality to media texts that give rise to fandoms: (7) nostalgia. Many media fans have lived their entire lives with their favorite texts, having grown up with them. It is almost a cliché within *Dark Shadows* fandom that fans of a certain age remember running home from school everyday to watch it on television every afternoon. Thus for some members of a fan community, participating in a fandom may be a way of reconnecting with one's youthful or past pleasures. Such reading practices across the decades also underscore the historical "situated-ness" of media reception: what a young boy or girl might have enjoyed about *Dark Shadows* during its initial run (mild G-rated scares) perhaps today gives way to an amused nostalgic appreciation of the show's cheap sets and flubbed lines. As a way of perhaps acknowledging nostalgia, some long-running franchises even thematize time-travel, creating a space-time in which characters from earlier iterations of the franchise may "loop back" into newer episodes. *Star Trek, Dark Shadows*, and *Doctor Who* (1963–) have all developed this trait within their primary texts, in effect merging older versions of the franchise with newer ones, in the process exposing newer fans to older characters, all the while invoking nostalgia in older fans. And as certain franchises continue to produce new films and TV shows, parents and children can enjoy them together, making their appeal trans-generational, and obviously more lucrative in the process.

Henry Jenkins, "Textual Poaching," and shipping

Much of the first generation of scholarship on fan cultures (written in the 1980s and 1990s) was performed by researchers like Henry Jenkins, Camille Bacon-Smith, John Tulloch, and Constance Penley, all of whom focused on science fiction and fantasy fan cultures. Henry Jenkins's book *Textual Poachers: Television Fans and Participatory Culture* (1992) is exemplary and among the best known works; in it, Jenkins uses the term **textual poaching** to describe and theorize the activities of media fans, whom Jenkins sees as "poaching" ideas, characters, settings, plots, and pleasures, from mainstream media texts. Historically, a poacher was someone who hunted game illegally on land belonging to someone else, as when a serf hunted on his feudal lord's land without permission. In Jenkins's formulation, fans borrow, steal, or otherwise **reappropriate** mainstream media texts in order to produce their own, homegrown interpretations or versions of them—versions that speak to fans in ways inspired by the original text but also in ways more personal and idiosyncratic. As per Jenkins then, fandom involves (1) a certain mode of reception, with fans intensely watching and re-watching their favorite shows and/or movies, looking for aspects and connections that more casual viewers might miss.

As such, fandom is also (2) a mode of criticism and interpretation, as fans seek to make connections between different iterations of the franchised texts under consideration, seeking to create what some scholars call a **hyperdiegesis**, a sort of all-encompassing timeline that relates all official episodes/installments of a given franchise to one another. Fans sometimes refer to the official storyline created by TBTB—"the powers that be"—as the franchise's **canon**. Jenkins's similar term **meta-text** encompasses all the official iterations of the text as well as fan-based additions and modifications, what the fans sometimes refer to as a **fanon**. Fandom is also a basis for (3) consumer activism, as when fans of a certain TV show or TV character influence producers to change or expand upon some aspect of the show. Perhaps most famously, the briefly canceled animated TV sitcom *Family Guy* (1999–2003, 2005–) was put back into production after fans' response to **strip-syndicated** reruns and DVD releases singled ongoing interest in the show. Fandom is also (4) a basis for creative cultural production: anything from water-cooler discussions, to original fan-written stories, poems, drawings, songs, dioramas, costumes, and even novels and scripts meant to expand upon the original diegetic universe of a given franchise or show. Finally, fandom serves as (5) a basis for community, whether in local fan clubs, large multinational conventions, or in cyberspace itself. Friendships forged in fandoms can be deep and long lasting, even after a TV show or franchise has come to its end.

Jenkins's work on fans draws upon and expands ideas developed by John Fiske in his 1987 book *Television Culture*. In it, Fiske usefully distinguishes between primary texts, secondary texts, and tertiary texts. The term **primary text** refers to the main text(s) under consideration: the films and TV shows that comprise the *Star Trek* franchise, for example, or even individual texts like *The Wizard of Oz*, *The Rocky Horror Picture Show*, or *All My Children* (1970–2011) that engender a large fan following. It is the primary text(s) that media fans revere and adore. As an expression of that ardor, some fans try to collect as many ancillary products related to their favorite primary texts as they can. These **secondary texts** (sometimes called **paratexts** by other scholars) include things like film reviews, posters, novelizations, music CDs or downloads, video games, autographed portraits, toys, models, and all sorts of memorabilia, all of which exist to promote, publicize, spread, and merchandise the brand. (One might note again here the importance of genre to franchising and fandoms: producing and marketing secondary texts that recall strange objects from science fiction or fantasy universes is far easier than merchandising props from fairly realistic texts like soap operas.) The important thing about secondary texts is that they are created for profit—just as primary texts are—with most of that profit going back to the companies or corporations that own the primary film, TV show, and/or franchise. Thus Paramount owns the *Star Trek* brand and franchise: periodically they create new movies or TV shows (**primary texts**) while also licensing their brand to toy manufacturers and other businessmen who produce **secondary texts** related to the brand or franchise. Like most labels, these too can get slippery: what is the primary text for a fan who first comes to *Harry Potter* via *Harry Potter* novels? He or she might consider the books to be primary texts, while for most other fans of the movies, the books might be considered to be secondary texts.

Arguably the most important type of text for fan studies is the **tertiary text**, which refers to the objects, activities, and original texts created by the fans themselves, with no official licensing from the owners and creators of the primary (or secondary) text(s). Not all fans are content to consume only primary and secondary texts; such highly motivated fans produce a wide (and often quite surprising) range of tertiary texts. They do not do it for profit—and indeed it would be illegal to sell **tertiary texts** without a licensing agreement—but out of their love for a film, TV show, or a media franchise. To a great extent, fans create tertiary texts for other fans: it is a way to share one's intense interest in a text with others who feel similarly. Tertiary texts may include **fan fiction** or **fanfic** (fan-written stories of varying lengths), poems, comic books, and lyrics; fan-written lyrics based on a primary text and its characters can be set to new or pre-existing melodies and they are known as **filk songs** (allegedly derived from the term folk songs). Fans also make art: drawing, painting and even sculpting favorite characters in a variety of media. Some fans rework secondary texts, carving into or otherwise altering professionally produced models or toys to express their own interests (see Figure 11.1). Another of the more interesting tertiary texts of recent years is the phenomenon of **cosplay** (from "costume play") in which fans first make costumes for themselves based upon those worn in the primary text, and then meet to enact vignettes or just simply to role play. And as new media technologies have increasingly allowed fans to manipulate the images from primary texts, whole new forms of fan-made videos ("fanvids") have appeared, from faux documentaries, to music videos (montages of primary-text clips set to new music), to mash-up videos (that combine two or more fandoms or characters), and even **machinima** videos (wherein fans re-purpose video game software to create new scenes featuring favorite characters or situations). Perhaps the most pervasive form of tertiary text is simply the viewer-generated discussion that transpires on hundreds if not thousands of websites and other online forums.

But it is **fan fiction** that initially drew the attention of many media scholars. In *Textual Poachers*, Henry Jenkins surveyed the many different genres of fan writing produced within 1970s and 1980s science fiction and fantasy fandoms. While fan fiction is potentially infinite in form and scope these days, it is useful to review Jenkins's "Ten Ways to Rewrite a Television Show" (162–77). The first of these is (1) *recontextualization*, wherein fans write stories that attempt to explain or refigure certain behaviors or developments in the primary text. Often these stories try to explain seemingly out-of-character behaviors that have piqued the fans' interests but which remain unanswered within the primary texts. The next genre of fan fiction that Jenkins identifies is (2) *expansion of the timeline*—stories that explore what characters did before or after the time periods depicted in the primary texts. A story focusing on the adventures of Harry Potter in the Hogwarts Retirement Home is a hypothetical example of this genre. Jenkins also identifies (3) *refocalization* as a genre of fan writing; in this format, fans write about minor or one-off characters who appear briefly within the franchise, expanding their stories well beyond what is featured in the primary text. An entire story devoted to Mrs.

Figure 11.1
From *Trekkies* (1997): a **secondary text** (a *Star Trek: The Next Generation* [1987–94] action figure) becomes a **tertiary text** when its owner alters the figure's hair and moustache to resemble the character's new look on the show.

Hudson (Holmes and Watson's landlady on the BBC series *Sherlock* [2010–]) would be a good example of refocalization. (4) *Moral realignment* is an extreme form of refocalization, a genre of fan fiction that turns villains into heroes and heroes into villains. This genre perhaps owes its existence to the original *Star Trek* episode "Mirror, Mirror," which centered on an alternative universe Enterprise manned by duplicitous fascists out to exploit the universe, not benignly explore it. The popular book and musical play *Wicked* is another good example of *moral realignment*, refiguring *The Wizard of Oz*'s Wicked Witch of the West not as a monster but as a noble heroine fighting for social justice. Yet another popular form of fan fiction is (5) *genre shifting* wherein figures from one genre (like those in science fiction) are written about as if they were in a romance novel, mystery, or court room drama. The original *Star Trek* again perhaps inspired this form of fan fiction: several primary episodes have the crew visiting a western planet, a gangster planet, and a Nazi planet. Similarly, *Star Trek: The Next Generation* (1987–94) featured several episodes devoted to the crew solving Sherlock Holmes mystery adventures via the Enterprise's virtual reality "holodeck," another good example of *genre shifting* occurring within a primary text.

One very popular form of fan fiction involves what Jenkins calls (6) *crossovers*. These texts combine characters from two or more fandoms into one story, such as Harry Potter meeting up with Frodo for an adventure in Middle Earth. Jenkins's category of (7) *character dislocation* is today more commonly called **alternate universe** (AU) storytelling, in which familiar characters from one franchise are reimagined within new diegetic contexts. Common AU story genres today include animal AU (wherein human characters are reimagined as animals), high school AU (wherein primary characters are written as though they were still attending high school), and kidfic (which imagines what canonical characters might have been like when they were children). Another form of fan fiction Jenkins describes is (8) *personalization*, in which the author of a story writes him or herself into the diegetic world of the primary text. One better known (and much maligned) form of personalization is the "Lt. Mary Sue" story, so named because such stories originally focused on a pretty young female officer (the generic "Lt. Mary Sue") who is transferred to the Starship Enterprise and falls into a passionate romance with Captain Kirk or Mr. Spock. Writers of fan fiction often deride this type of fan fiction as lazy wish-fulfillment, some even branding the *Twilight* novels as "Lt. Mary Sue" stories because they arose from author Stephenie Meyer's own romantic fantasies. (Meyer even describes her *Twilight* heroine Bella Swan in terms that mirror Meyer's own looks.) As should be clear, character development and (9) *emotional intensification* play large roles in fan fiction, as does (10) *eroticization*, terms that are perhaps self-explanatory.

Many contemporary fans use the term **shipping** (derived from "relationship") to describe any fanfic, fanvid, or fan art that pairs up favorite characters in sexual, romantic, or otherwise intensely emotional ways. Shipping can occur within a single fandom (as in a sexual vignette between Spike and Buffy from *Buffy the Vampire Slayer*), or across fandoms (as in a pairing between Buffy and *Doctor Who*). Shipping is often written to explore the sexual and/or romantic dimensions of characters who may or may not be overtly paired or romanticized in their primary text(s). To some fans who create this type of tertiary text, these relationships represent a given fan's preferred "take" on their favorite characters, and are sometimes dubbed a "One True Pairing." Some subgenres of **shipping** or pairing, such as "Hurt/Comfort," explore sadomasochistic fantasies, as do fanfics that depict bondage, domination, slave narratives, and/or non-consensual sex. (It is worth noting at this juncture that the *Fifty Shades of Grey* novels began their life as sadomasochistic *Twilight* fan fiction.) Adult-oriented and overtly sexualized stories are common within many fandoms, and many fans use the MPAA rating system to classify their work from G to NC-17, in order to make sure it finds its proper readers.

Broadly, explicit heterosexual (Het) stories are usually designated in fanzines and on websites with a diacritical slash mark, as in "m/f," or Spike/Buffy or Harry/Hermione (see Figure 11.2). On the other hand, *nonsexual* stories ("genfic") based on the same characters are more likely to be designated as Spike & Buffy or Harry & Hermione. Such stories might also be classified as "fluff" or "curtain-fic," the latter genre so named because it tends to dramatize a "One True Pairing" performing quotidian activities like grocery shopping or picking out a new set of draperies. Yet another variation of shipping involves writing stories that replace the characters from a given text with the actors who play them. In this way, fans also explore their attraction to and desire for certain actors, as well as the characters they play on screen. For example, it is easy to find shipping fanfic or fanart about Benedict Cumberbatch and Martin Freeman, the actors who play Holmes and Watson on *Sherlock*.

The "slash" mark used to indicate adult or sexualized fan fiction derives from one of the most interesting aspects of fan fiction, also referred to as **slash**: stories, drawings, or videos that imagine a close, loving, and frequently sexualized relationship between two same sex characters—characters who in the original primary texts are not depicted as sexual partners or lovers *per se*. The genre got its name from the convention that evolved among early slash writers for placing a slash mark between the two characters' initials or names to indicate the homosexual nature of the story, as in Kirk/Spock, Draco/Harry, Edward/Jacob, or Aragorn/Legolas (from *The Lord of the Rings* franchise). Thus, Western fanfic about two

Fig 11.2
Erotic fan art displayed in *Trekkies* (1997), depicting Data (Brent Spiner) and Tasha Yar (Denise Crosby) from *Star Trek: The Next Generation* (1987–94) as sexual intimates.

male characters in a sexual relationship is referred to as **slash fiction** (or slash fic), and within **manga** or **anime** fandoms it is known as "yaoi." Western fanfic about two female characters is sometimes referred to a **femme slash** (or fem slash), while within manga or anime fandoms it is known as "yuri." Among the first slash fictions to be studied by scholars were what fans designated K/S stories, which paired up *Star Trek*'s Kirk and Spock in various intimate situations. Slash videos and gifs are increasingly prevalent on YouTube and Tumblr for most major fandoms and can be quite imaginative: one K/S video cuts together intense, violent, and homoerotic buddy scenes between Kirk and Spock (culled from the primary episodes) and sets them to the Nine Inch Nails song "Closer," creating a **queer** sadomasochistic effect. Watching a video such as this one might make the viewer question the nature of the homosocial bonds between Kirk and Spock, which is precisely the point.

According to many of the scholars who first studied the phenomenon, most of the first slash fictions were written by heterosexual women, often female fans of a show who were dissatisfied with the gendered inequities built into heterosexual relationships on the primary text (as well as in "Lt. Mary Sue" fanfic) (see Figure 11.3). In this way, slash authors could and did imagine their favorite male characters in equally gendered sexual and romantic partnerships, in the process expanding the homosocial bonds of the primary text into homosexual ones. Still other scholars see slash as a type of heterosexual female porn, similar to the "girl-on-girl" scenes featured in much pornography aimed at straight men. Today it should probably be acknowledged that all sorts of different people write slash fiction or create slash videos for all sorts of different reasons. For younger queer fans, slash fiction may be a way of imagining and exploring their own same-sex desires, just as heterosexual females who write slash use the genre to explore and share their own fantasies. Slash fiction, like fan fiction in general, is likely to have as many reasons for its existence as there are people who write it and read it.

As this brief discussion has hopefully demonstrated, there are many different

Fig 11.3
A fan who writes **slash fiction** is interviewed in *Trekkies* (1997).

ways to be a media fan, and many different ways to write fan fiction or create tertiary texts. Not all fans (nor the owners of the primary texts) agree on what sorts of representations should be "allowable" within fandoms. Most famously, in the 1980s George Lucas sent his lawyers after *Star Wars* fans who were publishing adults-only fan fic about "his" characters. As in many venues on the Internet, flame wars can and do occur between different types of fans, which is why so many fans try carefully to label their work *before* someone reads it and becomes offended. There is even the fascinating phenomenon of the **anti-fan**, someone who spends time and energy reviling and/or critiquing a given cultural or media text, especially when that text is a drunk and disorderly "celebutant" like Paris Hilton, Kim Kardashian, or any of the denizens of *Jersey Shore* (2009–12). Other anti-fans save their venom for film or TV texts they personally revile, as when male heterosexual vampire fans disparage *Twilight*'s "sparkling" vampire lovers whom they find to be effeminizing, or feminists who critique the same text for what they feel are its outmoded patriarchal attitudes towards women and heterosexual romance. One thing is certain: fan fiction is now a huge cultural phenomenon with websites like FanFiction.net listing hundreds of thousands of stories devoted to *Harry Potter*, *Twilight*, *Glee* (2009–15), *Supernatural*, *Sherlock*, *Doctor Who* and numerous **anime** titles. Arguably there is fan fiction written by (and for) every type of fan, from stories that remain canonical, to those who imagine wildly different contexts and situations for their beloved characters. In so doing, fan fiction and fandom in general can and does serve as a research laboratory for studying human behaviors and human interactions in our ever-mediated world.

Case study: *Star Trek* (1966–9) and *Trekkies* (1997)

Arguably, *Star Trek* has been one of the longest running and most influential media franchises in Western history. As of this writing, it consists of six somewhat interlocking television series (arguably the franchise's **primary texts**), 13 feature films that draw on the first two live-action TV series, one web series, hundreds of *Star Trek* books released by professional presses (**secondary texts**), hundreds if not thousands of *Star Trek* toys and models (also **secondary texts**), and thousands if not hundreds of thousands of fan-made **tertiary texts** (explored in greater detail below). The original *Star Trek* was the brainchild of TV producer Gene Roddenberry, who created the first prime time *Star Trek* show for NBC, a weekly science fiction **series** centered on the outer space adventures of the Starship Enterprise, helmed by Captain Kirk (William Shatner), Mr. Spock (Leonard Nimoy) and Dr. "Bones" McCoy (DeForrest Kelley) (see Figures 11.4 and 11.5). From its inception, Roddenberry was interested in using science fiction to address the tumultuous political issues of the late 1960s—including sexism, racism, environmentalism, the war in Vietnam—and felt he could safely address such issues within a science fiction context. He pitched the series to studio executives as a sort of "western in outer space," but when his pilot episode featured a female officer as the spaceship's second in command, he was sent back to the drawing board. Studio executives felt that no one in the audience would accept a woman in such a position of power. The somewhat less diverse cast that resulted (in addition to Kirk, Spock, and McCoy) included an Asian navigator (George Takei), a Scottish engineer (James Doohan), and a black female telecommunications officer named Lt. Uhura (Nichelle Nichols) (see Figure 11.6). The Starship Enterprise also featured two other sporadically occurring female characters: Janice Rand (a sort of secretary to Kirk),

Fig 11.4
Captain Kirk (William Shatner) as he appeared in the original *Star Trek* TV show (1966–9).

Fig 11.5
DeForest Kelley as Dr. McCoy and Leonard Nimoy as Mr. Spock in the original *Star Trek* TV show (1966–9).

and Nurse Chapel (who worked in the Sick Bay with Dr. McCoy). While commentators of the era might have been impressed to find women in such professional roles in a science fiction text, later critics have pointed out that those three female officers embody the sexist archetypes of "the telephone operator," "the secretary," and "the nurse." Furthermore, each character was routinely costumed in mini-skirts and go-go boots, as often were the "starlets of the week," alien women with whom Kirk often had a romantic-sexual fling (see Figure 11.7). Nonetheless, *Star Trek* was trying to **hegemonically negotiate** with the dominance of patriarchal attitudes in late 1960s television.

Star Trek also used multiple science fiction tropes to address race and racism. In addition to casting prominent African American and Asian American actors as both regulars and guest stars, the show also used the literary devices of metaphor and allegory to address racial issues. For example, Mr. Spock is posited as a hybrid subject—half-human and half-Vulcan (an alien race dedicated to logic), making him an apt metaphor for issues faced by biracial people: several episodes explore the biases and

Fig 11.6
Lt. Uhura (Nichelle Nichols) was an African American female officer in the original *Star Trek* TV show (1966–9), a bold casting choice that broke with usual stereotypes of black women in film and television.

Fig 11.7
Captain Kirk in one of his numerous sexual/romantic dalliances, seen here with France Nuyen in the episode "Elaan of Troyius" (1968).

confusions experienced by subjects "caught" between two different racial or cultural identities. Indeed, any number of the show's various alien races might also be taken to represent social **Others** here on Earth, whether they be racial, national, or whatever. *Star Trek* is also remembered for presenting one of the first interracial kisses on television (between Captain Kirk and Lt. Uhura), even if they were "forced" into that kiss by mind-controlling alien villains, which arguably still suggests the "inappropriateness"—or at least volatility—of such a kiss in the late 1960s. The episode "Let That Be Your Last Battlefield" is one of *Star Trek*'s most obvious "race problem" episodes. In it, one alien feels superior to another because the left side of his face is white while the right side is black: his enemy's face has the opposite configuration (see Figures 11.8 and 11.9). In this way, *Star Trek* presented a liberal critique of racism, hegemonically negotiating with dominant racist ideologies of 1960s America. That said, the original series also regularly used racial markers to suggest villainy: two of the Enterprise's chief adversaries were the Klingons and Romulans, two alien "races" represented as having darker skin tones and vaguely Asiatic features (such as Fu Manchu beards) (see Figure 11.10).

Although the original *Star Trek* lasted only three seasons on TV, it soon returned as an animated Saturday morning cartoon series (1973–5) and a series of popular Hollywood blockbusters starting with *Star Trek: The Motion Picture* (1979). When the television series was rebooted as *Star Trek: The Next Generation* (1987–94), hegemonic negotiations in race and gender were again apparent. For example, the Enterprise was now captained by the less aggressive and more thoughtful Jean-Luc Picard (Patrick Stewart). Diegetically, Picard and his crew explored the galaxy some 200 years after Kirk and his crew had. In addition to Picard's traditionally masculine "Number Two," Commander William Riker (Jonathan Frakes), Picard was aided and abetted by two professional women: Dr. Beverly Crusher and Counselor Deanna Troi. Rounding out the main cast was LeVar Burton as the ship's blind African American navigator, and Lt. Commander Data (Brent Spiner) an artificial life form whose hybrid status allowed him to explore questions related to the meanings of being human. Also on the bridge was Lt. Commander Worf, a Klingon officer; in the first series, the Klingons had been the mortal enemy of the United Federation of Planets, for whom Kirk and crew explored the galaxy. Worf's inclusion in the rebooted series suggested that past enemies could become loyal comrades in the future (a trait of both

Fig 11.8
In the *Star Trek* episode "Let That Be Your Last Battlefield" (1969), the crew of the Enterprise encounters two aliens locked in mortal hatred of one another ...

Fig 11.9
... solely based on the color configuration of their faces, a thinly disguised allegory about racism.

Fig 11.10
While trying to be multicultural in one sense, the original *Star Trek* (1966–9) also used racial/racist signifiers to suggest villainy: alien races like the Klingons and the Romulans often had darker skin tones and sported Fu Manchu beards.

liberal thinking and serial narrative!). Perhaps the most interesting change between the two series was the rewriting of the Captain's opening monologue, heard each week over the opening credits. For Captain Kirk, the Enterprise's mission was "to explore strange new worlds, to boldly go where no *man* has gone before." For Captain Picard, the mission was now "to boldly go where no *one* has gone before." While such a change in rhetoric may seem small, it nonetheless reflects the impact of second wave feminism on popular culture. The more inclusive term "one" was used as a way to mitigate the patriarchal nature of the term "man."

These gendered and racial casting choices continued throughout the other *Star Trek* television shows that followed. African American actor Avery Brooks played Captain Benjamin Sisko on *Star Trek: Deep Space Nine* (1993–9); in addition to commanding a space station, Sisko was also a single father raising a teenage son. Arab-British actor Alexander Siddig was cast as Dr. Bashir in the same series, and Armin Shimerman as Quark introduced a new alien race into the *Star Trek* universe called The Ferengi. The Ferengi's greed and avarice were perhaps meant to be a critique of capitalist excesses (and Hollywood in general), even as some viewers complained they were invoking age-old stereotypes of Jewish moneylenders. The fourth live action series, *Star Trek: Voyager* (1995–2001) finally put a woman in the Captain's chair: Kate Mulgrew as Captain Kathryn Janeway, a no-nonsense leader whose gender never hindered her command. Janeway was supported by Chakotay (Robert Beltran) an officer of Native American heritage, a Vulcan played by an African American actor (Tim Russ), and Chinese American actor Garrett Wang as Harry Kim. The final *Star Trek* television series (to this point in time) was *Star Trek: Enterprise* (2001–5), set 100 years *before* the first series supposedly began. Its cast was arguably less diverse, as it tried to recapture some of the action-adventure feel that some fans felt had slowly ebbed out of the other *Star Trek* series in favor of dealing with social issues in science fiction settings. This action-adventure rather than social problem approach to *Star Trek* is also evident in its recent Hollywood film reboots (2009–), films that go back to the original *Star Trek* characters and adventures of Captain Kirk and Mr. Spock.

As mentioned earlier, *Star Trek* was instrumental in creating what we think of as modern media fandoms. According to some sources, the first *Star Trek* **fanzine**

(*Spockanalia*) was published in 1967, during the run of the first series. **Secondary texts** like toys, models, novelizations, and episode guides proliferated throughout the 1970s. By the 1990s, however, with additional primary and secondary texts, *Star Trek* fandom had grown from a niche phenomenon into such a massive pop cultural one, in the process becoming the subject of a feature-length documentary entitled *Trekkies* (1997). (The film too should be considered a secondary text within *Star Trek* fandom, because it was licensed and released by Paramount Pictures, the owners of the *Star Trek* brand.) The title of the film derives from a somewhat contested term used to describe *Star Trek* fans. A mash-up of "Trek" and "groupie," the term was used by many *Star Trek* fans of the 1970s until it was decided that the term had negative connotations arising from the slang word "groupie" (a young woman whose central purpose is to have sex with male rock musicians, often following them from town to town hoping to be selected). As such, the term "Trekker" evolved from "Trekkie." As Kate Mulgrew (the actor who played Captain Janeway) puts it in the documentary film *Trekkies*, Trekkers are fans who "are walking with us" [the show and its diegetic characters] rather than fans who are there to worship the primary text unconditionally all-the-while gobbling up secondary materials. As mentioned earlier, the "Trekkie/Trekker" debate again suggests a form of **Othering**, as Trekkers often consider themselves to be better and more serious fans than Trekkies.

Its title aside, *Trekkies* explores the wide world of *Star Trek* fans, what they do, and what the show means to them. (Actually, *Trekkies 2* [2004] takes a much more international look at the *Star Trek* phenomenon, focusing on fans from round the globe; it also includes a section on Klingon cover bands, in which fans perform their favorite songs in Klingon personas.) Our guide to the world of *Star Trek* fans in both films is Denise Crosby, the actor who appeared in *Star Trek: The Next Generation* as Lt. Tasha Yar. In this way, one might say she is both a **participant** in *Star Trek* culture as well as an **observer**, making her an ideal host for the film's ethnographic project. The film also opens with a delightful visual metaphor for *Star Trek* fandom: multiple close-up shots of multi-colored wool stitches, coupled with the audio babble of divergent voices, slowly pull back to reveal a needlepoint portrait of Denise Crosby as Lt. Tasha Yar (see Figure 11.11). In its

Fig 11.11
A fan-made needlepoint portrait of actor Denise Crosby as Lt. Tasha Yar from *Star Trek: The Next Generation* (1987–94), used in *Trekkies* (1997) to exemplify the diverse yet unified nature of *Star Trek* fandom.

opening credit sequence, *Trekkies* celebrates all the diverse elements and voices of fan culture, each of which contributes to and coalesces into a portrait of *Star Trek* fandom, here represented by the fan-made portrait of Tasha Yar.

True to the nature of most fandoms, the film does focus on the erotic or romantic responses some fans exhibit towards the franchise and its characters. One of the film's most memorable subjects describes herself as a "Spiner-Femme" because of her intense devotion to actor Brent Spiner (Data on *Star Trek: The Next Generation*). She shows off her memorabilia (much of which is kept in a locked safe-deposit box in her closet) including hundreds of photographs of actor Brent Spiner she took at a *Star Trek* convention. Her sequence in the film ends when she shows Denise Crosby a hill beyond her own apartment complex, a hill where Brent Spiner allegedly has a home (see Figure 11.12). This connection—however ephemeral—to the object of her devotion obviously gives her great pleasure—she says she often comes out on the patio when stressed to take a little "Brent Break." In another vein of romantic/erotic fascination, slash fiction is discussed by some of the women who write it (recall Figure 11.3), even as one slash writer who appears in the film has opted to have her face shot in darkness and her voice electronically altered due to what she feels is the still controversial nature of her chosen genre of fanfic. In another sequence, both fans and *Star Trek* executives discuss tertiary texts that reconfigure Captain Janeway as an S&M dominatrix needing to discipline her crew in sexualized ways (see Figure 11.13). The cultural critic might analyze these tertiary texts as negotiating gender against and through pre-existing (and arguably patriarchal) models of powerful phallic women such as alien sexual predators (in films like *Species* [1995]), femme fatales (any **film noir**), and even the lesbian vampire.

Still other fans have produced a Klingon sex manual, one rule of which is there is no such thing as foreplay in the Klingon culture. Klingons are known for their gruff and almost bestial nature, but when two African American fans dressed as Klingons express "desire" for another through physical violence, their roleplaying starts to look uncomfortably close to old-fashioned racist beliefs that figured blacks as more animalistic than whites. The film does not comment on the implied racism inherent in such characterizations, although the cultural critic of the film *Trekkies* might readily

Fig 11.12
In *Trekkies* (1997), a self-proclaimed "Spiner-femme" shows Denise Crosby her view of the hill where actor Brent Spiner (Data from *Star Trek: The Next Generation* [1987–94]) allegedly has a home.

Fig 11.13
Tertiary texts: fan-made comics that depict the crew of *Star Trek: Voyager* (1995–2001) in bondage and domination scenarios.

do so. Instead, *Trekkies* presents the issue of race within the history of *Star Trek* as a positive, progressive one, discussing how the original show had significant impact on young African Americans of the late 1960s and 1970s. Nichelle Nichols, the actor who played Lt. Uhura on the original series, relates an anecdote told to her many years later (see Figure 11.14). In it, a young African American girl was stunned to see a strong beautiful black woman on her TV set, one not playing a **mammy** or a maid. The young girl realized she could grow up to be anything she wanted, and in fact did grow up to be Oscar-winning actress and comedian Whoopi Goldberg, who herself has appeared in the *Star Trek* franchise as the *Next Generation* bartender and confidant Guinan.

Ultimately, *Trekkies* celebrates creator and **showrunner** Gene Roddenberry and his vision of a diverse and peaceful future, a philosophy known within *Star Trek* fandom as "IDIC"—"Infinite Diversity in Infinite Combinations." Lesbian and gay fans talk about their desire to belong to a future that does not stigmatize them based on their sexuality, as do racial minorities. One fan compares his interest in *Star Trek* to his interest in his Native American heritage. Women talk about how they can watch Captain Janeway on *Voyager* with their daughters and share what they feel to be a highly positive role model for young women (see Figure 11.15). Scientists and astronomers speak about the ways that *Star Trek* inspired their careers, and a psychotherapist discusses the usefulness of *Star Trek* metaphors like "raising the deflector shields" in his clinical practice. Other fans try to carry on Roddenberry's vision of a better future by performing community service, using local fan clubs to outreach and make connections with like-minded individuals. Although some fans seem content to buy expensive memorabilia at fan conventions and/or auctions, or collect as many secondary texts as they can (see Figure 11.16), many others create some quite remarkable artifacts. Sixteen-year-old Gabriel Koerner, for example, who many viewers of *Trekkies* might initially read as a "nerd," wrote his own *Star Trek* movie and designed computer graphics for it—on a MAC from the 1990s (see Figure 11.17). Since then Koerner has had a professional career as a digital effects artist in Hollywood.

Fig 11.14
In *Trekkies* (1997), actor Nichelle Nichols relates an anecdote about how the young Whoopi Goldberg was inspired by her character Lt. Uhura on the original *Star Trek* (1966–9).

Fig 11.15
Captain Janeway from *Star Trek: Voyager* (1995–2001) served as a role model for many women seeking representations of strong female characters on TV.

Audiences read *Trekkies*—as they do all cultural artifacts—in various negotiated ways. As an ethnographic documentary, the film runs the risk of Othering its subjects and making fun of them, even with the presence of Denise Crosby as participant/observer. Some viewers of the documentary feel it does exploit its subjects, especially the fans in the film who exhibit what many might call extreme behaviors—the family who runs a *Star Trek*-themed dental practice, the "Spiner-Femme" mentioned above, the fan who wore her *Star Trek* uniform to the President Clinton-connected Whitewater trial, or the man who is considering having his ears surgically altered to look like Vulcan ears. Yet, before we judge any of those people, let us remember it should be everyone's right to express him or herself as they choose, and to wear whatever clothes or uniforms we want. One scene in *Trekkies* addresses this directly, when a group of fans in Klingon uniforms

Fig 11.16
A *Star Trek* fan surrounded by his collection of **secondary texts**, from *Trekkies* (1997).

Fig 11.17
Fan Gabriel Koerner wearing his fan-made (**tertiary**) Star Fleet uniform in *Trekkies* (1997), while also showing off his collection of **secondary** texts.

confront a group of fast food workers in theirs: the fans might seem odd, but they have chosen to wear what they are wearing, as opposed to the restaurant workers who were probably forced to buy their uniforms in order to earn a minimum wage slinging burgers. (The scene also underscores the fact that being a media fan entails a certain level of middle class wealth.) One might also note that cosmetic surgery is a booming medical specialty that tens of millions of people undergo each year, even as many (if not most) of those procedures are designed to make women look more like idealized air-brushed versions of patriarchal femininity than "real" people. Why shouldn't there be more Vulcan ears on human heads? In many ways the film sums up its attitudes towards it subjects in a comment from actor Brent Spiner. When asked about the odd or peculiar nature of many *Star Trek* fans, he simply opines, "I don't think I've ever met anyone—*Star Trek* fan or not—who wasn't peculiar. I mean, we're all peculiar aren't we?"

Conclusion

Rather than saying that the *Star Trek* franchise—like most other popular media franchises—is somehow feminist or anti-racist (a claim I have tried to complicate in the case study above), it nonetheless demonstrates the **hegemonic negotiation** of issues like gender and race across 50 years of American television and cinema history. The franchise self-consciously attempted to become more inclusive over the years, minimizing certain biases and stereotypes, and aiming for more multicultural casting choices—even as in other ways it arguably reasserted hegemonically dominant ideologies. For many of the franchise's fans, such as those profiled in *Trekkies*, this impetus towards diversity and peaceful co-existence, remains an important one. And as discussed in Chapter 2, hegemonic negotiation itself presents us with a sort of "glass half full, glass half empty" situation. Challenges may be presented (and changes may be made) to the dominance of white patriarchal capitalism in media and society, even as white patriarchal capitalism is rarely dislodged from its position of dominance. Nonetheless, the historical study of franchises and fandoms can and does reveal interesting things about how those hegemonic processes can and do occur in textually and culturally specific ways.

That said, franchises and fandoms are ultimately still dependent on the **culture industries**. The industry used to mock media fans, but currently it wants to encourage them, and in the process it may be curtailing or short-circuiting some of the creativity expressed by earlier generations of media fans, instead channeling their energies into studio-created websites and the purchasing of more and more expensive franchised tie-ins. While fandom may still carve out a space for non-normative people and practices, fandom is still a capitalist enterprise, and white male characters and actors (however kinder or gentler) are still usually the central figures of most franchises as well as the objects of devotion within most fandoms. To invoke the **Frankfurt School** once again, perhaps media fandoms are just another way the culture industries seek to distract us from the material world around us, cajoling us to buy and consume their products in ever-fanatical ways. The scornful declaration to media fans made in previous decades—that they needed to "Get a Life!"—is now rarely heard. Instead, the media industries themselves have developed ways to promote and encourage the rise of fandoms, and in so doing, they continue to profit from them.

Questions for discussion

1   Do you consider yourself a media fan? If so, of what media texts or franchises are
    you a fan? Why? What are the specific pleasures you derive from your favorite texts?
    How involved are you in the creation of **tertiary texts** devoted to your chosen
    fandom?
2   Compare a media franchise you like with the criteria discussed on pages 225–227.
    Does your text or franchise fit into the model described? In what ways does it differ
    from the model described?
3   Can you list other examples of "nerd chic," either in real life or in other media
    artifacts? Do you see any concomitant shift in gender roles for women? How does
    race, class, ethnicity, or sexuality relate to any contemporary shifts in gender you
    may have identified?

References and further reading

Bacon-Smith, Camille. *Enterprising Women: Television Fandom and the Creation of
    Popular Myth*. Philadelphia, PA: University of Pennsylvania Press, 1992.
Benshoff, Harry. *Dark Shadows*. Detroit, MI: Wayne State University Press, 2011.
Bernardi, Daniel. Star Trek *and History: Racing Toward a White Future*. New
    Brunswick, NJ: Rutgers University Press, 1998.
Duffett, Mark. *Understanding Fandom: An Introduction to the Study of Media Fan
    Culture*. London and New York: Bloomsbury, 2013.
Fiske, John. *Television Culture*, Second Edition. New York and London: Routledge,
    2010 (first edition 1987).
Gerrold, David. *The World of* Star Trek. New York: Ballantine Books, Inc., 1973.
Gray, Jonathan, Cornel Sandvoss, and C. Lee Harrington, eds. *Fandom: Identities
    and Communities in a Mediated World*. New York and London: New York
    University Press, 2007.
Hills, Matt. *Fan Cultures*. London and New York: Routledge, 2002.
Hills, Matt. "Defining Cult TV: Texts, Inter-texts, and Fan Audiences," in Robert
    C. Allen and Annette Hill, eds. *The Television Studies Reader*, London and New
    York: Routledge, 2004. Pp. 509–23.
Jeffords, Susan. *Hard Bodies: Hollywood Masculinities in the Reagan Era*. New
    Brunswick, NJ: Rutgers University Press, 1994.
Jenkins, Henry. *Convergence Culture: Where Old and New Media Collide*. New York:
    NYU Press, 2008.
Jenkins, Henry. *Textual Poachers: Television Fans and Participatory Culture*. New York
    and London: Routledge, 2012 (1992).
Penley, Constance. *NASA/TREK: Popular Science and Sex in America*. London:
    Verso, 1997.
Radway, Janice. *Reading the Romance: Women, Patriarchy and Popular Literature*.
    Chapel Hill, NC and London: The University of North Carolina Press, 1991
    (1984).
Reagin, Nancy, ed. Star Trek *and History* (Wiley Pop Culture and History Series).
    Hoboken, NJ: John Wiley and Sons, 2013.
Roberts, Robin. *Sexual Generations:* Star Trek: The Next Generation *and Gender*.
    Champaign, IL: The University of Illinois Press, 2013.

Tulloch, John and Henry Jenkins. *Science Fiction Audiences: Watching* Dr. Who *and* Star Trek. London and New York: Routledge, 1995.

Whitfield, Stephen E. *The Making of* Star Trek. New York: Ballantine Books, Inc., 1968.

CHAPTER 12

Beyond identity politics: Contemporary thinking on nation, race, gender, and sexuality

This chapter explores some of the ways that contemporary scholars think about issues related to social difference, since social reality is deeply imbricated in mediated forms of communication like film and television (and vice versa). And as is hopefully a given by now for readers of this textbook, culture influences film and television texts, and film and television texts influence culture—that is to say, how real people get treated in the real world. In 2012, when Vice President Joe Biden was asked how and why his views on lesbian and gay people had changed over the years—allowing him to come out in support of marriage equality—he answered "I think *Will & Grace* [1998–2006] probably did more to educate the American public than almost anything anybody's ever done so far." Extrapolating from Biden's comment, one might say that images of "positive" or "normalized" (whatever those terms might mean) gay and lesbian people on television has had a significant impact on changing Western culture's understanding of homosexuality. Indeed, over the decades the connotations of homosexuality have changed significantly—from those of secrecy, deviancy, pathology, disease, and sin—to those of likable people next door who deserve the same rights and freedoms as do all people.

Recall that in the United States and other Western nations, the **counterculture** movement of the 1960s sounded a forceful critique of **dominant (white, patriarchal, capitalist) ideologies**, opening up new social spaces and cultural venues within which the voices of women, racial and ethnic minorities, and even lesbian and gay people could be heard. These disparate groups were also linked to the anti-war in Vietnam protests, and other movements devoted to social justice, combatting poverty and classism, and educating the populace about ecology. While the success of these various movements can be debated, in many cases they did help to create changes in the media's representation of minority peoples; *vice versa*, media images of diverse peoples helped to expose differing viewpoints to mainstream audiences and spur social change. Remember (from Chapter 11) the impact a black female Star Fleet officer on the TV show *Star Trek* (1966–9) had on young African American girls of that era. Seeing characters at the movies or on television that "look like you" can be tremendously validating to many minority groups and minority individuals, especially as such images challenge demeaning stereotypes or even lift a cloak of invisibility.

In terms of African Americans, the 1960s saw the first central and continuing black characters on TV since the early 1950s, when the **sitcom** *The Amos 'n Andy Show* (1951–3), based on a radio show by two white men who imitated black characters, aired on CBS. Late 1960s shows that created new roles for African American characters included not just *Star Trek*, but also *I Spy* (1965–8), a black and white buddy action show starring Bill Cosby and Robert Culp, and *Julia* (1968–71), a sitcom starring Diahann Carroll as a middle-class nurse raising her son. Other shows from *Hogan's Heroes* (1965-71) to *The Mod Squad* (1968–73) featured integrated casts, and as was explored in Chapter 4, Norman Lear created several successful sitcoms focused on African American families, both wealthy and poor, during the 1970s. At the movies, the early 1970s saw the explosion of **blaxploitation filmmaking**, a movement of cheaply made action films that allowed African American heroes the chance to "kick whitey's butt" and win the day. These films—which most famously include titles like *Shaft* (1971), *Super Fly* (1972), *Blacula* (1972), *Coffy* (1973), and *Foxy Brown* (1974)—were controversial upon their release and remain so for some critics (see Figure 12.1). They were accused of recirculating negative stereotypes while filling white Hollywood's coffers. But they were also popular with many audiences of all races, and helped open doors in Hollywood to black filmmakers and (especially) black musicians.

Before the 1960s, there was little organized study of film and television, and very little attention paid to the white patriarchal dominance of the film and television industries, and the images they produced. More concerted efforts to think about the rights and representations of minority groups began (for some groups) during World War II, as when the NAACP met with Hollywood executives to protest negative images of African Americans within Hollywood films. Such thinking about identity and representation continued throughout the postwar era, and flourished during the 1960s and 1970s, as film studies became a discipline within academia. Recall from Chapter 8 that **feminist film criticism** arose during this era, alongside the civil rights movement, the Chicano

Fig 12.1
Pam Grier starred in many **blaxploitation films** of the 1970s (such as *Foxy Brown* [1974]) as a strong and sexy action hero.

movement, the anti-war movement, the gay and lesbian movement, *et al*. All of these movements shared the strategy of what might be called **identity politics**, a term that describes a strategy for minority empowerment, chiefly through a given social group coalescing around a single label or a key identity that they wish to empower or redefine. Within identity politics, diverse members of any given group are expected to put aside their differences *within* the group, and to support the goals of the overall group identity, whether it be black, feminist, Chicano, or gay. In this case, fluid social categories like race, gender, ethnicity, or sexuality tend to get fixed and defined in monolithic and essentialist terms. For example, women of the era were urged to forego their differences from one another (based on class, color, sexuality, regionality, etc.) and present a strong unified front under the banner "Women's Liberation." As one can easily see, what oftentimes gets lost within the practices of identity politics are the various differences that make up any single minority group. For example, black people are female and male, rich and poor, straight and gay, from Atlanta and from the Bronx. They might all coalesce under the idea of "the black community" for certain political goals, but in reality every community is really a collection of communi*ties*. There may be just as many differences within any given community as between allegedly disparate communities.

Some theorists today use the term **strategic essentialism** to refer to the way that groups of people can and do come together under a single label (as in identity politics) in order to fight for social change. The idea is that intra-group differences must be muted or downplayed in order to create a united front, a kind of critical mass of people demanding social change. To give a more recent example, many lesbian and gay people critical of America's military goals in the Middle East put aside those qualms in order to fight for the repeal of "Don't Ask, Don't Tell," the federal policy discriminating against lesbian and gay soldiers in the Armed Services (which indeed did end in 2011). In this example, equal rights for lesbian and gay soldiers was felt to be more important (at least by some activists) than critiquing the wars in the Middle East. Similarly, during the 1960s and 1970s, many black women were expected to silence their own feminist goals in order to support the black civil rights movement, led primarily by heterosexual men. Many black women were made to feel that if they supported feminist causes, they were somehow negating or ignoring black causes. This is somewhat analogous to issues faced by people of mixed racial heritage, who often feel they must "choose" which race they "truly" belong to, all the while facing opprobrium for not being "white enough" or "black enough."

The critical method for analyzing film and TV images during the era of identity politics was **image** or **stereotype analysis**. Popular culture in general (and film and television in particular) have always traded in **stereotypes**, images and tropes that reduce any given social group's diversity and complexity into superficial markers, often derogatory, that come to represent the entire group in some readers' minds. The goal of the media analyst during this era was to identify and challenge the prevailing stereotypes of a given cultural group. Books by Marjorie Rosen and Molly Haskell (discussed in Chapter 8) identified prevailing stereotypes of women in Hollywood film. Donald Bogle's book *Toms, Coons, Mammies, Mulattoes, and Bucks*, first published in 1973, is also exemplary of this type of work. In an almost exhaustive fashion, Bogle scoured Hollywood film history and identified five stereotypes of African Americans—those that comprise the title of his volume.

Each of these stereotypes reduce the complexity and humanity of the black people to simplified (and often forthrightly derogatory) images that all of America consumed for decades, if not centuries.

In Bogle's analysis, the **Tom** (or **Uncle Tom**) stereotype refers to an older male house servant who only thinks to serve his white master. Uncle Tom was meant to be beloved (to white audiences) because of his gentle albeit simple wisdom and loyalty to his white masters/employers. Examples of the Tom include Uncle Remus in Disney's *Song of the South* (1946), or almost any black porter, butler, or shoeshine boy in countless classical Hollywood films. By the 1960s, the image of the Uncle Tom was scorned if not reviled by many blacks. The **coon** stereotype was meant to be similarly innocuous and powerless. The coon is a black buffoon—an illiterate, shuffling, mush-mouthed fool who amuses white audiences with his slowness and stupidity (recall Fig. 1.1). The **mammy** is the Tom's counterpart in the master's house, an overweight asexual black woman devoted to raising her white charges. The **mulatto** and the **buck** are more frightening stereotypes that some theorists argue arose after the Civil War to scare white people into keeping blacks oppressed. While the Tom, coon, and mammy are docile and harmless figures—supposedly representing the beneficence of slavery—the mulatto and the buck are sexual threats. The outdated term mulatto refers to a person of mixed race, and s/he symbolizes the alleged dangers inherent in interracial sex. In Bogle's analysis, this figure is usually female and always meets a tragic fate, dragging the men who desire her—whether they be white or black—down with her. Finally, the buck is the stereotype of a black man as hypermasculine and hypersexual, a figure used to terrify whites and especially white women, as he represents the ever-present threat of bestial, interracial rape. By the 1970s, the black buck (and other) stereotypes were ripe for parody, as in Mel Brooks's *Blazing Saddles* (1974) when Cleavon Little as "Black Bart" taunts the KKK with the inflammatory question "Where are the white women at?" By the twenty-first century, a film like *Django Unchained* (2012) could even reconfigure its Uncle Tom character (played by Samuel L. Jackson) into the ultimate villain: hypocritical and self-serving, Jackson's character Stephen was made up and costumed to look like a benign Uncle Tom, but he was clearly a hateful traitor to his own race (see Figure 12.2).

As important as that era's stereotype or image analysis was and is, it also has its limitations. As just noted, the use of stereotypes in *Blazing Saddles* and *Django Unchained* are not merely replicating them in an un-thinking way: they are instead

Fig 12.2
Samuel L. Jackson in Quentin Tarantino's *Django Unchained* (2012) up-ended the **Uncle Tom stereotype** by making his character truly despicable.

critical of dominant ideology's *use of stereotypes*. Through parody and satire (forms of **deconstructive genre filmmaking**) *Blazing Saddles* and *Django Unchained* call attention to the absurdity of such stereotypes (as well as their prevalence in twentieth-century popular culture). Stereotype or image analysis is also often predicated on the idea of negative or positive images—i.e. is the stereotype thought to be more or less harmful to how dominant culture understands a given minority group? But that raises the question of what "negative" or "positive" images might exactly be, and to whom. The bad-ass hero of a blaxploitation action film might be seen as a positive image by one member of the audience, but just an updated black buck figure by another, and therefore a negative image. In another good example, are the women of *Sex and the City* (1998–2004) truly emancipated feminists, or just shopaholic man-chasers?

One of the more important ideas to take away from image analysis, even as we move into more recent ideas that complicate those approaches, is that *stereotypes linger*: they transform and mutate, and can often be invoked subconsciously. For example, some critics have accused the character of Jar Jar Binks from George Lucas's *Star Wars* franchise as being an updated coon stereotype. Other critics have wondered whether white Americans adore Oprah Winfrey because she is a sort of updated mammy figure. Are hypermasculine black rappers and sports stars simply new versions of the black buck stereotype, even as today they are usually celebrated (rather than feared) by white Western culture? When does any given black comedian become a coon stereotype? These are all salient questions that have to be looked at in careful and individuated historical ways: one of the primary goals of both **poststructuralist** and **cultural studies** criticism. Recall that one of the central points of contemporary cultural criticism is to underline differences and/or slippages in the meanings of the object(s) of study, and not reproduce reductive essentialisms. Thus, when looking at specific images and/or stereotypes, there is the need to understand them within their various contexts: historical, industrial, socio-cultural, etc.

Today's approaches to understanding questions surrounding identity have moved beyond the rather essentialist practices associated with both identity politics and basic image analysis. These ideas—known variously under labels such as **critical race theory**, **postcolonial theory**, **anti-essentialist** and/or **third wave feminism,** and **queer theory**—all share some common ideas about identity and meaning drawn from the theoretical advances of the last several decades. Since it would take many, many books to recount the changing histories and ways of thinking about each and every minority group in Western culture in relation to the history of film and television, this chapter first attempts to introduce some of the general (and generalizable) concepts related to many of these struggles. Specific concepts related to race and nation, and gender and sexuality, follow in subsequent subsections.

Ten trends in contemporary thinking about identity

As this book has explored throughout its length, thinking about media and culture has evolved a great deal from earlier decades, and it continues to change and grow as scholars contest old paradigms and elaborate new ones. Some of today's more interesting ideas about identity—both that of individuals and that of groups or even nations—have drawn upon concepts central to psychoanalysis, first wave and second wave feminism, cultural studies, phenomenology and reception, postmodernism, and poststructuralism in general. As such, these new theoretical paradigms are (1) highly **interdisciplinary**. The ideas associated with them can be and are discussed in film and media departments, history departments, philosophy departments, all sorts of cultural studies departments, as well as the disciplines of sociology, psychology, and medicine. To take a quick example of how these latter disciplines are rewriting or rethinking identity, researchers in those fields now realize that "gay" as a category of sexual orientation is a limited and almost useless label when dealing with certain ethnic or regional populations. Sociologists and those in associated medical fields now often use the terms "Men who have Sex with Men" (MSM) and "Women who have Sex with Women" (WSW) instead of gay or lesbian, because some people who participate in homosexual acts do not self-identify as gay or lesbian, terms they or their cultures perhaps feel are derogatory, or too associated with white bourgeois Western cultures. As such, sociological and medical researchers might miss important data if they only ask their subjects if they identify as gay or lesbian. Real life is almost always more complicated than the words and images we use to understand it.

As cultural studies insists, questions of representation are very important to how we understand ourselves and others. Film and television images (2) shape our understandings of everything, from social difference to climate change. Recall that cultural studies examines the *struggle* for meaning within cultures—in this case the meaning of human differences and human identities. People are treated in the "real world" based on how others perceive them. How any given culture defines the terms and meanings of social identities (or more broadly social issues) directly impacts on the ways it writes its social policies and laws, elects politicians, and even starts or ends wars. In the end, human lives are often at stake in these struggles over meaning. Thus, contemporary cultural theory might ask questions like these: How do cultural artifacts like film and television texts contribute to the meanings of the term Muslim? How do representations of white Muslims differ from those of black Muslims? Or Muslims of Middle Eastern descent? What does it mean to be a Muslim in America versus Great Britain? Those are all questions that move and expand cultural analysis beyond the labeling of diverse individuals or cultures as simply "Muslim." Whether we are talking about race, nation, gender, or sexuality, many of these new theoretical paradigms share common goals and assumptions. All of them are (3) attempts to *move beyond the basic essentialisms associated with identity politics*, and theorize something more complex and actually descriptive of the world in which we live.

As noted above, many of these new approaches to understanding identity owe a great deal to (4) **poststructuralist** thinking, which insists that identity and meaning are linguistically, historically, and socially constructed—not somehow essentially or biologically determined. We can only know reality through pre-existing symbolic sign systems—whether they be coarse systems of stereotypes or more subtle **discourses** within which reality is spoken or constructed. For example, **Michel Foucault**, in his book *The History of Sexuality*, famously argued that our understanding of sex and sexuality in Western cultures is not in effect repressed or silenced, but rather produced through the various discourses within which it is spoken. Thus legal discourses tends to frame sexuality as an issue that is either lawful or not; medical discourses approach it as something biological, and judge it as either healthy or diseased; while religious discourses understand sexuality as a moral issue to be regulated through church doctrine or else disparaged as sin. The very words and signs we use to express meaning themselves shape and delimit what they can and do express.

One of the more important contemporary approaches to understanding questions around identity was theorized by feminist philosopher **Judith Butler**, who introduced and elaborated upon (5) the concept of **performativity** in her books and essays. Writing primarily about gender, Butler argues that what we call gender is actually created through a series of performative acts—the very enacting or "doing" of gender is what constitutes it. In this formulation, there is no original gender, but rather only a series of shifting codes and ways to enact gender. Similar to some Eastern philosophies, the idea of performativity suggests that *doing* is what constitutes our sense of *being*, and not *vice versa* (as Western thinking had suggested for centuries). According to Butler, human identity is not a stable thing (as with the metaphor of the rugged individualist who make conscious "free will" choices about what he or she does), but rather the opposite: doing—moving through the world on a day to day basis—creates the concept of identity or individuality in the first place. Importantly, **performativity** is *not* performance, which suggests a voluntary or conscious choice to dress or act a certain way. Performativity is the overall system that *constitutes the subject* as gendered, or to extrapolate: raced, sexualized, classed, nationalized, etc.

Butler's ideas about performativity are mostly consistent with other ideas already explored in this book such as **phenomenology** and **interpellation**. Phenomenology draws our attention to understanding the self as lived experience, while interpellation suggests we are all caught up in (and move throughout our lives within) inescapable ideological structures. Again, consider gender as a set of overdetermined ideological structures. In many places throughout the West, from the moment we are born, we are placed into a pink blanket or blue blanket; we are immediately interpellated into a structure of gender (here one based on medical discourses and color coding). As we go through life we will continue to "do" or create our gender identities based upon our involvement with other ideological structures such as our families, our schools, sports (both as active team members and spectators), and especially the heavily gendered aisles of toy stores. As such, (6) identity is **anti-essentialist**; it is always in flux. While we may feel like a unified subject, in fact we behave in different ways at different times in different social and cultural contexts. As human subjects, we may feel united under supposedly stable signifiers like "I" or "me" or the term "individual" itself, but those terms should be considered linguistic crutches or even **cultural fictions**, hiding the actual complexity of human subjectivities in flux.

Thus, within most contemporary anti-essentialist thinking about race, class, gender, sexuality, and nation, etc., (7) labels are seen as problematic. Like stereotypes, labels tend to reduce the complexity of human identities (or the complex varied identities of human social groups) to one simplified and monolithic meaning. Psychoanalytic theory also cautions against simplistic labeling and the social classifications associated with it, noting that (8) our sense of our selves is always dependent upon the concept of **Othering**. Recall that according to psychoanalysis, the self is always defined against the Other, and that the Other represents that which the subject has repressed within him or herself. As such, the alleged self/Other binary is false, as each term contains some component of its "opposite" (however deeply repressed it might be). As we saw in Chapter 3, binaristic thinking lends itself to stereotypes and essentialisms. Common usage of binary terms such as white and black when talking about race provide an excellent example. First of all, no one on earth is the color of this page or the ink upon it; use of the terms black and white in this context thus **reifies** race as something beyond actual reality—literally a product of linguistic production. In further reductive and essentializing ways, the binary suggests that all people can be defined by two terms and only two terms; use of the terms elides the vast complexities that exists within any community, and especially the ways that white and black people can and do share many common goals and aspirations. As yet other theorists have noted, binaries also give rise to hierarchies, in which one term is privileged over the other. Thus binary thinking subtly creates desire for the first term while relegating the second to (literally) second class status. Think how the meaning of "race" would change if we only spoke about the "human race" without acknowledging color. Use of race in this way would imply shared human qualities rather than assumptions about the (allegedly lacking) humanity of **Others**.

In fact, among some poststructuralist thinkers, there is a felt need to move beyond the discourse of race itself. Recognizing that race is an artificial linguistic and cultural construction based on hundreds if not thousands of years of Eurocentric thought, these critics have introduced the term **racialism** to define the ways that popular culture continues to use race as a meaningful term. A prime example of racialism in the popular press is the continued referral to and naming of President Barack Obama as the "first black President" of the United States, instead of calling him the nation's first *biracial* President, which is more accurate, as he is the son of a black man and a white woman. In refusing or eliding the term "biracial," popular discourse surrounding the President ignores the complexity of twenty-first-century human identities, many if not most of which are increasingly mixed according to race, ethnicity, region, and nation. This is not to suggest in some facile way that Western culture is now miraculously beyond race or is **post-racial**, as some naïve commentators have proposed. In fact, categorization by gendered or raced labels—as the earlier discussion of **strategic essentialism** hopefully demonstrated—has been and can still be an important tool for groups seeking social change, allowing them to coalesce and achieve a kind of "critical mass" of people fighting for one specific goal. As such, race maintains its status as a central (if hopefully declining) organizing principle in Western thought; use of the terms and significations of "black" and "white" still remain endemic to much Western thought, as much as poststructuralist thinking might wish to **deconstruct** them. As we have seen elsewhere in this book, ideologies (like stereotypes) rarely disappear overnight; even if we pass civil rights legislation or elect a biracial President, ideas associated with race (and, most virulently, racism itself) linger and persist. However, by trying to think and speak about race in more complex ways, and by critiquing the ways popular culture (including film and television) continues to use race as a meaningful term, we may contribute to the ongoing unraveling of the concept itself.

As may already be apparent, all these new ways of thinking about gender, race, sexuality, *et al.* draw upon (9) various metaphors that help deconstruct socio-cultural binaries and emphasize the diversity within social groups. Terms such as **hybridity**—originally drawn from biology and botany—are used by some contemporary thinkers to describe how cultures and identities are always mixtures of various other cultures and identities. Similarly, the term **intersectionality** is used to emphasize how what we think of as identity is actually a composite thing, made up of various forms and aspects of social difference, all of which intersect within individual subjects. Another way to think about intersectionality is to realize that race is always gendered (i.e. men and women within any given racial group may have different concerns and ways of thinking). Likewise, sexuality intersects with and is shaped by race, by gender, by region, etc. Each aspect of our identities overlaps and intermingles with the others, giving rise to an infinite number of specific human subjects based upon our own unique social and cultural experiences.

Finally, as with most aspects of contemporary cultural theory, these new ways of thinking about race, gender, sexuality, nation, *et al.* are (10) deeply committed to the doctrines of human rights: goals that include equity and fairness under the law for all people, peace on (and ecological care for) the planet, and the end of various forms of cultural practice that cause misery and exploitation. In terms of race, ethnicity, and nation, the goal is to become aware of the overdetermined ideologies of **Eurocentric** thinking, the lingering and contemporary effects caused by imperialism and neo/colonization, as well as ongoing discourses of racism and racialism. In terms of gender and sexuality, the goal is to undermine **heteronormativity**, a complex term that brings together second wave feminist critiques of patriarchy with more nuanced arguments about gender and sexuality. Put simply, heteronormativity might be thought of as the cultural idea that the only proper or normal sexual activity is "heterosexual-monogamous-married-white-man-on-top-of-white-woman-for-procreation-only" sex; the discourses of heteronormativity effectively hide the diversity of heterosexual as well as homosexual sexualities, while also maintaining privilege of the former over the latter. Put together, a central goal of contemporary cultural theory is to mount a challenge to white **heteronormativity**, to ensure the fair and equitable treatment of all human beings regardless of class, gender, race, nation, sexuality, age, ability, and so forth. And as media critics and/or media makers, those who study film and television have the ability—and the ethical responsibility—to shape and influence these debates, whether via cultural criticism or through new ways of representing the complex, ever-changing world in which we live.

Basic concepts of postcolonial and critical race theory

To understand contemporary thinking about race, ethnicity, and nation, it is necessary to understand the history of **Western Imperialism**, the centuries-long program of state-sanctioned exploration and colonization by Western European nations of much of the rest of the world. Areas of the globe so exploited include—but were not restricted to—the Middle East, China, India and South East Asia, Africa, South America, Central America, North America, and Australia, as well as many smaller island nations in the Atlantic and Pacific. While other nations in previous historical eras have also practiced imperialism, Western Imperialism followed upon the discovery of America in 1492 and the subsequent rise of Spanish, Dutch, French, and British fleets of warships and merchant vessels. Desire for exotic products that could be shipped from around the globe (and the profits they generated) helped fuel **colonialism**, the practice of settling in and annexing various global territories in the name of European nations. The intertwining goals of both imperialism and colonialism, as noted above, were economic. For Western

European nations, the so-called New World contained many new resources, including land, labor, and precious minerals. The British Empire, which was the largest of the European empires, included territories in North America, India, China, and Australia. The extent and breadth of the British Empire—an old adage quipped that "the sun never sets on the British Empire"—arguably contributed to the dominance of the English language (as well as many aspects of British culture) around the globe today. Similarly, the prevalence of Spanish speaking nations in South and Central America is a direct result of their having been primarily colonized by Spain for hundreds of years. Similarly, the dominant language spoken in Brazil today is still Portuguese, because Brazil had been a colony of Portugal from the sixteenth through the nineteenth centuries.

The structural, linguistic, national, economic, and cultural frameworks that were created by imperialism and colonialism are still being critiqued and examined as central discourses of **Eurocentrism**. The term **postcolonial studies** encompasses this broad theoretical and historical project. What is at stake here is the theorization of how nations, cultures, and individuals have been transformed (and continue to be transformed) under *and after* centuries of colonialism. Thus, the term **neo-colonialism** (unlike postcolonialism, which perhaps implies a moving past the colonial era) suggests the ongoing and pervasive nature of colonialism via non-military means such as global corporate capitalism and/or cultural imperialism. In the twenty-first century, most Western nations no longer rule over other nations with warships and invading armies, but neo-colonialist theory explores how the influence and dominance of colonizing forces can be and still are felt in other areas of (allegedly decolonized) life—specifically in the ideological spheres of culture, religion, politics, and especially economics. The Oscar-nominated documentary feature *Virunga* (2014) puts an all-too-human face on such processes. The film explores how a British oil company (Soco International) subcontracted international firms who then subcontracted local militias to do the oil company's dirty work—violently forcing people off their land and in this case, away from the Virunga National Park whose oil deposits the First World corporation hoped to exploit.

Imperialism and colonialism in the "New World," like much unfettered capitalist practice, led to much misery and suffering, not only for native populations overrun by European settlers, but also for Africans sold into slavery to fuel the economic engines of empire. In many cases, Europeans settlers themselves were mistreated by their European masters and some rebelled, creating their own sovereign nation-states, as did the United States in 1776. Over the next several centuries, other colonized nations gradually declared and/or won their independence (often at great human cost), or were "granted" sovereignty. The era of the (official) British Empire is usually said to have ended in the years immediately following World War II, when Great Britain granted independence to most of its colonized territories. However, for many new nation-states, the granting of independency was just the beginning of a new era of exploitation and instability, one based more on economic and **cultural imperialism** and less on direct rule by the colonizers and their military forces. The term **economic underdevelopment** is sometimes used to refer to how the economies of these newly independent nation-states were (and continue to be) deformed by the practices of European colonialism. In many cases, when the colonizers went home, they left their former territories worse off than before they arrived. While they were developed in one way (to the good of the colonizers), they could also be said to be underdeveloped in others. Like a vampire draining his or her victim, colonialist interests grew wealthy feeding on the free resources and cheap labor of their colonies, then transferred their economic success back to their original nations; this left their former territories emaciated and weak, the state of economic underdevelopment. In many cases, these newly sovereign states lacked any sort of stable economic or political infrastructure, and many fell into civil wars and murderous dictatorships whose effects are still being felt in the twenty-first century.

Colonialism also created devastating effects on questions of identity, both individual and national. In some cases, people in colonized nations were encouraged to study in and acculturate to the colonizing nation, in effect creating **hybridized** identities. Others were not so lucky, as churches, colonial governments, and other colonizing forces actively sought to eradicate "original" cultures in the name of Western Civilization. During the twentieth century, people in colonized nations increasingly began to speak about how their minds (and those of their countrymen and women) had also been colonized by imperialist invaders. Theorists like **Frantz Fanon** (1925–61) and filmmakers like Ousmene Sembene (1923–2007) explored in eloquent detail how colonized people become "split" in their thinking and in their cultural allegiances. Fanon's *Black Skin, White Masks* (1952) and *The Wretched of the Earth* (1961) drew upon his interests in psychopathology and Marxism; both are key texts of postcolonial theory. Senegalese filmmaker Sembene recalled his youth watching Hollywood *Tarzan* movies, all of which depicted Africa and Africans as backwards and primitive, an image that was far from his everyday experience. His feature films (from *Black Girl* [1966] to *Moolaadé* [2004]) set out to correct those imbalances. Postcolonial thinking about identity can be traced at least back to the influential writings of African American theorist W. E. B. Du Bois (1868–1963), if not further. In his book *The Souls of Black Folk* (1903) Du Bois spoke about the **double consciousness** suffered by African Americans, a term that refers to how black people understand the world through simultaneous and often contradictory perspectives: that of the white culture that imposes certain "truths" on all of its subjects, and that of the black subject, who recognizes those truths to be ideological inventions.

After World War II, the terms First World, Second World, and Third World were often used to describe various aspects of global economics and politics. The term **First World** referred to areas encompassing North America, (Western) Europe, and Australia, nations and regions who embraced capitalism and the free market, and who generally had been the victors in the recent World War. The term **Second World** referred to the communist bloc nations of Europe and Asia—primarily China, the USSR, and its satellite nations in Eastern Europe. The term **Third World** was used to describe everyone and everywhere else—the formerly colonized regions of Africa, Central and South America, and portions of the Middle East. As is hopefully immediately apparent, the use of three terms to describe an entire world of people and national cultures is grossly reductive. Although the terms afforded some Third World nations a handy label under which to coalesce and share their issues and struggles (as many did at the 1955 Bandung Conference), the term implies that the issues and struggles of peoples and new nations in every corner of the globe were somehow the same, and not mitigated by specific national, economic, historical, and postcolonial forces. Nonetheless, the terms were influential throughout the 1960s and 1970s, and a movement of filmmaking calling itself **Third Cinema** arose in some Third World nations, including Cuba, Brazil, Argentina, and some African nations. Third Cinema differentiated itself from the First Cinema (Hollywood), and the Second Cinema (the European art film), and sought to use film as a sort of agitprop (agitation and propaganda) tool designed to educate and engage its viewers in the political struggle against neo-colonial exploitation.

Continuing the critique of essentialist and reductive terms like First World, Second World, and Third World, some theorists began to use the term **Fourth World** to describe the existence and exploitation of native or indigenous populations within (but often overlooked by) terms like First, Second, and/or Third World. Still other theorists deployed terms like **micro-regionalism** to refer to the ways that some (if not all) nations can be thought of as containing discrete populations within the whole. The Basque region in Spain and France (centered around the Pyrenees Mountains) would be a good example of a **micro-region** because it has its own history, language, and culture distinct from the rest of Spain or France. In the United States, one might consider the Southern Bible Belt to be a micro-region, that is, an area within national borders that can be both geographically and culturally distinguished from the rest of the nation. Similarly, the term **macro-region** has been invoked to describe areas that encompass and traverse national boundaries, usually because of shared histories, languages, and culture. Today, much Spanish language media plays to a broad macro-region of Spanish-speaking people in nations in Europe as well as in South, Central, and North America.

Yet another term from postcolonial theory that seeks to "muddy the waters" of supposedly pure national or ethnic/racial identity is **diaspora**. Diaspora refers to ways that cultural identities—whether individual, national, or ethnic/racial—are constantly **hybridized** as they move across the globe in space and time, coming into contact with other cultures. It is common now to speak of the Jewish diaspora, which over the course of centuries has spread from Eastern to Western Europe and beyond into the Americas, Israel, and elsewhere. The idea of diaspora suggests that whatever Jewish identity was hundreds of years ago in Europe, it is today both similar to and different from what it was in that previous place and time. It is also common to speak of the African diaspora which describes the spreading out of African cultures across the Atlantic Ocean via slavery, into the Caribbean Islands, the Americas, and back across the ocean to Europe. A good example of the cultural hybridization which occurs along the way is voodoo, a religious practice that developed among slaves in the New World as a sort of amalgamation of native African beliefs and Roman Catholicism (imposed on them by colonizers). Recently, some critics have used the term diaspora in relation to Western gay identities, as the concepts and signifiers germane to many late twentieth-century American and European homosexual identities—gay pride, rainbow flags, pink triangles—are making inroads into very different cultural contexts in India, China, and other areas of Southeast Asia.

Another important concept of postcolonial theory is **Orientalism**, an idea that draws partly on psychoanalysis as it might relate to culture and race. Developed and published in a book of the same name by cultural theorist **Edward Said** in 1978, Orientalism refers to the way that Western cultures have in the past constructed (and continue to construct) images and ideas about the Orient (here referring mainly to the Middle East) based less on actuality and more on their own repressed and projected desires and fears about the **Other**. If the West sees itself as logical, lawful, and moral, Said argued, then Western writers and artists construct the East as irrational, unlawful, and licentious. If the West sees itself as cool, strong, and masculine, it will construct the East as violent, exotic, and sensual. These processes have occurred throughout centuries of European imperialism, and can be expanded to explore almost any representations of minority cultures made by those in a dominant culture. More recently, the term Orientalism might be invoked to describe how popular Western discourses describe their own belief systems as legitimate "religions," while positing those of the East as dangerous "cults." One can see Orientalism at work in both classical and contemporary Hollywood film and television that depict decadent harem scenes or lost exotic cities such as Shangri-La (as in the *Lost Horizon* films [1937, 1973]). Orientalist motifs have been used almost randomly within science fiction and fantasy genres to suggest exotic others, "decadent" interracial sexualities, and monstrous Others. In the *Flash Gordon* serials of the 1930s, Ming the Merciless, despite allegedly coming from the planet "Mongo," wears Oriental robes, a Fu Manchu moustache, and summons his servants with a Chinese gong. More recently, one might cite Jabba the Hutt and his sexualized enslavement of Princess Leia in the *Star Wars* franchise as an Orientalist trope. More broadly, Orientalism underscores the dangers inherent in any **ethnographic** project (discussed more fully in Chapter 11), where an observer from outside of a given culture imposes his or her own views and interpretations on the culture being studied.

Another term meant to confuse and confound the simple binaries of self and Other, or nation and territory, is the term **glocal**, a portmanteau word comprised of and invoking the various meanings of global and local. Glocal refers to the need to understand culture and identity as simultaneously engaged with (and determined by) specific local concerns as well as broadly global ones. The term might be invoked to describe a range of complex issues related to, for example, South African Bushmen encountering a Coca-Cola bottle—the very subject of the film *The Gods Must be Crazy* (1980). Glocal might also be invoked by studies that explore how Middle Eastern youth cultures make sense of the global popularity of *Titanic* (1997, see further reading by Barbara Klinger), and is encapsulated by the bumper sticker that exhorts us to "Think Globally, Act Locally." Like the terms hybridity, intersectionality, and diaspora, the term glocal impels us to think of the world through increasingly complex and intermingling lenses of nation, region, religion, politics, media, representation, etc. in the era of global corporate capitalism.

Finally, as explored above in relation to the concept of **racialism**, contemporary cultural theory (whether global or local) is invested in deconstructing race as a meaningful term. The term race is based on outdated science and Eurocentric models about human beings (and their subsequent worth) as marked by superficial physical qualities such as skin tone, hair texture, and physiognomy. Such markers of human difference have been challenged in recent years by genetic studies that show that people within one "race" may have vastly different genetic markers from one another, and in fact, may have more similar genetic markers to people from other races. Actually, the concept of **ethnicity**—which refers more to the ways that cultural groups express their identities through **performative** gestures—remains more in line with critical thinking about "race" than does the concept of race itself. Race may be a biological fantasy, or disproved theory, but its concepts still impact upon lived experience. As such, other theorists have called for the need to examine what it means to be "white" in the first place, in the process furthering the process of deconstructing **whiteness**, thinking about it as a **structuring absence**. Thus, instead of studying the images of African Americans or Asian Americans in film and television (as scholars have been doing for decades now), critics have begun to examine how the dominant white race passes itself off as "natural" or given, how being white is the implied state of being human or "normal" within Eurocentric discourses. In film studies, Richard Dyer's 1997 book *White* has been particularly influential in this regard, as have books like Daniel Bernardi's *The Birth of Whiteness: Race and the Emergence of United States Cinema* (1996) and *Classic Hollywood, Classical Whiteness* (2001).

In summation, when thinking about film and television in relation to nation, "race," and ethnicity, it is important for media critics to be aware of the Eurocentric biases that still underlie many media representations. It is important to analyze how the representations of other nations and cultures may be distorted when they are presented from a white, Western point of view. It is important to note the lingering effects of decades-long (if not centuries-long) cultural stereotypes, effects that may, for example, influence the media industries to "green light" (finance for production) film and television texts that showcase images of black buffoonery over black drama. And while the poststructuralist, postmodern cultural critic needs to be aware of these (and many other) complex dynamics when examining film and television texts, contemporary media producers should also be aware of them. Film and television producers in the twenty-first century need to pay heed to the ideas that generations of global cultural critics have formulated, and strive to make their work as culturally relevant and free from bias as possible. They should avoid or challenge stereotypes, fight for new and different types of color-blind casting, and acknowledge their biases where they exist. The media industries have a built in economic motive to produce work that replicates the themes and images of work that has been financially successful in the past. It may be difficult or impossible to change that imperative overnight, but through new generations of media producers and critics continuing to challenge the status quo, images and the worlds they represent will continue to change via the processes of hegemonic negotiation. Film and television—if they exist at all in the future—may look very different from what they do today. They already look very different from what they did three decades ago, or even yesterday.

Further thinking about gender and sexuality

As Chapter 8 suggested, thinking about gender and sexuality in relationship to film and television continues to be an important area of scholarly inquiry. And just as second wave feminist media critics did, so do contemporary film and television scholars seek to understand the complex relationships between images of gender and sexuality and the complex ways people actually live their lives. But whereas most second wave critics would probably have argued that film and television images reflected pre-existing notions of masculinity and femininity, **third wave feminists**—drawing on the linguistic bases of **poststructuralism** and ideas associated with **queer theory**—approach gender and sexuality from a much more **anti-essentialist** perspective. Drawing on the work of Michel Foucault, third wave feminists are likely to understand gender as fluid and socially constructed, inflected in different ways as it is spoken of within different discourses. Drawing on the work of Judith Butler, third wave feminists are likely to understand gender in terms of **performativity**, seeing it as a category based not on biological criteria but rather one constructed by a series of enacted behaviors that constitute a sense of gendered identity. Butler famously referred to a gender as **simulacra**—a copy of something that has no original—and the phrase is provocative as well as illuminating. What was the original expression of femininity? Of masculinity? Even if we believe in the creation story of Adam and Eve, how did those two individuals express their genders? We can never know, only projecting backwards onto them our own ideas about gender and sexuality. Similarly, if we believe that the human race has been evolving for millions of years, it is almost impossible to know how gender was expressed at any given point along that timeline (later centuries notwithstanding). Gender expressions have evolved along with the human species, and they will continue to do so. There is no original or proper gender role in nature—only ones constructed in specific times and places and deemed to be so.

Along with such theoretical or philosophical considerations, third wave feminism also developed in part because much of second wave feminism had overlooked differences within the category of gender—that men and women are also marked by class, race, region, nation, sexuality, and so forth. During the 1970s, many women of color and lesbians felt left out of the mainstream feminist movement, because they felt it focused too much on issues of importance to white, middle class, heterosexual women. Many lesbian feminists became separatists, cutting themselves off from mainstream (straight) feminism. Similarly, many African American women became more comfortable identifying with the label **womanist**, a nineteenth-century term given new meaning by novelist Alice Walker in her 1983 book *In Search of Our Mothers' Gardens: Womanist Prose*. Definitions of womanism differ somewhat depending upon who is asked, but most would likely agree it refers to the gender-based struggles of people of color, and especially women of African American descent. As with **lesbian feminist separatism**, the term womanist was used to mark a break with mainstream feminism, which was seen as too white, too middle class, and too unaware of how race impacted upon gender. (For other theorists, womanism also contains a spiritual or Christian dimension.) While the term womanism has caught on among many women of color, other critics see it is as a distraction from creating a critical mass of people centered on invoking reforms based on gender (rather than race, or gendered race). And as with all labels, still other critics see the term as limiting—suggesting that all women of color face the same issues, which of course may differ greatly between First Nations women, Chicano women, Iranian women, etc. And although third wave feminism attempts to include and speak for women of all colors, classes, and sexualities, many women still feel excluded from mainstream feminist movements, creating the urge for more specific labels and (organizing) focused on causes related both to feminism and other forms of social inequity.

Besides women (and men) of color, and academic theorists, the term third wave feminism is also used to describe newer, younger generations of women seeking to extend the activism of second wave feminism. Like the queer activists discussed below, many younger third wave feminists focus on more activist and in-your-face tactics meant to bring issues of gender bias to the mainstream. For example, the **Riot grrrl** movement of the mid-1990s used punk rock and underground fanzines to express their concerns about gender inequity. In 1993, the Barbie

Liberation Organization exchanged the voice boxes in hundreds of talking Barbie and G. I. Joe dolls, and returned them to the store, where they were bought by unsuspecting consumers. When they got home, they found their Barbie dolls saying things like "Vengeance is mine!" and "Eat lead, Cobra!" The G. I. Joe dolls, now speaking with Barbie's voice, uttered prerecorded phrases like "Let's plan our dream wedding!" and "Will we ever have enough clothes?" Targeting the same toy company (Mattel), feminist activists protested when it released a talking Barbie doll that said "Math class is tough!" Rightly so, these activists argued that children's dolls like these were good examples of ideological apparatuses shaping gender: the dolls teach boys that men are aggressive and violent, and teach girls that young women are mindless consumers who struggle with math and science.

It is important to differentiate third wave feminism, and the ongoing feminist activism associated with it, from what the popular press has termed **postfeminism**. Like all "post" terms, postfeminism suggests we have achieved and moved beyond feminism—specifically the goals of second wave feminism. Perhaps it is true that many white middle-class heterosexual women now have the opportunities and equality (however that might be defined) for which their foremothers fought. Yet, as media scholars like Yvonne Tasker and Diane Negra have shown, the discourses of postfeminism work to cloak the concerns of women who are not white, middle class, and heterosexual (just as second wave feminism had allegedly done). Also greatly concerning is that postfeminist discourse suggests that a woman's way to freedom and happiness is not through collective action and political gain, but through her "freedom to choose" how she wants to live her life (again, a freedom allegedly secured by second wave feminism). Thus, postfeminism suggests that contemporary women (who have money) are free to live (purchase happiness) as they see fit. *Sex and the City*—both as a cable television show (1998–2004) and as two Hollywood movies (2008, 2010)—is "storm central" for many of these debates, with many third wave feminists seeing the text(s) as the epitome of postfeminist discourse. Carrie, Miranda, Charlotte, and Samantha appear to be modern, urban, liberated women, making their own choices about careers, motherhood, and relationships. Yet Carrie, Miranda, Charlotte, and Samantha are also white and earn enough money to live in swanky Manhattan, and their main personal goals still seem to be finding Mr. Right and purchasing expensive designer shoes. Is this what second wave feminism was really all about? It is not that the show is necessarily unrealistic—there are wealthy white heterosexual women in Manhattan who can afford to buy expensive shoes—but it tends to suggest (as postfeminist discourse does in general) that all women now enjoy the freedoms that Carrie, Miranda, Charlotte, and Samantha do. And although the show rarely critiques the idea that their freedom and happiness are based on consumerism and courtship, third wave feminists have already begun to do so.

The discourse of postfeminism is part of a larger **heteronormative** consumer culture that tells everyone—men and women alike—that happiness can be purchased, and that happiness is found in love, sex, marriage, and successful relationships based on traditional (although often exaggerated and unreachable) gender ideals. Why does almost every ad for men's shaving cream end with a beautiful blond bombshell stroking a male model's perfectly chiseled cheek? While the advertising industries are perhaps more responsible for spreading heteronormative consumer culture than are film and television, it is nonetheless true that film and television are deeply imbricated in those industries, via direct advertising and sponsorship, product placement, and simple role modeling: in most film and television shows, the "good looking" guy always ends up with the beautiful young woman. Whether it is *Sex and the City* or the latest postfeminist romantic comedy, film and TV constantly barrages us with the message that men and women can increase their chances of finding happiness by buying designer clothes and expensive hair product. In more extreme cases, happiness can be purchased with cosmetic surgery, breast implants, labial reconstruction, and/or laser hair removal. Is a young woman who chooses to appear naked in a *Girls Gone Wild* video exercising her hard-won feminist freedoms (a potentially postfeminist claim), or is she merely being used as a tool of patriarchal consumer capitalism?

These are but some of the issues explored by contemporary third wave feminists and queer media critics, many of whom draw on concepts broadly grouped under the label **queer theory**. As with all contemporary thinking about identity, queer theory seeks to move beyond—deconstruct or complicate—simplistic **binaries** (straight versus gay, male versus female, feminine versus masculine, black versus white) as well as essentialist models of gender and sexuality rooted solely in biology. While gender and sexuality do have bases in biological differences (genitals, hormones, chromosomes, etc.), queer theorists—like third wave feminists—are much more interested in looking at how culture and history shape and delimit the ways that gender and sexuality can be expressed. The term "queer" is itself contentious, having been used in the West throughout much of the twentieth century as a negative epithet (similar to the use of the word "nigger") meant to dehumanize and shame homosexuals. The term began to be **reappropriated** in the 1980s and 1990s by activists and scholars. Activists fighting for causes associated with the AIDS crisis (faster drug trials, governmental spending on health care), as well as gay and lesbian rights advocates, started using the term in group names like Queer Nation and slogans like "We're here! We're queer! Get used to it!" This was partly a way to shock a complacent mainstream society into sitting up and taking notice, but also a reflection of the fact that AIDS activists were not just gay, but also lesbian, straight, bisexual, transgender, IV drug users, hemophiliacs, Haitians—in fact, members of every community imaginable. While some people today still prefer to use (ever-lengthening) acronyms for the queer community, like LGBTTQQIA2 (which stands for Lesbian, Gay, Bisexual, Transgender, Transvestite, Queer, Questioning, Intersex, Asexual, and Two-Spirited), many AIDS activists opted for the shorter and more urgent term queer, which was meant to reflect the myriad forms of identity drawn together by the AIDS crisis. (Two-Spirit refers specifically to Native American or Aboriginal people who are [by Western definitions] homosexual, transgender, or queer—qualities that were often celebrated by indigenous cultures and not denigrated, as in the West and elsewhere until very recently.)

In academia, queer theorists arose from different disciplines, including literary studies, cultural studies, philosophy, history, women's and gender studies, and the fledgling discipline of gay and lesbian studies. Academic queer theorists tended to shun queer activists' more essentialist use of the term queer in favor of theorizing sexuality as fluid and socially determined. Queer is about challenging **heteronormativity**, the assumption that white, married and monogamous, procreative heterosexuality is the "normal" sexuality of human beings. In fact, there are myriad ways to be homosexual, heterosexual, and everything in between. Just as whiteness studies seek to expose whiteness as a dominant Eurocentric discourse,

some queer theorists study the various shifting meanings of heterosexuality as it too intersects with history class, race, etc. While there are different ways to "do" queer theory, many scholars approach queer theory as a process or method meant to deconstruct binaristic thinking in order to explore gender and sexuality within specific and diverse contexts. In this sense, one can speak of something not only as being queer, but also as "doing" queer work, or **queering**. One might say *Brokeback Mountain* (2005) queers the Hollywood western while *Far From Heaven* (2002) queers the Hollywood melodrama, both by exploring sexuality in specific regional, historic, and social contexts. *Brokeback Mountain* also queers the line between "straight" **homosocial desire** and **homosexual desire** (recall Figure 10.3). It could be easily argued that *Mad Men* (AMC 2007–15) does queer work, by historicizing gender and sexuality within the 1960s Manhattan advertising industry.

As with third wave feminism, many of the concepts and ideas related to queer theory have yet to make it into the mainstream media, many of whom simply understand queer to be another synonym for gay and/or lesbian, thus reinforcing the original straight–queer binary that queer theory seeks to complicate. We can see this use of the term in the title of the briefly popular reality TV show *Queer Eye for the Straight Guy* (2003–7), which did very little to deconstruct the straight–gay binary. In fact, the whole show was based on the allegedly essentialist differences between (fashion challenged) straight men and (chic and sophisticated) gay men. Furthermore, how groundbreaking was the show's stance on (homo) sexuality when it arguably re-circulated age-old stereotypes of gay men as hairdressers and fashion designers? (Perhaps a hypothetical show like *Queer Doctor for the Straight Heart Attack* would have challenged more assumptions!) But lest we forget, the whole *raison d'être* of a show like *Queer Eye for the Straight Guy* is economic: the show is an attempt to guilt trip men into buying cosmetics, hair products, and new clothing, much as the fashion industry has been targeting women for decades if not centuries. In a somewhat different fashion, calling *Brokeback Mountain* a "gay cowboy movie" is incorrect, since neither of the two central characters claims a gay identity. The much repeated phrase "gay cowboy movie" works to reduce the film's depiction of complex queer sexualities (both Ennis and Jack marry and have children) into (yet once again) the simplistic essentialist binary of gay versus straight.

Queer theory has arguably had a greater impact on film (and to a lesser extent television) than has third wave feminism, thanks to an entire movement of independent films made in the 1990s that drew upon queer activism and did the queer work of complicating human sexualities. Those films most famously include *Paris is Burning* (1990), *Poison* (1991), *My Own Private Idaho* (1991), *Edward II* (1991), *Zero Patience* (1993), *Go Fish* (1994), and *Watermelon Woman* (1996). Arguably, those films led the way for more recent critically acclaimed films like *Gods and Monsters* (1998), *Boys Don't Cry* (1999), *American Beauty* (1999), *Far From Heaven*, *The Hours* (2002), *Monster* (2003), *Capote*, *Brokeback Mountain* (2005), *Milk* (2008), and *The Imitation Game* (2014)—films that focus on the historical construction of homo/sexuality (often by examining actual historical figures) or by exposing and complicating the false binaries of gender and sexuality. Television has also done queer work, mostly by presenting an increasingly broad range of visible queer characters, even as the first among them tended to be middle-class white gay men (a charge also leveled at many of the films mentioned above). Not only do such characters hide or elide other types of queer experiences, but their

generic moorings (in many cases film comedies or television sitcoms) allow for the easy replication of pre-existing stereotypes, as in shows like *Will & Grace*, *Modern Family* (2009–) and *Glee* (2009–15). However, queers of color continue to be introduced in TV shows like *Brooklyn Nine-Nine* (2013–), *The Fosters* (2013–), and *Empire* (2015). So too have transgender characters and storylines been featured in recent (streaming) TV shows, like *Orange is the New Black* (2013–) and *Transparent* (2014–). In this way, aspects of the cultural superstructure are helping shift national debates on the meanings of homosexuality, gender and gender identity, marriage, and family.

Case study: *Paris is Burning* (1990)

The observational documentary film *Paris is Burning* became an art house hit when it was first released, and it is today a much loved cult film among many queer and queer-friendly audiences. The film has also generated controversy and a good amount of academic writing (by bell hooks and Judith Butler, notably), including most recently a book-length monograph by Lucas Hilderbrand exploring the film's production history and lasting cultural significance. Like *Trekkies*, *Paris is Burning* is an ethnographic exploration of a particular subculture that defines itself to a great extent in relation to pop culture. However, while the subjects of *Trekkies* were a diverse group of middle-class consumers of a mass-produced and endlessly franchised text, *Paris is Burning* centers on an underground and/or little seen subculture: poor urban queers of color living in and around late-1980s New York City negotiating with white patriarchal capitalism in interesting and provocative ways. The film explores the world of its subjects' underground drag balls, wherein competing teams walk and/or dance the runway in an contest to pass as "real"—real fashion models, movie stars, and even business executives. As one of the film's subjects puts it, "This is our Hollywood." While a few critics (such as bell hooks) fault the film and its director (white female Jennie Livingston) for exploiting its subject matter, many others argue that the film deeply humanizes its subjects, and presents a fascinating meditation on the mechanisms of cultural (re)appropriation, performance and performativity, all the while queerly deconstructing binaristic identity categories.

As one of the first films to be associated with the New Queer Cinema movement, *Paris is Burning* certainly challenges static notions of race, gender, and sexuality while also keeping class issues clearly in the foreground. Although these people are poor, non-white, and queer, many of their fantasies—as acted out in the drag balls—are directly linked to the ideals of white patriarchal capitalism, ideals that they see endlessly represented in the mainstream media that surrounds them. (They directly reference the characters of *All My Children* [1970–2011], *Dynasty* [1981–9], and the fashion industry as the types of people they want to emulate.) Some of them speak of wanting to be spoiled white rich girls whose husbands will (allegedly) provide for their every need. Late in the film, when Willi Ninja has found some measure of monetary success, he takes great pride in acknowledging his ability to pay for things, proudly asserting his ability to finally be part of the consumer economy. Thus, even as many viewers might consider the subjects of *Paris is Burning* to be a highly oppositional subculture, the film dramatizes their internalization of dominant ideologies, and how subcultures are always in some form of hegemonic negotiation with dominant culture.

The film also confounds and complicates our most basic assumptions about gender, sexuality, and race. Its wide array of men, women, drag performers, transvestites, and

transsexuals—most of whom are not identified as one gender or the other— confound simplistic binaries of gender. Some performers appear to be female—but are they? Some of them speak about having male genitalia, and some are desirous of a sex change while others are adamantly not. Throughout, the film asks us to examine our own assumptions about what it means to be male or female, and consider the physical markers we use to make those distinctions. Similarly, race too is categorically blurred, with participants exhibiting a range of skin tones and social identities that might be considered white, African American, biracial, Hispanic, and so forth. One of the older drag performers, Dorian Corey, strikes many viewers initially as white until he reveals his own self identity as linked to Lena Horne (a light-skinned African American actress in 1940s Hollywood) (see Figure 12.3). One of the central and most light-skinned characters in the film is Venus Xtravaganza (most of the characters adopt last names based upon the "house" to which they belong) (see Figure 12.4). Venus's race or ethnicity is not readily known,

Fig 12.3
Dorian Corey in the New Queer Cinema hit *Paris is Burning* (1990), discussing his career as a professional entertainer.

Fig 12.4
Venus Xtravaganza in *Paris is Burning* (1990) desires what she believes are the perks of being white, wealthy, and female.

although she associates herself with best friend Angie Xtravaganza ("mother" of the House of Xtravaganza) who presents herself as Hispanic. The point of all this is that the usual categories of gender, race, sexuality, etc. are broken down by the film and the people in it. None of the people in it can be identified by simplistic binary labels such as male or female, black or white, or straight or gay.

Like any subculture, poor queers of color in mid-1980s New York City had their own forms of expression, the balls themselves being the most prominent. But language, behavior, style, and bodily movement are also key in defining a subculture. The term "voguing"—drawn from the fashion magazine of the same name—best describes the kind of dancing the ball walkers innovate (and then see appropriated two years later in the film's final segment). Voguing itself is discussed as a form of historical appropriation drawing its moves from Egyptian hieroglyphics, break dancing, and of course high fashion modeling. The terms "house" and "mother" are reworked from dominant culture to mean a group of queer friends who treat one another like family, overseen by a smart and caring leader (see Figure 12.5). Similarly, Dorian Corey explains how "reading" (the "art form of insult") then evolved into "throwing shade" (conveying an insult through attitude alone) that then also became incorporated in the vogue dance. Another discusses the practice of "mopping," which basically means stealing. During the final credits, another of the film's subjects explains an entire language system (**langue**) used by some members of the community.

Some of the more interesting segments of the film explore gender in a more straightforward way. Willi Ninja, for example, one of the biggest proponents of voguing, works a day job where he teaches women how to be "properly" feminine—how to walk and comport themselves as such (see Figure 12.6). This and other sections of the film asks us to understand gender as a performance, a set of gestures that constitute an identity (and not the other way around, as theorized by the model of performativity). For example, when the film cuts from the ball participants to "everyday" white people on the streets of New York City, one realizes that they are just as costumed and made up as are the ball participants (see Figure 12.7). Masculinity and femininity are revealed as performances, whether on the floor of the dance contest or in the halls of Wall Street. Willi's instruction in femininity recalls the larger fashion industry in general, wherein

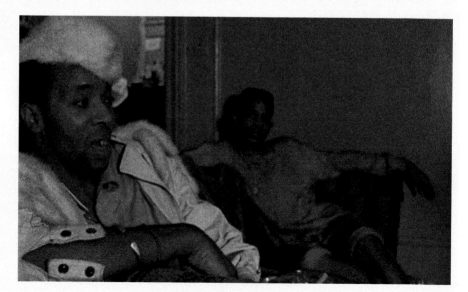

Fig 12.5
In *Paris is Burning* (1990), Pepper LaBeija discusses the discrimination he faced from his biological family, as a younger member of the House of LaBeija looks on knowingly.

Fig 12.6
Willi Ninja teaches women how to walk and act like runway models in *Paris is Burning* (1990).

Fig 12.7
When *Paris is Burning* (1990) cuts from its primary subjects to random strangers on the street, it becomes apparent that every expression of gender is some form of performance.

men (often gay) dictate what women are supposed to wear, what they are supposed to look like, and how they are supposed to behave. In another section of the film, Octavia St. Laurent attends an Eileen Ford model agency search, passing effortlessly among the other contestants. Eileen Ford of the modeling agency professes that girls must be cooperative and cheerful if they hope to become succesful models, and that girls will be girls no matter what. However, Octavia's presence in this scene demonstrates that in fact boys might be girls as well (see Figure 12.8).

The final section of the film is set in 1989 and dramatizes how ball culture has moved from a subcultural artifact to a more mainstream one. Willi Ninja talks about his successful introduction of voguing to Japan. A celebrity panel appears at a voguing contest designed to raise funds for AIDS services, and it is covered by a local news team. (Although not featured in *Paris is Burning*, Madonna's 1990 music video "Vogue" is another good example of how the formerly subcultural dance style was severed from its roots,

Fig 12.8
Octavia St. Laurent at the
Eileen Ford model search
contest featured in *Paris is
Burning* (1990).

and incorporated into mainstream culture for profit) (see Figure 12.9). The film ends on
a sobering note: Angie tells the camera how she had to recover Venus's murdered body
from a city morgue, highlighting the tremendous amount of prejudice and violence still
often directed at transgender individuals (see Figure 12.10). While the **culture industry**
snapped up voguing for a brief period of time—earning profits for its executives and
shareholders by exploiting the latest subcultural dance-music innovation—the people
who actually innovated the dance style did not share in those profits. In fact, they were
subject to discrimination and violence. Their dreams of becoming as rich and famous as
the stars and models they emulated never materialized.

However, 20 years later the media industry has once again found a way to capitalize
on the talents and energies of drag queens and queers of color. The reality game
show *RuPaul's Drag Race* has been a hit show on the cable network LOGO since 2009.

Fig 12.9
Madonna's video
"Vogue" cashed in on the
dance craze and culture
innovated by the subjects
of *Paris is Burning* (1990).

Fig 12.10
At the end of *Paris is Burning*, Angie Xtravaganza tells the camera how she had to recover the unclaimed body of her murdered friend Venus.

In true hegemonic form, the show brings forward the images and concerns of queer men (and queer men of color) even as they are presented within a commercial format that endorses capitalism: the show is structured as a competition for a cash prize. How one feels about the folks on *RuPaul's Drag Race*, or those featured in *Paris is Burning*, ultimately depends on the individual viewer. Those so inclined may see them as stereotypes (or worse), while others may applaud their charisma, uniqueness, nerve, and talent. In either case, they (and the media in which they appear) continue to impact upon the changing social meanings of race, gender, sexuality, and class.

Questions for discussion

1   How do you know what you know about any cultural group that is not your own? If you have never had direct personal contact with a given cultural group, how have your opinions of it been shaped by the media?

2   How would you describe your own identity? Out of all the possible traits a human being might have, which are the ones you most usually use to describe yourself? Do any of the traits that make you "you" seemingly contradict or conflict with any of the others?

3   Think about your favorite film or TV text: how might changing the race, gender, or sexuality of its characters change the meanings of the text? Perhaps more importantly, how might changing the race, gender, or sexuality of the characters change *your perception* of the text?

References and further reading

Anzaldua, Gloria. *Borderlands/La Frontera: The New Mestiza*. San Francisco: Aunt Lute Books, 1987.

Benshoff, Harry M, and Sean Griffin. *America On Film: Representing Race, Class, Gender, and Sexuality at the Movies*. Malden, MA: Wiley-Blackwell, 2009 (2004).

Bernardi, Daniel, ed. *The Birth of Whiteness: Race and the Emergence of United States Cinema.* New Brunswick, NJ: Rutgers University Press, 1996.

Bernardi, Daniel, ed. *Classic Hollywood, Classical Whiteness.* Minneapolis, MN: University of Minnesota Press, 2001.

Bogle, Donald. *Toms, Coons, Mulattoes, Mammies, & Bucks: An Interpretive History of Blacks in American Films,* Fourth Edition. New York and London: Continuum, 2002 (1973).

Butler, Judith. *Gender Trouble: Feminism and the Subversion of Identity.* New York: Routledge, 1990.

Dines, Gail and Jean M. Humez, eds. *Gender, Race, and Class in Media: A Critical Reader,* Third Edition. London: Sage Publications, Inc. 2010.

Du Bois, W. E. B. *The Souls of Black Folks.* Printed by CreateSpace: Millennium Publications 2014 (1903).

Dyer, Richard. *White.* New York: Routledge, 1997.

Fanon, Frantz. *Black Skin, White Masks.* Trans. Richard Philcox. New York: Grove Press, 2004 (1952).

Fanon, Frantz. *The Wretched of the Earth.* Trans. Richard Philcox. New York: Grove Press, 2005 (1961).

Foucault, Michel. *The History of Sexuality, Volume One, An Introduction.* Trans. Robert Hurley. New York: Vintage 1990 (1977).

Hilderbrand, Lucas. Paris is Burning: *A Queer Film Classic.* Vancouver: Arsenal Pulp Press, 2013.

hooks, bell. *Black Looks: Race and Representation.* Boston, MA: South End Press, 1992.

Klinger, Barbara. "Contraband Cinema: Piracy, *Titanic,* and Central Asia," *Cinema Journal* 49:2 (2009). Pp. 106–24.

May, Vivian M. *Pursuing Intersectionality, Unsettling Dominant Imaginaries.* New York and London: Routledge, 2015.

Rich, B. Ruby. *New Queer Cinema: The Director's Cut.* Durham, NC: Duke University Press, 2013.

Said, Edward. *Orientalism.* New York: Vintage, 1979.

Shohat, Ella and Robert Stam. *Unthinking Eurocentrism: Multiculturalism and the Media.* New York: Routledge, 1994.

Sullivan, Nikki. *A Critical Introduction to Queer Theory.* New York: New York University Press, 2003.

Tasker, Yvonne and Diane Negra, eds. *Interrogating Postfeminism: Gender and the Politics of Popular Culture.* Durham, NC: Duke University Press, 2007.

Walker, Alice. *In Search of Our Mothers' Gardens: Womanist Prose.* New York: Mariner Books, 2003 (1983).

Glossary

A pictures – prestige films made within classical Hollywood cinema that featured large budgets, big stars, well-known directors, and an aspiration towards quality or artistry.

abject – within psychoanalysis, the (generally taboo) aspects of the "self" that immediately become "not-self" the moment they leave the body, such as urine, feces, blood, toenail clippings, etc.; the abject is fraught with psychic meaning because it always threatens to destabilize one's sense of self as stable, whole, and unified.

abstract expressionism – late movement of modernist art in which the medium of the art form became the subject of the work, as in Jackson Pollock's "action paintings," wherein the subject of the work is arguably the placement and form of the paint upon the canvas.

aesthetics – a branch of study or philosophy that attempts to define the nature of beauty and artistry.

Age of Enlightenment – also known as the Age of Reason (roughly the seventeenth and eighteenth centuries), a period in which science, logic, and rationality dominated culture, art, and politics.

ahistoricity – the postmodern idea that contemporary culture has become "unstuck" in time, that history (if remembered at all) is often remembered via nostalgic simulacra; Fredric Jameson likens this state to one of schizophrenia.

alienation – within basic Marxism, the idea that the masses who produce consumer goods suffer a disconnect from those material goods as well as from one another (and the larger issues of economic domination and subordination).

alienation effect – part of Brecht's concept of Epic theater: any self-reflexive theatrical device that breaks the fourth wall, destroying theatrical realism and calling attention to the politics of the play.

alternate universe – a type of fan fiction that places characters from a canonical primary text into a different diegetic setting, often to imagine how the characters would behave under new circumstances.

Althusser, Louis (1918–90) – French Marxist theorist who reworked basic (vulgar) Marxist principles to account for how class and economic determinism relate to the political structures of twentieth-century Western nations.

anal stage – the second stage of Freud's model of infantile sexuality, wherein the child learns to control his or her execratory organs.

anime – Japanese animation, often centered around science fiction and fantasy tropes.

anthropology – academic science dedicated to studying the origins and variations of human beings as well as their interactions with the environment and one another.

anti-essentialist – as opposed to essentialist claims, anti-essentialist positions stress that meaning is never closed or absolute, that complex human systems cannot be reduced to simplified essences, labels, or sound bites.

anti-essentialist feminism – comparable to third wave feminism, ways of thinking about gender and sexuality that do not understand biology as a determinant of gender; instead, anti-essentialists argue that gender is a socially constructed product of pre-existing patriarchal cultures and languages.

anti-fan – a person who positions him or herself as overtly antagonistic to a cultural text or media artifact.

apparatus theory – broadly, a model of how cinema works as almost a psychic-physical machine, drawing on ideas from psychoanalysis, structuralism, and ideology.

audience/reader – in Stuart Hall's model of "Encoding/Decoding," this term refers to the actual people who receive (decode) media texts, each of whom is uniquely situated culturally with regard to the texts under consideration.

audience studies – the (often ethnographic) study of how actual audiences make sense of texts, as well as what audiences/fans might create in response to them.

auteur-structuralism – a shift in thinking about auteur theory that focused less on the director as an actual human being, and more on the idea of the director as a set of formal and thematic traits that could be found within his or her films.

auteur theory – broadly, the idea that the director of a film should be considered its author, as he or she is thought to unite a diverse creative staff into one artistic vision. The film auteur is somewhat similar to a TV show's creator or "show runner."

avant-garde – a type of artistic production that is thought to be ahead of its time, more experimental or creative than usual.

B pictures – low budget films made within the classical Hollywood cinema that featured lesser-known stars and directors, often meant to fill out the second half of a double bill. More broadly, B film can refer to any cheaply made film.

Bakhtin, Mikhail (1895–1975) – Russian literary critic and semiotician who theorized several ideas that would become germane to cultural studies, including the "Carnivalesque," the chronotope, dialogism (an early theorization of intertextuality), and heteroglossia.

baroque – broadly, a work of art characterized by excessive or ornate detail.

baroque genre phase – the fourth and final phase of genre scholar Thomas Schatz's model of genre evolution, it occurs when the conventions of any given genre become so well known to both filmmakers and filmgoers that their conventions can be "played with"—parodied, hybridized, deconstructed, etc. Examples might include the "anti-western" *Little Big Man* (1970) and the western parody *Blazing Saddles* (1974).

Barthes, Roland (1915–80) – French post/structuralist important to the rise of cultural studies; his work was among the first to apply principles of structural anthropology to the study of popular/mass culture.

base-superstructure model – within basic Marxism, the idea that any given culture's socio-cultural and ideological institutions (its superstructure) are determined by that culture's economic base, whether capitalist, communist, socialist, etc.

basic repression – according to Freud and some of his followers, basic repression is needed for any form of human subject formation and/or the formation of a civilized state.

Baudrillard, Jean (1929–2007) – postmodern theorist known for the 1981 book *Simulacra and Simulation*.

Baudry, Jean-Louis (b. 1930) – French theorist whose ideas contributed to the development of apparatus theory.

binary oppositions – terms like night and day, or male and female, that are usually considered to be opposites; contemporary theory critiques binary terms as essentialist and ahistorical, as they tend to obscure the fact that one term can and often does "bleed into" its alleged opposite, as in dawn and dusk, or in the case of intersex individuals.

blacklist – lists maintained during the Red Scare (roughly the 1950s) containing the names of alleged communists who were not to be hired; these lists had a major impact on people working in the media industries, who lost jobs or even saw their careers destroyed.

blaxploitation filmmaking – a movement of American filmmaking circa the early 1970s, in which African American actors played leading roles in cheaply made genre films, including *Shaft* (1971), *Super Fly* (1972), and *Blacula* (1972).

blurring of boundaries – a major trait of both modernist and postmodernist art and culture, such as the mixing of genres, high and low arts, historical eras and styles, etc.

bourgeoisie – the middle class; within classical Marxism, this group is also contiguous with the ruling class, i.e. those who own the means of production.

box office returns – weekly accounting of how much money any given film earns in the US or global marketplace.

brand – name, term, or logo that identifies a certain product or type of text; some TV formats might be thought of as brands to be licensed in other regional markets.

bread and circuses – a phrase attributed to the Roman empire, which refers to the fact that if the populace was fed ("bread") and entertained ("circuses") the rule of the empire could be easily maintained.

Brecht, Bertolt (1898–1956) – German Marxist playwright who championed the idea of the "Epic theater," an anti-realist theatrical style designed to make the audience aware it was watching a constructed piece of theater; a later generation of film theorists and filmmakers would also champion the need for cinema to be as anti-realistic as possible in order to undermine and call attention to its ideological underpinnings.

bricolage – within postmodern aesthetics, the combination of radically different styles in one single text.

buck – stereotype of the black male as an aggressive, hypersexual threat.

Butler, Judith (1956–) – feminist philosopher known for her work on gender and performativity.

camera-stylo – literally "camera pen," a term coined in 1948 by Alexandre Astruc, who suggested filmmakers should use their cameras as an author might use a pen; Astruc's ideas eventually contributed to the formulation of the auteur theory.

canon – in fan studies, this term refers to the totality of narrative and diegetic elements that create a franchise's universe, as described by the franchise's primary texts. In cultural history more generally, the term refers to a group of texts that are thought to be more important than others, allegedly because they are brilliantly creative and hold universal truths.

capitalism – economic and political system based on private or corporate ownership of goods and industries, organized to maximize profit.

castration anxiety – the terrifying fantasy central to the Oedipal narrative, wherein the boy fears he may lose his own penis and the patriarchal power it represents.

CGI – see **computer generated imagery**.

chain of signification – semiotic concept that suggests one sign may give rise to another in an infinite chain of meaning, that signification is potentially endless or open.

chanbara **film** – Japanese film genre centered on samurais and sword play; examples include *The Seven Samurai* (1954) and *Yojimbo* (1961).

chick flick – comparable to the rom-com (romantic comedy), a colloquial term used to describe contemporary films aimed at women, such as *Bridget Jones's Diary* (2001) or *The Notebook* (2004).

Cinémathèque Française – archive and cinema in Paris run by curator Henri Langlois that became the center of postwar French cinephilia and by extension postwar French film theory.

classical art – see **classicism**.

classical era – see **classicism**.

classical genre phase – the second phase of genre scholar Thomas Schatz's four-point model of genre evolution, it occurs when a genre is named and recognized by both filmmakers and filmgoers alike; this occured for many genres in the 1930s, when horror films, musicals, biopics, gangster films, etc. were regularly produced within the assembly-line structure of the studio system.

Classical Hollywood cinema – term referring to films and the industrial conditions that produced them, i.e. the studio system as practiced by the eight most important motion picture production companies during the 1930s and 1940s.

classical realism – a style of filmmaking (often associated with classical and post-classical Hollywood) that emphasizes linear narrative, continuity editing, and other formal features designed to create a sense of the film's world being real or plausible while simultaneously hiding the fact that it is itself an artifact constructed under certain ideological and industrial pressures.

classical realist film – see **classical realism**.

classicism – broad period in Western art history predating modernity and modernism; classic art strives for unity, balance, harmony, and mimesis.

closed text – this term is used to describe a text whose singular meaning is readily discerned; fairy tales with explicitly stated morals are good examples of closed texts, as are most mainstream narrative films and TV shows.

code – in semiotics, how certain signs are organized/deployed in specific ways throughout a given text.

collage – art form in which fragmented elements are combined into one text.

colonialism – the practice of settling in and taking control over another country or region of the globe for the goals of economic exploitation and cultural expansion.

commercialized postmodernism – the majority of postmodern artifacts, those whose politics are either incoherent or reactionary; they are sold as visual extravaganzas but rarely rework their nostalgic tropes into something new or critical of the past.

commodification – literally turning something into a commodity, be it a person, thing, or idea; for example, rap music was sold as a commodity to mainstream audiences in the 1980s and 1990s, despite the fact that it was in many ways critical of dominant ideologies of race, class, and capitalism.

commodity fetishism – within Marxism, the idea that people overinvest meaning into the things they buy—coveting name brands or expensive items just for the sake of owning them.

communism – a system of economic and political organization based on the even redistribution of society's wealth among all of its members; in order to achieve this end, the means of production must be owned by the state or other commonality.

computer generated imagery – pervasive special effects technology used in much contemporary Hollywood filmmaking used to create "realistic" images of sets, characters, lighting effects, etc.

condensation – within psychoanalytic dream theory, the way that more than one issue or trauma may be mapped onto a single symbol or symptom; thus making that symbol or symptom overdetermined.

conditions of projection – within apparatus theory, this term refers to how cinematic spectators sit passively in the dark, with projection occurring from behind, a physical set-up that allows for regression and projection.

connotation – in semiotics, connotation refers to all the meanings a sign gives off after its first order or denotative meaning; connotation is potentially infinite, as one sign (signifying meaning) always give rise to another sign (signifying another meaning).

conscience – similar to the superego, one's conscience is that part of the mind that makes one think about the consequences of acting on id urges or drives.

conscious mind – the waking state or self-aware ego part of the human mind.

consumer capitalism – type of contemporary capitalism associated with global corporate capitalism and the production and consumption of disposable goods rather than necessities.

contemporary cultural criticism – the types of analyses explored in this book, drawn from a broad set of interdisciplinary ideas about how cultural artifacts reflect the contexts within which they are produced and consumed.

continuity editing – see **Hollywood continuity editing**.

coon – stereotype of an African American man as a bumbling, uneducated fool.

co-opted postmodernism – see **commercialized postmodernism.**

cosplay – a type of tertiary (fan-made) text or practice, cosplay involves making and wearing costumes that suggest a primary text's characters.

counterculture – umbrella term used to describe the various socio-political movements of the 1960s, including the anti-war movement, the civil rights movement, feminism, etc., all of which defined themselves against dominant culture and ideologies.

critical postmodernism – see **deconstructive postmodernism**.

critical race theory – broadly, an academic discipline exploring how white supremacy pervades Western culture, and how it might be countered or undone.

cross-cutting – editing technique that cuts back and forth between two separate strands of action occurring simultaneously; the cross-cutting usually ends when the two strands of action converge.

cubism – modernist movement in arts that breaks reality into fragments and reassembles them in abstract form, as in the works of Pablo Picasso or Georges Braque.

cultural artifact – another term for text.

cultural exhaustion – the postmodern idea that everything has already been said or done, that contemporary artists can only recycle, remake, and repackage what has come before.

cultural fictions – term meant to problematize the popular narratives a society tells itself about itself.

cultural hegemony – see **hegemony**.

cultural imperialism – the domination of other nations or regions not through colonialism or violence, but through the dissemination of cultural artifacts (texts) that represent and normalize the dominance of one culture over another.

cultural studies – broadly, an interdisciplinary field that seeks to understand texts (cultural artifacts) in relation to their socio-historical contexts.

culture – within contemporary cultural studies, the characteristic features, behaviors, and texts related to a given group or class. The term "culture" used to come with elitist connotations, in that "having culture" often meant one was more educated and refined than other people or groups; some societies were deemed "primitive" and without culture altogether. Today we recognize that all societies have cultures that are unique.

culture industry – term coined by the Frankfurt School to describe how popular culture is mass produced as if on an assembly line.

culture jamming – guerrilla tactic designed to question or expose social and cultural systems of domination and/or exploitation.

cycle – term related to genre that is often applied to a small number of films that copy an initial highly succesful film; for example, following the success of *Jurassic Park* (1993), a small cycle of giant dinosaur films were produced.

dada – modernist movement that rejected traditional notions of beauty and form in favor of the abstract and nonsensical.

de Saussure, Ferdinand (1857–1913) – Swiss linguist whose ideas helped lay the groundwork for the fields of semiotics and structuralism.

decoding – in Stuart Hall's model of "Encoding/Decoding," this term refers to the ways that individual people make sense of cultural artifacts like films or TV shows, based upon their own specific social subjectivities.

deconstruction/deconstructive criticism – associated with poststructuralism and especially theorist Jacques Derrida, deconstruction is a philosophy and form of analysis that attempts to unravel or pull apart linguistic/formal structures; it sees all meaning as relational and infinitely mutating.

deconstructive genre film – a film that may look like it belongs to a classical genre, but whose thematic myth subverts or inverts that of the classical genre, as in "anti-Westerns" like *Little Big Man* (1970) or *McCabe & Mrs. Miller* (1971).

deconstructive postmodernism – a (rare) type of ideologically consistent postmodernism that uses postmodern aesthetics to mount a critique of dominant ideologies or dominant forms.

deep structure – see **thematic myth**.

defense mechanism – within psychoanalysis, any psychic manipulation or process that hides unacceptable id urges or traumatic events from the conscious mind.

denial – within psychoanalysis, a basic defense mechanism wherein a trauma or unacceptable id urge is vociferously negated (or denied); the subject may loudly insist upon the very opposite of the unconscious truth.

denotation – in semiotics, this term refers to the first order of signification that arises from a given sign; the denotative meaning of the sign "X" might thus be two short lines that cross in the middle. Meanings such as "the letter X" or "the Roman numeral 10" would be considered second or third order significations; i.e. connotations or connotative meanings.

Derrida, Jacques (1930–2004) – French poststructuralist philosopher who theorized the ideas and processes of deconstructive criticism.

diaspora – the spread of a culture across time and space as it incorporates new elements or loses older ones.

diegesis – the world of the film's story.

disavowal – within psychoanalysis, a tricky defense mechanism wherein a trauma or unacceptable id urge exists in a sort of "yes, but no" formation; see also **fetish**.

discourse – associated most clearly with the work of Michel Foucault, a discourse is a socially produced and/or institutionalized way of speaking such as those found within academic disciplines or social institutions like the legal system, medicine, psychiatry, the military etc.; discourses shape and limit the meanings of what can be expressed within them, and thus shape the meanings of power and knowledge.

dispatcher – one of Vladimir Propp's seven character types found in Russian folk-tales, this character sends the hero on his quest.

displacement – within psychoanalysis, a basic defense mechanism wherein a trauma or unacceptable id urge is psychically moved out of the subject's unconscious mind and attributed to someone or something else; see also **projection**.

domestic sitcom – a sitcom that generally revolves around a family; i.e. *The Cosby Show* (1984–92) or *Modern Family* (2009–).

dominant-hegemonic reading – see **preferred reading**.

dominant ideology – the ideologies that are most prevalent and pervasive in any given place and time; in the Western world, dominant ideologies include the alleged superiority of lighter skinned peoples over those with darker skin, men over women, capitalism over other forms of economic organization, and Judeo-Christian ethics over other forms of religion.

donor – one of Vladimir Propp's seven character types found in Russian folk-tales, this character gives the hero his special powers.

doppelgänger – an imaginary(?) character or double who may or may not be reflective of some aspect of the subject's mind; literature and the media arts are full of figures that could be considered doppelgängers, such as Dr. Frankenstein and his creation.

double consciousness – term coined by early African American race theorist W. E. B. Du Bois (1868–1963) referring to how the psyches of black people are split between a central sense of the true (African) self versus a sense of how one is seen within racist, white culture.

economic determinism – the idea that all culture (elements of the superstructure) arises from and is structured (or determined) by the economic system at its base.

economic underdevelopment – term referring to the depleted wealth and shattered infrastructure of nations that have been colonized, their wealth and resources having primarily benefited only the colonizing nation.

écriture féminine – literally "female writing," a type of writing meant to oppose or critique phallogocentric language structures.

ego – within psychoanalysis, one of three parts of the mind; the ego is the waking conscious part of the mind, distinct from the id and the superego.

ego ideal – in Lacanian theory, this is the image that the child sees of itself in the mirror; the child assumes that the image is better and more independent than it truly is, thus it is an ideal version of the self.

Electra complex (or Electra narrative) – the female analog to the Oedipal narrative, how the female infant attains her gendered subjectivity by realizing that her own lack of a penis matches that of her mother's; subsequently she models herself on her mother.

encoding – in Stuart Hall's model of "Encoding/Decoding," this term refers to the ways that not only individual people but also media institutions, economic imperatives, and industrial parameters instill meaning into a cultural artifact (such as a film or TV show) during its production.

epic westerns – blockbuster westerns prevalent in the 1920s and 1960s that specialized in grand themes and visual spectacle.

epistemology – study of the ways and means we come to know what we know.

Eros – within psychoanalysis, the life drive, which also contains sexual desire (libido).

essentialism – the ideological belief that cultural artifacts and groups of people can be defined by static, trans-historical characteristics and meanings; for example, that all women tend to be passive and nurturing due to their biological nature.

essentialist claims – assertions that tend to reduce the complexity of things into basic, easily assimilated sound bites, often misrepresenting reality by oversimplifying it.

ethnicity – socially defined group of people who share common traits, behaviors, and cultures; the term is increasingly preferred over race which has biological connotations long since disproven.

ethnography – from the Latin, "writing about a culture;" ethnographers first observe and participate in the culture they wish to study, then produce a written or filmic account of that culture.

Eurocentrism – broadly, a narrative or discourse that suggests that Europe and the Western world represent the apex of human accomplishment; in general, it finds the accomplishments of other nations or regions to be negligent.

exchange-value – within basic Marxism, the idea that a material good's worth may be more than its use function; i.e. a shirt may cost $20 to produce but its exchange-value might be $100 if people are willing to pay that amount.

exegesis – see **textual analysis**.

exhibitionism – sexual pleasure in exposing oneself to unsuspecting viewers.

existentialism – a broad movement in twentieth-century philosophy, art, and culture that posits the thinking human being as a subject with free will; existentialism often focuses on the nature of what it means to be human.

experimental film – a type of film that plays with the usual conventions of the medium; they are often self-reflexive and "difficult," and might include films made in modernist or avant-garde styles.

experimental genre phase – the first phase of genre scholar Thomas Schatz's four-point model of genre evolution; it occurs when a genre has not been identified as such by filmmakers or filmgoers, although certain generic elements are beginning to appear in numerous films.

expressionism – modernist art movement that distorts reality as a means of expressing a subjective or critical viewpoint.

false hero – one of Vladimir Propp's seven character types found in Russian folk-tales, this character appears to be a help to the hero but then is revealed to be villainous.

fan – derived from fanatic, a person who is especially enthusiastic about something, such as sports, a particular musical artist, or some aspect of contemporary media culture.

fan fiction – writing (tertiary texts) produced by fans based on a primary media text or franchise; fan fiction encompasses multiple genres and multiple uses.

fandom – term used to describe a fan culture positioned around a given text or set of texts, as in *Harry Potter* fandom or *Star Trek* fandom.

fanfic – see **fan fiction**.

fanon – in fan studies, this term refers to the totality of narrative and diegetic elements that create a franchise's universe, as described by both the franchise's primary texts and the fans' embellishments of those events as described within tertiary texts. See also **meta-text**.

Fanon, Frantz (1925–61) – French Caribbean psychiatrist and cultural theorist whose writings in the 1950s helped form the bases for post- and neo-colonial theory.

fanzines – fan-made (tertiary) texts circulated among like-minded individuals, often including conference updates, trivia, episode guides, or original fan fiction and fan art.

femininity – the gender role expected of infants born female.

feminism – broadly, a critique or social movement dedicated to critiquing gender inequity.

feminist film criticism – arising within second wave feminism in the 1970s, this movement critiques the sexist imbalances in film (and later television and new media).

feminist film theory – see **feminist film criticism**.

femme slash – fan fiction that depicts a sexualized relationship between two female characters.

fetish – within psychoanalysis, an overinvestment of libidinal energy into/onto some object such as a shoe or under garment, thought to "cover over" the threat of castration. A fetish is dependent upon the defense mechanism of disavowal, and thus symbolizes both the threat of castration (lack) as well as the phallus itself, which is why it is so over-charged with psychic energy.

fetishistic scopophilia – a final stage of objectification according to feminist film theory: as per Laura Mulvey, even objectified female characters still represent a threat to the male spectator, so those bodies are further fragmented into fetishistic close ups of body parts.

fetishization – within psychoanalysis and apparatus theory, the tendency to overvalue or overinvest psychic energy into some thing or some experience.

filk songs – tertiary texts that wed new lyrics about a fan's favorite media text with new or pre-existing melodies.

film noir – French term meaning "black film" or "dark film"—referring to the expressionist detective/crime/mystery films of the post-WWII era; examples include *The Big Sleep* (1946) and *Kiss Me Deadly* (1955). Critics and scholars often debate whether film noir should be considered a genre, a style, or perhaps a movement?

films d'art – a movement of Eurocentric filmmaking in the 1910s that positioned itself as "high art," chiefly by adapting famous plays and novels, and occasionally importing actors from the "legitimate stage."

first wave feminism – movement critiquing gender inequity (circa the late nineteenth century through the 1920s) that focused on issues like women's suffrage, working conditions, and (in some cases) temperance.

First World – term coined in the post-World War II era, used to refer to the Western bloc nations (and often former colonialists) who practiced capitalism.

flow – concept accredited to Raymond Williams that describes how television is a

never-ending text; some scholars now study televisual flow, rather than individual TV texts.

folk culture – culture produced by a specific group of people primarily for consumption by that same group of people; examples might include folk celebrations, ethnic food, "street arts" like break dancing, etc.

formalism – in art and media studies, this term refers to the aesthetic tendency to foreground style over content.

format – similar to film genre, a TV format refers to a branded premise that can be sold to other nations or regions and then tailored specifically to those cultures; examples include *Who Wants to be a Millionaire?*, a format that has been re-developed and aired in over 100 national/regional contexts.

Foucault, Michel (1926–84) – French poststructuralist whose work on power, knowledge, and discourse helped shape much contemporary critical cultural theory.

Fourth World – term coined in response to the "Three World" model to acknowledge the indigenous populations within First, Second, or Third World nations.

fragmentation – a trait of modernist and postmodernist art and culture, favoring smaller and smaller disjointed units rather than unity and wholeness.

franchise – in the contemporary media landscape, a series of related texts that often encompass various media forms, such as books, TV, movies, video games, etc. *Star Wars* and *Harry Potter* are two large and very popular media franchises.

Frankfurt School – body of thinkers circa World War II and after (including Max Horkheimer and Theodor Adorno) who theorized popular culture as the product of the "culture industries"; they argued that mass culture produced passive and conformist consumers.

French impressionism – a modernist movement in the arts, including film, that often emphasized soft focus, pastel colors, fragmentation, and/or rapid editing and superimpositions; examples include the paintings of Claude Monet and Pierre-Auguste Renoir and the films of Abel Gance and Germaine Dulac.

French New Wave – movement of innovative and influential filmmaking centered in Paris during the 1960s; many New Wave directors—Truffaut, Godard, Rohmer—had formerly been film critics at *Cahiers du cinema*.

Freud, Sigmund (1856–1939) – considered the "Father of Psychoanalysis," Freud theorized about the workings of the human mind, creating a legacy of psychotherapeutic methods as well as multiple models of cultural analysis.

gender – the social roles that male or female subjects are expected to perform or fulfill; gender roles can vary greatly according to place and time, since they are socially constructed.

gender anti-essentialism – see **anti-essentialist feminism**.

gender essentialism – ways of thinking that understand gender as intrinsically tied to sex; that "biology is destiny" in that being born male or female predetermines later gender expression.

genital stage – the fifth and final stage of Freud's model of infantile sexuality that occurs during or before puberty; when the child attains its "proper" adult heterosexual gender role.

genre – broadly, type. More narrowly, a type of fictional film made within an industrial context such as Hollywood. Genres are frequently discussed as having a surface structure (iconography) and a deep structure (ideological problematic or thematic myth).

genre hybrid – film that combines or "mashes up" two or more genres, such as the musical horror film *Sweeney Todd: The Demon Barber of Fleet Street* (2007) or the western science fiction film *Cowboys & Aliens* (2011).

genre theory – see **genre**.

German expressionism – a modernist movement in the arts, including film, that often emphasized bizarre color design, angular, anguished distortion, and/or high contrast black and white cinematography; examples include the paintings of Georges Grosz and Paul Klee as well as films like *The Cabinet of Dr. Caligari* (1920) and *Nosferatu* (1922). German expressionist film style is central to the visual look of classical Hollywood horror films and later films noir.

global corporate capitalism – type of contemporary capitalism associated with consumer capitalism wherein the flow of money and goods is controlled by vast transnational corporations.

glocal – portmanteau word combining global and local, referring to a perspective that is simultaneously international and local.

gothicism – similar to romanticism, gothicism arose in Europe in the late eighteenth century as a response to Age of Enlightenment thinking; gothic literature like *The Castle of Otranto* or *Frankenstein* focuses on crumbling castles, morbid themes, sensation, and/or stylized subjectivities.

Gramsci, Antonio (1891–1937) – Italian Marxist credited with the theory of cultural hegemony, i.e. how a state or class maintains control through constant ideological negotiation.

Hall, Stuart (1932–2014) – Jamaican-born British scholar who helped to innovate the field(s) of cultural studies; his work centered on race and class but also television as in his seminal essay "Encoding/Decoding."

hard sciences – empirical fields like biology, chemistry, and physics that generate knowledge through the use of the scientific method, relying on laboratory experimentation to quantify the meanings of repeatable and observable data.

hegemonic negotiation – the process by which dominant ideology is always in flux or contestation with non-dominant ideologies; from the dialectic negotiation of such forces, new social forces may emerge, even as dominant ideologies often remain central (if somewhat altered).

hegemony – the dominant powers and ideologies of the ruling class which structure a given culture; hegemony is never static but must be constantly re-won and re-negotiated. See also **hegemonic negotiation**.

helper – one of Vladimir Propp's seven character types found in Russian folk-tales, this character aids and abets the hero on his quest.

hero – one of Vladimir Propp's seven character types found in Russian folk-tales, this character is also known in media studies as the protagonist.

heteroglossia – the idea that some texts are written with many different tongues or voices, and can thus mean different things to different readers; similar to an open text.

heteronormativity – the assumption that white, married, monogamous, procreative heterosexuality is the only "normal" sexuality of human beings.

high art – see **high–low dichotomy**.

high–low dichotomy – refers to the way cultural artifacts are often thought to be (1) either art or not art, or (2) either good art (high) versus bad art (low). Contemporary cultural studies seeks to elide those highly subjective distinctions, although certain forms like ballet or opera still carry high art connotations while comic books and Hollywood genre films generally carry low art connotations.

historical reception study – a field of inquiry within cultural studies that explores how film and TV texts are positioned (by the culture industries) to be received, as well as their actual reception.

historicization – analyzing and situating a text within its historical context.

Hollywood continuity editing – set of rules for editing (including eye-line matches, matches on action, obeying the 180 degree law) that attempts to hide the cuts in classical narrative filmmaking, spoon feed information to the audience, and present a unified sense of the diegetic world as real.

Hollywood montage sequence – a technique that compresses the passing of diegetic time and space into a brief sequence of cuts, dissolves, and superimpositions, held together by unified extra-diegetic music, as in a training montage from a 1980s sports film.

Hollywood studio system – the assembly line-like mode of film production that was innovated by and central to the American film industry (Hollywood) from roughly the 1920s to the 1950s.

homophobia – fear and hatred directed towards people whose sexual orientation is gay or lesbian (homosexual); the term "queer-phobia" is sometimes used to describe the same feelings towards anyone whose sexual and gender identity is non-heteronormative.

homosexual desire – feelings of love and sexual desire between people of the same sex, as opposed to heterosexual desire, feelings of love and sexual desire between people of the opposite sex.

homosocial desire – non-sexual feelings and relationships between people of the same sex, as might be shared by members of a fraternity or sorority, or between characters in a buddy film or bromance.

horror genre – Western film genre that focuses on some sort of monstrous threat to either psychic or social "normality."

hybridity – broadly, a mixture; in contemporary cultural criticism, the term refers to how human identities are always mixtures of various elements (racial and otherwise).

hyperconsciousness – a self-reflexive hyperawareness found in many postmodern texts, as in texts that acknowledge their own cultural status as texts.

hyperdiegesis – a sort of all-encompassing space and time-line that links up and relates all of the primary texts within a given franchise, creating a fictional universe. See also **canon**.

hyperreality – in postmodern theory, a digitally constructed "reality" often mistaken for actuality.

hyphenate auteur – a filmmaker who not only directs his or her film, but perhaps also serves as its producer, writer, star, composer, etc.

hypodermic needle model – a phrase sometimes used to refer to the Frankfurt School's critique of the culture industries, describing the way that (according to that model) passive media consumers are allegedly "shot up" with dominant ideologies.

icon – see **iconic sign**.

iconic sign – in semiotics, one of three types of signs: an iconic sign is a sign whose signifier looks like or suggests qualities of its signified. A drawing of a cat, as in a cartoon or comic strip, is an iconic sign, in that its meaning can probably be recognized by people who speak different languages.

iconography – as per genre scholar Thomas Schatz, the sights and sounds common to any given film genre; the iconography (also called surface structure) of the western would include cowboys, Indians, guns, saloon girls, and tumbleweeds.

id – within psychoanalysis, that part of the mind that contains repressed urges and traumas.

idealist ideology – within apparatus theory, a sense of knowing more or seeing more than one normally would, created by the interlocking effects of the cinematic apparatus.

identity politics – social and political arguments based on some (often essentialized) shared group marker, such as race, gender, or sexuality; more recent thinking about identity often seeks to problematize or deconstruct those very categories and the binaries inherent within them.

ideological message – see **ideology**.

ideological problematic – a range of ideological positions that a single text or group of texts may express, rather than one clearly expressed point of view.

ideological state apparatuses (ISAs) – an important part of Althusser's contribution to neo-Marxist theory, ISAs are social institutions such as religion, the family, political parties, sports, and especially the *media* whose overdetermined ideologies are actually responsible for maintaining political rule in Western nations. Compare to **repressive state apparatuses**.

ideology – systemic or structural beliefs (both conscious and unconscious) that are held by groups of people that shape their understanding of the world around them.

image analysis – one of the first ways that minority groups began to critique mainstream representations of themselves; looking through a body of texts to identify underlying patterns of representation and/or stereotypes.

Imaginary, the – Lacanian term analogous to Freud's pre-Oedipal, before the child enters the Symbolic (the realm of language); the Imaginary is a sensate world of images, sounds, and touches wherein the infant has yet to acquire a sense of its own body as separate from the Mother's.

impressionism – see **French impressionism**.

incorporation – how potentially adversarial texts and ideologies are drawn within the realm of the hegemonic, usually via commodification and the "watering down" of those adversarial ideas.

index – see **indexical sign**.

indexical sign – in semiotics, one of three types of signs: an indexical sign is one whose signifier could not be produced without the presence of the thing it signifies, as with a photograph. Indexical signs of a cat would thus include a photograph of a cat, a recording of its meows and purrs, a footprint, or cat fur—all of which could only be produced by the actual material cat.

individual – a model of human identity that suggests identity is more or less biologically determined and relatively static.

industrial capitalism – type of factory-based capitalism associated with the Industrial Revolution and the rise of modernism/modernity.

Industrial Revolution – in the West, the period (circa eighteenth and nineteenth centuries) during which factory life and machine-age industrial manufacturing flourished, giving rise to both modernity and modernism.

infantile sexuality – broadly, Freud's theory of how the infant attains subjectivity by mapping its own body in a series of biologically occurring stages.

infomercial – a portmanteau word describing 30 or 60 minute television shows that are basically advertisements for some given product.

interdisciplinarity – the sharing of ideas and methods across differing academic disciplines.

interpellation – an important part of Althusser's contribution to neo-Marxist theory, this idea posits that ideology is structural and "always, already" present in the subject's life; as soon as one accedes to a place in the world, one has become interpellated into its ideological structures. For example, most Western babies are born into (interpellated into) pre-existing and overdetermined ideologies of gender.

interpretant – another sign (or signs) that is used to explain a first sign; many signs like "faith" or "hope" do not have material referents—they can only be explained through the use of other signs, known within semiotics as interpretants.

intersectionality – a term used to emphasize how identity is a composite thing, made up of various aspects of social difference (race, class, gender, etc.), all of which combine within individuals in unique and interdependent ways.

intersex – a range of biological or physical syndromes wherein subjects are born with or develop both male and female sex characteristics.

intertextuality – most broadly, how one text relates to another, often through allusion, reference, quotation, etc. Intertextuality is a common feature of many postmodern texts.

irony – stylistic device that suggests a critical distance from something, especially to comment upon or critique it; a statement or situation that is expressed in one way but meant to be understood in another, even opposite way.

Jameson, Fredric (1934–) – postmodern theorist who famously dubbed it "The Cultural Logic of Late Capitalism."

journalistic criticism – a type of criticism often found in newspapers, websites, and classic TV shows like *Sneak Previews* (which "starred" the critics Roger Ebert and Gene Siskel); it relies mostly on the critic's subjective aesthetic criteria for rating a film as either good (worth spending money on) or bad (don't waste your money).

Judeo-Christian religions – the mainstream religious denominations of the Western world, that base their dogma on the Old and New Testaments of the Bible.

kiaju eiga – Japanese film genre centered on giant monsters; examples include *Godzilla* (1954) and *Rodan* (1956).

kinescope – a copy of a live broadcast created by filming a TV monitor as it is transmitted; this was a way of preserving television shows before the advent of video tape.

La Politique des Auteurs – term innovated by the critics at *Cahiers du Cinema* in the 1950s that would eventually be translated into English as the auteur theory.

Lacan, Jacques (1901–81) – French psychoanalyst who rewrote Freud's Oedipal narrative in linguistic-semiotic terms.

lack – within psychoanalysis, the absence of the phallus, represented by the mother and other women.

Langlois, Henri (1914–77) – curator of postwar Paris's Cinémathèque Française, whose programming is often thought to have influenced the development of the auteur theory. His temporary removal from that post in 1968 was an event that helped politicize film studies.

langue – in semiotics, a language system with its own rules, syntax, and grammar, all of which pre-exist individual speakers or speech acts; langue might be seen as analogous to certain filmic or televisual formats such as the western, the sitcom, or the horror film, all of which are pre-existing structures or signifying systems within which media producers may choose to create texts.

latency period – the fourth stage of Freud's model of infantile sexuality, wherein the child shows very little interest in libidinal pleasures or the opposite sex.

Leavisite Criticism – a type of literary criticism that flourished in England throughout the twentieth century; like New Criticism, it tends to be formalist and dependent on close textual analysis, finding a work's chief significance in its internal aesthetic devices.

Lévi-Strauss, Claude (1908–2009) – French thinker who applied principles of structuralism to the fields of anthropology and ethnography, a move that helped critique the Eurocentrism of more traditional approaches to people and cultures.

lesbian feminist separatism – socio-political movement of the 1970s in which many lesbians isolated themselves from gay male culture as well as mainstream feminism, neither of which they felt addressed their concerns.

liberal humanism – a broad philosophy often found within twentieth-century academic institutions, emphasizing science, reason, justice, and human agency over superstition and religion; for some thinkers, liberal humanism has been displaced by the ideas and theories of post/structuralism.

libido – psychoanalytic term for the sex drive.

linguistics – the study of language—in a general sense—including grammar, syntax, basic forms and units, etc.

low art – see **high–low dichotomy**.

machinima – a type of fan-made video that repurposes video game software in order to create new (tertiary) scenes.

macro-region – a term used in contemporary thinking about global cultures, it refers to an area that encompasses many nations that are nonetheless united through similar cultural expressions such as language; the Spanish-speaking diaspora might be considered a macro-region when studying Spanish language media.

Madonna/whore dichotomy – see **virgin/whore dichotomy**.

male gaze – within feminist film theory, the idea that classical Hollywood film form creates a male subject position and plays to the fantasies of the male unconscious.

mammy – stereotype of an African American female as an overweight, asexual house slave or nanny, dedicated to raising white children and/or helping white people.

manga – Japanese comic books or graphic novels.

manifest destiny – the United States' nineteenth-century imperialist and expansionist policy to colonize North America and other areas of the globe; this was tied into the spread of Christianity and Western culture throughout allegedly "primitive" regions. Vestiges of manifest destiny lingered into the twentieth century and can still be found within the discourse of American exceptionalism.

Marxism – most broadly, a critique of social inequity based on class.

masala **film** – Indian (Mumbai) film genre that combines many different genres, including romance, action, comedy, and the musical, examples include *Amar Akbar Anthony* (1977) and *Om Shanti Om* (2007).

masculinity – the gender role expected of infants born male.

mass communication – area of academic inquiry that studies the mass media (including journalism, public relations, and advertising) via social science paradigms; usually more quantitative in approach than cultural studies' approach to media.

mass culture – texts and artifacts produced by the mechanized culture industries; texts and artifacts (like film and TV) that are produced in vast quantities and allegedly consumed by vast numbers of people.

master narratives – broad stories (or metanarratives) that cultures tell themselves about themselves, such as the flourishing of civilization from ancient Greece to the modern Western world, or a teleological approach to history that suggests steady progress towards a future utopic state; postmodern and poststructuralist thinkers often challenge such grand discourses as essentialist.

media criticism – most broadly, researching and writing about media—including film and television—from a variety of theoretical positions, i.e. auteur criticism, or genre criticism.

media economics – an approach to studying film and TV (and media in general) that focuses on the flow of money, i.e. how economic policies and practices shape the media marketplace.

media fandoms – see **fandoms**.

media producer – in Stuart Hall's model of "Encoding/Decoding," this term refers not only to the people but also the institutions and industrial parameters that surround the creation of any cultural artifact such as a film or TV show.

medium specificity – an aspect of modernist art that self-reflexively emphasizes the unique qualities of a given art form, as in foregrounding brush strokes in painting or revealing the means of production in film or TV.

melodrama – see **woman's film**.

mental machinery of spectatorship – within apparatus theory, the psychoanalytic processes that allow for regression and identification with the apparatus and subsequently with characters on screen.

meta-text – Henry Jenkins's term for a fan-based canon including both primary and tertiary texts.

metteurs-en-scène – as per auteur theorist François Truffaut, directors who film pre-packaged screenplays (often of literary classics) in uninspired ways, rather than someone who uses the camera in a truly creative manner (i.e. the auteur).

Metz, Christian (1931–93) – psychoanalytic and structuralist film theorist whose ideas became important to apparatus theory.

micro-region – a term used in contemporary thinking about global cultures, it refers to an area within a national border that maintains a culture distinct from its larger national one; examples include the Basque Country within Spain.

mimetic art – similar to realist art, mimetic art seeks to render the subject of the work as true to life as possible.

miniseries – a limited serial form of television meant to be shown over several nights or several weeks; examples include *Roots* (1977) and *The Bible* (2013).

mirror stage – in Lacanian theory, the stage when the child develops a sense of its own identity as distinct from the mother's; this can happen in front of the mirror when the child sees an image of itself in the mirror.

miscegenation – outmoded term used to describe sexual or romantic relationships between people of different races; the Hollywood Production Code technically prohibited miscegenation onscreen from 1930–66.

mis-recognition – in Lacanian theory, this is what happens when the child sees itself in the mirror; it is a mis-recognition because the indexical image of the child and the child itself are not the same thing.

modernism – a broad movement in Western arts (roughly the 1880s–1950s) that reacted to the realist styles of classical art by emphasizing fragmentation, medium specificity, and new ways of seeing/thinking/being. Individual "schools" within modernism include surrealism, expressionism, and impressionism.

modernist era – see **modernism**.

modernity – the ways that life was experienced during the Industrial Revolution, including urbanity, factory life, class struggle, and eventually World War I.

monoglossia – the idea that some texts are written with a single tongue or voice, and are thus fairly closed to different interpretations or readings.

monomyth, the – a supposedly universal narrative structure associated with the work of mythologist Joseph Campbell; some filmmakers including George Lucas have consciously created their films according to its principles.

movement of filmmaking – as distinct from film genre, a film movement is usually based in a given place and time; examples would include the French New Wave or blaxploitation filmmaking, each of which contained various genres.

mulatto – outmoded term used to refer to people of mixed racial status; in Donald Bogle's formulation, mulattos in Western culture tend to be female and are often sources of tragedy for those who interact with her.

multi-accentuality – the idea that words or texts can mean different things depending on who is speaking them; speakers inflect meaning into words or texts according to their own subjective or ideological positions.

multiculturalism – a movement in the Western humanities (following the civil rights era) that acknowledges and addresses how disparities in race, gender, class, sexuality, etc. play out across culture and the media, emphasizing the need for cultural diversity in all aspects of society.

Mulvey, Laura (1941–) – published "Visual Pleasure and Narrative Cinema" in 1975, an essay that argued (via psychoanalysis and apparatus theory) that Hollywood film form itself constructs a patriarchal bias, the so-called "male gaze."

narcissism – within psychoanalysis and apparatus theory, the love of self; the narcissistic gaze refers to the gaze that encourages spectators to identify with characters on screen.

narrowcasting – as opposed to broadcasting, this term refers to the way contemporary film and television markets itself to hundreds if not thousands of niche cultures, rather than producing texts designed to appeal to all segments of the audience.

negotiated reading – in Stuart Hall's model of "Encoding/Decoding," a reading made when an audience member decodes a text partially in line with how it has been encoded and partially in ways antithetical to its preferred (dominant) meaning; i.e. they decode *Raiders of the Lost Ark* (1981) as a thrilling action film that also celebrates racist, sexist, and Eurocentric ideologies. To a certain extent, all readings are negotiated readings.

negotiating – see **hegemonic negotiation**.

neo-colonialism – control of a region or nation not through military force or direct political rule, but rather through economic policies and cultural imperialism; the critique of neo-colonialism is an important part of postcolonial studies.

neuroses – within basic psychoanalysis, mental disorders such as obsession, hysteria, fetishization, depression, etc. whose symptoms can/could be best cured through psychoanalysis.

New Criticism – a type of literary criticism that flourished in Western nations throughout the twentieth century; it is highly formalist and dependent on close textual analysis, finding significance only in the text's internal aesthetic devices.

New Queer Cinema – independent film movement of the early 1990s that sought to incorporate postmodern and queer ideas into film form and content.

niche culture – culture produced by the culture industries that is generally aimed at a specific section (demographic) of the population; examples might include the SyFy channel, BET, or Adult Swim.

Nielsen ratings – quantitative system meant to monitor television usage, specifically how many people are watching any given television show.

nostalgia – within postmodern aesthetics, a trend to focus on the forms and stories of earlier eras, often bathing the past in a sentimental rosy glow.

nostalgic Hollywood blockbuster – term used to describe big budget action films that seem to recall earlier forms of Hollywood cinema; examples include *Star Wars* (1977) and *Raiders of the Lost Ark* (1981).

objectification – the process of turning a human subject into an object, as when the male gaze of Hollywood cinema reduces female characters to sex objects or mere love interests.

observation – a central tenet of ethnographic practice, the careful study of a culture, subculture, or cultural phenomenon.

Oedipus complex (or Oedipal narrative) – a basic formulation of psychoanalytic theory, broadly this refers to the way that the male infant attains gendered subjectivity by rejecting the Mother (the feminine) and aligning with the Father (the masculine).

oeuvre – a body of work related to a single author; for example, all the films of Alfred Hitchcock would be considered Hitchcock's oeuvre.

ontology – a field of philosophical inquiry that explores the nature of being or existing.

open text – this term is used to describe a text that potentially gives off a wide array of meanings, as in many avant-garde or experimental films or videos. See also **heteroglossia**.

oppositional reading – in Stuart Hall's model of "Encoding/Decoding," a reading made when an audience member decodes the text "against the grain" of the way it was consciously encoded; i.e. they decode *Raiders of the Lost Ark* (1981) not as a thrilling action film but rather as a racist, sexist, imperialist text that validates the discourses of Eurocentrism.

oral stage – the first stage of Freud's model of infantile sexuality, wherein most or all of the stimulation that the child receives is centered around its mouth and lips.

Orientalism – theory developed by Edward Said that suggests the West constructs a fantasy version of the East out of its own repressed desires.

Other/Othering – the Other is that which has been repressed in the subject and projected onto someone or something else, this might also be called repression-displacement or repression-projection.

overdetermination – a concept germane to both psychoanalysis and Marxist theory, it means that some phenomena may be caused (or determined) by multiple forces; ideology is said to be overdetermined when it is promoted by multiple spheres of culture, i.e. patriarchy is overdetermined because it is promoted by ideological state apparatuses like religion, politics, sports, the nuclear family, and most aspects of the media.

P and O – see **participation** and **observation**.

paradigm – see **paradigmatic axis**.

paradigmatic axis – in semiotics, this term refers to all of the other signs that might potentially fill a slot at any given point along a syntagmatic axis, including (in

describe the id-like functioning of the infant; as the child matures, these will be replaced by the functions of the secondary processes.

primary sex characteristics – biological term used to assign sex (male versus female) based on sexual organs and their reproductive functions.

primary text – in the study of media fans, this term usually refers to the films and/or TV shows that are the focus of a fan's enthusiasm.

princess – one of Vladimir Propp's seven character types found in Russian folk-tales, this character is also known in media studies as the love interest.

producers – within cultural studies, this term refers to all of the people, institutions, social parameters, and historical forces involved in the creation of a cultural artifact (text). See also **encoding** and **decoding**.

projection – within psychoanalysis, a basic defense mechanism wherein a trauma or unacceptable id urge is attributed to ("projected onto") someone or something else; for example, if the subject unconsciously hates his father but denies it, he might also make the repetitive observations that other people hate their fathers. See also **displacement** and **Othering**.

proletariat – see **working class**.

Propp, Vladimir (1895–1970) – Russian formalist who studied the structure of folk-tales, identifying seven principle character types and 31 possible narrative events. His work on folk-tales can be used to explore the structure of classical Hollywood films as well.

pseudo-individuation – a trait of the culture industries, this term refers to the way that similar products (like soap, lipstick, soft drinks, or Hollywood movies) are marketed as having significant differences, when in fact they are manufactured as standardized artifacts; pseudo-individuation creates an illusion of choice for the consumer.

psychoanalysis – a theory of the mind (human subjectivity and its development) popularized by Sigmund Freud and his followers throughout the twentieth century.

psychoses – mental disorders like schizophrenia in which the patient has lost touch with reality, generally considered more severe (and biological in origin) than neuroses.

qualitative approaches – approaches to understanding culture and the world around us—common to disciplines within the humanities such as history, comparative literature, and media studies—that believe numbers cannot be used to measure complex social phenomena; these disciplines attempt to describe and relate social phenomena to their larger contextual settings.

quantitative approaches – approaches to understanding culture and the world around us—common to the hard sciences, mass communication studies, and other social sciences—that use numbers to measure social phenomena and then draw conclusions (findings) based on them.

quantitative audience studies – reception research that makes use of questionnaires with proscribed questions and a proscribed range of answers that can then be evaluated numerically.

queer/queer theory – broadly speaking, anything not thought of as heteronormative; queer theory explores the potentially infinite forms of socially constructed sexualities that exist in time and place.

queering – calling attention to or deconstructing the heteronormative aspects of a text, a genre, or other cultural artifact.

racialism – continued use of the term "race" as if it were a meaningful biological category, and not a socio-cultural label in need of deconstruction.

reader-response criticism – a form of reception or audience studies found especially within literary studies.

readerly text – Roland Barthes's term for a type of text that is easy to consume, one that rarely challenges its readers.

readers – within cultural studies, this term refers to actual human subjects who interact with cultural artifacts (texts). See also **encoding** and **decoding**.

Real, the – in Lacanian theory, an abstract realm that represents an unknowable reality—unknowable because we can only have access to the real through Symbolic sign structures.

realism – style of making art that seeks to be mimetic, presenting its subject as objectively as possible. See also **classical realism**.

reality television – broad label defining TV shows that feature real people in dramatic, difficult, or intriguing situations; example might include everything from game shows to talk shows to *Girls Gone Wild*.

reappropriation – the "taking back" of a previously negative term, re-infusing it with new and confrontational meanings; examples include "black" in the 1960s and "queer" in the 1990s. Alternatively, the reworking of certain media tropes within new contexts.

rebooting – term used in contemporary Hollywood to refer to the remaking of a previously succesful movie or (more regularly) a highly successful franchise. The *Star Trek* films of the twenty-first century might be said to be rebooting the original *Star Trek* television show (1966–9), in that they focus on the original *Star Trek* characters in new and different ways.

reception studies – similar to audience studies, a subset of cultural studies that explores how media texts are positioned to be (and sometimes actually are) decoded by readers.

Red Scare – post-World War II fear in the United States that communists were infiltrating various sectors of American life, politics, and culture.

referent – the material real-word thing to which a sign refers; for example, a sign of the Eiffel Tower (such as a photograph of it) makes us recall the real Eiffel Tower (the referent of the sign).

refined genre phase – the third phase of genre scholar Thomas Schatz's four-point model of genre evolution, it occurs when a genre is up-scaled from B movie to A movie status; refined genre films are likely to win Oscars as did the refined musicals *An American in Paris* (1951) and *West Side Story* (1961).

regression – within psychoanalysis, a basic defense mechanism wherein the subject retreats to an earlier stage of psychic development, thus avoiding a trauma or unacceptable id urge.

reification – in Marxism, a form of alienation in which human beings are treated as things, rendering them passive and open to exploitation.

reimagining – term used in contemporary Hollywood to refer to the remaking of a previously successful movie; reimagining implies a creative rethinking of the project, while remaking implies a less creative, more imitative endeavor.

relative autonomy – an important part of neo-Marxist theory, the term describes how elements of the superstructure have some ability to influence one another and be somewhat distanced from the economic base.

Renaissance perspective – a way of seeing and making visual texts based on objective mathematical formulae, creating a sense of depth and realism organized around a "vanishing point."

repetition compulsion – within psychoanalysis, the way repressed guilt or trauma strives to return to consciousness, often literally by obsessively repeating a symptom linked to it; for example, a murderer may repeatedly wash his or her hands as a means of expressing and perhaps expunging unconscious guilt.

repression – within psychoanalysis, a basic defense mechanism; if something exists only in the unconscious mind it is said to be repressed.

repressive state apparatuses (RSAs) – an important part of Althusser's contribution to neo-Marxist theory, RSAs are defined as social institutions that use violence or the threat of violence to maintain social control; RSAs thus include military force, terrorism, torture, and execution. Compare to **ideological state apparatuses**.

return of the repressed – within psychoanalysis, a basic maxim that refers to the ways that anything that has been banished to the unconscious will strive to make itself known (return to consciousness); this formulation also describes a basic functioning of the horror film genre.

rhetorical mode – a term coined by TV scholar Robert Allen to refer to a mode of address (common to various forms of reality television) that seems to simulate a face-to-face encounter or two-way communication between TV personality and home viewer.

Riot grrrl – broad term referring to the underground punk feminist movement of the 1990s, addressing the concerns of young women through music, zines, and other forms of political activism.

romanticism – a broad movement in Western arts—roughly the start of the nineteenth century—that reacted to the Age of Enlightenment's scientific rationalism by celebrating passion, feeling, and sensation, as in the works of Edgar Allan Poe or Peter Ilyich Tchaikovsky.

ruling class – within classical Marxism, the group that controls the means of production, maintaining both economic and ideological dominance over all other classes.

rural sitcom – a popular type of sitcom associated with CBS in the 1960s such as *The Andy Griffith Show* (1960–8), and *Green Acres* (1965–71); CBS replaced its rural sitcoms in the early 1970s with more urban and topical sitcoms.

sadism – within psychoanalysis, taking libidinal pleasure in inflicting pain or exerting control.

Said, Edward (1935–2003) – Egyptian neo-colonial theorist who coined the term and concept of Orientalism.

scopophilia – within psychoanalysis and apparatus theory, the love of looking or watching, which has libidinal (sexual) implications in many if not all cases.

screen memory – within psychoanalysis, a basic defense mechanism wherein a trauma or unacceptable id urge is repressed and replaced with a completely new "memory"—actually a fabrication of the subject's mind that covers over the traumatic event.

Screen **theory** – the theoretical and political ideas about film originally expressed in the scholarly journal *Screen* in the late 1960s and 1970s; this term is sometimes used synonymously with apparatus theory.

second wave feminism – in the Western world, the feminist movement of the 1960s and 1970s that focused on issues like reproductive rights, equal pay, and (in the United States) the passage of the Equal Rights Amendment.

Second World – term coined in the post-World War II era used to refer to the communist bloc nations, primarily China, the USSR, and its satellite nations in Eastern Europe.

secondary identification – within apparatus theory, the processes that allow for spectators to identify with individual characters within the film.

secondary processes – following the id-like functioning of the primary processes, this term is used to describe those functions the maturing child attains through repression and the creation of the superego.

secondary sex characteristics – biological term used to assign sex (male versus female) based on an individual's developing physical features such as breast development or facial hair.

secondary sources – in historical scholarship, those sources that build upon and synthesize original, primary documents (those directly tied to and contemporary with the issue/text being studied). This book would be considered a secondary source on film and TV methods, as the ideas it discusses come from primary sources.

secondary texts – in the study of media fandoms, this term refers to paratexts like toys, games, reviews, tie-in soundtrack albums, etc. that relate to and promote primary texts; secondary texts are usually licensed by and generate profits for the owners of primary texts.

self-reflexivity – the aesthetic trait of calling attention to an art form's materiality or medium specificity, for example, a film about filmmaking.

semantic/syntactic approach – genre scholar Rick Altman's preferred terms for describing and identifying genres; similar to iconography, a genre's semantic axis refers to its often-repeated signs and symbols, while similar to thematic myth, a genre's syntactic axis refers to how those semantic elements are combined in order to create meaning.

semiology – see **semiotics**.

semiotic excess – the bombardment of signs endemic to postmodern culture and media.

semiotics – the study of signs and how they signify (make meaning).

serial television – broadly defined form of television that tells complex stories with multiple characters over weeks or years; examples include soap operas, telenovelas, or "quality TV" dramas like *Lost* (2004–10), *Breaking Bad* (2008–13), and *Game of Thrones* (2011–).

series television – broadly defined form of television that tells a complete story within its given weekly time slot, such as anthology shows like *The Twilight Zone* (1959–64) or classical sitcoms like *All in the Family* (1971–9). Series TV has become increasingly serialized in the postmodern era.

sex – a categorization of male versus female often based on biological considerations such as chromosomes, and primary and secondary sex characteristics.

sexism – an ideology that blatantly accepts the alleged superiority or importance of one sex over the other; many if not most global cultures are patriarchal, valuing men and masculinity more than women and femininity.

shipping – fanfic, fanvid, or fan art that pairs up favorite characters in sexual, romantic, or otherwise intensely emotional ways.

showrunner – similar to the film auteur, the person often credited with creating, producing, and/or writing a TV show.

sign – in semiotics, the smallest unit of meaning and analysis, usually a single word or image; all signs are made up of two parts, a **signifier** and a **signified**.

signified – that part of the sign that exists in the mind of the one encountering it—the meaning to which the sign gives rise.

signifier – that part of the sign that exists in the material word, for example, a word upon a printed page or a mark upon a blackboard.

simulacrum – a copy of something that has no original.

simulation – in Baudrillard's formulation, the fourth and final stage of how signs relate to reality; in this final stage, signs have no relationship to reality at all.

singing cowboy film – a genre hybrid film (combining the musical and the western) popular in the United States in the 1930s and 1940s.

sitcom – an enduring form of series television, sitcoms are usually 30 minute shows that focus on 4–6 recurring characters (often in a domestic or workplace setting) who humorously grapple with and then resolve a "situation of the week"; examples include *The Dick Van Dyke Show* (1961–6), *WKRP in Cincinnati* (1978–82), and *Modern Family* (2009–).

situation comedy – see **sitcom**.

slash fiction – a type of fan fiction that imagines same sex desire between two male characters, often expanding upon homosocial bonding depicted in a fandom's primary texts.

soap opera – one of the first forms of serial television, these were ongoing daytime dramas whose name was derived from their sponsorship (frequently companies who sold household cleaning products); by the twenty-first century, soap operas became increasingly expensive to produce, and only a few remain such as *General Hospital* (1963–) and *The Young and the Restless* (1973–).

social problems films – classical realist texts that engage with social issues like race (*Guess Who's Coming to Dinner* [1968]) or AIDS (*Philadelphia* [1993]).

social sciences – academic disciplines like sociology, economics, and communication studies that tend to generate knowledge through the use of the scientific method, sometimes using qualitative methodologies but more often using quantitative ones.

socialism – originally synonymous with communism, today the term refers to a sort of hybrid social and economic system in which some aspects of culture are owned or controlled by the state while also preserving free market capitalism in most other arenas.

sociology – an academic discipline that studies human (sub)cultures, institutions, and social relations.

spaghetti westerns – a group of westerns made in Europe in the 1960s and 1970s, often featuring American or international stars; they were usually more violent and cynical than classical Hollywood westerns.

spectator – within apparatus theory, the slot in the machine into which real life subjects insert themselves when going to the cinema; although the term is sometimes used in media studies interchangeably with audience member or reader, within apparatus theory it refers to a position, not an actual person.

stereotype – a simplified image or trope that reduces any given social group's diversity and complexity onto superficial markers, often derogatory, that come to represent the entire group in some readers' minds.

stereotype analysis – see **image analysis**.

strategic essentialism – when a cultural group overlooks or downplays its own internal differences in order to express a unified critical mass of voices needed to achieve certain goals or effect social change.

strip syndication – a method for repositioning television re-runs; programming a once-weekly TV show into a regular Monday through Friday time slot.

structural anthropology – field innovated by Claude Lévi-Strauss, who applied the principles of structuralism to the study of human cultures.

structural/materialist filmmaking – highly medium-specific movement of experimental filmmaking (circa 1960s–70s) that took cinema itself as its subject; examples include Michael Snow's *Wavelength* (1967) and Ernie Gehr's *Serene Velocity* (1970).

structuralism – broadly, a set of ideas that suggest social relations should be understood in relation to one another, and thus to larger or deeper systems that permeate all culture. In media studies, structuralism helps explain the recurring forms and themes of a given set of texts.

structured polysemy – literally "many signs arranged in some ordered way." All texts are structured polysemies in that they are made up of a multitude of signs that are nonetheless organized in some way. Their polysemic aspect may give rise to diverse readings, while their structured aspect attempts to contain diverse readings. See **open** and **closed texts**.

structuring absence – in critical theory, a pronounced elision of a concept or issue from a text or textual system from which a theorist might begin to deconstruct the text.

subconscious – similar to the unconscious, that part of the mind accessible to the waking subject (conscious mind) only through dreams or psychoanalysis.

subgenre – a subset of a genre; the slasher film is a subgenre of the larger horror film genre.

subject – a model of human identity that suggests that identity is always in flux, more or less subject to or shaped by the ideological structures and institutionalized forces of a given society.

subjectivity – broadly, how we think about identity; cultural critics have various models for understanding subjectivity, from Althusserian interpellation to Freud's Oedipal narrative.

sublimation – within psychoanalysis, a basic defense mechanism wherein a trauma or unacceptable id urge is channeled into some more socially acceptable behavior. See also **displacement**.

superego – within psychoanalysis, that part of the mind that acts as a sort of internal censor or policeman, keeping id urges in check.

superstructure – within Marxism, all the social, political, and cultural elements that arise from and relate back to a given society's economic base.

suppression – within psychoanalysis, a basic defense mechanism, that occurs when a trauma or unacceptable id urge is consciously "tamped down" or ignored (unlike repression, wherein the trauma or unacceptable id urge has no conscious component).

surface structure – see **iconography**.

surplus repression – within psychoanalysis, the extra repression needed to maintain a certain type of society; for example, in patriarchy, women and the feminine must be repressed.

surrealism – a modernist movement in the arts, including film, that often attempted to visualize the unconscious mind through distorted and frequently sexualized or violent imagery; examples include the paintings of Salvador Dali and Max Ernst as well as films like *Un Chien Andalou* (1929) and *L'Age d'Or* (1930).

suture – within psychoanalysis and apparatus theory, this term refers to how the classical realist text draws the spectator into the diegetic space of the film.

symbol – see **symbolic sign**.

symbolic sign – in semiotics, one of three types of signs: a symbolic sign is one in which there is only a shared cultural connection between its signifier and its signified, as with words and languages. For example, there is no reason "CAT" means a furry domestic pet except that people who speak English agree that it does.

Symbolic, the – Lacanian term analogous to Freud's post-Oedipal; it refers to the state of being that occurs when the child leaves behind the Imaginary and enters the realm of language.

symptoms – within psychoanalysis, the mental or physical effects (symbols) of a patient's underlying disorder; examples might include paralysis, amnesia, hallucinations, or other odd behaviors.

syntagm – see **syntagmatic axis**.

syntagmatic axis – in semiotics, this term refers to ways in which signs can be combined in a linear order across time, as in a sentence, or shots in a scene, or frames in a comic strip.

taxonomy – classification by type; a primary goal of basic genre theory.

technical base – in apparatus theory, this term refers to those material elements of cinema that create certain idealist effects, including camera, lighting, film stock, choice of lens, etc.

telenovela – a form of serialized TV show popular in Asia and Spanish-speaking regions, telenovelas usually have a limited run (unlike Western soap operas); the popular American prime time serial *Ugly Betty* (2006–10) began its life as the Columbian telenovela *Yo soy Betty, la fea* (1999–2001).

televisuality – term coined by John Caldwell referring to the highly detailed *mise-en-scène* of television programming since the 1980s.

tertiary text – in the study of media fandoms, this term refers to the cultural artifacts that fans themselves produce in relation to their favored primary texts.

text – in cultural studies, any cultural artifact that can be studied in relation to the culture that produces and consumes it; infinite examples include subcultural style, a song, a painting, a poem, or for the purposes of this book, any given movie or TV show.

textual analysis – within cultural studies, the process of relating a text's formal properties to its conditions of production, circulation, and reception, in order to understand or explain how a given text creates meaning(s). See also **decoding**.

textual poaching – a way to describe some fan activities—how fans borrow or reappropriate characters and elements from chosen primary texts in order to express their own desires, interests, and concerns.

Thanatos – within psychoanalysis, the death drive.

thematic myth – also known as a genre's deep structure or ideological problematic, thematic myth refers to a genre's cultural-ideological meaning or significance. Many scholars understand the thematic myth of the western to be about American policies of **manifest destiny**.

theory – a proposed model or structure that seems to explain observable phenomenon, even if direct proof is absent. In most hard sciences, a theory will be abandoned if the data does not support it. Many theories—like the theory of evolution—remain highly useful to scientists since all observable data support the verity of the theory. In media studies, the term theory refers to the many ways that scholars have sought to explain the multifarious relationships between film, TV, the spectator, culture in general, etc.

Third Cinema – term coined in the post-World War II era, used to refer to a sort of agitprop (agitation and propaganda) cinema designed to educate and engage its viewers in the political struggle against neo-colonial exploitation.

third wave feminism – a term mostly used in academia to address new ways of thinking about gender and sexuality that arose in (roughly) the 1980s and 1990s; third wave feminism is anti-essentialist and explores gender and sexuality in relationship to other social factors such as class, region, nation, race, etc.

Third World – term coined in the post-World War II era used to refer to all nations not identified as First World or Second World, including formerly colonized regions of Africa, Central and South America, and portions of the Middle East.

Tom – stereotype of a black man as a servile house slave or menial worker.

torture porn – cycle or subgenre of the horror film that arose at the start of the twenty-first century that emphasized physical suffering; examples include *Saw* (2004) and *Hostel* (2005).

traditional cultural criticism – often centered on the formation of canons of "great art," this type of criticism usually ignores the cultural contexts of art or literature, focusing instead on the chosen text's alleged universal significance and artistic merit.

transcendental signified – in semiotics this term refers to the place where a chain of signification is forced to stop, where the play of meaning comes to an end. A child's desire to question his parent's authority might thus meet up with the transcendental signified of the statement "Because I am your Father and I say so!" … thus ending any debate on the topic.

transcendental spectator position – within apparatus theory, the omniscient, all-seeing, all-knowing subject position created by the cinematic apparatus and the classical realist text.

transgender – term preferred by many people who might be classified as transsexual by the medical community; there are infinite ways transgender people might choose to express their identities and live their lives. Some people who identify as female refer to themselves as transwomen, while those who identify as male often refer to themselves as transmen.

transmedia storytelling – using various media forms (films, TV, comics, websites) to tell a single large and expansive narrative.

transsexual – medical term given to individuals whose external sex characteristics differ from their internal or psychic sense of their sex or gender.

uncanny – within psychoanalysis, an object that seems strangely familiar, or a reality that seems slightly odd; the uncanny is thought to suggest or recall the subject's own unconscious thoughts.

Uncle Tom – see **Tom**.

unconscious – that part of the mind accessible to the waking subject (conscious mind) only through dreams or psychoanalysis; the unconscious is the site of unacceptable id urges and other repressed traumas.

underdevelopment – a state of economic affairs in which a formerly colonized nation or region is not merely undeveloped, but actually worse off than before the colonizers arrived, its wealth and resources having been drained or exploited by the colonizing nation.

uneven development – an important part of neo-Marxist theory, this refers to how various aspects of the superstructure are situated in relation to the economic base, some being closely aligned to it while others are less so.

uni-accentuality – a situation that occurs when a word or concept is given only a single meaning by the powerful person or institution that speaks it, thus coopting and perhaps closing off its possible *meanings* in favor of the one spoken by the dominant discourse.

use-value – within basic Marxism, the value of a good for what it is: a chair or a shirt; it is opposed to exchange-value which is the price an item may sell for in excess of its use-value.

vaginal symbols – things in culture that resemble or recall the female genitals; Georgia O'Keeffe's paintings of flowers are well-known for their vaginal symbolism.

villain – one of Vladimir Propp's seven character types found in Russian folk-tales, this character is also known in media studies as the antagonist.

virgin/whore dichotomy – a way of thinking about women in Western culture; it defines women solely by their sexuality, classifying them as either the virgin (good girl, princess) or whore (sexualized plaything or perhaps femme fatale).

Voloshinov, Valentin (1895–1936) – Soviet linguist who argued that meaning and signification is not static but is given different inflections by its users; meanings are regulated and shaped by their social usages.

voyeur – one who derives sexual gratification from secretly watching people, i.e. a Peeping Tom.

voyeurism – within psychoanalysis and apparatus theory, sexual pleasure in watching others; the voyeuristic gaze allows for spectators to observe characters on screen in an erotic way.

vulgar Marxism – basic Marxism, referring to ideas before the rise of cultural studies and more nuanced understandings of culture and ideology.

Warhol, Andy (1928–87) – American Pop artist famous for blurring high and low art forms in his work.

weepie – see **woman's film**.

Western imperialism – broadly, the conquering, colonization, and/or economic exploitation by European nations of vast regions of the globe throughout much of the eighteenth and nineteenth century.

white supremacist – adjective describing the complex overdetermined ideologies that promote the superiority of the Caucasian race.

whiteness studies – interdisciplinary field that explores the culture, history, social construction, and ongoing assumptions of superiority associated with people identified as white, i.e. Caucasian.

Williams, Raymond (1921–88) – a founding figure of British cultural studies, whose objects of study ranged from literary theory to television.

womanism – term coined in the wake of second wave feminism, meant to draw attention to the concerns of women of color, who often felt that mainstream second wave feminism had ignored them.

woman's film – sometimes called the Hollywood melodrama, this was a genre of films circa the 1920s–1960s that focused on the trials and tribulations of central female protagonists; examples include *Stella Dallas* (1925, 1937), *Imitation of Life* (1934, 1959), and *Peyton Place* (1957).

working class – within classical Marxism, the wage-earning laborers who are exploited by the ruling class (those who own the means of production).

workplace sitcom – a sitcom that generally revolves around a group of friends or co-workers; for example, *WKRP in Cincinnati* (1978–82), *Seinfeld* (1989–98), or *Friends* (1994–2004).

writerly text – Roland Barthes's term for a type of text that is difficult to consume, one that challenges its readers to "do work" in order to make sense of it.

yakuza **film** – Japanese film genre focusing on gangs and gangsters; examples include *Tokyo Drifter* (1966) and *Ichi the Killer* (2001).

zines – see **fanzines**.

Index

Page references to illustrations are indicated in **bold**.

torture porn 86
Toulouse-Lautrec, Henri de 177–8
Tourneur, Jacques 66
"Tradition of Quality" filmmaking 69
traditional cultural criticism 6–7
"tragic mulatto" stereotype 152
transcendental signified 49–50
transcendental spectator position 132, 133
transgender/transgender characters 103, 147, 260–7; *see also* queer/queer theory
transmedia storytelling 183, 226
Transparent (2014–) 103, 164, 262
transsexual *see* transgender
trauma 108–11, 121–5
"Trekker" 222, 237
"Trekkie" 222
Trekkies (1997) 233, 237–41, 262
Trekkies 2 (2004) 237
Treme (2010–11) 64
Trip, The (1967) 89
Triumph of the Will (1934) 92, 186
True Blood (2008–14) 12, 64, 183
True Grit (films, 1969, 2010) 91
Truffaut, François 68
"truthiness" 185
Turner Classic Movies 6, 12
Twilight franchise (2008–12) 119, 183, 225, 226, 230, 231, 233

Ugly Betty (2006–10) 96
Ugly Duckling, The (1939) 14
uncanny 122
unconscious mind 105–25, 174
underdevelopment 253–4
underground film 84
uneven development 29–30, 204
uni-accentuality 205–6
United States of Tara (2009–11) 164
Universal Studios 32, 66, 86, 90
University of Birmingham 200–2
Upstairs Downstairs (1971–5) 200
urbanity/urban audiences 10, 21, 23, 35, 99, 102, 173
use-value 24

vaginal symbols 112, **113**
Valdez, Luis 27

Vampire Lovers, The (1970) 152
vampires 119
variety show 11, 98
Vertigo (1958) 134, 156
Vertov, Dziga 24
video blogs 53
video games 183
Videodrome (1983) 116
Vietnam War 80, 91, 244
View, The (1997–) 159, 206
villain (character type) 54–5
Vincent (1982) 75, **77**
Virgin Suicides, The (1999) 157
virgin-whore dichotomy 152, 153
Virunga (2014) 253
"Vogue" (music video) **266**
"voguing" 264
Volosinov, Valentin 205–6
Von Stroheim, Erich 66, 68
voyeur/voyeurism/voyeuristic gaze 133–6, 155–9
vulgar Marxism 23

Walker, Alice 73, 258
Walt Disney Company 32, 71, 75, 107–8, 166, 178, 206, 247
war movie 84, 226
Warhol, Andy 176, 178–9, 190
Warm Bodies (2013) 85
Watermelon Woman (1996) 261
Wavelength (1967) 176
Wayans Bros., The (1995–9) 102
Wayne, John 22, 44, 91
Weber, Lois 152
Weekend (1967) 26
weepie *see* woman's film
Welcome to the Doll House (1995) 56, 60
Welles, Orson 7, 66, 68, 191
West, Mae 152, 153
West Side Story (1961) 91
western (genre) 2, 11, 33, 44, 51, 83, 84, 85, 87–91, 117, 226, 261
Western Imperialism 252–7
Whale, James 90
Whedon, Joss 64
white patriarchal capitalism 262–7, 73–4; *see also* dominant ideology
whiteness 20–1, 33, 37, 88, 90–1, 119, 252–7; *see also* race/racism